International Military Missions and International Law

International Humanitarian Law Series

VOLUME 31

The International Humanitarian Law Series is a series of monographs and edited volumes which aims to promote scholarly analysis and discussion of both the theory and practice of the international legal regulation of armed conflict.
The series explores substantive issues of International Humanitarian Law including,

- protection for victims of armed conflict and regulation of the means and methods of warfare
- questions of application of the various legal regimes for the conduct of armed conflict
- issues relating to the implementation of International Humanitarian Law obligations
- national and international approaches to the enforcement of the law and
- the interactions between International Humanitarian Law and other related areas of international law such as Human Rights, Refugee Law, Arms Control and Disarmament Law, and International Criminal Law.

The titles published in this series are listed at brill.nl/ihul.

International Military Missions and International Law

Edited by

Marco Odello and Ryszard Piotrowicz

MARTINUS
NIJHOFF
PUBLISHERS

LEIDEN • BOSTON
2011

Printed on acid-free paper.

Library of Congress Cataloging-in-Publication Data

International military missions and international law / edited by Marco Odello and Ryszard Piotrowicz.
p. cm. -- (International humanitarian law series ; v. 31)
Includes bibliographical references and index.
ISBN 978-90-04-17437-5 (hardback : alk. paper)
1. Peacekeeping forces. 2. War (International law) I. Odello, Marco. II. Piotrowicz, Ryszard W.
KZ6374.I583 2011
341.5'84--dc23

2011035285

ISBN 978 9004 17437 5

Table of Contents

List of Contributors

Susan Breau LLM, PhD (LSE) is Professor of International Law, Flinders Law School, Flinders University in Adelaide, Australia where she researches in the areas of the law of armed conflict, international protection of human rights and the law of international organisations. Prior to this appointment she held academic appointments as Reader in International Law at the University of Surrey, the Dorset Fellow in International Law at the British Institute of International and Comparative Law and Lecturer in International Law at the School of Law, Queen's University Belfast. She obtained her PhD at the London School of Economics. She has published extensively and her current monograph, co-authored with Kerim Yildiz, is *The Kurdish Conflict: International Humanitarian Law and Post-Conflict Mechanisms* published by Routledge.

Ulf Häußler is Assistant Legal Advisor Operational Law at Headquarters, Supreme Allied Commander Transformation (NATO HQ SACT) on secondment from the Legal Service of the German Armed Forces. He has previously held positions as Legal Advisor, Military Prosecutor and Lecturer in Law within the German Armed Forces. He served on active duty on deployments to KFOR (2006) and SFOR (2004) and was seconded to the Legal Office, NATO International Staff (2006). Prior to joining the Legal Service of the German Armed Forces, he was a Research Fellow and Lecturer in International Law and Public Law (1997-2002), and a Research Fellow for Justice LWH Ackermann at the Constitutional Court of South Africa (1997).

Ben F. Klappe (Colonel) is a military judge at the District Court Arnhem, the Netherlands and Senior Lecturer at the Netherlands Defence Academy. Previously, he served as the Special Assistant to the UN Military Adviser (2002-2006) and as Acting Director, Military Department at the International Institute of Humanitarian Law in San Remo, Italy (1999-2002). During his career, Klappe has commanded logistic and training units. He served as legal advisor at division and corps headquarters in the Netherlands and Germany respectively. Klappe holds a Masters of Law degree from Leyden University and contributes world-wide to seminars and training sessions on peacekeeping and international law.

Paolina Massidda is Principal Counsel within the Office of Public Counsel for Victims at the International Criminal Court since 2005. A lawyer since 1994, she is specialised in human rights and international humanitarian law and she holds a

Master degree in international criminal law. She has practiced before national and international jurisdictions, representing *inter alia* victims of gender crimes and handling mass claims cases. Before joining the Court, she worked as Legal Adviser in Chambers at the International Criminal Tribunal for the former Yugoslavia. She also worked for the International Federation of the Red Cross and Red Crescent Societies as delegate for the dissemination of international humanitarian law in several countries.

Marco Odello, (LLM, PhD), is Lecturer in Law at the Department of Law and Criminology, Aberystwyth University. He is a member of the International Institute of Humanitarian Law, where he is involved in teaching and training programmes. He has published articles and contributions in the areas of International Law, Human Rights, Humanitarian Law and International Organisations. Co-author of *La Convenzione Internazionale sui Diritti del Minore e l'Ordinamento Italiano* (Napoli, 1994); Mazzarelli & Odello (eds), *L'insegnamento dei Diritti Umani* (Roma, 1999); co-author of *Problemas actuales del derecho público en México* (México DF, 2004). He is General Editor of *The Cambrian Law Review.*

Ryszard Piotrowicz is Professor of Law at the Department of Law and Criminology, Aberystwyth University. He previously taught at the Universities of Glasgow, Durham and Tasmania, where he was Dean of Law. He is an Alexander-von-Humboldt Fellow. He has lectured on IHL in many countries and has worked closely on dissemination of IHL with national Red Cross Societies in Germany, Romania, Poland, Latvia, Lithuania and Estonia as well as with the ICRC throughout Europe.

Noëlle Quénivet, (LLM, PhD), is Senior Lecturer in the Department of Law of the University of the West of England. She has published several articles relating to international humanitarian law and the use of force, co-edited *International Humanitarian Law and Human Rights Law: Towards a New Merger in International Law* (Nijhoff, 2008) and *International Law and Armed Conflict: Challenges in the 21st Century* (Asser Press, 2010) and authored *Sexual Offences in Armed Conflict and International Law* (Transnational Publishers, 2005), winner of the Francis Lieber Honorable Mention Award. She is co-Editor-in-Chief of the *Journal of International Humanitarian Legal Studies.*

Katie E. Sams joined the International Committee of the Red Cross in 2000. A lawyer specialised in international humanitarian law, she is currently Head of the Civil Society Relations Unit at the ICRC headquarters in Geneva. From 2005 to 2008, she was Head of the Education and Behaviour Unit. She previously served as a Delegate to Academic Circles and as a Protection Delegate. Her professional experience outside the ICRC includes working as a Research Fellow at the United Nations Institute for Disarmament Research (Geneva) and as a Visiting Researcher at the Institute for Security Studies (Pretoria). She has published on a range of international peace and security issues.

Nicholas Tsagourias (LLM, PhD) is Professor of International Law and Security at the University of Glasgow. His main research interests are in the law of armed conflict (use of force and humanitarian law); international criminal law; international and European constitutional theory. He is on the editorial board of the *Journal of Conflict and Security Law* (OUP) and has published widely in scholarly publications. Among his publications are the book *Jurisprudence of International Law: the Humanitarian Dimension* (MUP, 2000) and the edited book *Transnational Constitutionalism: International and European Models* (CUP, 2007).

Nigel D. White is Professor of Public International Law at the University of Nottingham, formerly Professor of International Law at the University of Sheffield. In addition to publishing numerous articles and essays, he is author of several books including *Keeping the Peace: The United Nations and the Maintenance of International Peace and Security* (2nd ed, 1997), *The Law of International Organisations* (2nd ed., 2005), *The UN System: Toward International Justice* (2002), and *Democracy Goes to War: British Military Deployments under International Law* (2009). He is also editor of a number of leading collections, primarily *Collective Security Law* (2004), and co-editor of *The UN, Human Rights and Post Conflict Situations* (2005), *International Conflict and Security Law* (2005), and *European Security Law* (2007). He is co-editor-in-chief of the *Journal of Conflict and Security Law*, published by Oxford University Press.

Abbreviation List

AMISON	African Union Mission in Somalia
AMO	Area of Maritime Operations
ANC	Armeé Nationale Congolaise
AP	1977 Additional Protocol to the Geneva Conventions
ARIO	Articles on Responsibility of International Organizations
ASR	Articles on State Responsibility
AU	African Union
CEMAC	Economic Community of Central African States
CENTCOM/CC	United States Central Command – Coalition Countries
CFSP	Common Foreign and Security Policy
CIL	Customary International Law
CIS	Commonwealth of Independent States
CRDF	Collective Rapid Deployment Force
CSTO	Collective Security Treaty Organisation
DPKO	Department of Peacekeeping Operations
DRC	Democratic Republic of Congo
DUF	Directives for the Use of Firearms
ECHR	European Convention for the Protection of Human Rights and Fundamental Freedoms
ECJ	European Court of Justice
ECOMOG	Economic Community of West African States Monitoring Group
ECOWAS	Economic Community of West African States
ECtHR	European Court of Human Rights
ESDP	European Security and Defense Policy
EU	European Union
EUNAVFOR	European Union led Naval Force
GA	General Assembly
HQ	Headquarters
HRC	Human Rights Committee
IAC	International Armed Conflict
IBRD	International Bank for Reconstruction and Development
ICC	International Criminal Court
ICCPR	International Covenant on Civil and Political Rights
ICESCR	International Covenant on Economic, Social and Cultural Rights

ICJ	International Court of Justice
ICRC	International Committee of the Red Cross
ICTY	International Criminal Tribunal for the Former Yugoslavia
IED	Improvised Explosive Device
IHL	International Humanitarian Law
IHR	International Human Rights
IHRL	International Human Rights Law
ILC	International Law Commission
IMF	International Monetary Fund
IMM	International Military Missions
INTERFET	International Force for East Timor
IO	International Organisation
ISAF	International Stabilization Force
JP	Joint Publication
KFOR	Kosovo Force
KWSA	Kigali Weapons Secure Area
MFO	Multinational Forces and Observers
MNB	Multinational Brigade
MONUC	United Nations Organization Mission in the Democratic Republic of the Congo
NAC	North Atlantic Council
NATO	North Atlantic Treaty Organisation
NIAC	Non-International Armed Conflict
OECD	Organisation for Economic Cooperation and Development
ONUC	United Nations Operation in the Congo
ONUCA	United Nations Observer Group in Central America
ONUMOZ	United Nations Operation in Mozambique
ONUSAL	United Nations Observer Group in El Salvador
OSCE	Organisation for Security and Co-operation in Europe
PCIJ	Permanent Court of International Justice
PISG	Provisional Institutions of Self-Government
PSI	Proliferation Security Initiative
PSO	Peace Support Operations
QRF	Quick Reaction Force
R2P	Responsibility to Protect
RGF	Rwandese Government Forces
ROE	Rules of Engagement
RPF	Rwandese Patriotic Front
S-G	Secretary-General
SC	Security Council
SFI	Stabilization Force Iraq
SFOR	Stabilization Force in Bosnia and Herzegovina
SOFA	Status of Forces Agreement
TCC	Troop Contributing Country
TCN	Troop Contributing Nations
TFG	Transitional Federal Government

ToA	Transfer of Authority
UDHR	Universal Declaration of Human Rights
UKTS	United Kingdom Treaty Series
UN	United Nations
UNAMID	African Union-United Nations Hybrid Mission in Darfur
UNAMIR	United Nations Assistance Mission for Rwanda
UNAMSIL	United Nations Mission in Sierra Leone
UNAVEM	United Nations Angola Verification Mission
UNCLOS	United Nations Convention on the Law of the Sea
UNEF	United Nation Emergency Force
UNFICVP	United Nations Force in Cyprus
UNFICYP	United Nations Peacekeeping Force in Cyprus
UNIFIL	United Nations Interim Force in Lebanon
UNIIMOC	United Nations Iran/Iraq Military Observer Group
UNIKCOM	United Nations Iraq/Kuwait Observer Mission
UNITAF	Unified Task Force
UNMBIH	United Nations Mission in Bosnia and Herzegovina
UNMEE	United Nations Mission in Ethiopia and Eritrea
UNMIK	United Nations Interim Administration Mission in Kosovo
UNMIT	United Nations Integrated Mission in Timor-Leste
UNOCI	United Nations Operation in Côte d'Ivoire
UNOSOM	United Nations Operation in Somalia
UNPD	United Nations Procurement Division
UNPREDEP	United Nations Preventive Deployment Force
UNPROFOR	United Nations Protection Force
UNSCR	United Nations Security Council Resolution
UNSF	United Nations Security Force in West New Guinea
UNTAC	United Nations Transitional Authority in Cambodia
UNTAET	United Nations Transitional Administration in East Timor
UNTAG	United Nations Transition Assistance Group
UNTS	United Nations Treaty Series
VBSS	Visit, Boarding, Search and Seizure
WEU	Western European Union
WFP	World Food Program
WMD	Weapons of Mass Destruction

Abbreviation of Journals

AFLR	Air Force Law Review
AJIL	American Journal of International Law
All ER	All England Law Reports
AYIL	Australian Yearbook of International Law
Can.Y.B. Int'l Law	Canadian Yearbook of International Law
Columbia HRLR	Columbia Human Rights Law Review
Cornell JIL	Cornell Journal of International Law
ECHR	Reports of Judgements and Decisions of the European Court of Human Rights
EHRLR	European Human Rights Law Review
EHRR	European Human Rights Report
EIR	Executive Intelligence Review
EJIL	European Journal of International Law
HILJ	Harvard International Law Journal
HRLR	Human Rights Law Review
ICLQ	International and Comparative Law Quarterly
IJHR	International Journal of Human Rights
ILM	International Legal Materials
ILR	International Law Reports
IOLR	International Organizations Law Review
IRRC	International Review of the Red Cross
Isr.Y.B.Hum.Rts.	Israel Yearbook on Human Rights
J. Mil. Ethics	Journal of Military Ethics
JCSL	Journal of Conflict and Security Law
JICJ	Journal of International Criminal Justice
JIL	Journal of International Law
Neth.Y.B. Int'l Law	Netherlands Yearbook of International Law
NILR	Netherlands International Law Review
NZAFLR	New Zealand Armed Forces Law Review
OJ	Official Journal of the European Communities
RBDI	Revue Belge de Droit International
RGDIP	Revue Générale de Droit International Publique
RIAA	Reports of International Arbitral Awards
UNTS	United Nations Treaty Series
YIHL	Yearbook of International Humanitarian Law

Foreword

The definition and clarification of international legal rules that should apply to international military operations is a major challenge today. In recent years the United Nations and other regional organisations, such as the North Atlantic Treaty Organisation, the European Union, the African Union and the Organisation of American States, have become increasingly involved in peace-keeping and peace-support operations.

Still, the rules which regulate those missions, which often imply the use of force to protect the local population and to restore a secure and peaceful environment, need further clarification. International Humanitarian Law, Human Rights Law, specific United Nations mandates, Memorandums of Understanding, Status of Forces Agreements, Rules of Engagement and States' national law have been taken into consideration in this book, to provide a comprehensive analysis of legal regulations that can apply to military personnel in the field.

Since the beginning of the United Nations deployment in international peace operations, the International Committee of the Red Cross has supported the idea that fundamental rules of International Humanitarian Law, such as common Article 3 to the four 1949 Geneva Conventions, would apply in the conduct of international operations. The development of International Human Rights Law and its possible extraterritorial application add new and more stringent rules to the protection of civilians where the troops, civilian and police components of multi-functional peace operations are deployed.

In 2008, the International Institute of Humanitarian Law devoted a Seminar and a major Round Table specifically to discussing these important and topical issues. Furthermore, the Institute is particularly involved in teaching and disseminating the fundamental rules that apply in contemporary armed conflicts, including the rules that should regulate peace-keeping operations.

This book, written by very distinguished academics and practitioners, is a particularly welcome contribution to the legal debate surrounding the clarification of the law applicable to international military operations. By looking at essential legal aspects, including human rights, humanitarian law and international criminal law, it provides an important input to the work that international organisations and individuals are offering for the understanding of complex legal structures, and it can be used as a tool for the training of experts and practitioners in the field of international peace operations.

Ambassador Maurizio Moreno
President of the International Institute
of Humanitarian Law, Sanremo

Introduction

The changing nature of armed conflicts poses complex challenges to the legal regulation of the behaviour of the protagonists as well as the protection of victims. The dilemma of a body of law elaborated to address mainly international armed conflicts yet having somehow, through common Article 3, an increasingly irrelevant second Additional Protocol to the 1949 Geneva Conventions, and a reliance on the vagaries of customary international law – however helpful the International Committee of the Red Cross's (ICRC) 2006 Study may have been – to regulate opposing forces in civil wars, has become far greater under the challenge of other developments. One of the most significant is the increasing use of international military missions (IMMs), both by the United Nations (UN) and other groups of States in a variety of situations, not all of which are by any means amenable to straightforward regulation by the Geneva Conventions.

With the end of the Cold War, the distension between different ideological blocks and the emerging new forms of conflict, different types of military operations are increasingly deployed internationally to address a variety of crisis situations which constitute a potential threat to international peace. However, the empirical development of international or multinational operations operates in a rather unclear legal framework, which does not facilitate operational work in what is in any case a usually very uneasy context. The UN, which developed the practice of military contingents in peace-keeping operations (PKOs), has never clearly stated which rules would regulate the acts of its forces engaged in such operations. Only in 1999, under pressure from the ICRC, the UN Secretary-General adopted a Bulletin with fairly general principles related to the application of International Humanitarian Law (IHL) in PKOs. Only in 2008, the Capstone Doctrine, adopted by the UN Department for PKOs, sought to focus on this issue, albeit still in quite general terms, by defining 'principles and guidelines'.

The diverse nature of contemporary armed conflicts and situations of violence, and the different types of missions which are sent to address a variety of threats and challenges, has not been adequately addressed. The law is a mess, or it just isn't. Nobody quite agrees on who is bound by what. The expanding use of military forces and other types of personnel, including police units and civilian experts, in a variety of contexts raises the problem of which rules are, or should be, applicable by and to them.

Many legal scholars and official documents have addressed some of the issues involved; however there is a need to address them in a more comprehensive way, and that is what this book seeks to do.

The type and forms of military operations which are addressed in this book include mainly PKOs, which are deployed under UN mandate, as they represent the most established model of international operations with military components, and due to the limitations on the use of force established under the UN Charter. However other IMMs, for instance under the control of international organisations, or coalition forces (White, Chapter 1) which seem to have an unclear legal status, have been addressed in the book. As the title clearly suggests, the main focus is on IMMs and therefore on military personnel engaged in this type of operation. In some chapters there is reference to cases where police and private contractors are involved in security and other operations which may work together with military contingents, to clarify some rules that may apply to the different types of personnel.

The purpose of this book is to explore the main topics concerning the often unclear regulation of international military forces involved in international operations. It seeks to highlight different existing rules, with special attention to international legal obligations, which play a relevant role in defining the types of legal standards applicable to military personnel.

Therefore, the aim of this book is to provide a documented analysis of the legal regulations applicable to IMMs. This means looking at rules and principles which may be relevant in shaping the legal framework of IMMs (Odello & Piotrowicz, Chapter 2). These may include general international law, both customary and conventional law, international humanitarian law (Sams, Chapter 3; Breau, Chapter 4) and human rights law (Quénivet, Chapter 5). Other types of existing rules can be relevant in the context of international military operations, such as the Rules of Engagement (RoE) which are provided to multinational forces when engaging in the field (Klappe, Chapter 6). Other issues discussed include the development of international criminal law (Massidda, Chapter 8), and the responsibility of international organisations under whose mandate military forces act (Tsagourias, Chapter 9). One chapter is dedicated to the still quite unexplored but emerging area of crisis operations in the maritime environment (Häußler, Chapter 7).

The book avoids addressing the special cases of internal disciplinary issues related to the misconduct of peacekeepers. While this is certainly a most topical issue in the context of UN and other international missions, this matter relates mainly to criminal acts and disciplinary behaviour that should be addressed under national criminal law either of the sending State or of the host State.

The practice of States and multinational coalition forces is also considered, as evidence of the evolution of legal and policy principles, to identify applicable rules and the general practice of States and international organisations.

We hope that this work may contribute to focussing the attention of the international community to address the legal and interpretative gaps, lacunae and occasional overlaps with which the present international system is afflicted. This is not a mere scholarly exercise: we think that clarity of rules makes the work of those involved in military operations more efficient. This book therefore aims at providing also a tool for practitioners and legal experts who have to advise governmental and international institutions that deploy international military missions under different mandates. We also hope that the book may be a useful training tool for military lawyers and policy makers. Finally, with the development of international studies on international organisations and international law addressing this specific subject matter, this book could be used as a teaching tool for postgraduate students and academics who want to explore this complex area of international law.

Special thanks go to each individual contributor for the efforts made in delivering their chapters whilst busy in many other professional activities, to Jill St George and Daniele Perissi for their support in the editing of the final manuscript, to Lindy Melman and Bea Timmer, from Martinus Nijhoff Publishers, for all their support and patience in dealing with this publication in all its stages.

Marco Odello,
Ryszard Piotrowicz,
Aberystwyth

Chapter 1

Towards Integrated Peace Operations: The Evolution of Peacekeeping and Coalitions of the Willing

Nigel D. White

1. Introduction

Historically the United Nations (UN) has concerned itself with defining and developing the concept of peacekeeping since the first full UN peacekeeping force in the Middle East of 1956-67 (UNEF). Peacekeeping was more finely crafted during the Cold War, but in traditional terms reached both its climax and its low-point with the largely unsuccessful peacekeeping operation in Lebanon (UNIFIL) in place since 1978. Such operations are voluntary and are based on consent and co-operation. Generally such operations consist of contributing States' military contingents under UN command and control, specifically the Secretary-General acting under delegated authority from the Security Council, exceptionally the General Assembly. This should be contrasted with the enforcement model that emerged out of Chapter VII of the Charter under which a Coalition of the Willing is authorised by the Security Council with command and control being delegated to the contributing State(s) or organisation.

With disagreements over the composition of any 'standing' UN force and the pervasive use of the veto in the Security Council, Article 42, which empowers the Security Council under Chapter VII of the Charter to take military enforcement action 'by air, sea, or land forces as may be necessary to maintain or restore international peace and security', was largely inoperable during the Cold War. The only significant exception was the Korean War from 1950-3, in which a US-led force received UN authority in the absence of the Soviet Union from the Security Council, to combat North Korean aggression. The Korean episode apart, the superpowers, while not countenancing the development of Article 42, were prepared to allow the development of a much more limited military deployment, namely peacekeeping forces that seemed to fall more on the Chapter VI side of the Security Council's powers, though there is no specific mention of peacekeeping in the Charter.

In general peacekeeping was acceptable during the Cold War because it was kept distinct from military enforcement action. Such a limited military operation not only suited the veto-wielding powers in the Security Council, it also met with the approval of the Non- Aligned states. Indeed the values of peacekeeping – non-intervention and non-aggression - reflected very much the values of the Non-Aligned movement, and more crucially, fundamental principles of international law. It is no coincidence that the major troop contributors to peacekeeping forces during

M. Odello and R. Piotrowicz (eds.), International Military Missions and International Law.
2011 Koninklijke Brill NV. Printed in The Netherlands. ISBN 978 9004 17437 5. pp. 1-23.

the Cold War were smaller volunteer States drawn from outside the five permanent members of the Security Council and their immediate allies.

With the end of the Cold War peacekeeping changed, with operations becoming multi-functional combining peacekeeping with limited peacebuilding, usually centred around the holding of elections as the pivotal event between conflict and a stable state. Such operations were a mixed success, with a number failing because the holding of elections did not engage the factions sufficiently to prevent a fresh outbreak of fighting. Since the Brahimi Report of 2000 we have seen the emergence of more integrated and more ambitious peace operations, which combine peacekeeping with more ambitious peacebuilding, consisting of much more than the crude introduction of democracy to an often alien environment. Given that such operations are often conducted in fragile or failed States, there has been a trend towards enabling the military element of such an operation to use force beyond the traditional limited form of self-defence used by peacekeepers. The emergence of peace operations with Chapter VII elements in effect brings together the doctrines underlying the two forms of international military missions that had emerged during the Cold War – peacekeeping based on traditional international legal principles of consent, non-intervention and non-aggression; and military enforcement based on one of the Charter exceptions to the ban on the use of force. This chapter will trace the legal evolution of the doctrines of peacekeeping and military enforcement, and the problematic move towards convergence.

2. Second Best: The Development of Coalitions of the Willing

The Organisation's collective security role was premised in 1945 on the ability of its primary organ, the Council, ultimately to use military measures to enforce the peace, under Chapter VII specifically Article 42. Article 43 detailed the mechanism whereby armed forces were to be made available, namely by 'special agreements' to be arrived at by members of the UN, detailing the numbers, location and the state of readiness of such forces. These agreements were to be reached as soon as possible. However, although the Military Staff Committee, established under Article 47 of the Charter, did report to the Security Council by April 1947 on the basic principles that should govern the UN's armed forces, Cold War tensions prevented any overall consensus.[1]

With no likelihood of consensus between the permanent members the idea of a UN army was shelved. The collective security vision of UN authority and UN command and control of military enforcement action was therefore unachievable. What developed instead, starting with Korea in 1950, was a partially decentralised system of collective security whereby the UN delegated authority to a state or group of states acting under Chapter VII to take military enforcement action on behalf of the UN. This in essence brings military enforcement action under Article 42 of Chapter VII very close to the system envisaged for regional organisations under Chapter VIII. Article 53 of Chapter VIII provides that 't]he Security Council shall, where appropriate, utilise such regional arrangements or agencies for enforcement action

1 UN SCOR, 2nd Sess., Special Supp. No.1, 1947.

under its authority'. The UN's supremacy in collective security matters of a coercive nature is underlined by the same article when it goes on to state that 'no enforcement action shall be taken under regional arrangements or by regional arrangements without the authorisation of the Security Council'. Although there are debates as to whether regional organisations have autonomy in the field of economic sanctions, it is clear that the Charter prohibits military enforcement action taken without UN authority. Collective defensive military action by regional organisations or *ad hoc* alliances is permitted by Article 51 of the Charter when a member State has been the subject of an armed attack but only until 'until the Security Council has taken measures necessary to maintain international peace and security'.

In the absence of agreements under Article 43 of the Charter, the Security Council has produced a loose decentralised system of collective security. The norm is for the Security Council to authorise a State or group of States under Chapter VII of the UN Charter to take military action to maintain or restore international peace and security. Command of these operations is vested in those States forming the multinational force (or coalition of the willing). The Security Council's main mechanism for controlling the operation it has sanctioned comes in the form of the enabling resolution and a reporting system. Under this the contributing States provide information to the Security Council, usually via the Secretary-General, on the military action taken in pursuance of the mandate. This is a far cry from the formal provisions of Chapter VII of the UN Charter whereby command and control was meant to be centralised under the Military Staff Committee and ultimately the Security Council.[2]

Strategic control by the Military Staff Committee and overall political control by the Council appear necessary for the achievement of the collective security model envisaged by the Charter. This calls into question the Council's practice to date, when it has delegated authority and control to a State or group of States. However, simply to dismiss an alternative system because it does not match the text of the Charter is to adopt a textual approach with little regard to context.[3] The Council may simply authorise one State to use force to achieve an objective within the ambit of the UN's security role. Despite the fact of being performed by one State, it is still a collective authorisation to use force in that it is being performed to carry out the collective will of the Council on behalf of the UN. This is all the more so when the Council authorises a group of States to carry out such a function.[4] It is argued here that the provisions of Chapter VII are processes which, if in operation, would facilitate the exercise of power contained in Article 42. They can be seen as just one method of

2 Articles 45-47 of the UN Charter, 24 October 1945, 1 UNTS XVI.

3 *But see* J. Quigley, 'The United States and the United Nations in the Persian Gulf War: New Order or Disorder?' (1992) 25 *Cornell JIL* 1.

4 This seems to be envisaged by Article 48 of the UN Charter which provides in paragraph 1 that 'the action required to carry out the decisions of the Security Council for the maintenance of international peace and security shall be taken by all the Members of the United Nations or by some of them, as the Security Council may determine'. *See also* paragraph 2, which envisages such action by member states acting in 'appropriate international agencies'.

allowing the Council to fulfil its collective security function. Thus, it would appear to be unnecessary to make these methods a prerequisite to the use of military enforcement action by the Council.[5]

Though the system that has emerged is not *ultra vires* the UN Charter it has problems that call into question its legitimacy. Whereas an ideal collective security system envisages aggression and threats to the peace being met whenever they occur, the decentralised system is erratic. Its operation often occurs only when dominant States' interests are at stake, and it can easily be blocked by the veto when a permanent member sees its interests as being threatened. It must be pointed out that a veto-bound Council is a flaw that undermines both the original centralised security scheme and the second best decentralised one that has in effect replaced it.

Having said that, with the end of the Cold War, the collective security system started to operate in a fashion closer to that envisaged in 1945. What is clear at the moment is that the Council has not yet 'decided' to use military force, it has simply recommended or authorised States, on a voluntary basis, to use force in particular situations and for particular purposes. Inevitably, the voluntary nature of the military option undermines the collective security ideal that every aggression is met with counter-force, since there may be no willing volunteers or, indeed, those initially volunteering may withdraw without any legal hindrance.[6] However, it is difficult to argue against the volunteer system of UN-authorised military action under Chapter VII when Chapter VIII explicitly accepts it under Article 53 as regards regional arrangements.

2.1 Coalitions in Action

Although not matching the original Charter scheme, the decentralised military option which has been developed by the Security Council to deal with acts of aggression (Korea in 1950 and Kuwait in 1991), and threats to the peace (such as found in Somalia in 1993, Haiti in 1994 and again in 2003, Bosnia in 1995, Albania in 1997, East Timor in 1999, and the DR Congo in 2003) is a lawful development of its powers to maintain or restore international peace and security. This does not mean that the system does not have any legal parameters. *De minimis* there must be an authorising resolution from the Security Council,[7] which given its import and the fact that it is purporting to delegate potentially devastating powers to States must be construed narrowly.[8] In the United Nations there is consensus that the phrase 'all necessary measures' or 'all necessary means' in combination with an 'authorisation' 'under

5 T.D. Gill, 'Legal and Some Political Limitations on the Power of the UN Security Council top Exercise its Enforcement Powers under Chapter VII of the UN Charter' (1995) 26 *Netherlands YBIL* 61.

6 *But see* D. Sarooshi, *The United Nations and the Development of Collective Security* (Clarendon, Oxford, 1999) 150.

7 J. Lobel and M. Ratner, 'Bypassing the Security Council: Ambiguous Authorizations to Use Force, Cease-Fires and the Iraqi Inspection Regime' (1999) 93 *AJIL* 124, 125-7.

8 *Sarooshi* (n 6) 44.

Chapter VII' signifies that military enforcement action is being sanctioned. Other language will not do.

The UN collective security system clearly overlaps with the collective self-defence regime when the international community is responding to a case of armed aggression when one State invades another. In the two cases where the UN has authorised a response to aggression it has been argued by some jurists that the UN is simply legitimating a response which is clearly already legally based on the right of collective self-defence enshrined in Article 51 of the UN Charter.[9] However, for the States involved in the operation as well as the State members of the organisation authorising the military action, the legal basis of the operation is Chapter VII of the UN Charter, specifically Article 42. It is a UN military operation fulfilling UN aims and objectives,[10] rather than those defined by the customary law of self-defence. Clearly the UN has the legal power to authorise responses to aggression under Articles 39 and 42 of the Charter, and in the case of Korea in 1950 and Iraq in 1990 the organisation did just that.

In the case of Korea in 1950 the Security Council recommended 'that the Members of the United Nations furnish such assistance to the Republic of Korea as may be necessary to repel the armed attack and to restore international peace and security in the area'.[11] The mandate clearly goes beyond the purely defensive, which would be restricted to repelling the attack by North Korea. It seems to permit the UN authorised army to take offensive action if necessary to restore international peace and security. The mandate is clearly too ambiguous to be fully acceptable, but doubts as to whether the Security Council mandate was adequate for a crossing of the 38th parallel into North Korea by the UN authorised, US-led operation seemed to be dispelled by the General Assembly's supporting resolution.[12] The General Assembly had to take over as the organ of authority with the Soviet Union having returned to the Security Council ensuring deadlock in that chamber.

The UN authorised response to the North Korean intervention eventually led to a return to the status quo in the Korean peninsula, although only after the US-led operation had been pushed out of North Korea by the Chinese army. The dangers of attempting to enforce peace on an aggressor seemed to influence the extent of the military operation undertaken against Iraq in 1991, following that country's aggression against Kuwait. Council Resolution 678 of 29 November 1990 authorised member States 'to use all necessary means to uphold and implement Security

9 J. Stone, *Legal Controls of International Conflict* (Stevens, London, 1954) 234-7; E.V. Rostow, 'Until What? Enforcement Action or Collective Self-Defense?' (1991) 85 *AJIL* 506-10; O. Schachter, 'United Nations Law in the Gulf Conflict' (1991) 85 *AJIL* 452, 459-60; R. Lavalle, 'The Law of the United Nations and the Use of Force under Relevant Security Council Resolutions of 1990 and 1991 to Resolve the Persian Gulf Crisis' (1992) 23 *Netherlands YBIL* 3, 62.

10 N.D. White and O. Ulgen, 'The Security Council and the Decentralized Military Option: Constitutionality and Function' (1997) 44 *NILR* 378; D.W. Bowett, *United Nations Forces* (Stevens, London, 1964) 45-7.

11 *UNSC Res. 83* (27 June 1950).

12 *UNGA Res. 376* (7 October 1950).

Council resolution 660 and all subsequent resolutions and to restore international peace and security in the area', unless Iraq withdrew before 15 January 1991. Despite the wider permissive phrase, the coalition of forces again commanded by the US restricted its operation to the removal of Iraq from Kuwait. Although the air campaign did penetrate deep into Iraq and was aimed at industrial as well as military targets, and the ground offensive did involve a temporary occupation of large parts of southern Iraq, these actions seemed only to be those necessary to ensure the successful liberation of Kuwait.

Both the Korean and Kuwaiti operations were successful in that they achieved the aim of repelling the aggressor. The wider aims of collective security – in particular in trying to tackle the source of the aggression - though have presented problems. In the case of Korea, this nearly resulted in a worldwide conflagration as the UN authorised army's crossing into North Korea provoked a massive Chinese military intervention. In the case of Iraq it was decided by the Security Council to deal with Iraq in a non-military way after the coalition had freed Kuwait, by the continuation of sanctions and an enhanced inspection regime.[13] Frustration at the perceived lack of success of this regime led western States to step outside UN authority when taking military actions culminating in the invasion of Iraq by the US and UK in 2003, despite attempts to stretch the cloak of UN resolutions over their actions.

The UN's response to threats to the peace is equally patchy. During the Cold War the response was non-existent at least at the military level, with the possible exception of the authorisation to the UK for the Beira patrol to stop the importation of oil by southern Rhodesia in breach of the Security Council's sanctions regime.[14] After 1990 the UN has been much more active, though with varying levels of success. On the one hand there have been the debacles of Somalia (1993-5), Rwanda (1994) and Bosnia pre-Dayton (1993-5), balanced by the successes in Haiti (1994), Albania (1997) and East Timor (1999). In the balance hangs the UN authorised operations in Bosnia (1995-) and Kosovo (1999-). These conflicts are far too complicated to offer any in depth analysis of UN involvement in the space of this chapter, although a few general comments can be made as regards some of the UN authorised operations to date.

The danger of 'mission creep' was particularly prevalent in Somalia where the initial humanitarian aims of the UNITAF operation stated in 1992[15] were supplanted by the desire to build a State in Somalia. While State building is a legitimate and desirable aim, particularly when faced with a 'failed State', the lesson of Somalia is that it cannot be achieved easily by force of arms. The failure to quell the factions in Somalia and the resultant ignominious withdrawal of UNITAF's successor UNOSOM II in 1995 are testament to this. Some degree of consent is needed. Even then more time and resources are needed for the restoration of both a negative and a positive peace within the country than were exerted in the initial military operation.

13 *UNSC Res. 687* (3 April 1991).

14 *UNSC Res. 221* (9 April 1966).

15 *UNSC Res. 794* (3 December 1992).

The initial success of the mere threat of a US-led intervention in Haiti in 1994,[16] must be soberly balanced against the struggles of the UN peacekeeping and peacebuilding operations thereafter. Further evidence of this can be found in the UN authorised operations in Bosnia after the Dayton Agreement of 1995, and in Kosovo from June 1999 following the unauthorised NATO bombings of the FRY. The cycle of violence that has stretched back for centuries in this region is not going to be broken easily and requires a long-term commitment both in terms of a military presence and in terms of civilian administration, with the EU taking the lead in both Bosnia and Kosovo. There are no short-term solutions to the underlying problems. States must be prepared to support, resource and fund continuing multi-faceted operations if peace is to be permanently brought to these zones of violence.[17]

3. Third Best: The Creation of Peacekeepers

Peacekeeping was defined by the UN at the end of the Cold War in 1991 as an 'operation involving military personnel, but without enforcement powers, undertaken by the United Nations to help maintain or restore international peace and security in areas of conflict. These operations are voluntary and are based on consent and co-operation'.[18] The superpowers, while not countenancing the development of Article 42, were prepared to allow the development of a much more limited military deployment, as a third best military option after the original Charter scheme for military action (the best option) and the coalitions of the willing that replaced it as a second best option.

The acceptability of a peacekeeping force lies in the fact that it usually has limited objectives, normally by helping to maintain a cease-fire and a separation of the belligerents, not by enforcement but by consent and co-operation. Hence peacekeeping is still stated by the General Assembly's Special Committee on Peacekeeping to be based on a trinity of virtues – consent, impartiality, and restrictions on the use of force.[19] While the latter clearly includes a peacekeeper using force in defence of his own life, his 'comrades and any person entrusted in [his] care, as well as defending [his] post, convoy, vehicle or rifle',[20] there has been a lack of clarity as to whether the force could also 'defend' its mandate. As Secretary-General Hammarskjold recognised in 1956 the wider the right of self-defence is drawn the more blurred

16 *UNSC Res. 940* (31 July 1994).

17 *See* 'Report of the Panel on United Nations Peace Operation (The Brahimi Report)' (21 August 2000) UN docs. A/55/305, S/2000/809.

18 *The Blue Helmets: A Review of United Nations Peacekeeping* (2nd ed, United Nations, 1990). *See also* the International Court's advisory opinion in which it endorsed the development of peacekeeping – *Certain Expenses of the United Nations* (Advisory Opinion) [1962] ICJ Rep. 151.

19 Special Committee on Peacekeeping, 'Comprehensive review of the whole question of peacekeeping operations in all their aspects Report' (28 March 2003) UN Doc. A/56/767 para. 46.

20 'General Guidelines for Peace-Keeping Operations' (1995) UN Doc. UN/210/TC/CG95.

the distinction between peacekeeping and enforcement action under Chapter VII becomes.[21] Secretary-General Waldheim's 1973 guideline, which stated that 'self-defence would include resistance to attempts by forceful means to prevent the force from discharging its duties under the mandate of the Security Council',[22] seemed to raise the prospect of a widely drawn mandate giving rise to enforcement action, though in practice rules of engagement were drawn quite conservatively.[23] In general peacekeeping was acceptable during the Cold War because it was kept distinct from enforcement action. Such a limited military operation not only suited the veto-wielding powers in the Security Council, it also met with the approval of the Non Aligned States. It is no coincidence that the major troop contributors to peacekeeping forces during the Cold War were smaller volunteer States drawn from outside the five permanent members of the Security Council and their immediate allies (with the exception of the UK in Cyprus).

3.1 Multi-Dimensional Peacekeeping

Classically peacekeeping was kept separate from peacebuilding, so that for example the efforts of the Secretary-General to find a permanent peaceful solution to the Cyprus problem has not been integral to the presence of the blue-helmeted force that has been on the island since 1964 (UNFICYP), helping to keep the parties apart but in so doing helping to maintain the continuing division of the island. However, even in the Cold War there were exceptions to this separation of keeping the peace to building the peace, one forceful (ONUC in the Congo 1960-64), and one consensual (UNSF in West Irian 1962-3). Though these were not called peace operations they were early instances of such.

The post-Cold War peace operations, where peacekeeping was combined with peacemaking under the principles of consent, impartiality and the limited use of force, started with the UN operation in Namibia (UNTAG) in 1989. In the early 1990s the UN rapidly developed a multi-dimensional peacekeeping and peacebuilding model, a number of examples of which were successful in achieving their more ambitious mandates, for example in Nicaragua (ONUCA 1989-92), in El Salvador (ONUSAL 1991-5), in Cambodia (UNTAC 1991-3), and in Mozambique (ONUMOZ 1992-4), though a number struggled, most notably UNAVEM in Angola (1989-97).

In straightforward terms such operations took the form of a combined military/civilian mission which supervised the end of the hostilities, and oversaw peacebuilding including an election process with the aim of producing a stable State. The

---

21 'Report of the Secretary-General on UNEF I' (1956) UN Doc. A/3943 para. 179.

22 'Report of the Secretary-General on the Implementation of Security Council Resolution 340' (1973) UN Doc. S/11052/Rev.1.

23 M. Goulding, 'The Evolution of United Nations Peacekeeping' (1993) 69 *International Affairs* 451, 455. Rules of engagement 'provide as clearly as possible the parameters within which armed military personnel assigned to a peacekeeping operation may use force' – R. Zacklin, 'The Use of Force in Peacekeeping Operations' in N. Blokker and N. Schrijver (eds), *The Security Council and the Use of Force* (Martinus Nijhoff Publishers, The Hague, 2005) 100.

force consisted of a military component whose function was to 'serve in a supporting role: to guarantee and maintain a secure environment in which the civilian components' could work, by helping to maintain a cease-fire, and by the cantonment or withdrawal and disarmament of factions as provided by the peace agreement. Mine clearance was also included in most. Secondly, a police element with a role that was 'between the military and civilian actors' by assisting in maintenance of public order, by crowd control, law enforcement and training local police officers. This was often accompanied by the development or reform of the judicial system. Finally there was a sizeable civilian component consisting of both IGO and NGO actors with political, electoral, human rights and humanitarian functions. The political function included overall guidance in the peace process and help with rebuilding or developing political institutions. The electoral function included advice, education, monitoring and verification of the electoral process. The human rights function consisted of promoting, educating, monitoring, and investigating abuses. Finally, the humanitarian function included the delivery of aid, the implementation of the right of return for refugees, and the re-integration of former combatants.[24] All of these elements are found and developed in complex peace operations reviewed below. Such developments have led to what has been labelled the 'civilianisation' of peace operations whereby the still large military peacekeeping component is matched by the inclusion of 'civil administration, humanitarian assistance, policing, electoral, human rights monitoring, economic revival functions and personnel', which have not always been effectively co-ordinated.[25]

3.2 Peacekeeping plus Peace Enforcement

The crucial problem with the development of peace operations from a practice and doctrinal basis in consensual and limited peacekeeping, is that while peacekeeping and peacemaking can be perfectly compatible and complementary when both are based on negotiated peaceful solutions with the consent of all the parties (and not just the government), difficulties arise if the peacebuilding element is, or becomes, undertaken in an environment that is 'non-consensual' or at best 'semi-permissive',[26] for example through the actions of factions (commonly referred to as 'spoilers') who would undermine the process. Spoilers were defined by the High Level Panel in 2004 as 'factions who see a peace agreement as inimical to their interests, power or ideology, use violence to undermine or overthrow settlements'.[27] The need for coercive enforcement action in these circumstances becomes difficult to avoid, especially

24 W. Hansen, O. Ramsbotham and T. Woodhouse, *Hawks and Doves: Peacekeeping and Conflict Resolution* (Berghof Research Centre for Constructive Conflict Management, 2004) 5.

25 J. Cockayne and D. Malone, 'United Nations Peace Operations: Then and Now' (2005) 9 *International Peacekeeping: The Yearbook of International Peace Operations*, 1, 18.

26 *Hansen, Ramsbotham, and Woodhouse* (n 24) 6.

27 'High Level Panel Report, Report of the High Level Panel on Threats Challenges and Change, A More Secure World: Our Shared Responsibility' (2004) UN Doc. A/59/565, 222.

given the need to prevent repetition of the failures of the UN forces in Rwanda in 1994 and at Srebrenica in 1995. In such situations the traditional principles of peacekeeping cannot be fully upheld, which will make it problematic in the long term for states to agree to peacekeeping forces or even to contribute to them if there is a possibility that such forces will be used to enforce the peace when it has been breached.

Though not using the term 'peace operation', Secretary-General Boutros-Ghali paved the way for the development of a more integrated approach to combined civilian/military operations in his Agenda for Peace report of 1992, which was to contain proposals for strengthening and making more efficient such operations in the post-Cold War era. Though in elaborating the elements of what have become known as peace operations, the Secretary-General seemed to maintain a consensual view of such operations, he did imply that peacekeeping forces could be deployed without consent if necessary.[28] The report further recommended the deployment of better armed 'peace-enforcement units' forcefully to 'restore and maintain' a ceasefire that had been breached.[29] Beyond this it did not attempt to change the classical principles of peacekeeping, and certainly in the light of the Brahimi Report and other conceptions of peace operations, Agenda for Peace was not such a radical document. It was rather the Secretary-General's instrumental role in the disastrous UN operation in Somalia (UNOSOM 1993-5), where a peacekeeping force was given an enforcement mandate under Chapter VII, which led to both him and the UN as a whole reconsidering the question of whether it was desirable to move peacekeeping away from the values of non-aggression and non-intervention. In the Supplement to an Agenda for Peace of January 1995, the Secretary-General admitted that the forces in Somalia and Bosnia (UNPROFOR 1992-95) 'were given additional mandates that required the use of force and therefore could not be combined with existing mandates requiring the consent of the parties, impartiality and the use of force'. He concluded by stating that 'nothing is more dangerous for a peace-keeping operation than to ask it to use force when its existing composition, armaments, logistics support and deployment deny it the capacity to do so'.[30]

Thus, conceptually as well as practically, there seems to be a divide between peacekeeping and military enforcement action. They share a military heritage but 'the logic of peace-keeping flows from political and military premises that are quite distinct from that of enforcement; and the dynamics of the latter are incompatible with the political process that peace-keeping is intended to facilitate'. Boutros-Ghali concludes that to 'blur the distinction between the two can undermine the viability of the peace-keeping operation and endanger its personnel'.[31] The problem remains though that peacekeepers will be faced not only with the actions of those

28 Report of the Secretary-General Pursuant to the Statement Adopted by the Summit Meeting of the Security Council on 31 January 1992, 'An Agenda for Peace' (17 June 1992) UN Document A/47/277 – S/24111, para. 20.

29 Ibid. para. 44.

30 'Supplement to an Agenda for Peace: Position Paper of the Secretary-General on the Occasion of the Fiftieth Anniversary of the United Nations' (3 January 1995) UN Document A/50/60 and S/1995/1 para. 35.

31 Ibid.

who may wish to undermine the peace, but with actions that violate the fundamental human rights of civilian populations. Both the Independent Report into Rwanda,[32] and the Secretary-General's Report into Srebrenica,[33] highlighted the inadequacies of peacekeeping as a tool for dealing with situations of massive human rights abuse, by concluding that in such situations 'the neutral, impartial and mediating role of the United Nations was proving woefully inadequate'.[34] The desire to tackle this issue, as well as reform the creaking peacekeeping function whose credibility had suffered greatly in the mid-1990s, led the UN Secretary-General Kofi Annan to establish the Panel on United Nations Peace Operations chaired by Lakhdar Brahimi. The aim of this Panel was not simply to address the issue of how peacekeepers should approach human rights violations but went much wider to try in effect to address the tension between the traditional values of peacekeeping and the need for greater effectiveness of the UN in intra-State conflict situations.[35]

4. Towards Integrated Peace Operations

According to the Henry L. Stimson Center:

> Peace operations comprise peacekeeping – the provision of temporary post-conflict security by internationally mandated forces – and peacebuilding – those efforts undertaken by the international community to help a war-torn society create a self-sustaining peace.[36]

This succinct definition provides a starting point to analysing a concept that has emerged in the post-Cold War period, reaching its solidification in the Brahimi Report of 2000. Whereas peacekeeping forces are largely military in composition, peace operations will have a variety of professionals and experts, from soldiers, to police, relief workers, election monitors, human rights workers, development advisers and so on. In the post-Cold War period 'most peace operations are conducted in weak/fragile or failed States', which 'has implications both for the security environment and for the mandates of such missions'.[37]

The Brahimi Report of 2000 outlined the three principal elements of UN peace operations:

---

32 'Report of the Independent Inquiry into the Actions of the United Nations during the 1994 Genocide in Rwanda' (16 December 1999) UN Doc. S/1999/1257.

33 'Report of the Secretary-General pursuant to General Assembly Resolution 53/35: The Fall of Srebrenica' (15 November 1999) UN Doc. A/54/549.

34 *Hansen, Ramsbotham and Woodhouse* (n 24) 6.

35 C. Gray, *International Law and the Use of Force* (2nd ed. Oxford University Press, Oxford, 2004) 238.

36 *Compare* <www.stimson.org.> It is also interesting to note that the Pearson Peacekeeping Centre now commonly uses the term 'peace operations' rather than peacekeeping operations – *cf.* <www.peaceoperations.org.>.

37 Challenges Project, *Meeting the Challenges of Peace Operations: Cooperation and Coordination* (Elanders Gotab, Stockholm, 2005) 38.

1. Conflict prevention and peacemaking. Conflict prevention normally being diplomatic activity while peacemaking also uses the tools of diplomacy and mediation but addresses conflicts in progress.
2. Peacekeeping has evolved from the traditional military model of observing cease-fires and forces separation best suited to inter-state conflicts, to 'incorporate a complex model of many elements, military and civilian, working together to build peace in the dangerous aftermath of civil wars'.
3. Peacebuilding 'defines activities undertaken on the far side of conflict to reassemble the foundations of peace and provide the tools for building on those foundations something that is more than just the absence of war'. It includes the reintegration of former combatants into civilian life, strengthening the rule of law (e.g. police and judiciary, prisons); improving respect for human rights; providing technical assistance for democratic development; and promoting conflict resolution and reconciliation techniques.[38]

It has been seen how peacekeeping and peacebuilding (elements 2 and 3) can be combined though this may produce tension between the cardinal principles of peacekeeping reflecting a non-interventionist approach, and the desire for effectiveness. However, the inclusion of 'conflict prevention and peacemaking' (element 1) within the overall concept of a peace operation is problematic since these are really the processes that occur at the diplomatic level before, during and after conflicts, making it difficult to see them as part of an 'operation', a term which connotes a organised team on the ground. Though there can be preventive deployments of peacekeepers (for example UNPREDEP in Macedonia 1995-99), this is relatively rare and so maybe the clearer definition is that of the Stimpson Center which sees a peace operation as consisting of peacekeeping and peacebuilding (elements 2 and 3). However, building a conflict resolution function into both the peacekeeping and peacemaking elements by including civilian and military negotiators, might be a more effective way forward, complementing higher level but perhaps more remote diplomatic activity. Negotiators or individuals with negotiating skills embedded in the peace operation may well be able to keep the peace process on track by utilising greater local knowledge and contact with leaders at various levels.

4.1 Peacebuilding

Probably with such failures as the mission in Angola in mind, the Brahimi Report recognises that free and fair elections are just part of a process of building 'governance institutions', democratisation, the protection of human rights and the development of civil society.[39] The peace operation aims to develop a partnership with the local population and time is taken in developing political and civil processes. In a number of early peace operations 'hasty elections' took the 'place of finding legitimate inter-

38 *Brahimi Report* (n 17) paras. 10-13.

39 *Brahimi Report* (n 17) para. 38.

locutors'.[40] Thus there is no quick fix in which the international community supervises elections and then leaves, though there has to be a developed exit strategy based on a clear timetable under which a stable government and society is formed. Once it is clear that the people have exercised their right of self-determination (which does not mean simply holding elections) and secure institutions and processes are in place, then the sovereignty and independence of the people and the country should be respected and the operation withdrawn, unless a small residual operation is left in a more symbolic role.[41] The problems in Bosnia (UNMBIH 1995-2002) and Kosovo (UNMIK 1999-2008) in which peace operations struggled to establish such conditions, are a salient reminder that these are ambitious projects. An essential element is that the process must engage the local population and ensure that they are the main stakeholders as well as the beneficiaries of the process. Fundamentally, the process should allow for the local population to shape the society, not for that to be shaped by the outside actors.

In this respect, it is important that the peacekeepers and peacebuilders are accountable for their actions, and are not allowed to hide behind their immunities as has hitherto often been the case. Sexual abuse of women and girls by some individuals in the Congo operation (MONUC 1999-) is a recent example. Though actions before the local courts may be counter-productive, individuals (including private contractors engaged to fulfil certain aspects of the peace operation) guilty of criminal acts or human rights abuse should be punished and not simply repatriated. Agreements should be made between contributing States and the international organisation dealing with the issue of punishment. In addition, it would enhance the legitimacy of the operation if each had an ombudsman to receive and process complaints of ill-treatment. The legitimacy of the operation is undermined if the international components are seen as above the law, while at the same time promoting the rule of law within the country itself.

In addition to enhanced security provided by international peacekeepers and police, peacebuilders are concerned to promote reconciliation, governance, humanitarian assistance and development.[42] Peacebuilders promote reconciliation by refugee return, peace education, but also methods and processes for dealing with the 'psycho-social trauma' of the conflict, which may include a truth and reconciliation commission. In these situations the peacebuilders have to try and reconcile the need to negotiate with those who may have abused human rights with the longer-term end of promoting reconciliation and justice.[43]

Concern has been expressed about the need to preserve 'humanitarian space' for the civilian humanitarian and development agencies to operate, by the military component in particular respecting those agencies' principles of impartiality and humani-

40 *Challenges Project* (n 37) 48.

41 *See* current role of UNMIT in East Timor.

42 *Hansen, Ramsbotham and Woodhouse* (n 24) 18.

43 E.B.Eide, A.T. Kaspersen, R. Kent and K. von Hippel, *Report on Integrated Missions* (Independent Study for the Expanded UN ECHA Core Group, 2005) 7.

ty.[44] The development of civil/military Provincial Reconstruction Teams (for example as part of ISAF in Afghanistan from 2001) has blurred the line between humanitarian and military operations, and has led to 'concerns in the humanitarian community regarding the primary motives of the military and what many humanitarians believe to be the distortion of humanitarian principles and policies'.[45] The solution may be to recognise that the military element of the peace operation should only be involved in humanitarian assistance in certain limited circumstances of extreme need, or extreme violence. Normally the military and police elements of the operation will concentrate on providing a secure environment in which humanitarian and other civilian agencies may operate.

The promotion and protection of both civil and political rights, and economic, social and cultural rights, is essential in developing fair and effective governance. Peacebuilders should be careful to promote the different types of rights equally, and not see civil and political rights as a priority (whether for ideological or practical reasons). Only in so doing can the right to self-determination in both its political and economic aspects be promoted. Of importance for the economic aspect of the right to self-determination is the task of development and relief which will include at the lowest level the meeting of basic needs (the fulfilment of the basic human rights to life, food, water and shelter),[46] and then the development of the economic and social infrastructure. Clearly there is a danger here of interfering in the choices a society might make about economic, social and political development, and so the local population should have a clear say in these choices. 'The aim of any international support should not be to create replicas of their own home paradigms',[47] but should be to facilitate choices and decision-making by the local population.

The reality though might not be so impartial. Roland Paris has argued that 'most international organisations engaged in peacebuilding have internalised the broadly liberal political and economic values of the wealthy and powerful industrialised democracies', and have in effect 'transplanted' those values (elections, civil and political rights and market reforms) into weak countries in which peace operations have been located. This is most evident in cases of 'proxy government' by the UN in Kosovo and East Timor (UNTAET 1999-2002) though it is not only in these obvious cases, but in other multifunctional operations such as occurred in Cambodia and Mozambique. This process he argued amounts to the 'globalisation of the very idea of what a State should look like and how it should act'.[48] However, while the consensus in the UN General Assembly is to support democratisation, built around the minimal requirements of free and fair elections,[49] the long-term economic reform

44 Ibid. 28.

45 *Challenges Project* (n 37) 46.

46 *See* N.D. White, 'Towards a Strategy for Human Rights Protection in Post-Conflict Situations', in N.D. White and D. Klaasen (eds), *The UN, Human Rights and Post-Conflict Situations* (Manchester University Press, Manchester, 2005) 465-6.

47 *Challenges Project* (n 37) 21.

48 R. Paris, 'International Peacekeeping and the 'Mission Civilisatrice' (2002) 28 *Review of International Studies* 637, 638-9.

49 N.D. White, 'The United Nations and Democracy Assistance: Developing Practice

of a country is in the hands of the IMF, IBRD and other lenders, which, arguably, have different agendas to the UN Assembly and UNDP. Though part of the UN system, the Bretton Woods Organizations enjoy far more autonomy than other specialised agencies, and because of their weighted voting system, have agendas that can be set by the OECD countries. The conditionalities imposed by the IBRD on loans to post-conflict States intrudes into their sovereignty by requiring market-oriented economic and political reforms,[50] which leads them inevitably down the path towards market economies. It is questionable whether these organisations are or should be fully included within the concept of a peace operation for their ideologies are different to the other elements, in that they seem more about State-building than peacebuilding. On the other hand, to bring them into the overall operation and to recognise that they are bound by the same principles of impartiality and consent may be a more compelling argument. It is doubtful whether the newly created Peacebuilding Commission in developing integrated strategies for post-conflict rebuilding and recovery will usher in a renewed impartiality to peace operations. In recommending the establishment of the new commission at the World Summit in 2005, the General Assembly merely stated that the World Bank and the IMF should be invited to participate in all the Peacebuilding Commission's meetings.[51]

4.2 Peacekeeping

Peacekeeping is clearly the well-established element of a peace operation. As recounted in the Brahimi Report, during the Cold War peacekeeping was the dominant function and generally included the monitoring of a cease-fire and the withdrawal of troops under an agreement of the former belligerent parties. Peacebuilding was a separate function, which meant that peacekeeping forces could be in situ for decades. Although such forces have still been deployed in the post-Cold War era (for example UNMEE emplaced between Ethiopia and Eritrea in 2000), they are difficult to justify unless accompanied by 'serious and sustained peacemaking efforts that seek to transform a ceasefire accord into a durable and lasting peace settlement'.[52]

Such criticisms, plus the less restrictive atmosphere of the post-Cold War period, led the UN to combine peacekeeping with peacebuilding in 'complex peace operations deployed into settings of intra-State conflict'.[53] Currently, these are in place in Kosovo, the Democratic Republic of the Congo, Liberia, Côte d'Ivoire, Haiti and Sudan. In such operations the complexity of the task and the complexity of the still volatile and hostile environment with any number of actors being involved or having

---

within a Constitutional Framework' in P. Burnell (ed), *Democracy Assistance: International Co-operation for Democratization* (Frank Cass, London, 2000) 74-6.

50 *Paris* (n 48) 644; *See* N.D. White, *The United Nations System: Towards International Justice* (Lynne Rienner, Boulder, 2002) 281-2 for a discussion of Article 4(10) of the IBRD Articles of Agreement which prohibit the Bank from interfering in the political affairs of States.

51 *UNGA Res. 60/1 (24 October 2005)* para. 102.

52 *Brahimi Report* (n 17) para.17.

53 Ibid. para. 28.

an interest make it very difficult for the operation to fulfil its mandate. In these situations 'United Nations missions put not only their own people but peace itself at risk unless they perform their tasks with the competence and efficiency that the situation requires and have serious great power backing'.[54]

Some protection for peacekeepers is provided by the 1994 Convention on the Safety and Security of UN and Associated Personnel, which prohibits attacks on peacekeepers and imposes a duty on host States to prosecute or extradite those accused of committing violence against peacekeepers.[55] However, such protection ceases to apply to enforcement actions under Chapter VII where UN personnel are engaged as combatants, in which case international humanitarian law applies.[56] Thus it is important to determine whether UN peacekeepers are engaged as combatants or not in order to determine the level of protection that applies to them. More widely, the development of complex peace operations to include peacebuilding has inevitably led to the inclusion of powerful States in such operations, and consequently has diluted the cardinal principles of peacekeeping based on respect for non-intervention and sovereignty.

In the period after 2000 complex peace operations have regularly been given certain Chapter VII or enforcement powers to enable them to fulfil aspects of their mandates, tasks undertaken by the peacekeeping element, which is clearly a departure from traditional peacekeeping values.[57] In fact from the turn of the century it has become normal practice for a Chapter VII mandate to be given to peace operations on the basis 'that even the most benign environment can turn sour when spoilers emerge to undermine a peace agreement and put civilians at risk'.[58]

Impartiality will be justifiably impaired if peacekeepers are under a duty to protect civilians within their care, for they will sometimes have to use aggressive force to repel attacks on civilians as well as themselves. In such an environment the Brahimi Report recommended that peace operations be bigger and better equipped, so that they can deal with 'spoilers' and also protect civilians where necessary. The idea is that such forces would act as a credible deterrent, in contrast to traditional peacekeeping forces, which were more symbolic and non-interventionist. Contributing States in such peace operations must be prepared to allow their troops to operate under robust rules of engagement and run the risk of casualties and, while still supporting the peacekeeping principles of consent, impartiality and the use of force only in self-defence, the Report represented an attempt to draw the peacekeeping line nearer to Chapter VII than Chapter VI.[59] Impartiality has become lack of partiality in the

54 Ibid.

55 *Zacklin* (n 23) 101-3. *See also* Article 8(2)(b)(iii) of the Rome Statute of the International Criminal Court (adopted 17 July 1998, entered into force 1 July 2002) (1998) 2187 UNTS 3.

56 Article 2(2) of the 1994 Convention.

57 *Zacklin* (n 23) 91.

58 *High Level Panel Report* (n 27) para. 213.

59 *Brahimi Report* (n 17) paras. 48-52.

carrying out of the mandate, as opposed to the traditional approach that interpreted impartiality as neutrality and non-intervention.

Overall though, the function of the peacekeeping element of the peace operation is to provide security by overseeing the cease-fire, by protecting human rights,[60] by demobilising the armed factions, by disarming and de-mining, and by police and army reform. The peacekeeping force should not only protect the human rights of individuals within its area of deployment (which might require forceful intervention on occasions), but must be human rights compliant in its own activities (for example when detaining spoilers), and when engaged in conflict it must respect the principles of international humanitarian law contained in the Geneva Conventions (including distinguishing between combatants and non-combatants, and distinguishing between military and civilian targets).[61] In 2006 the Security Council stated that peacekeeping and peacebuilding missions should, where appropriate, have a mandate that includes the 'protection of civilians, particularly those under imminent threat of physical danger, within their zones of operation' and stated its intention that such 'protections mandates' are implemented.[62] Certainly this is reflected in the more coercive mandates of recent UN peace operations. Arguments have been made that this reflects an emerging wider norm of a collective responsibility to protect in the event of genocide and other large scale killings, ethnic cleansing or serious violations of international humanitarian law which sovereign governments have proved powerless or unwilling to prevent.[63]

In sum peace operations commonly have the following elements: (i) they are based on an internationally brokered peace agreement (ii) they are normally mandated by the Security Council increasingly utilising Chapter VII (iii) sometimes the operation draws on a number of organisations – the UN, EU, NATO, OSCE etc (iv) they do not simply observe the status quo but they have the more ambitious aims of managing transitions – assisting in post-conflict rebuilding (v) they are involved in the restoration of stability, law and order, the protection of civilians, and providing the basis for long-term recovery development and democratic governance (vi) to this end they are constructed around three functions involving differing actors – peacekeeping, development and humanitarian actors (vii) because of the varied nature of the post-conflict situations in which such operations operate there is no set template for such operations and the overall guide should be that 'form must follow function'.[64]

For the future peace operations should ideally be 'integrated missions' which have been defined as:

---

60 *See* MOU between UN High Commissioner for Human Rights and UN DPKO.

61 Secretary-General's Bulletin: 'Observance by the United Nations Forces of International Humanitarian Law' (6 August 1999) UN Doc. ST/SGB/1999/13.

62 *UNSC Res. 1674* (28 July 2006).

63 *High Level Panel Report* (n 27) para. 203. *See* more qualified version in UNGA Res. 60/1 (24 October 2005) para. 139.

64 *Eide and others* (n 43) 10-12, 17.

> An instrument with which the UN seeks to help countries in the transition between war and to lasting peace, or address a similarly complex situation that requires a system-wide UN response, through subsuming various actors and approaches within an overall political-strategic crisis management framework.[65]

From multi-functional operations of the 1980s, to post-Brahimi peace operations, towards 'integrated' missions, each represent greater attempts to effectively co-ordinate the 'security, political, human rights, rule of law, humanitarian and development components of the mission'.[66] The newly created Peacebuilding Commission should improve coordination and effectiveness of peacebuilding operations in the future.[67] However, it will be seen that, especially in 'hybrid' operations that involve two or more organisations, it is very difficult to achieve integration, which remains a goal rather than the practice.

5. Peace Support Operations

From Brahimi onwards the 'aim is to avoid any failure to protect civilians' learning from experiences in Bosnia and Rwanda, and also to 'ensure that there are adequate self-defence mechanisms for peacekeeping forces and UN staff', learning from Sierra Leone and East Timor in 1999, when UN staff were kidnapped and killed by mobs and militia.[68] Though Brahimi marked the turning point, 'the shift in peacekeeping was principally initiated by the national defence academies of countries that had participated in the larger-scale deployments in the 1990s', and who would 'no longer agree to send their military forces into conflict for which they were inadequately prepared and supported'.[69] The more ambitious and complex mandates of the post-Cold War period meant that the hitherto non-involvement of powerful States in peace operations had to be reversed. With the involvement of these States there came demands for more effective operations. This is exemplified by the development by the UK of the concept of 'peace support operations' in 1999.[70] In its latest version a peace support operation is defined as:

> An operation that impartially makes use of diplomatic, civil and military means, normally in pursuit of United Nations Charter purposes and principles, to restore

65 Ibid. 14.

66 'Guidance on Integrated Missions, Note from the Secretary-General' (9 February 2006) <www.undg.org/docs/8483/8039-SG_s_Note_of_Guidance_on_Integrated_Missions__Feb__2006.pdf>.

67 Kofi Annan, 'In Larger Freedom: Towards Development, Security and Human Rights for All' (21 March 2005) UNGA Doc. A/59/2005 para. 115.

68 *Hansen, Rambotham and Woodhouse* (n 24) 7.

69 Ibid.

70 UK Ministry of Defence, *Peace Support Operations: JWP 3-50* (Ministry of Defence, London, 1999).

> or maintain peace. Such operations may include conflict prevention, peacemaking, peace enforcement, peacekeeping, peacebuilding and/or humanitarian operations.[71]

The difference between this and peace operations is to emphasise enforcement and de-emphasise the principles of peacekeeping. Impartiality becomes the only remaining element and that is used in a way that would not be recognised in an orthodox peacekeeping operation. In practice though, with an increasing use of Chapter VII by the Security Council, the doctrines of 'peace operations' and 'peace support operations' are not clearly distinct. First introduced to the discussion by The Agenda for Peace, peace enforcement has become more central to peace operations after Brahimi (although not clearly included in the definitions in that Report). Peace enforcement does not mean military victory over the enemy, so distinguishing it from pure enforcement action under Chapter VII. Impartiality and consent are still the goals of any peace operation, though the former becomes the more important concept if factions indicate the withdrawal of their consent by attempting to undermine the peace.

Furthermore, in such situations, according to the equivalent NATO peace support doctrine:

> consent from the warring factions may be minimal and amount to nothing more than a phoney tolerance of the operation, whilst the rest of the population may be desperate for intervention and assistance.[72]

Furthermore, according to NATO 'should the level of consent be uncertain, and the potential for opposition exist, it would be prudent to deploy a force capable of enforcing compliance and promoting consent from the outset'.[73] Such operations must be 'sufficiently flexible, robust and combat ready', exemplified by NATO-led KFOR in Kosovo and the Australian-led INTERFET in East Timor, both deployed in 1999, and the role of British force in support of the UN force in Sierra Leone in 2000. 'PSO doctrine recognises that the military's role, while robust, must also be a limited one: its objective is to create and safeguard the secure space within which humanitarian and civilian components can work to re-establish peace'.[74] Whereas pure Chapter VII enforcement action attempts to impose a solution by force, a peace support operation is engaged in preventing violence that will undermine the participation of the parties and the population as a whole in achieving peace. The aim of peace support operations is to achieve a political end-state, not victory over an enemy.[75]

---

71 UK Ministry of Defence, *The Military Contribution to Peace Support Operations: JWP 3.50* (2nd ed. MOD, London, 2004) 7.

72 NATO Allied Joint Publication (AJP) 3.4.1, Peace Support Operations, para. 508.

73 Ibid.

74 *Hansen, Ramsbotham and Woodhouse* (n 24) 7.

75 *NATO AJP 3.4.1.* (n 72) para. 0204.

PSO doctrine has been arguably implicitly adopted by the EU in the development of its Petersberg tasks namely 'humanitarian and rescue tasks, peacekeeping tasks and tasks of combat forces in crisis management, including peacemaking',[76] and in its practice in the deployment of EUFOR, replacing the NATO-led SFOR in Bosnia in 2004. NATO has explicitly adopted it in 2001 defining peace support operations as:

> Multi-functional operations, conducted impartially, normally in support of an internationally recognised organisation such as the UN or the [OSCE], involving military forces and diplomatic and humanitarian agencies. PSOs are designed to achieve a long-term political settlement or other specified conditions. They include Peacekeeping and Peace Enforcement as well as conflict prevention, peacekeeping, peace building and humanitarian relief.[77]

It must not be assumed that these definitions are universally accepted. The NATO doctrine suggests that such operations would not necessarily require UN authorisation even though they include elements of enforcement,[78] while the British version suggests such operations might not be undertaken in pursuit of UN purposes and principles. Both doctrines suggest that regional organisations could act autonomously from the UN, though normally they would act in 'support' of it and its principles.

In contrast to this more interventionist PSO doctrine. The UN's Special Committee on Peacekeeping has, as recently as 2003, reiterated that the traditional virtues of peacekeeping 'such as the consent of the parties, impartiality and the non-use of force' are essential to its success. This was preceded in the report by the Committee emphasising respect for the principles of the UN Charter, especially sovereignty and non-intervention.[79] It may be that the UN Committee's continuing support for the view that peacekeeping is essentially of a non-interventionist nature can be explained because of a narrow doctrinal approach to peacekeeping, rather than the wider notion of a peace operation or a peace support operation. However, the Committee on Peacekeeping seemed to view such operations as within its purview when it mentioned a number of times the increasing complexity of peacekeeping operations.[80] The failure by the Committee to develop the doctrine of peacekeeping to accurately reflect its role in peace operations is unsatisfactory, but may reflect the divisions within the UN, with some States being unhappy about the increasingly interventionist nature of peace (support) operations.

---

76 Article 17(2) Treaty on European Union (TEU) – *see generally* R.A. Wessel, 'The State of Affairs in WEU Security and Defence Policy: The Breakthrough in the Treaty of Nice' (2003) 8 *Journal of Conflict and Security Law* 265.

77 *NATO AJP 3.4.1* (n 72) para. 0202.

78 Contrary to Article 53 of the UN Charter.

79 *Special Committee on Peacekeeping (2003)* (n 19) paras. 45 and 46.

80 Ibid. para.42.

6. Regional Organisations and Peace Operations

The end of the Cold War has also allowed regional organisations to take up more active roles often in operations that have the characteristics of peace support,[81] in that they have more coercive mandates than either the complex peace operation or the traditional peacekeeping force. The actions of ECOWAS in Liberia and Sierra Leone, NATO in Bosnia, Kosovo and Afghanistan, and the EU in the Congo and Bosnia are based on them having enforcement powers when necessary – they are in effect 'Chapter VII' operations in a UN sense. While there remains a peaceful situation on the ground these forces may have the appearance of traditional peacekeepers, supporting the job of peacebuilding, but when the peace breaks down they have the authority and capability of dealing with the 'spoilers' and protecting civilians. In many ways, SFOR (now EUFOR) in Bosnia from 1995, KFOR in Kosovo from 1999, ISAF in Afghanistan from 2001, the EU's Operation Artemis in the Democratic Republic of Congo in 2003, and ECOMOG in West Africa in the 1990s share the characteristics of Coalitions of the Willing authorised by the Security Council under Chapter VII to undertake enforcement action, and have been included in the analysis of that concept above. Coalitions of the Willing act under UN authority but they are not UN commanded and controlled operations in the peacekeeping/peace operation sense. The Australian led force in East Timor (INTERFET) fits this pattern as well, though this was an *ad hoc* force. They are not necessarily fighting a full-scale war, but they are war fighting or have war fighting potential rather than just a peacekeeping function. It is interesting to note that, with the exception of the West African forces, the regional forces are undertaken by the 'global north' in contrast to peacekeeping operations (either traditional or as part of a peace operation) which are undertaken by the 'global south',[82] though the peacekeepers may be supported by separate enforcement elements drawn from the north.

In general there needs to be better co-operation and co-ordination between the UN and other organisations engaging in collective security:

> Increasingly, operations have taken on a hybrid character, with two or more organizations responsible for different elements of the international response. Differences in circumstances have led to no standard form being adopted, and thus the UN has sometimes deployed troops alongside those of other organizations with or without formal coordination, or preceded or followed a multinational, regional or bilateral force, with responsibilities changing as the mission matures.[83]

It would of course be better to have an 'integrated operation' with a 'single chain of command and control, if not a co-ordinated operation' where the UN and regional organisations have separate command structures but liaise closely, rather than a 'parallel operation' where there is no formal coordination. 'Sequential operations' when

81 M. Bothe, 'Peace-keeping' in B. Simma (ed), *The Charter of the United Nations: A Commentary* (2nd ed. Oxford University Press, Oxford, 2002) 696-8.

82 *Cockayne and Malone* (n 25) 13.

83 *Challenges Project* (n 37) 12.

the UN precedes or follows a regional operation are unlikely to be integrated but should be closely coordinated.[84]

The UN's Special Committee on Peacekeeping recognises the significant contribution that regional organisations can make to peacekeeping, but has stressed that this must be in accordance with Chapter VIII of the UN Charter. The Committee put particular emphasis on Article 53 of the UN Charter, which states that enforcement action undertaken by regional organisations requires the authorisation of the Security Council.[85] The High Level Panel endorsed this in 2004, and because of the propensity of modern peace operation to use force more widely, stated that all regional peace operations, including those undertaken by NATO must have the authority of the Council, except in urgent situations when it could be sought after the operation had started.[86] This exceptional approach of retrospective authorisation utilised in the past in relation to ECOWAS clearly presents difficulties if the Security Council is deadlocked. Arguably in these cases authority should be sought from the General Assembly under its exceptional competence for peace and security.

The UN's Special Committee has stressed the need for enhancement of African peacekeeping by developing a close relationship with the African Union,[87] perhaps in response to the constituent treaty of the new AU in 2000 that seemed in Article 4 to permit enforcement action to combat crimes against humanity without the need for Security Council approval. The Committee's report though clearly does not accept that the AU can act autonomously in the field of enforcement action, even to combat grave and widespread breaches of human rights. Though the AU and the UN have co-operated and co-ordinated their efforts in response to the crisis in Darfur caused by the crimes against humanity being committed there since 2003, the hybrid UN/AU force (UNAMID 2007-),[88] had only deployed 7,000 troops by January 2008 far short of the 26,000 required.

The advantages of regional organisations becoming involved in peace operations is that they 'often enjoy a special legitimacy amongst local actors', they will be 'more familiar with local conditions' and in some ways they 'have a greater incentive to stay the course and implement long-term conflict prevention and monitoring strategies'.[89] However, they may be dominated by regional hegemons that will push them towards higher levels of enforcement than may be necessary (for example Nigeria's domination of ECOWAS). Alternatively, some organisations (for example the AU) may not have the resources to mount an effective peace operation of any sort. The better approach is to develop 'an interlocking system of peacekeeping capacities that will enable the United Nations to work with relevant regional organizations'.[90]

84 Ibid. 36.

85 *Special Committee on Peacekeeping (2003)* (n 19) paras. 161-2.

86 *High Level Panel Report* (n 27) paras. 272-3.

87 *Special Committee on Peacekeeping (2003)* (n 19) paras. 165-9.

88 *UNSC Res. 1769* (31 July 2007).

89 *Cockayne and Malone* (n 25) 11.

90 *In Larger Freedom* (n 67) para.115.

7. Towards Effective and Equitable Peacc Operations

There is now a broad spectrum of collective military operation from the consensual peacekeeping force on the one end, to the military enforcement action to combat aggression on the other. Currently peace operations are in between these two poles, which make them difficult to analyse is legal terms since the military component of these operations may move from being peacekeepers to war fighters in the constantly changing conditions of a volatile post-conflict environment in which violence is still endemic and may flare up at any moment. Though fluid and difficult to classify, it is possible to make suggestions for the improvement of modern peace operations that would still respect, as far as practical, the foundational principles of peacekeeping.

The High Level Panel in 2004 stated that a credible and sustainable collective security system must be effective, efficient and equitable. The latter means that such a system should 'promote security for all its members without regard to the nature of would be beneficiaries, their location, resources or relationship to Great Powers'.[91] To this end it would be good practice for all actors within peace operations to be coordinated under clear achievable mandates, perhaps leading to agreements between the UN and regional organisations on the command and functioning of peace operations. Greater work should be undertaken on bringing together the peace operations doctrines of the UN and key security actors such as NATO, the EU, AU and ECOWAS. This should lead to a common peace operation doctrine respecting the traditional principles of impartiality, consent and limited use of force, but recognising that the dual needs to deal with spoilers and to protect civilians will require a coercive mandate and clear rules of engagement to that effect. In these circumstances the traditional principles must be returned to as soon as practicable.

Further work needs to be done on identifying the principles underlying peace operations. It is suggested here that fundamental human rights, including the right of self-determination, should be an important part of the framework within which peace operations operate. This is reflected in the recognition in practice that peace operations must be undertaken with the cooperation of the local peaceful population. The achievement of self-determination by the expression of the will of the people through stable democratic structures also provides a clear exit strategy for each operation. Self-determination must be exercised freely without outside interference in the substantive political and economic processes. Peace operations should not only promote human rights but should respect them in their operations and activities. In this regard the UN and other actors should provide avenues and mechanisms of accountability for victims of human rights abuse by UN personnel.

91 *High Level Panel Report* (n 27) paras. 31 and 40.

Chapter 2

Legal Regimes Governing International Military Missions

Marco Odello and Ryszard Piotrowicz

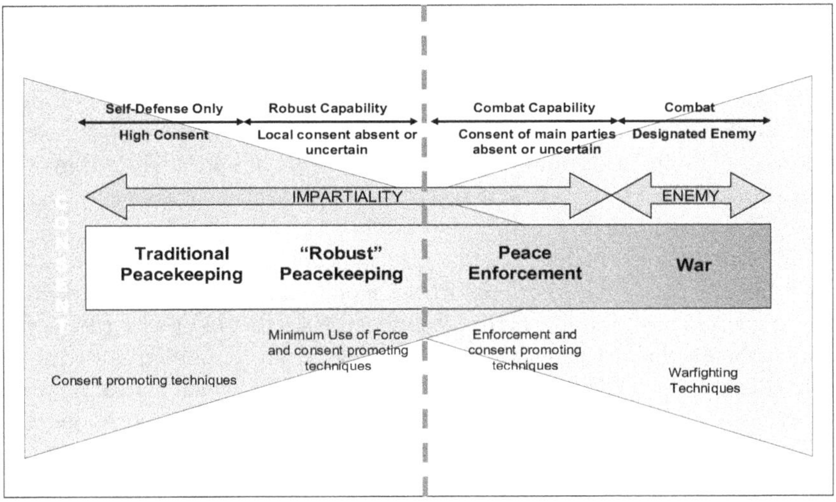

Picture taken from Capstone Doctrine for United Nations Peacekeeping Operations – Draft 2 *(7 August 2006), p. 27, available at: <www.challengesforum.org/cms/images/doc/UN_Capstone_Doctrine_Summary_Rev2_26-2_8_Sep_2006.doc>.*

1. Introduction

International military missions (IMMs) are not a new phenomenon. However in recent years they have come to be deployed in increasing numbers and varying formats. The changing nature, structure and purposes of IMMs, and the diverse types of conflict where they are deployed, raise several important legal issues. United Nations (UN) peacekeeping operations (PKOs) and other related military operations have evolved from relatively modest engagements, in the form of observation missions acting in situations of crisis and armed conflict, to more robust operations with major involvement in the armed conflict, and more often in post-conflict operations leading to forms of international administration of territories. The emergence of Peace

M. Odello and R. Piotrowicz (eds.), International Military Missions and International Law.
2011 Koninklijke Brill NV. Printed in The Netherlands. ISBN *978 9004 17437 5. pp. 25–44.*

Operations and Peace Support Operations[1] with a variety of potential tasks poses the question: which rules should apply during this type of military operation and to the military personnel involved?[2] The aim of this chapter is to provide an analysis of the applicability of international rules to IMMs, with particular consideration of missions established under an International Organisation's (IO) mandate. More specific rules and areas of international law will be analysed in other chapters.

The main issues include the identification and discussion of which rules should or could apply to IMMs under international law, in particular under International Humanitarian Law (IHL) and International Human Rights Law (IHRL). This includes two main areas of reflection: 1) the influence of the justification and mandate for international military actions on the applicable rules on the ground; and 2) the rules that should be considered applicable once the IMMs are deployed and operating in the field. It is not the purpose of this chapter to focus on the legal justification for the use of IMMs under international law, as this is a matter mainly related to the law regulating the use of force and *jus ad bellum* concerns. Nevertheless, the possible influence of justifications for the use of force, based on humanitarian concerns, might influence the type of rules that should be applied. IMMs may have specific tasks which shift on a wide spectrum of operational engagements, and they have changed with the practice of States and IOs.

The first issue is whether the clear-cut distinction between *jus ad bellum* and *ius in bello* is applicable to IMMs. Secondly, the applicability of rules other than rules of IHL is considered in the context of the different tasks that IMMs have to perform. Thirdly, some examples are considered regarding the applicability of different legal regimes and the possible relevance of other types of rules, which may be more suitable for this kind of military operation, as they include also police components and civilian personnel. Finally, the increasing influence of the so-called Responsibility to Protect principle[3] and its possible implications in the conduct of international peace operations will be addressed.

This chapter considers the complex reality of rules and practice that may apply during IMMs, with particular attention to the Capstone Doctrine,[4] in the context of UN PKOs.

---

1 *See* P.F. Diehl, *Peace Operations* (Polity Press, Cambridge, 2008); Donald C.F. Daniel, Patricia Taft & Sharon Wiharta (eds), *Peace Operations: Trends, Progress, and Prospect* (Georgetown University Press, Washington D.C., 2008); Michael W. Doyle & Nicholas Sambanis, *Making War and Building Peace: United Nations Peace Operations* (Princeton University Press, Princeton, 2006); Lorraine M. Elliott & Graeme Cheeseman (eds), *Forces for Good: Cosmopolitan Militaries in the Twenty-First Century* (Manchester University Press, Manchester and New York, 2004).

2 *See* Nigel White, Chapter 1.

3 International Commission on Intervention and State Sovereignty, *The Responsibility to Protect* (International Development Research Centre, Ottawa, 2001).

4 UNDPKO, *United Nations Peacekeeping Operations: Principles and Guidelines* (New York, 18 January 2008).

2. Different Types of Personnel and Applicable Rules

Contemporary PKOs are very complex. They may include a variety of personnel who can be governed by different rules. This issue has been addressed in cases of human rights violations by peacekeepers in the Zeid report.[5] At least five categories of personnel have been identified, including: UN staff; UN Volunteers (UNV); individual contractors and consultants; civilian police and military observers; and military members of national armed forces.[6] The alleged violations and the subsequent legal analysis have revealed the difficulties in defining which rules apply to whom.[7] Here the focus is on the rules applicable to the military personnel, the so-called blue helmets.

The most obvious assessment as to which rules apply to them is that IHL does apply, because it is the law applicable to armed forces during armed conflict. However, this is not uncontroversial. First of all it is important to distinguish between the use of military operations under PKOs and the use of force authorised by the UN or other IOs in the field of collective security measures. In the latter case, if it is accepted that the use of force is authorised to oppose or address threats to international peace and security, the application of IHL is not disputed. Collective security action, like the 1950 Korean War, and later the 1991 Iraq War, was regulated by IHL because the military operations concerned the armed forces of two or more opposing States.

When it comes to PKOs, however, this rule has not been always clear.[8] The difficulty in defining the rules applicable to PKOs and to similar IMMs may be traced to the initial development of peace-keeping practice within the UN. Due to the fact that PKOs were introduced as an implied power of the UN in the maintenance of international peace and security, no detailed rules were adopted from the outset regarding their regulation. Initial operations were based on full respect for State sovereignty, including agreement of all the parties involved, and the impartiality of the

5 UNGA, 'A comprehensive strategy to eliminate future sexual exploitation and abuse in United Nations peacekeeping operations' (24 March 2005) UN Doc. A/59/710, (hereinafter *Comprehensive strategy*, or *Zeid Report*).

6 Ibid. paras. 15-22.

7 *See* M. Odello, 'Tackling Criminal Acts in Peacekeeping Operations: The Accountability of Peacekeepers' (2010) 15(2) *Journal of Conflict & Security Law*, 347-391; T. Dannenbaum, 'Translating the Standard of Effective Control into a System of Effective Accountability: How Liability Should be Apportioned for Violations of Human Rights by Member State Troop Contingents Serving as United Nations Peacekeepers' (2010) 51 *Harvard International Law Journal Online*, 113-192; J.J. Paust, 'The U.N. Is Bound By Human Rights: Understanding the Full Reach of Human Rights, Remedies, and Nonimmunity' (2010) 51 *Harvard International Law Journal Online*, 1-12; P. Rowe, 'United Nations Peacekeeping Forces and Human Rights Violations: the Role of Military Discipline' (2010) 51 *Harvard International Law Journal Online*, 69-81.

8 U. Palwankar, 'Applicability of International Humanitarian Law to United Nations Peace-keeping Forces' (1993) 294 *International Review of the Red Cross*, 227-240.

international action,[9] often referred to as the so-called 'trinity of virtues': consent, impartiality and restriction.

However, the practice of contemporary PKOs, including the use of IMMs by other IOs, indicates a rather wide variety of rules that could be applicable rather than a possible legal vacuum or gap. These might include:

- International Humanitarian Law
- International Human Rights Law
- General International Law
- UN Security Council Mandate
- Rules of Engagement
- Status of Forces Agreements and Memorandums of Understanding
- Domestic law:
  - Sending State
  - Host State

Clearly, the range of potentially applicable rules is extensive and this may cause either confusion or doubt as to the identification of those rules applicable to a specific IMM. In this context the main international rules will be discussed to see how they interrelate, overlap or integrate in the context of PKOs and IMMs. Some military and governmental experts prefer to maintain a clear distinction between peace-keeping, based on impartiality and agreements among the major actors, and peace-enforcement, which entails participation in the conflict, and therefore loses the impartiality requirement.[10]

3. International Rules and International Military Missions

In seeking to identify the rules applicable to IMMs, we should think of these rules and, indeed, the international system, in a more interactive way. It is difficult to maintain that the rules applicable to armed forces are only those defined in the main international instruments related to the law of armed conflict (LOAC) or IHL. Given the existence of a broad set of rules, from human rights to international criminal law, and considering the importance of general customary rules that can bind all subjects of international law, including IOs, it is not always possible to apply international legal rules in separate compartments. This is particularly resonant in the long-lasting debate concerning the relationship between the rules of IHL and the rules of

9 Generally referred to as *observation missions*, i.e. United Nations Truce Supervision Organization (UNTSO) in Palestine (1948) and United Nations Military Observer Group in India and Pakistan (UNMOGIP) (1949).

10 *See* S. Trzeciak, *Between Peacekeeping and Peace Enforcement: Does the NATO Intervention in Kosovo Provide a New Formula of Peace Operation?* (NATO-EAPC Research Fellowship, Final Report, June 2003); R. Thakur, 'From Peacekeeping to Peace Enforcement: The UN Operation in Somalia' (1994) 32(3) *The Journal of Modern African Studies*, 387-410; George F. Oliver, 'The Other Side of Peacekeeping: Peace Enforcement and Who Should Do It?' (2002) 8 *International Peacekeeping: The Yearbook of International Peace Operations*, 99-117.

IHRL. It is not our purpose here to deal with this issue, nor the theoretical distinctions between what is considered to be *lex generalis* (IHRL) and *lex specialis* (IHL),[11] and the possible complementarities between IHL and IHRL. It may be too extreme to envisage a total merging of IHL and IHRL. Particular prohibitions and duties exist under IHL compared to the more general language of IHRL.[12] Moreover, different standards and principles apply in armed conflict compared to time of peace, for instance in the domains of right to life, protection of property and collateral damage. Nevertheless, a certain relationship, and mutual influence, between IHL and IHRL should not be seen as blasphemy, and this area is yielding new studies and analyses in the academic context,[13] in decisions by international tribunals,[14] but also with possible relevant applications in the field.

One of the principal issues is to determine which rules, if any, should be applied in all circumstances regardless of the definition or classification of the context in which armed forces are deployed. This implies looking at different sources of international and national law that may apply to IMMs and to other components of international peace operations. They include at least IHL, IHRL, international criminal law, national criminal law, national administrative law, national constitutional law and national military law.[15] Other rules can also be relevant, such as international and national rules concerning the financial and economic sector when reconstruc-

---

11 *Legality of the Threat or Use of Nuclear Weapons* (Advisory Opinion) [1996] ICJ Rep. 1996 (I), para. 25; *Legal Consequences of the Construction of a Wall in the Occupied Palestinian Territory* (Advisory Opinion) [2004] ICJ Rep. 2004, para. 106 [hereinafter Wall Advisory Opinion]; Heike Krieger, 'A Conflict of Norms: The Relationship Between Humanitarian Law and Human Rights Law in the ICRC Customary Law Study' (2006) 11 *JCSL* 265, 268-276.

12 Louise Doswald-Beck & Sylvain Vité, 'International Humanitarian Law and Human Rights Law' (1993) 293 *IRRC* 94-119.

13 *See* R. Arnold and N. Quénivet (eds), *International Humanitarian Law and Human Rights Law* (Martinus Nijhoff Publishers, Leiden-Boston, 2008); C. McCarthy, 'Legal Conclusion or Interpretative Process? *Lex Specialis* and the Applicability of International Human Rights Standards' in *idem*, Chapter III; R. Provost, *International Human Rights and Humanitarian Law* (Cambridge University Press, Cambridge, 2002); G.I.A.D. Draper, 'The Relationship between the Human Rights Regime and the Laws of Armed Conflict' (1971) 1 *Isr.Y.B.Hum.Rts.*191; R.E. Vinuesa, 'Interface, Correspondence and Convergence of Human Rights and International Humanitarian Law' (1998) 1 *YIHL* 69-110; H.-J. Heintze, 'On the Relationship between Human Rights Law Protection and International Humanitarian Law' (2004) 86 *IRRC* 798; N. Szablewska, 'Non-state Actors and Human Rights in Non-international Armed Conflicts' (2007) 32 *South African Yearbook of International Law* 345.

14 *See Legality of the Threat or Use of Nuclear Weapons* (n 11) para. 25; *Legal Consequences of the Construction of a Wall in the Occupied Palestinian Territory* (n 11) paras. 106-113; Inter-American Court of Human Rights, *Bamaca Velásquez v. Guatemala*, Judgment (25 November 2000), para. 207; UN Human Rights Committee, *General Comment No. 31* (26 May 2004) CCPR/C/21/Rev.1/Add.13, para. 11.

15 I. Österdahl & E. van Zadel, 'What will jus post bellum mean?' (Paper presented at the BISA Annual Conference 2008, Uppsala University, 15-17 December 2008) 10.

tion is foreseen, as well as the foundation treaties of IOs, administrative and personnel regulations.

IMMs perform many tasks, including arresting and detaining civilians, providing order in the areas under their control, disarming rebel groups and factions, and arresting indicted persons for international crimes. This requires that we identify and clarify the rules applicable to IMMs in a more objective, coherent and structured way, rather than referring to the occasional willingness of the States involved in sending their troops to identify on an *ad hoc* basis the rules that would be applicable. As things currently stand, there is a risk of uncertainty and gaps; these do nothing to facilitate the task of military personnel in the field, raising doubts about legality or even perceived illegitimate actions, affecting the support of the local populations, and therefore the overall success of an international operation. Furthermore, there are issues regarding international responsibility[16] and the extraterritorial applicability of IHRL[17] to troops and personnel involved in Peace Operations and IMMs.

Therefore, a set of rules that could be tailor-made, or at least a minimum set of rules that might constitute the core of *jus post bellum,* would be most desirable as a basic set of legal obligations for all IMMs.[18]

4. International Humanitarian Law

IHL clearly affirms that it applies whenever armed forces of a State act in the territory of another State. This is based on the fact that traditional military actions were conducted amongst States with the purpose of conquest of territory and in highly confrontational circumstances, the main objective being the defeat of the enemy. But the development of the UN practice of PKOs, and later of peace-enforcement and peace-building operations of regional organisations, with the sending of military missions abroad, without the purpose of defeating the enemy and acquiring part or all of another State's territory, has changed the perspective, the philosophy and the justification of international actions by military forces. Is it right that different rules should apply in those cases compared to the rules that were adopted for conflicts between States – rules that enjoy universal acceptance? Is this shifting of the purposes and aims of IMMs for the protection of human rights, restoration of peace, security and stability in a certain territory, or in a region, under the mandate of an IO, justified under the *jus ad bellum*? Is this approach also influencing the rules for the conduct of military forces, and therefore the rules of IHL and military occupation?

16 *See* N. Tsagourias, Chapter 9 in this book.

17 *See Legal Consequences of the Construction of a Wall in the Occupied Palestinian Territory* (n 11) and Armed Activities on the Territory of the Congo *(Democratic Republic of the Congo* v. *Uganda),* Judgment [2005] ICJ. Rep. 168.

18 *See* UN Security Council, Report of the Secretary-General, 'The Rule of Law and Transitional Justice in Conflict and Post-Conflict Societies' (August 2004); C. Turner, 'Delivering Lasting Peace, Democracy and Human Rights in Times of Transition: The Role of International Law' (2008) 2 *The International Journal of Transitional Justice*, 126-151.

Challenging the application of IHL to IMMs has been highly criticised for different reasons. First, tampering with existing established and generally accepted legal rules threatens the legal certainty related to the use of force, with the possible risk of lowering or damaging the protection standards foreseen by IHL. Legal categories, once established, create legal certainty for all the actors involved in their application. Dismissing agreed rules and establishing new ones, particularly in international law, may create gaps and uncertainties.

Second, armed forces are trained to use legal principles and rules based on the distinction between *jus ad bellum* and *jus in bello*. This distinction is crucial from a humanitarian perspective, as it enables the acceptance of neutral and objective rules for the protection of the victims of armed conflicts, which should not be influenced by the reasons behind the use of force.

Third, the shifting from a more objective to a subjective applicability, based on States' differing characterisation of their military activities, of the rules in case of armed conflict could create gaps and uncertainty which can have very negative results for the protection of the parties involved in the conflict and for the protection of civilians, which are amongst the most important objectives of IHL.

From the outset, PKOs and their military components were not considered strictly bound by IHL. This was due to the fact that the 1949 Geneva Conventions mention the 'parties to the conflict' and, as treaties, they bind States, identified as the High Contracting Parties.[19] The UN and the Troop Contributing Countries (TCC), not being or acting as States, did not consider themselves parties to the conflict when establishing PKOs. Furthermore, the UN, not being a State, has not ratified the Geneva Conventions, nor other relevant IHL treaties.[20] This raised several concerns and criticism in the international community, in particular from the ICRC, as the depository and international body responsible for the promotion of the application and dissemination of the Geneva Conventions, as well as in the literature.[21] The issue was eventually partly clarified with the adoption of the UN Secretary-General's Bulletin in 1999.[22] This affirms that UN forces are bound by 'principles and rules' of IHL included in the Bulletin 'when in situations of armed conflict they are actively engaged therein as combatants, to the extent and for the duration of their engagement'.[23] It refers in particular to the protection of the civilian population,[24] to the means and methods of combat,[25] to the treatment of civilians

19 *See* Common Article 1 to the four 1949 Geneva Conventions.

20 *See* R. Gutman, 'United Nations and the Geneva Conventions' in *Crimes of War: A to Z Guide*, available at: <www.crimesofwar.org/thebook/un-geneva.html>.

21 R. Murphy, 'United Nations Military Operations and International Humanitarian Law: What Rules Apply to Peacekeepers?' (2003) 14 *Criminal Law Forum* 153-194; P. Benvenuti, 'The Implementation of Humanitarian Law in the Framework of Peacekeeping Operations' (1995) 1 *Law in Humanitarian Crises* 83.

22 Secretary-General's Bulletin: 'Observance by United Nations Forces of International Humanitarian Law' (1999) U.N. Doc. ST/SGB/1999/13.

23 Ibid. Section 1.1.

24 Ibid. Section 5.

25 Ibid. Section 6.

and persons *hors de combat*,[26] to the treatment of detained persons,[27] and to the protection of the wounded, the sick and medical and relief personnel.[28] Yet, the Bulletin contains extremely limited and general obligations compared to the elaborate set of rules under IHL. It also affirms that national contingents are still bound by their respective national law during the duration of the mission.[29] However, there is no clear reference to human rights obligations, in particular under international law. These issues will be discussed in the subsequent sections when dealing with IHL and other legal obligations.

5. Justifications and Legal Rules

The three terms *jus ad bellum*, *jus in bello* and *jus post bellum* identify the rules that apply to all situations related to an armed conflict. In particular, the distinction between *jus ad bellum*, the right to recourse to force under international law,[30] and *jus in bello*, the rules applicable during the conduct of hostilities and armed operations, has been considered a fundamental feature of international law applicable to armed conflicts.[31] The purpose of this distinction is to avoid any negative correlation between the reasons for the recourse to armed force and the rules applicable in the field. Due to abuses that occurred in the past, in particular under the doctrine of just war,[32] IHL has tried to establish a clear cut differentiation between the justification for the use of force and the actual regulation of military activities: the reasons behind the use of force should not influence the applicability of IHL. The spirit and purpose of IHL is to provide protection for those affected by the conflict irrespective of the reasons behind that specific conflict, and to ensure the equality of belligerents before IHL.[33] A third category of rules, *jus post bellum*, has been considered a possible way to address situations where IMMs are involved, particularly in the post-conflict scenarios, often identified as peace-building operations. In this section the three issues are briefly considered in relation to their applicability to IMMs.

26 Ibid. Section 7.

27 Ibid. Section 8.

28 Ibid. Section 9.

29 Ibid. Section 2.

30 *See generally* Christine Gray, *International Law and the Use of Force* (2nd ed.) (Oxford University Press, Oxford, 2004).

31 C. Greenwood, 'The Relationship Between *jus ad bellum* and *jus in bello*' (1993) 9 *Review of International Studies* 221-234.

32 M. Walzer, *Just and Unjust Wars: A Moral Argument with Historical Illustrations* (Basic Books, New York, 1977); Ivan Shearer, 'A Revival of the Just War Theory?' in M.N. Schmitt and J. Pejic (eds), *International Law and Armed Conflict: Exploring the Faultlines – Essays in Honour of Yoram Dinstein*, 1-20 (Martinus Nijhoff Publishers, Leiden-Boston, 2007) 1.

33 H. Meyrowitz, *Le principe de l'égalité des belligérants devant le droit de la guerre* (Éditions A. Pédone, Paris, 1970) 418.

5.1 Jus ad bellum

International law, under the UN Charter, prohibits the use of force between States. Article 2(4) prohibits the 'threat or use of force against the territorial integrity or political independence of any State'. The only exceptions to this rule are the right to individual and collective self-defence by States,[34] under Art. 51 of the Charter, and the authorisation to use force by the UN Security Council, in dealing with cases of threat to the peace, breach of the peace and acts of aggression under Chapter VII. The *jus ad bellum* regulates and defines the right and conditions to use force in those cases.

Due to the limited powers of early PKOs, there was limited discussion on the rules applicable to them, as they were mainly observation missions, deployed with the consent of the States concerned and with limited powers of self-defence in case of attack. As self-defence is a well established rule not only in international law but in all domestic legal systems, there was little doubt that if peacekeepers were the object of an attack, they should be entitled to defend themselves.

When the PKO mandate involves a certain amount of force to protect the civilian population which may lead to stronger intervention in the conflict, some legal problems emerge. In particular, the relationship between State sovereignty and the use of force by other UN member States has become a difficult issue. This has led to a conflict between one of the pillars of international law: the respect for, and protection of, State sovereignty and independence of States on the one hand; and the mandate provided under the UN Charter to promote universal respect for, and observance of, human rights, on the other.[35]

Armed conflicts and gross violations of human rights could be considered within the areas of concern, and possible action, by the UN, in particular when they represent a threat to international peace and security, and trigger Chapter VII powers under the UN Charter. This type of situation implies the application of Art. 42 of the Charter and the use of force not only to protect military personnel, but also to protect a population that is suffering massive violations of human rights. More robust and more complex PKOs and peace-enforcement operations need stronger powers, and therefore they may be a significant limitation on State sovereignty. This issue was addressed in the 2000 Millennium Report by the UN Secretary-General, Kofi Annan, who stated:

> [I]f humanitarian intervention is, indeed, an unacceptable assault on sovereignty, how should we respond to a Rwanda, to a Srebrenica—to gross and systematic violations of human rights that offend every precept of our common humanity?[36]

---

34 *See* T. Gazzini, *The Changing Rules on the Use of Force in International Law* (Manchester University Press, Manchester, 2005). It is not intended here to discuss the possible legality of humanitarian intervention.

35 *See* Art. 55 UN Charter.

36 Millennium Report of the Secretary-General, 'We the Peoples: The Role of the United Nations in the 21st Century' (UN Department of Public Information, New York, 2000) 48; Secretary General's Speech to the 54th Session of the General Assembly (20 September 1999) UN Doc. SG/SM/7136 GA/9596.

Use of stronger force to stop humanitarian catastrophes means that military force could be used to stop atrocities, fight those responsible for the atrocities, and eventually to restore peace. The use of such armed force is extremely problematic within the current positivist international law paradigm because of the seemingly clear and limited justifications permitted by Art. 2(4). The practical consequences are seen in humanitarian tragedies across the world. While it is very difficult, and perhaps even dangerous, to look outside the Charter to legitimise the use of force, nevertheless in recent times there has emerged another perspective that aims, not to deny the limitations of the Charter but rather to seek and elucidate ways in which the Charter might justify other force other than in the currently rather widely accepted restricted circumstances. Such developments raise also the interesting possibility of other bases upon which to found the actions of IMMs. Perhaps the most influential of such developments has been the emergence of the notion of the Responsibility to Protect.

5.2 The Responsibility to Protect

The so-called 'responsibility to protect'[37] in its most famous manifestation is already nearly ten years old and it has provoked significant discussion in recent years. This is of course primarily an aspect of the *ius ad bellum*, not the *ius in bello*. However, while this book is primarily concerned with the *conduct* of IMMs, it must also be considered, we suggest, whether we have now arrived at a situation whereby particular scenarios may trigger an obligation to act; and whether such obligation can apply to IMM as well as to States as such.

That the R2P has ramifications for the conduct of peacekeeping operations appears to be accepted, although what this means in practice is not so clear. In 2009 the Secretary-General stated:

> Peace operations led by DPKO – through their human rights, rule of law, political affairs, civil affairs, child protection, gender, *military*, and police components, and within the limits of their mandates and capacities – respond to past and ongoing violations and help to prevent their recurrence, including genocide....[38]

However, in the subsequent outline of the ways in which these responses are carried out, there is no mention of specific military activities that might take place nor how they might be regulated. It is stated that PKOs work '...to ensure the protection of civilians under imminent threat of physical violence'.[39] This certainly suggests that peacekeepers may become involved in situations that run the risk of armed force being used but remains silent on how they conduct themselves.

R2P is fundamentally a 21st century spin on the right of humanitarian intervention. The controversy over whether States have a right to intervene in other States in order to stop serious violations by a State of the human rights of its own citizens or

37 *The Responsibility to Protect* (n 3).

38 Report of the Secretary General, 'Implementing the responsibility to protect' (January 2009) UN Doc. A/63/677, para. 18 (emphasis added).

39 Ibid.

residents is well known. No such right is specifically authorised in the UN Charter; consequently some States argue that it is never permissible because only the use of force clearly authorised by the Charter can be in accordance with international law. On the other hand, this raises the dilemma: how to deal with a situation like Rwanda in 1994, when flagrant, serious and mass violations of human rights are taking place? It seems almost nonsensical to await some, possibly never forthcoming and, even if forthcoming, inadequate mandate from the Security Council. That is why some States have argued for a limited right of humanitarian intervention: there must be, because there *ought* to be, a right to take action to stop – preferably even prevent – such acts. But international law is not based on wishful legal thinking: if there is not a treaty or a rule of customary international law to justify an act then it is extremely difficult to argue for its legality. There is certainly no treaty to justify humanitarian intervention, and the practice is far too inconsistent, and too much opposed, to assert a positive right to intervene.

This is where R2P comes in:

> ... the idea that sovereign States have a responsibility to protect their own citizens from avoidable catastrophe – from mass murder and rape, from starvation – but that when they are unable or unwilling to do so, that responsibility must be borne by the community of States.[40]

The essence of the concept, as outlined above, is elaborated in the Synopsis of the Report.[41] The crucial element here is what the authors term 'the responsibility to react: to respond to situations of compelling human need with appropriate measures, which may include coercive measures like sanctions and international prosecution, and in extreme cases military intervention'.[42] It is perhaps unreasonable to isolate this part from the overall context, which is very clearly stressed by the authors; nevertheless this is surely the most contentious element: the assertion of a right to intervene in another State without its consent in order to protect human rights and prevent their further violation.

The issue whether the R2P might justify armed intervention – and it is intervention, however one chooses to justify it or name it – has to be considered in light of the mandate of the particular IMM. If the mandate is from the Security Council under Chapter VII of the Charter, then there may be no problem, as long as the wording is clear enough. In other words, it would probably have to use the phrase 'all necessary means' rather than, for instance, 'serious consequences'. In that situation, however, there is no need to rely on the putative R2P. If the IMM is actually a UN force it would be highly contentious for it to go beyond its mandate given that the Security Council would be most unlikely to agree to an implied use of force. This was precisely the reason for the argument over the legality of the invasion of Iraq in

40 *The Responsibility to Protect* (n 3) viii.

41 Ibid. xi-xiii.

42 Ibid. para. 3B, at xi.

2003, when the USA and the UK argued that force was a legitimate option based on the relevant SC Resolutions on Iraq.

The more problematic scenario is where the mandate of an IMM purports to rely on the R2P to justify the intervention. That option would arguably entail going beyond the existing parameters for the use of force as they are currently understood. That orthodoxy has been challenged by Shearer, who has argued recently that 'the orthodox interpretation of international law governing the use of armed force in international relations, which admits of no exceptions to the authorisations specified in Chapter VII of the Charter, is by reason of that inflexibility no longer able to serve the interests of world order'.[43] The authors of the R2P Report did not quite argue this; rather, they sought to show how the Charter could be used more effectively to justify action for the maintenance of international peace and security, where that was threatened by mass violations of human rights, if the Security Council were only able to act more effectively.

The notion of R2P has attracted significant and substantial support – but not from States. Even if States come to endorse it, its potential use as a basis for intervention will remain just that in the absence of real change in the way the Security Council operates. Accordingly, it is problematic at this stage to look to the R2P as a means to justify the acts of IMMs. Shearer argues that it is time to consider a 'more elastic' interpretation of Article 2(4) that would provide States with the legal foundation upon which to act where the kind of situations addressed in the R2P Report arise:[44] we do not need new law; just a more flexible way of using the existing law in light of modern challenges, and that Article 2(4) is amenable to such interpretation if States have the will. Ultimately, in the absence of authorisation by the Security Council where that body has failed to approve a proposal or to deal with it in a reasonable time, R2P even anticipates the possibility of action by 'regional or sub-regional organizations under Chapter VIII of the Charter, subject to their seeking subsequent authorization from the Security Council'.[45] Note, the obligation would be to seek – not necessarily obtain – the Council's approval. So, the aim is to work within the UN system but to bypass it if necessary – a potentially highly risky prospect.

Depending on how one sees this, it may be considered either as a proposal *de lege ferenda* – and as such a threat to the stability of the international security regime founded upon the Charter; or else it can be taken as a suggestion as to how the Charter may be interpreted so as to enable the international community to face serious challenges to the protection of, and respect for, human rights during and after armed conflicts. The expansion in the number of IMMs, as well as in the range of their activities and mandates, was also not foreseen in the Charter, yet they have become a fact of international life. As things currently stand, reliance upon R2P to justify military action by an IMM would be contentious but it would not be *ipso facto* in breach of international law.

---

43 *Shearer* in *Schmitt and Pejic (eds), International Law and Armed Conflict* (n 32).

44 Ibid. 19-20.

45 *The Responsibility to Protect* (n 3) para. 3.E.II, at xiii.

The R2P is not the only initiative dealing with interrelated strategies to keep the peace, including early warning and prevention, robust reaction by the international community and comprehensive rebuilding. Other documents include the 1992 Agenda for Peace,[46] by Boutros Ghali, the 1999 UN Secretary-General's Bulletin,[47] the 2000 Brahimi Report,[48] the 2007 UN Peacekeeping Best Practices and the 2008 United Nations Peacekeeping Operations: Principles and Guidelines.[49]

This policy was then reaffirmed by the 2005 UN General Assembly:

> [W]e are prepared to take collective action ... through the Security Council, in accordance with the Charter, including Chapter VII... should peaceful means be inadequate and national authorities...manifestly [fail] to protect their populations from genocide, war crimes, ethnic cleansing and crimes against humanity.[50]

The R2P might also have an impact on Rules of Engagement (RoE) because the 'use of only minimal force in self-defence that characterises traditional peacekeeping would clearly be inappropriate and inadequate for a peace enforcement action'. It is therefore suggested that the RoE should be 'clear and robust'.[51]

The question is whether international law supports this position and which rules should be applied by IMMs involved in this type of operation.

In the field, the R2P affirms that the military option should be considered the last resort and that military action should be governed by the principle of proportionality in the sense that the scale, duration and intensity of planned military intervention should be the minimum necessary to secure the 'defined human protection objective'.[52] Furthermore, in exercising that responsibility, RoE must involve 'total adherence to international humanitarian law';[53] although that arguably begs the question, what does 'total adherence' mean for IMMs, if their obligations are in fact less than, or different from, those of States? The Report itself does not really clarify this matter. It simply states:

> In the context of interventions taken for human protection purposes, the ROEs for a military intervention must reflect a stringent observance of international law, and international humanitarian law in particular. They should include an acknowl-

46 UN Secretary-General, 'An Agenda for Peace: Preventive diplomacy, Peacemaking and Peace-Keeping' (17 June 1992) UN Doc. A/47/277 - S/24111.

47 *See Observance by United Nations Forces of International Humanitarian Law* (n 22).

48 'Report of the Panel on United Nations Peace Operations' (17 August 2000) UN Doc. A/55/305-S/2000/809 (The 'Brahimi' Report).

49 *See United Nations Peacekeeping Operations: Principles and Guidelines* (n 4).

50 UN General Assembly, 'Outcome Document of the World Summit' (24 October 2005) UN Doc. A/RES/60/1, para. 139.

51 *Brahimi Report* (n 48) para. 55.

52 *The Responsibility to Protect* (n 3) para. 2.C, at xii.

53 Ibid. para. 4.D, at xiii.

> edgment that certain types of arms, and particularly those which are banned under international agreements, may not be used.[54]

This is probably the best formulation that could have been adopted, inasmuch as any attempt even to address which obligations might be binding upon IMMs, as opposed to States, would have been extremely problematic and highly contentious. There is moreover another potential problem: in suggesting that certain types of weapon may not be used, the Report may have gone as far as it could. For instance, weapons that cause unnecessary suffering are surely banned in any case but of course there is disagreement about which weapons meet that criterion in particular circumstances. Moreover, while it may be desirable to exclude the use of weapons that are 'banned under international agreements', what implications does this have where a particular weapon is banned by treaty, but some States in an IMM have ratified that instrument while others have not done so, indeed even argue for the legitimacy of the use of such weapons?

It is uncontroversial that the R2P is not, in itself, legally binding. Nevertheless, it is particularly relevant to consider the existing legal rules, policy documents and State practice to identify which rules should be applied in the field by military forces.

From the perspective of the *jus in bello*, the R2P report accepts limitations and gradualism in the application of force, based on the fact that the main objective of IMMs is the protection of the population, and not the defeat of the enemy State. This may well affect the type of rules that should apply to the forces involved in the mission.

The UN experience and that of other international organisations show the development of different types of engagement[55] and the problems in addressing the protection of the civilian population. At the same time, they also show the problem in defining clear rules that should be applied by the military personnel in the field.

Multi-dimensional PKOs develop a series of tasks, based on combined military/civilian components, which should supervise the end of hostilities amongst the parties to the conflict, oversee peace-building actions, often to facilitate election processes, and promote stable statehood to provide permanent peace in the territories which are the object of the intervention.

5.3 Jus in bello

International law has tried to define when an armed conflict starts, and despite the use of declarations of war for a certain period of time,[56] the misuse of this practice has led modern IHL to affirm that 'an armed conflict exists whenever there is a resort to armed force between States, or in cases of protracted armed violence between governmental authorities and organised armed groups within a State'.[57] This rule is based

54 Ibid. para. 7.28.

55 *See* N. White, Chapter 1 in this book.

56 Hague Convention III 1907, Art. 1.

57 *Prosecutor v. Tadić* [1996] 105 ILR 419, 488; François Bugnion, 'Just Wars, Wars of Aggression and International Humanitarian Law' (2002) 84 *IRRC* 523.

on the fact that States may even deny the existence of a state of hostilities, and sometimes use diverse justifications for the recourse to force, avoiding the qualification of war, due to the prohibition under the UN Charter. Nevertheless, under Common Article 2 to the 1949 Geneva Conventions the rules applicable to the hostilities, *jus in bello*, should apply irrespective of the classification of the conflict by the parties,[58] and under the 1977 Additional Protocol I,[59] to all cases of partial or total occupation of the territory of a party, even if the occupation meets no armed resistance. These strict rules are framed to provide humanitarian protection to the victims of the conflict and therefore regulate the conduct of hostilities in an objective way, trying to keep separate the reasons for the use of force from the actual rules applicable during the use of force.

A further element to take into consideration is that IHL distinguishes between international armed conflict and non-international armed conflict, and the rules applicable in each are not always the same.[60] If the IMMs are constituted by national contingents which operate abroad, then the rules applicable to international armed conflicts would apply. This distinction, however, seems less relevant today, as many relevant provisions applicable in both international and non-international armed conflict seem to have merged as customary international law.

5.4 Jus post bellum

Finally, a third category of rules has been more recently revamped to address the regulation of international military activities and functions, particularly in post-conflict situations, where reconstruction and durable peace are considered essential tasks for the international community. The concept of *jus post bellum* tries to define the rules that should apply not only to armed force, but also to the police and other civilian actors in the context of States and territories under international control, following a situation of armed conflict.[61] The rules of military occupation apply to armed forces which exercise effective control over a territory.[62] However, in the case of IMMs, different rules can apply. If the IMM is agreed with the host State, military occupation does not apply and specific rules, based on agreement between the parties, would apply. Some IMMs, in particular those authorised under Chapter VII of the UN Charter, often called Peace Enforcement Operations, do not require the consent of the State which is the object of the intervention. In this case it is often difficult to define the rules which should apply. Here the possible interaction of *jus ad bellum*

58 Geneva Conventions I-IV (GC I-IV), Common Art. 2.

59 Additional Protocol I (API), Art. 1(3).

60 Hilaire McCoubrey & Nigel D. White, *The Blue Helmets: Legal Regulation of United Nations Military Operations*, (Dartmouth, Aldershot, 1996) Chapter 8.

61 C. Stahn & J.K. Kleffner (eds), *Jus Post Bellum: Towards a Law of Transition From Conflict to Peace* (Cambridge University Press, Cambridge, 2008); G.J. Bass, 'Jus Post Bellum', (2004) 32(4) *Philosophy & Public Affairs* 384-412; B. Orend, '*Jus Post Bellum*: The Perspective of a Just War Theorist' (2007) 20 *Leiden Journal of International Law* 571-591.

62 Hague Regulations 1907 (HR) Art. 42.

and *jus in bello* is evident, because the States acting under an IO's mandate deny that they are 'occupying a foreign territory', as they do not consider the State where their troops operate an 'enemy State'. They justify their action under concerns for the re-establishment of international peace and security, often under humanitarian concerns, and in particular for the protection of human rights of the civilian population affected by the conflict. This can have the effect that the State's characterisation of its activity may inhibit the full applicability of IHL.

Several justifications for *jus post bellum* are based on moral philosophy and political concerns, mainly linked to the traditional concept of just war and the idea of justice, and now revisited to deal with contemporary forms of armed conflict and justification for the use of force.[63] However the analysis tries to focus on the implications of an emerging international legal regime that addresses IMMs but where the law remains uncertain.

The separation between *jus ad bellum*, *jus in bello* and *jus post bellum* considers them to be three different stages that should not necessarily influence each other, so as to avoid never-ending disputes linked to the justifications and limits of international actions. Therefore *jus post bellum* should regulate the transition from conflict to peace and the administration of territories by international forces and components.[64] The rules should deal with the restoration of order, restoration of sovereignty, economic reconstruction, establishment of durable peace, ensuring post-conflict reparations and punishment of fundamental rights violators.[65] This means looking at a wide set of international rules which address all the facets of international operations, in particular the military components which are our specific concern in this book.

6. From IHL to Human Rights

Reference to IHL only is unrealistic when dealing with IMMs. When enforcement measures are authorised or required by UN mandate, in particular during peace-enforcement operations, the military action should be governed by IHL. This conclusion is based on the analysis and discussion between the UN and the ICRC in the 1990s, which led to the elaboration and adoption of the 1999 UN Secretary-General's Bulletin that specifies the 1949 Geneva Conventions and their 1977 APs applicable to UN forces.

Later on, the 2000 Brahimi Report affirmed that '...once deployed, United Nations peacekeepers must be able to carry out their mandates professionally and successfully and be capable to defend themselves, other mission components and the mission's mandate, with robust rules of engagement, against those who renege on their commitments to a peace accord or otherwise seek to undermine it by violence'.[66]

63 *See* M. Evans (ed), *Just War Theory. A Reappraisal* (Edinburgh University Press, Edinburgh, 2005); J. Rawls, *The Law of Peoples* (Mass., Harvard University Press, Cambridge, 1999); M. Walzer, *Just and Unjust Wars* (Basic Books, New York, 2000).

64 C. Stahn, *The Law and Practice of International Territorial Administration: Versailles to Iraq and Beyond* (Cambridge University Press, Cambridge, 2008).

65 *Österdahl and van Zadel* (n 15).

66 *Brahimi Report* (n 48) para. 49.

It is reasonable to assume that carrying out the mandate professionally and implementing the mission would require compliance with the rules of armed conflict. However, the debate on the applicable rules is not over: many problems regarding the applicability of IHL rules to international organisations remain unresolved.

Nevertheless, it is generally agreed that when military forces are employed in the enforcement of peace, and are engaged in military actions, they should respect, as a minimum, the rules identified in the Secretary-General's Bulletin. This only takes us so far, however, because of the general nature of that instrument. More specific rules are further defined in the RoE which are given to the military contingents when deployed.

Finally, other rules could and should be applied when military operations take place in a situation that is shifting from conflict to post-conflict and peace-building. This has been defined as the 'spectrum of conflict' and the 'continuum of operations' of peace operations,[67] even if this is not a well accepted concept in military circles,[68] as this would not clearly define the type of legal obligations for the military personnel in the field.

The law of armed conflict is based on the distinction between conflict and peace. But several situations in which IMMs are operating fit in the unclear terrain between armed conflict and peace. In many cases, ongoing fighting is present in some areas or territories whilst other areas are relatively peaceful. The question is: which rules would apply when actual conflict is not taking place, but other types of activity, including policing, security operations and public order or arrest, are conducted? In these cases, the rules of IHL are not particularly useful. Usually, IHL foresees that at the end of hostilities, the law of military occupation would apply. But military occupation is based on a set of conditions and hypotheses that are not always or easily applicable to peace-keeping operations. In particular the idea that military occupation is based on the administration of an occupied foreign, former enemy, territory would not fit the purposes of international military action, based on humanitarian purposes.

7. Applicability of IHL and IHRL to IMMs

The initial problem regarding the rules applicable during IMMs when deployed under IOs' mandates is to what extent the existing rules of IHL and IHRL would apply. When coalitions of States operate to provide humanitarian protection, the legal obligations seem clearer, as most States would be bound by IHL and IHRL treaties. In case of non-ratification of some of the major treaties, customary international law would apply as a minimum.

67 The Senate Standing Committee on Foreign Affairs, 'Defence and Trade, Inquiry into Australia's Involvement in Peacekeeping Operations', The Australian Federal Police Submission (March 2007) 5.

68 US, Field Manual No. 100-23 (Department of the Army, Washington D.C., 30 December 1994) 12; Field Manual No. FM 3-07 (20 February 2003) on stability operations, which include also peacekeeping and other types of missions.

The legal problem starts when IMMs act under IO mandate. International organisations are not generally parties to IHL and IHRL treaties, although in principle they may be parties to multilateral treaties. However, there remain several significant obstacles to the ratification of IHL and IHRL treaties by international organisations. For instance, the ICRC has clearly stated that only States can be parties to IHL treaties,[69] because only States have regular armies and can fulfil the relevant obligations,[70] based on common Article 1 to the four 1949 Geneva Conventions.[71]

Another example is the case of IHRL and the EU, with regard to the European Convention on Human Rights (ECHR).[72] The debate on the possible ratification of the ECHR by the EU has clearly stated the limits of a possible ratification. A solution has been the inclusion of some fundamental rights in the new Lisbon Treaty[73] which would bind EU member States, but what remains unclear is the effect on the EU itself under international law, when acting as an international actor.

In the case of IHRL, the concept of extra-territorial applicability of IHRL has been developed by the European Court of Human Rights (ECtHR), which has provided some justifications for the application of the ECHR to member States' troops deployed abroad, when the States involved exercise a certain amount of 'control' over the foreign territory.[74]

The same approach has not been adopted in the case of the applicability of IHL. Reference is made to the international obligations of TCC, but not to legal obligations of IOs more specifically. Due to the discussion and concerns raised by

---

69 ICRC Expert Seminars, *Improving Compliance with International Humanitarian Law* (Report prepared by the International Committee of the Red Cross, Geneva, October 2003) 2-7.

70 M. Sassòli, 'State responsibility for Violations of International Humanitarian Law' (2002) 846 *IRRC*, 401-434.

71 *See* L. Boisson de Chazournes & L. Condorelli, 'Common Article 1 of the Geneva Conventions Revisited: Protecting Collective Interests' (2000) 837 *IRRC*, 67-87.

72 European Convention for the Protection of Human Rights and Fundamental Freedoms, Nov. 4, 1950, 213, UNTS 221.

73 Treaty of Lisbon amending the Treaty on European Union and the Treaty establishing the European Community, signed at Lisbon (13 December 2007) OJ C 306, Volume 50 (17 December 2007).

74 *See Cyprus v. Turkey*, [1975] App. Nos. 6780/74, 6950/75, 2 Eur. Comm'n H.R. Dec. & Rep. 125; *Cyprus v. Turkey*, [1978] App. No. 8007/77, 13 Eur. Comm'n H.R. Dec. & Rep. 85; *Cyprus v. Turkey*, [1996] App. No. 25781/94, 86–A Eur. Comm'n H.R. Dec. & Rep. 104; *Gentilhomme v. France*, [2002] European Court of Human Rights (ECtHR) No. 48205/99, (14 May 2002) ; *Banković and Others v. Belgium and 16 Other Contracting States*, (dec.) [2001] [GC], No. 52207/99, ECtHR 2001-XII ; *Assanidze v. Georgia* [GC], No. 71503/01, ECtHR [2004]-II ; *Ilascu and Others v. Moldova and Russia* [2004] [GC], No. 48787/99, ECtHR 2004-VII; *Issa and Others v. Turkey*, [2004] ECtHR No. 31821/96, 16 (November 2004); D. Campanelli, 'The Law of Military Occupation Put to the Test of Human Rights Law' (2008) 871 *IRRC* 653-668; A. Roberts, 'Transformative Military Occupation: Applying the Laws of War and Human Rights' (2006) 100 *AJIL* 580-622. *Also see* N. Quénivet, Chapter 5 in this book.

the evolving nature of PKOs,[75] the issue was addressed by the UN and the ICRC,[76] leading to the adoption of the UN Secretary-General's Bulletin in 1999. The Bulletin affirms that the rules and principles identified 'are applicable to United Nations forces when in situations of armed conflict they are actively engaged therein as combatants, to the extent and for the duration of their engagement'.[77] It also affirms that the rules and principles are 'applicable in enforcement actions, or in peacekeeping operations when the use of force is permitted in self-defence'.[78] This statement raises some problems. First, the existence of an armed conflict is not clarified. Second, the type of engagement of military personnel is not always clear, due to the refusal of contributing States to consider their troops as 'parties to the conflict'. Third, paragraph 1.2 adds uncertainty in stating that the promulgation of the Bulletin 'does not affect the protected status of members of peacekeeping operations under the 1994 Convention on the Safety of United Nations and Associated Personnel or their status as non-combatants, as long as they are entitled to the protection given to civilians under the international law of armed conflict'.

Furthermore, under international criminal law, the killing of peacekeepers is considered to be an international crime. This can be problematic because if the peacekeeper should exceed his/her mandate and become engaged in combat, then that person is effectively acting as a combatant and as such would be a legitimate target. Accordingly the legal status of peacekeepers may still give rise to problems in practice.

8. Conclusions

It is reasonable to affirm that there are sufficient rules of international law that may apply to situations where IMMs are deployed. Either in the form of IHL or IHRL, specific rules and more general principles have been defined. States may be bound by specific treaty provision, but also in many cases by customary rules that have crystallised or emerged.

However, there is too much uncertainty. It would be highly desirable for States to clarify systematically, rather than on an *ad hoc basis*, which rules would apply to which IMMs. The UN could also contribute to clarifying the position of IMMs within the context of all military operations involving such personnel, through the adoption of an instrument by the DPKO, or even by the General Assembly, as part of the development of the legal regime of the organisation.

75 The legal discussion on the issue started with the 1950 Korean War, *see* ICRC, *Le Comité International de la Croix Rouge et le conflit de Corée*, (2 volumes) (CICR, Genève, 1952), and the 1960 UN Operation in Congo, *see* G. Abi-Saab, *The United Nations Operation in The Congo: 1960-1964* (OUP, Oxford, 1978); R. Higgins, *The United Nations Operation in the Congo*, (Royal Institute of International Affairs, London, 1980).

76 *See* D. Shraga, 'UN Peacekeeping Operations: Applicability of International Humanitarian Law and Responsibility for Operations-Related Damage' (2000) 94(2) *AJIL* 406-412.

77 *Observance by United Nations Forces of International Humanitarian Law* (n 22) para. 1.1.

78 Ibid.

The reference to the R2P does not necessarily mean better and clearer rules. Actually, existing rules in international law are more detailed and understandable on the ground. The R2P may be a useful political tool, to justify and guide international action in case of humanitarian catastrophes. From the operational point of view, it may support the identification of existing specific rules that overlap both IHL and IHRL, as part of the principle that UN operations are mainly justified for the protection of the civilian population affected by a conflict situation. But in itself, whatever impact it may have on the emergence of new rules applicable to the situations addressed in this book, the R2P does not have the same legal standing and authority as rules of IHL and IHRL.

The overall picture is one of significant complexity and even confusion. Clarification of the law, and perhaps even its development, can have important benefits for all of those directly affected by conflicts in which IMMs are involved. Furthermore, these benefits are not only conceptual in that they would offer greater certainty in the law; they would also contribute in real terms to the practical conduct of the personnel of IMMs and the protection of the civilian population and objects.

Chapter 3

IHL Obligations of the UN and other International Organisations Involved in International Missions

Katie E. Sams[1]

1. Introduction

Today, it is generally recognised that International Humanitarian Law (IHL) may apply to forces under the command and control of the United Nations and other international organisations (IOs) The facts on the ground determine the law's applicability in a given situation. Thus, to the extent that such forces are involved in combat operations that rise to the level of armed conflict, IHL is applicable. Similarly, the law of occupation may be a relevant normative framework in instances where forces under the command and control of the UN or other IOs exercise control over a territory and its inhabitants.

Despite the acknowledgement that IHL is applicable in such situations, the modalities and scope of its application are the subject of considerable debate. Beyond the issue of whether the UN and certain other IOs are subjects of IHL, the question arises whether they possesses rights and duties under IHL in a given instance and thus bear responsibility for violations of the law. Moreover, under some factual circumstances, it may be unclear when an armed conflict can be said to exist, and thus when IHL begins to apply. The matter of which rules of IHL – those governing international armed conflicts or those governing non-international armed conflicts – apply in situations where UN forces or forces of other IOs are involved in armed conflict also remains unsettled. In addition, the relationship between the rules of IHL as developed through treaty and customary law and other relevant legal and policy frameworks merits further clarification. In situations where UN forces or forces of other IOs exercise control over a territory, the question of whether the law of occupation applies *de jure* or *de facto* must be addressed. Whether the receiving State has consented to the presence of the force in question is relevant in this context. The fact that it is difficult to reconcile certain provisions of the law of occupation with the specific missions of such forces complicates the law's application. Finally, because the UN and other IOs cannot directly implement certain rules of IHL, there is uncertainty as to the content of applicable law.

---

1 This chapter reflects the views of the author alone and not necessarily those of the International Committee of the Red Cross (ICRC). The author would like to thank Eric Berman, Tristan Ferraro and Sylvain Vité for their comments on an earlier draft.

M. Odello and R. Piotrowicz (eds.), International Military Missions and International Law.
2011 Koninklijke Brill NV. Printed in The Netherlands. ISBN 978 9004 17437 5. pp. 45-71.

This chapter addresses such issues, examining the IHL obligations of the UN and other IOs involved in peace operations. Part I frames the discussion by describing the increasingly complex landscape of international missions undertaken by the UN, other IOs and *ad hoc* coalitions of States. Part II provides an overview of the broader normative framework that applies to such forces. Part III then reviews the *ratione personae* applicability of IHL to the UN and other IOs, presenting the contours of the debate over the legal basis for the law's applicability. Part IV considers the *ratione materiae* applicability of the law, based on the legal qualification of the situation on the ground as an armed conflict and the peace operation's involvement as a party to that conflict. Part V highlights key remaining issues related to the content of applicable IHL rules.

2. Background

Over the years, the spectrum of 'peace operations' undertaken by the UN and other actors has become increasingly broad, to encompass conflict prevention, peacemaking, peacekeeping, peace enforcement and peace-building dimensions.[2] Although these different dimensions generally correspond to distinct activities, the boundaries between them are sometimes blurred. To add to the confusion, a single peace operation often entails more than one dimension, and related activities are rarely carried out in a sequential manner.[3] The fact that the UN and others often conduct peace operations simultaneously or successively within the same context – and with varying degrees of coordination – is yet another complicating factor.

During the Cold War period, the scope of peace operations was generally confined to the peacekeeping dimension, and the UN was virtually the only actor involved.[4] Such operations were established sparingly, and generally fulfilled a conflict management role. The consent of the parties to a given conflict was a prerequisite for their creation. Once deployed, peacekeepers were expected to remain impartial and were prohibited from using force except in self-defence. In accordance with these principles, most UN peacekeeping missions involved positioning lightly-armed Blue Helmets between adversaries in order to monitor adherence to truces and preserve the *status quo*.

The end of the Cold War altered international peace and security realities and ushered in an initial wave of expanded UN peace operations.[5] In the post Cold War

2 *See United Nations Peacekeeping Operations: Principles and Guidelines* (United Nations Department of Peacekeeping Operations, New York, 2008) 17 – 18.

3 Ibid. 18 – 20.

4 In fact, peacekeeping developed as an impromptu reaction to the political constraints of the Cold War. The creation of a standing UN army composed of contingents from the armed forces of member States, as envisaged in Chapter VII of the UN Charter, became unachieveable with the onset of the Cold War. The five permanent members of the Security Council were unable to agree upon a collective security regime and the concept of peacekeeping emerged as a workable alternative.

5 Between 1987 and 1994, the number of UN peacekeepers grew from some 10,000 to some 78,000.

environment, such operations were able to move beyond peacekeeping to encompass peacemaking, peace enforcement and peace-building dimensions as well. Rather than simply preserve the *status quo*, they were intended to build a firm and sustainable peace and often included political, military, economic, social and humanitarian components. In 1992, then UN Secretary-General Boutros Boutros-Ghali noted that the UN's security arm 'has emerged as a central instrument for the prevention and resolution of conflicts and for the preservation of peace.'[6] In the process, the hallmarks of classical peacekeeping were abandoned; UN operations were established where consent was forfeited, impartiality was foregone and force was used other than in self-defence.

The abandonment of these principles in the face of new realities on the ground proved to be the UN's downfall, and the organisation subsequently reconceived its role in peace operations. In reviewing the UN's track record in 1995, Boutros-Ghali noted that it had been less successful in operations where it had departed from the principles of consent of the parties, impartiality and the non-use of force except in self-defence.[7] The UN operations deployed in the former Yugoslavia and Somalia between 1992 and 1995 were the most striking examples. In the wake of these failed ventures, the Security Council scaled back the organisation's commitments, proving increasingly reluctant to authorise large-scale, multi-functional operations, particularly those with an enforcement component.[8] During this retrenchment period, the Security Council was increasingly willing to allow regional and *ad hoc* initiatives in their stead.[9]

6 Report of the Secretary-General Pursuant to the Statement Adopted by the Summit Meeting of the Security Council on 31 January 1992 'An Agenda for Peace' (17 June 1992) UN Doc. A/47/277 – S/24111.

7 Position Paper of the Secretary-General on the Occasion of the Fiftieth Anniversary of the United Nations, 'Supplement to an Agenda for Peace' (3 January 1995) UN Doc. A/50/60 and S/1995/1, para. 33. Boutros-Ghali further indicated that peacekeeping and enforcement stem from different logics and cautioned against blurring the distinction between the two. Ibid. para. 35.

8 Looking back on that period, former UN Secretary-General Kofi Annan subsequently observed that, '[t]he United Nations' peacekeeping mechanism for a time became the international community's emergency services, fire brigade, gendarmerie, and military deterrent, even in instances where there was no peace to be kept'. Report of the Secretary-General, 'Renewing the United Nations: A Programme for Reform' (14 July 1997) UN Doc. A/51/950, para. 14. As of June 1999, some 12,000 Blue Helmets were deployed worldwide in 15 operations.

9 In fact, the size of non-UN peace operations had begun to grow during the early 1990s, paralleling the growth of UN missions. In 1994, about 150,000 troops and police were deployed in non-UN operations around the world. William J. Durch and Tobias C. Berkman, *Who Should Keep the Peace? Providing Security for Twenty-First-Century Peace Operations* (The Henry L. Stimson Center, Washington, D.C., 2006) 10. As the size and scope of UN peace operations diminished from 1994 to 1998, however, the share of non-UN operations expanded. In 1998, UN Blue Helmets accounted for only eight percent of the forces deployed. Ibid.

While the UN continued to shy away from extensive enforcement missions, opting to leave this task to others, it became progressively more involved in other types of peace operations. In 1999, the Security Council tasked the UN with developing transitional civil administrations in Kosovo and Timor Leste. These missions had far-reaching mandates, but they did not include military components; security was provided by a North Atlantic Treaty Organisation (NATO) force in Kosovo and an *ad hoc* coalition of States in Timor Leste.[10] Three more UN operations were established over the next year, in Sierra Leone, the Democratic Republic of Congo and in Ethiopia/Eritrea.[11]

As the size and scope of UN missions continued to grow, the organisation was endeavouring to clarify its role in future peace operations. In 2000, the UN Secretary-General convened a high-level panel to assess the UN's ability to conduct peace operations and to make recommendations for enhancing its effectiveness. While confirming that the principles of consent, impartiality and non-use of force except in self-defence should remain the bedrocks of UN peacekeeping, the panel reinterpreted them to give UN forces a stronger role.[12] It contended that UN troops 'must be prepared to confront the lingering forces of war and violence with the ability and determination to defeat them.'[13] It identified 'political support, rapid deployment with a robust force posture and a sound peace-building strategy' as the key conditions for the success of future complex operations.[14] At the same time, however, the panel highlighted the limits of the UN's capabilities and stressed the need for it to decline certain roles until it had reinforced its capacity.[15]

Meanwhile, the 'burden-sharing' trend first witnessed in the 1990s has continued. Even as the number of UN peacekeepers has grown,[16] the Security Council has

10 Marten Zwanenburg, *Accountability of Peace Support Operations* (Martinius Nijhoff Publishers, Leiden, 2005) 28.

11 *Durch and Berkman* (n 9) 10. A number of reasons have been given for this renewed upsurge in UN peace operations. For one thing, other organisations were confronted with the same challenges as the UN in contexts where the parties to the conflict were not committed to peace. Moreover, regional organisations were not appropriate for the task in instances where their member states were involved in the conflict. In addition, the UN offered a certain universal legitimacy that regional organisations did not. Finally, few regional organisations proved to have the necessary capacity to do the job. Jean-Marie Guéhenno, 'On the Challenges and Achievements of Reforming UN Peace Operations', *International Peacekeeping* (2002) No. 69, 71.

12 *Zwanenburg* (n 10) 29.

13 'Report of the Panel on United Nations Peace Operations' (21 August 2000) UN Doc. A/55/305 – S/2000/809, para. 1.

14 Ibid. para. 4.

15 *See* Ibid. para. 1.

16 The number of UN peacekeepers has risen steadily since 1999, finally exceeding the 1994 peak in 2006. In 2008, over 90,000 UN peacekeepers were deployed in 17 missions around the world. Statistics provided by UN Department of Peacekeeping Operations <www.un.org/Depts/dpko/dpko/contributors/index.htm>.

continued to rely on others to field multinational forces.[17] Among regional organisations, NATO, the European Union (EU), the African Union (AU), the Economic Community of West African States (ECOWAS), the Economic and Monetary Community of Central African States (CEMAC) and the Commonwealth of Independent States (CIS) have all deployed forces over the past decade – with many of them displaying a growing willingness to do so over time. NATO and the EU have fielded troops beyond their own political boundaries (so-called 'out-of-area' deployments). *Ad hoc* coalitions of States have also deployed significant forces in several instances over the same period.

Co-deployed, sequential and integrated operations involving the UN and other actors have become increasingly prevalent. For example, a NATO force of some 50,000 deployed in Kosovo alongside the roughly 3,000-strong UN Interim Administration Mission in Kosovo (UNMIK) in 1999, following a 78-day NATO air campaign. That same year, an Australian-led multinational force of some 10,000 troops in Timor Leste paved the way for the 10,000-strong peacekeeping component of the UN Transitional Administration in Timor Leste (UNTAET). In Sierra Leone, a 4,500 strong British contingent was deployed in 2000 to bolster the UN Mission in Sierra Leone (UNAMSIL), which included some 6,000 peacekeepers at the time. In 2001, a small UN civilian mission and the 5,000-strong, British-led International Stabilization Force (ISAF) were established simultaneously in Afghanistan. NATO took command of ISAF in 2003, which has grown to 51,000 troops at its height. Also in 2003, the EU deployed a 1,900-strong military force to support the larger UN Organisation Mission in the Democratic Republic of the Congo (MONUC). Since 2004, the UN Operation in Côte d'Ivoire (UNOCI), with an authorised strength of between 6,200 and 9,200 uniformed personnel, has worked alongside a French-led contingent comprising 5,000 troops at its height. The EU again deployed a 2,300-strong military force to support MONUC in 2006. In 2007, the UN Security Council authorised a 27,500-strong, hybrid UN – AU mission in Darfur. Most recently, the EU deployed a 3,300-strong force in the Central African Republic and Chad in 2008 to provide support to the small UN mission there.[18]

Operating environments and mandates of such operations have varied considerably, and no standard division of labour between the UN and other actors involved in peace operations has emerged. That said, the UN has tended to leave the provision of robust military support to others, with or without its authorisation.[19] It has often deployed comparatively limited peacekeeping missions alongside larger multi-

17 In 2006, some 70,000 non-UN troops were participating in multinational forces around the world. As of 2008, the number had risen to more than 80,000. Statistics taken from SIPRI Multilateral Peace Operations Database <http://conflict.sipri.org>.

18 Statistics taken from SIPRI Multilateral Peace Operations Database <http://conflict.sipri.org> and various documents issued by the UN and relevant regional organisations.

19 In Africa, however, the UN has only had limited success in finding other actors willing and able to respond militarily (at least until recently).

national forces. At the same time, the UN has taken on far-reaching tasks related to post-conflict reconstruction and nation-building.[20]

Different divisions of labour have given rise to different models of cooperation. Co-deployed operations feature regional or *ad hoc* military forces working simultaneously alongside the UN and other civilian components, but with separate command stuctures. In sequential operations, the UN replaces another actor or vice versa. Finally, integrated missions – the rarest forms of partnership to date – combine all mission components under a single line of authority.[21]

This complex international peace and security landscape often obscures the applicable normative framework. To discern and apply relevant legal regimes, it is necessary to distinguish between the broad array of actors, operations and cooperation models. Given the breadth of related issues, this chapter focuses on international missions carried out by the UN and other IOs.[22]

3. Normative Framework

The specific characteristics of peace operations are conditioned upon the normative framework applicable to them. In many instances, multiple legal regimes, comprising both international law and domestic law rules, govern their operation. Depending on the features of a given mission and the actors involved, international obligations may stem from the UN Charter and the constitutive documents of other concerned IOs, resolutions of the UN Security Council and of the peace and security organs of other IOs, mission-specific rules, and international law relevant to the force's activities.

International law on the use of force (*jus ad bellum*) provides the basis for determining the legality of military operations. The UN Charter obliges States to refrain from:

> the threat or use of force against the territorial integrity or political independence of any state, or in any other manner inconsistent with the Purposes of the United Nations.[23]

The Charter envisages two exceptions to this prohibition: Security Council action to maintain or restore international peace and security; and cases of individual or collective self-defence against armed attack.[24] The Charter also recognises an integral

20 UNMIK in Kosovo and the UNTAET in Timor Leste are two such examples.

21 Center on International Cooperation at New York University, 'Annual Review of UN Peace Operations 2008' Briefing Paper (March 2009) 10. *See also*, Bruce Jones with Feryal Cherif 'Evolving Models of Peacekeeping: Policy Implications and Responses' study prepared for the Best Practices Unit, UN Department of Peacekeeping Operations, (2004) 16 and *Durch and Berkman* (n 9) 3.

22 Chapter 4 of this book covers multinational forces fielded by States and *ad hoc* coalitions, given the different legal issues involved.

23 Article 2.4 UN Charter.

24 Ibid. Articles 42 and 51.

role for regional organisations in the maintenance of international peace and security.[25]

Although the concept of peace operations was not specifically envisaged in the UN Charter, the Security Council's competence to establish them is not contested. Such operations are generally established within the framework of Chapter VI or Chapter VII of the UN Charter, depending on their specific mandate. When a regional organisation undertakes an enforcement action, Chapter VIII of the UN Charter provides the relevant legal framework. Moreover, the constitutive documents of other concerned IOs may be relevant for defining the permissible scope of action for those organisations.

International military missions are often authorised in resolutions of the UN Security Council and of the peace and security organs of other IOs. Such resolutions may specify a peace operation's legal basis and outline its mandate. Generally, UN Security Council resolutions under Chapter VII of the UN Charter are deemed to be binding, whereas Chapter VI resolutions are considered as recommendatory. Beyond establishing UN missions, the Security Council has increasingly passed resolutions authorising other organisations to undertake enforcement actions in conformity with Chapter VIII of the Charter. The authority of decisions taken by the appropriate organs of other IOs varies according to their structures. While all such resolutions may not be legally binding, they are important sources of soft law.

Mission-specific rules also contribute to defining the legal framework applicable to peace operations. *Ad hoc* agreements on a force's establishment and operation may be concluded. For each of its operations, the UN generally concludes a status of forces agreement (SOFA) outlining the rights and duties of members of the UN force, with the host country.[26] In addition, the UN usually negotiates agreements with individual countries contributing personnel and equipment to govern their relationship.[27] In some instances, other IOs have also concluded agreements with the countries in which they are operating[28] as well as agreements with troop-contributing countries concerning their participation in the force.[29] Internal rules of the UN

25 Ibid. Articles 52, 53 and 54.

26 The UN Secretary-General developed a model for this type of agreement in 1990: 'Model Status-of-Forces Agreement for Peacekeeping Operations' (9 October 1990) UN Doc. A/45/594.

27 The UN Secretary-General also prepared a model agreement of this type in 1991: 'Model Agreement between the United Nations and Member States Contributing Personnel and Equipment to United Nations Peacekeeping Operations' (23 May 1991) UN Doc. A/46/185.

28 For example, NATO concluded a SOFA with Bosnia and Herzegovina prior to the deployment of the Implementation Force (IFOR) there. (*See Zwanenburg* (n 10) 42). However, it did not sign a SOFA with the Federal Republic of Yugoslavia covering the legal status of the Kosovo Force (KFOR) as the international community wished to isolate the regime of Slobodan Milosevic. Instead, the KFOR commander issued an 'Interim Status of Forces Policy', which was replaced by a joint KFOR – UNMIK declaration. Ibid. 46.

29 Chapter 6 of this book focuses specifically on Rules of Engagement and international military missions.

govern the functioning of the force. In this respect, the UN generally distinguishes between operations plans and rules of engagement (RoE). Operations plans generally provide a military interpretation of the force's mandate and are issued by the commander. RoE delineate the circumstances in which armed force can be used.[30]

Finally, in terms of international law, both international human rights law and IHL may impose important legal obligations on the actors involved. Yet applying these bodies of law in the context of international military missions raises a number of questions. Given the breadth of related issues, this chapter focuses on the IHL obligations of the UN and other organisations involved in international missions.[31]

4. *Ratione Personae* Applicability of IHL

The applicability of IHL to peace operations carried out under unified command and control has been the source of considerable debate over the years. The subject first emerged in the context of the UN's early military engagements, related to whether and how IHL could be applied to UN forces. As other organisations became involved in international missions, the issue was taken up with regard to them. Today, it is generally settled that the UN and certain other IOs are subjects of IHL. However, this is a separate issue from whether an IO possesses rights and duties under IHL in a given instance and thus bears responsibility for violations of the law. The level of effective control that the IO exerts over the conduct in question – an issue that it often difficult to gauge in practice – will ultimately determine where responsibility lies.

4.1 UN and other International Organisations as Subjects of IHL

The debate has essentially revolved around the legal basis for the law's applicability to the UN and other IOs. In 1949, the International Court of Justice (ICJ) determined that the UN has 'a large measure of international personality and the capacity to operate upon an international plane'.[32] It follows that the UN can be a subject of IHL; insofar as the UN can engage in armed conflict to achieve its goals and carry

30 Michael Bothe and Thomas Dörschel 'The UN Peacekeeping Experience' in Dieter Fleck (ed), *The Handbook of the Law of Visiting Forces*, (Oxford University Press, Oxford, 2001) 494 – 495. For several early missions, the UN established regulations setting forth relevant international standards describing the structure of the force, and outlining the rights and duties of its members.

31 Chapter 5 of this book focuses on international human rights law and peacekeeping operations.

32 *Reparation for Injuries Suffered in the Service of the United Nations* (Advisory Opinion) (1949) ICJ Rep. 11 April 1949, 179. The Court further noted: 'Whereas a state possesses the totality of international rights and duties recognized by international law, the rights and duties of an entity such as the Organization must depend upon its purposes and functions as specified or implied in its constituent documents and developed in practice.' Ibid. 180.

out its functions, the law governing such situations is applicable to it.[33] This debate has revealed a certain ambiguity about the source of the UN's IHL obligations, with different strategies being pursued at different times.[34] The same issue has arisen with regard to other IOs. To the extent that an IO has the authority to contribute to the maintenance of international peace and security by engaging in armed conflict, the rules of IHL are applicable to it.[35] In line with this logic, the rules of IHL are applicable to NATO, for example.[36]

In the early years of UN peacekeeping, the International Committee of the Red Cross (ICRC) stressed the law's relevance to the conduct of UN forces and regularly raised this issue with the UN and its member States. In virtually every conflict involving UN forces, the ICRC drew the UN Secretary-General's attention to the application of IHL to those forces.[37] The organisation periodically undertook broader 'macro'-level efforts to reinforce such context-specific initiatives. In 1961, for example, it submitted a memorandum to States party to the Geneva Conventions of 1949 and UN member States, calling upon States providing contingents to UN operations to respect and ensure respect for their IHL obligations under the Geneva Conventions.[38] The 1963 Council of Delegates adopted a resolution calling upon the

---

33 Christopher Greenwood, 'IHL and UN Military Operations' (1998) 1 *Yearbook of International Humanitarian* Law, 16. *See also* Robert Kolb, Gabriele Porretto and Sylvain Vité, *L'application du droit international humanitaire et des droits de l'homme aux organisations internationales* (Bruylant, Brussels, 2005) 124.

34 It was acknowledged early on that the UN was bound by customary IHL. Although not specifically designed to be applied by the UN, the rules of IHL extend to it *mutatis mutandis*. Given the uncertain content and scope of customary rules of IHL, however, various efforts were undertaken to secure the UN's formal commitment to respect the IHL treaties – whether by acceding to them or adopting a declaration. These efforts were ultimately unsuccessful, but the UN subsequently endeavoured to couch its relevant obligations in more concrete terms. Moreover, beyond the UN's obligations under customary IHL, troop-contributing countries remain obliged 'to respect and ensure respect for' IHL in accordance with Article 1 common to the four Geneva Conventions of 1949. *See* Dietrich Schindler 'United Nations Forces and International Humanitarian Law' in Christophe Swinarski (ed), *Studies and Essays on International Humanitarian Law and Red Cross Principles in honour of Jean Pictet* (Martinius Nijhoff Publishers, Dordrecht, 1984) 526 – 528.

35 Eric David, *Principes de droit des conflits armés* (2e édition, Bruylant, Brussels, 1999) 192; *Kolb, Porretto and Vité* (n 33) 127 – 28.

36 *See Kolb, Porretto and Vité* (n 33) 128 – 129. NATO's founding treaty of 1949, which establishes a Council to examine questions relative to the treaty's application and empowers the Council to establish subsidiary organs, affirms the organisation's international legal personality. NATO's scope of action was limited to individual or collective self-defence activities but in 1999, NATO member States extended the organisation's remit to 'crisis response operations'. *The Alliance's Strategic Concept* (24 April 1999) <www.nato.int>.

37 Daphna Shraga and Ralph Zacklin 'The Applicability of International Humanitarian law to United Nations Peacekeeping Operations: Conceptual, Legal and Practical Issues' in Umesh Palkankar (ed), *Report of the Symposium on Humanitarian Action and Peacekeeping Operations* (International Committee of the Red Cross, Geneva, 1994) 42.

38 'The Application of the Geneva Conventions by the Armed Forces Placed at the

UN to respect the Geneva Conventions and to adopt a 'solemn declaration' to that effect.[39] At the ICRC's recommendation, the 1965 International Conference of the Red Cross and Red Crescent adopted a resolution recommending that appropriate arrangements be made to ensure that contingents placed at the UN's disposal observe the Geneva Conventions.[40] During the expert conference preceding the diplomatic negotiations on the 1977 Additional Protocols, the ICRC submitted a draft protocol containing an article on the accession of inter-governmental organisations to the Geneva Conventions and the proposed protocol.[41]

The UN, for its part, hesitated to recognise the blanket applicability of IHL to peacekeeping forces under its command and control, underscoring related legal, political and practical difficulties. It asserted that a peacekeeping force is acting on behalf of international community at large in discharging its mandate and cannot be considered a 'party' to a conflict or a 'power' within the meaning of the Geneva Conventions. It further contended that the UN does not have the ability to fulfil many of the obligations laid down in IHL treaties, notwithstanding its status as a subject of international law. Finally, the UN asserted that it could not become a party to the Geneva Conventions as, by their terms, they do not provide for the participation of IOs.[42]

As peacekeeping missions became more robust in the early 1990s, however, the UN sought to reinforce the applicability of IHL to UN forces. In this new genera-

---

Disposal of the United Nations' *Memorandum of the ICRC to the Governments of States Party to the Geneva Conventions and Members of the United Nations*, reprinted in (1961) 1 *International Review of the Red Cross,* No. 9, 489 –491. Umesh Palwankar 'Applicability of International Humanitarian Law to United Nations Peacekeeping Forces' (1993) *International Review of the Red Cross*, No. 294, 230.

39 'Resolution of the Council of Delegates, Centenary Congress of the International Red Cross' reprinted in (1963) 3 *International Review of the Red* Cross, No. 31, 514. The Council of Delegates constitutes the assembly of representatives of different components of the Red Cross and Red Crescent Movement.

40 Resolution XXV, 'Application of the Geneva Conventions by United Nations Emergency Forces' *20th International Conference of the Red Cross*, Vienna (1965) reprinted in *Handbook of the International Red Cross and Red Crescent Movement (*13th Edition, International Committee of the Red Cross, Geneva, 1994) 748; *Palwankar* (n 38) 230. The International Conference brings together the States party to the Geneva Conventions and the components of the International Red Cross and Red Crescent Movement.

41 The UN Secretary-General noted that it was not possible for the UN to execute many of the obligations contained in the Geneva Conventions. The ICRC's proposal was ultimately rejected. *Schindler* (n 34) 525 – 526. Beyond the ICRC, a number of other organisations also affirmed the applicability of IHL to UN forces at the time. In 1963, for example, the International Law Institute indicated that obligations imposed on parties to a conflict by international law extend to actions undertaken by the UN. In 1966, the International Law Association recommended that the UN accept the Geneva Conventions and the 1954 Hague Convention on the Protection of Cultural Property. *Kolb, Porretto and Vité* (n 33) 126 – 127.

42 *Daphna Shraga and Ralph Zacklin* (n 37) 43; and Daphna Shraga 'The United Nations as an Actor Bound by International Humanitarian Law' in Luigi Condorelli, Anne-Marie La Rosa and Sylvie Scherrer (eds) *The United Nations and International Humanitarian Law* (Pedone, Paris, 1996) 323. *See also Greenwood* (n 33) 14 – 15.

tion of operations, the likelihood that UN troops could be called upon to undertake military operations involving the use of force increased, rendering IHL a potentially more relevant legal framework. In 1993, in the context of Rwanda, the UN undertook to ensure that its forces there would respect 'the principles and spirit' of the general IHL treaties (including the 1949 Geneva Conventions, their Additional Protocols of 1977 and the 1954 Hague Convention for the Protection of Cultural Property) and that participating military personnel would be fully acquainted with them.[43] This was the first time that the UN had assumed direct responsibility for ensuring respect for IHL by members of its forces *vis-à-vis* a particular State.[44] The same formulation was included in other SOFAs as well.[45]

Ultimately, however, the 'principles and spirit' clause proved too vague to be operationalised on the ground. UN personnel in contexts such as Somalia and the former Yugoslavia needed guidance on the law's practical application.[46] Although the content of the 'principles and spirit' of relevant conventions was seemingly not limited to customary IHL rules, its precise scope remained ambiguous.[47]

More concrete formulations of the UN's related obligations have subsequently emerged. The 1994 Convention on the Safety of United Nations and Associated Personnel acknowledges the applicability of IHL 'as contained in international instruments' – not only in their 'principles and spirit' – to UN personnel.[48] The UN Secretary-General's Bulletin on the Observance by United Nations Forces of International Humanitarian Law, issued in 1999, provides more explicit guidance on

43 Article 7 'Agreement on the Status of the United Nations Assistance Mission (UNAMIR)' United Nations Treaty Series, Vol. 1748 (5 November 1993). The Agreement imposed corresponding obligations in terms of the treatment of UN forces on the government of Rwanda. Ibid.

44 *See Shraga* (n 42) 324. Regulations for early UN peacekeeping missions merely contain a generic reference to the force's respect for the principles and spirit of IHL. The 1990 model agreement between the UN and States contributing to peacekeeping operations, which refers to the UN's obligation to observe and respect the principles and spirit of the relevant conventions and the participating State's responsibility for ensuring that its military personnel is acquainted with the principles and spirit of those conventions, does not establish a concrete obligation towards a third State. Ibid.

45 *See* Shraga 'UN Peacekeeping Operations: Applicability of International Humanitarian Law and Responsibility for Operations-Related Damage' (2000) 94 *American Journal of International Law* 407.

46 Ibid.

47 The 'principles and spirit' formulation was intended to underscore that IHL treaty law was designed to be applied to States, and that consequently, some of its norms could not be applied to IOs. *Kolb, Porretto and Vité* (n 33) 135 – 136.

48 The Convention's 'savings clause' provides: 'Nothing in this Convention shall affect. . . [t]he applicability of international humanitarian law and universally recognized standards of human rights as contained in international instruments in relation to... the responsibility of such personnel to respect such law and standards... .' Article 20 Convention on the Safety of United Nations and Associated Personnel, Annex (9 December 1994) UN Doc. A/RES/49/59. See also *Shraga and Zacklin* (n 37) 47.

the content of IHL rules applicable to UN operations.[49] Its promulgation marks an important step in the evolution of the UN's position regarding its responsibility to ensure respect for IHL by forces under its command and control.[50]

An administrative text issued by the Secretary-General in his capacity as 'commander in chief' of UN operations, the Bulletin purports to set out the 'fundamental principles and rules' applicable to forces operating under UN command and control.[51] It applies to such forces 'when in situations of armed conflict they are actively engaged as combatants, to the extent and for the duration of their engagement.'[52] The Bulletin aims to clarify pre-existing obligations by adapting them to the characteristics of the UN and to improve respect for the law on the ground.[53] It does not constitute an exhaustive list of applicable 'rules and principles,' but focuses on the core obligations for UN forces.[54]

In the intervening years, the UN has continued to affirm the applicability of IHL to UN forces. For example, in a 2001 report, the UN Secretary-General confirmed that the Bulletin 'signals formal recognition of the applicability of International Humanitarian Law to United Nations peace operations.'[55] The policy document on UN peacekeeping operations produced by the UN Department of Peacekeeping Operations in 2008 refers to the UN Secretary-General's 1999 Bulletin and provides that:

> United Nations peacekeepers must have a clear understanding of the principles and rules of international humanitarian law and observe them in situations where they apply.[56]

---

49 In an effort to move beyond the 'principles and spirit' formulation, the ICRC held a series of expert meetings in 1994 and 1995 to identify the core IHL rules applicable to UN operations. The resulting document served as the basis for the Secretary-General's Bulletin. *Shraga* (n 45) 407.

50 *See* Anne Ryniker 'Respect du droit international humanitaire par les forces des Nations Unies' (1999) 81 *International Review of the Red Cross*, No. 836, 799.

51 Secretary-General's Bulletin: 'Observance by United Nations Forces of International Humanitarian Law' (6 August 1999) UN Doc. ST/SGB/1999/13, introductory paragraph. The Bulletin is not, as such, a legally binding document. *Ryniker* (n 50) 804. The source of the legal obligation lies in the treaty-law provisions applicable to members of the force by virtue of their national laws or in the customary IHL rules that are independently binding on them. *Shraga* (n 45) 409.

52 *ST/SGB/1999/13* section 1.1.

53 Paolo Benvenuti 'Le respect du droit international humanitaire par les forces des Nations Unies: La Circulaire du Secrétaire-Général' (2001) 105 *Revue générale du droit international publique* No. 2, 357 – 358; *Kolb, Porretto and Vité* (n 33) 138 – 139.

54 *ST/SGB/1999/13* (n 52) section 2.

55 'Road Map Toward the Implementation of the United Nations Millennium Development Goals' (6 September 2001) UN Doc. A/56/326 para. 19.

56 *UNPO: Principles and Guidelines* (n 2) 15 – 16.

Recent SOFAs concluded between the UN and host countries refer to the UN's obligation to ensure that its forces respect the 'principles and rules' of relevant IHL treaties.[57] Other mission-specific rules and regulations also tend to refer to the UN's obligation to respect IHL.

Other organisations have also recognised the applicability of IHL to troops under their command and control. Like the UN, such organisations tend to refer to their obligation to respect IHL in their mission-specific rules and regulations. For example, the 2004 status of mission agreement on the establishment of an Africa Union ceasefire commission in Sudan provides that the AU shall ensure that the mission conducts its operations in Sudan with full respect for the 'principles and rules' of relevant IHL treaties.[58] The rules of engagement for NATO operations also clearly reflect the rules of IHL.[59]

Despite acknowledging the theoretical applicability of IHL to troops under their command and control, IOs often deny the law's actual applicability in concrete instances. Such denials attest to their reluctance to admit that they are taking part in an armed conflict and their desire to encourage the perception that they are an impartial and neutral force.[60] The ICRC maintains a dialogue with UN and regional forces on IHL-related issues at the operational level, drawing their attention to the applicability of IHL to such forces when the facts on the ground warrant it.[61]

57 *E.g.* Article 6(a) 'Agreement between the United Nations and Sierra Leone Concerning the Status of the United Nations Mission in Sierra Leone' United Nations Treaty Series, Vol. 2118 (4 August 2000); Article 6(a) 'Agreement between Ethiopia and the United Nations Concerning the Status of the United Nations Mission in Ethiopia and Eritrea', United Nations Treaty Series, Vol. 2141 (23 March 2001); Article 6(a) 'Agreement between the United Nations and the Government of Sudan Concerning the Status of the United Nations Mission in Sudan' United Nations Treaty Series, Vol. 2351 (28 December 2005). The same provision has been included in some SOFAs concluded between the UN and host governments, notwithstanding the fact that the country in question was not then experiencing an armed conflict (making the rules of IHL inapplicable in that context).

58 Article 8(a) 'Status of Mission Agreement (SOMA) on the Establishment and Management of the Ceasefire Commission in the Darfur Area of the Sudan (CFC)' (4 June 2004) downloaded from African Union Mission in the Sudan (AMIS) website <*www.amis-sudan.org/history.html*>.

59 *See* Alexandre Faite and Jérémie Labbé Grenier (eds), *Report of the Expert Meeting on Multinational Peace Opertaions: Applicability of International Humanitarian Law and Human Rights Law to UN Mandated Forces* (11-12 December 2003) (International Committee of the Red Cross, Geneva, 2004) 25 – 26.

60 Jakob Kellenberger, 'Keynote Address' in Gian Luca Beruto (ed), *International Humanitarian Law, Human Rights and Peace Operations, Proceedings of the 31st Round Table on Current Issues of International Humanitarian Law* (Institute of Humanitarian Law, Sanremo, 2009) 31.

61 In several recent instances, the ICRC has submitted a memorandum to the UN head of mission and force commander indicating that the UN force – as a party to an armed conflict – is obliged to respect IHL and outlining applicable IHL rules. The ICRC has submitted a similar memorandum to regional organisations and to individual troop-contributing countries IHL in several cases. In addition, it has made interventions to

4.2 Attributing the Conduct in Question to the UN or Other International Organisations

Concluding that IHL is applicable to the UN or another IO does not signify that every act committed in the framework of an operation conducted by that organisation is attributable to the organisation itself. An organisation's responsibility for acts committed by troops acting in its name hinges upon whether it – as opposed to its member States – has effective control over the conduct in question.[62] This relates to whether the control that the IO exerts is sufficiently independent from that of its member States to conclude that the organisation manages the conduct of operations.[63]

In principle, this is the case for UN peacekeeping operations, which are subject to the command and control of the United Nations.[64] The UN Security Council generally establishes such missions as subsidiary organs on an *ad hoc* basis, with personnel fielded by individual States. In theory, the UN acquires full authority over the deployment, organisation, conduct and direction of these forces, while troop-contributing countries retain authority in the administrative, disciplinary and penal domains.[65] In reality, however, the level of command and control that a UN force actually exhibits depends on national policies and practices of troop-contributing countries.[66] In some operations, the actual division of authority between the UN and troop-contributing countries on the ground has been ambiguous, calling into question the UN's effective control.[67]

---

forces under the command and control of regional organisations identifying specific events giving rise to questions regarding respect for the rules of IHL and highlighting particular practices.

62 Draft Article 5 of the Rules on the Responsibility of International Organizations, which was provisionally adopted by the International Law Commission in 2004, provides: 'The conduct of a State or an organ or agent of an international organization that is placed at the disposal of another international organization shall be considered under international law an act of the latter organization if the organization exercises effective control over that conduct.' Report of the International Law Commission: Fifty-Sixth Session (3 May – 4 June and 5 July – 6 August 2004) UN Doc. A/59/10, 99.

63 *Kolb, Porretto and Vité* (n 33) 151 – 152.

64 In UN operations, it is possible to distinguish between three levels of authority: [1] overall political direction, provided by the UN Security Council; [2] executive direction and control at the level of the UN Secretary-General; and [3] command in the field, residing in the head of mission. Report of the Secretary-General, 'Command and Control of United Nations Peacekeeping Operations'(21 November 1994) UN Doc. A/49/681, para. 4.

65 *See* Ibid. paras. 7 – 10.

66 Some States have laws prohibiting their military forces from taking orders from a foreign national. To get around such restrictions, orders are channeled through officers from participating States serving on the force commander's staff. *E.g.* Ray Murphy, (ed), *UN Peacekeeping in Lebanon, Somalia and Kosovo: Operational and Legal Issues in Practice*, (Cambridge University Press, Cambridge, 2007) 106 – 107.

67 For example, in the case of UNOSOM II – a UN operation which took over from a

For other IOs, their effective control will depend on the organisation and mode of functioning of a given operation. As with UN missions, indicators include the force's chain of command and the real division of authority between the IO and its member States on the ground. Assessing whether rights and duties vest in an organisation in a given instance – or rather remain with its member States – tends to be a more complicated determination for organisations that function on the basis of unanimous decisions taken by their membership. In this context, there has been some debate as to the degree of command and control actually vested in NATO during its various 'out-of-area' deployments.[68]

5. *Ratione Materiae* Applicability of IHL

After concluding that IHL is applicable to the UN and other IOs *ratione personae* as subjects of IHL possessing related rights and duties, it is necessary to examine whether the material conditions for the law's application are met in a given case. This hinges on the existence of an armed conflict in which the peace operation is participating. In analysing these issues, a number of subsidiary questions emerge related to the legal framework governing peace operations.

5.1 Existence of an Armed Conflict

The existence of an armed conflict triggers the application of international humanitarian law. Whether or not IHL applies to missions conducted by the UN and other organisations thus depends upon whether or not they are taking part in an armed conflict.[69] This is an objective determination, independent of the subjective justification for such action; the facts on the ground establish the applicability of IHL to a given situation.

US-led multinational force in Somalia in 1992 and operated alongside an independent US rapid intervention force – the straightforward command structure that existed on paper was not fully operational in practice. Certain contingents operating within UNOSOM II in fact took their orders from their own governments. Cases where UN forces were accused of violating IHL were addressed through national mechanisms and the UN's responsibility was never officially asserted. *Kolb, Porretto and Vité* (n 33) 155 – 158. *See also A/59/10* (n 62) 113 – 114.

68 For example, in the case of Operation Allied Force, NATO's 1999 air campaign in the Federal Republic of Yugoslavia, most authors have argued that the fact that NATO contingents preserved their own powers of operational command (under NATO's operational control) and could opt out of certain activities signified that NATO member States retained rights and obligations under IHL. They have asserted that as a result, NATO's international responsibility for illicit acts committed by its member States was not engaged. *See Kolb, Porretto and Vité* (n 33) 165 – 169; *but see Zwanenburg* (n 10) 41 – 49.

69 An IO is bound to comply with existing international law; therefore, when it becomes a party to a conflict, it must comply with IHL. *Faite and Labbé Grenier* (n 59) 9.

The relevance of a mission's mandate and rules of engagement for determining whether it is involved in an armed conflict has been raised. Regardless of the label and corresponding authority given to a peace operation, the fact of participating in the hostilities prompts the applicability of IHL. Thus, whether a UN operation is established under Chapter VI or Chapter VII of the UN Charter, IHL may be a relevant legal framework, depending on how the situation evolves on the ground.[70]

The issue has also arisen as to whether the general criteria for determining whether a given situation rises to the level of armed conflict should be adapted to the specific situation of peace operations conducted by the UN or other organisations. Some authors have argued that for situations involving international forces the threshold for determining whether an armed conflict exists should be different – whether lower, higher or variable.[71] Although States and IOs may have compelling *jus ad bellum* arguments for altering the applicable threshold, IHL provides no legal basis for maintaining that different criteria should obtain for determining the law's applicability to peace operations.[72]

In this context, the interplay between IHL and the protective framework established in the 1994 Convention on the Safety of United Nations and Associated Personnel becomes relevant. The 1994 Convention was specifically designed to meet the security needs of the UN and prohibit attacks on UN and associated personnel in certain circumstances.[73] It purportedly aims to differentiate its scope of application from that of IHL and ensure that the two legal regimes are mutually exclusive.[74] Accordingly, it distinguishes between UN operations 'conducted under United

70 *See Greenwood* (n 33) 11. While a particular mission's mandate and rules of engagement are not determinate when assessing whether IHL applies, they may be indicators of the probability that the force will be involved in armed conflict. *See Faite and Labbé Grenier* (n 59) 9.

71 A lower threshold would result in the broader applicability of IHL, potentially affording greater protection to the international force. A higher threshold would restrict the applicability of IHL and offer greater scope for protection according to the Convention on the Safety of United Nations and Associated Personnel. A variable threshold would permit a differentiated application of the IHL rules. *See* Robert Kolb, *Droit humanitaire et opérations de paix internationale (2e édition)* (Helbring and Lichtenhahn, Basel, 2006) 33 – 39 for a discussion of the possible legal bases for these different options.

72 The preamble to Additional Protocol I confirms the separation between *jus ad bellum* and *jus in bello*. It provides that the Geneva Conventions and Additional Protocol I 'must be fully applied in all circumstances to all persons who are protected by those instruments, without any distinction based on the nature and origins of the armed conflict or on the causes espoused by or attributed to the parties to the conflict'. Preamble, Additional Protocol I to the Geneva Conventions, 8 June 1977.

73 UN personnel includes '[p]ersons engaged or deployed by the Secretary-General o the United Nations as members of the military, police or civilian components of a United Nations operation' while 'associated personnel' covers '[p]ersons assigned by a Government or an intergovernmental organization with the agreement of the competent organ of the United Nations.' Article 1(a)(i) and Article 1(b)(i) UN Convention on the Safety of United Nations and Associated Personnel.

74 According to a participant in the negotiation process, '[t]he negotiators realized that it

Nations authority and control… [w]here the operation is for the purpose of maintaining or restoring international peace and security' (to which the Convention would apply) and those 'authorized by the Security Council as an enforcement action under Chapter VII of the Charter of the United Nations in which any of the personnel are engaged as combatants against organised armed forces' (to which IHL would apply).[75] The scope of these provisions is ambiguous, however.[76] In any event, the two legal regimes are not mutually exclusive; in some situations both IHL and the Convention apply.[77] This overlap could lead to situations in which attacks against UN or associated personnel engaged in hostilities with a combat function, though not prohibited by IHL, would constitute a crime under the 1994 Convention. Such an eventuality runs counter to one of IHL's basic tenets – the principle of equality between belligerents – which confers equal rights and duties upon all parties to a conflict.[78]

---

was necessary to have a clear separation between the new legal regime under the instrument being drafted and the Geneva Conventions, so that UN and associated personnel and those who attack them would be covered under one regime or the other, but not both. Evan T. Bloom 'Protecting Peacekeepers: The Convention on the Safety of the United Nations and Associated Personnel' (1995) 89 *American Journal of International Law* 625.

75 Article 1(c)(i) and Article 2(2) UN Convention on the Safety of United Nations and Associated Personnel. The Convention's 2005 Optional Protocol extends the definition of UN operations to cover operations established to deliver humanitarian, political or development assistance in peace-building or to deliver emergency humanitarian assistance. Article 2(a) and (b) Optional Protocol to the Convention on the Safety of United Nations and Associated Personnel, Annex (8 December 2005) UN Doc. A/RES/60/42.

76 For a discussion of related issues, *e.g.* Antoine Bouvier 'Convention on the Safety of United Nations and Associated Personnel: Presentation and Analysis' (1995) *International Review of the Red Cross*, No. 309, 660 – 664; *Shraga and Zacklin* (n 37) 335 – 337; and Claude Emanuelli 'Les forces des Nations Unies et le droit international humanitaire' in Luigi Condorelli, Anne-Marie La Rosa and Sylvie Scherrer (eds), *The United Nations and International Humanitarian Law*, (Pedone, Paris, 1996) 354 – 356. The wording of these provisions attests to the difficult negotiations related to delimiting the Convention's material scope of application and reflects compromises made. *E.g Bouvier* (above) 656 – 660.

77 The fact that an operation is 'authorized by the Security Council as an enforcement action under Chapter VII' does not determine the applicability of IHL. *See* Christopher Greenwood, 'Protection of Peacekeepers: The Legal Regime' (1996) 7 *Duke Journal of Comparative and International Law* 198-199. Indeed, the 'savings clause' of the Convention leaves open the possibility that the Convention and IHL could apply simultaneously. It provides that the Convention does not affect 'the applicability of international humanitarian law…in relation to the protection of United Nations operations and United Nations and associated personnel or the responsibility of such personnel to respect such law.' Article 20(a) UN Convention on the Safety of United Nations and Associated Personnel.

78 *Kellenberger* (n 60).

5.2 Involvement of the Peace Operation as a Party to the Armed Conflict

Simply being deployed in a situation of armed conflict does not make an international mission a party to that conflict.[79] It is necessary to gauge whether particular conduct by a peace operation constitutes participation in an armed conflict, in light of the broader context in which it occurs. Under certain scenarios, the use of force in self-defence may constitute participation in an armed conflict. The Secretary-General's Bulletin on Observance by United Nations Forces of International Humanitarian Law acknowledges this, indicating that IHL may be applicable to 'peacekeeping operations when the use of force is permitted in self-defence.'[80] In other instances, however, resort to force in self-defence may not trigger the applicability of IHL.[81]

One key element of the broader context to consider is the anticipated qualification of the situation as an international or a non-international armed conflict. On the one hand, an international armed conflict exists whenever one State resorts to armed force against another, regardless of the reasons for or intensity of the confrontation. Similarly, a situation in which one State occupies all or part of the territory of another State amounts to an international armed conflict.[82] On the other hand, a protracted armed confrontation between governmental armed forces and one or more armed groups, or between such groups, constitutes a non-international armed conflict.[83] Whereas virtually any hostile act carried out by one State against another can constitute an international armed conflict, the intensity of the violence and the level of organisation of the parties involved are important variables in determining whether a non-international armed conflict exists.[84] The international – non-international distinction is thus relevant for determining whether resort to force amounts to participation in armed conflict in a given instance.

---

79 If an international mission is not a party to the conflict, it will not be bound by the rules of IHL. However, it will benefit from the law's protection; its members will be considered civilians for the purposes of IHL.

80 *ST/SGB/1999/13* (n 51) section 1.1.

81 Whether force is used in self-defense or for some other purpose has no bearing on the applicability of IHL.

82 *See* 'How is the Term 'Armed Conflict' Defined in International Humanitarian Law?' *ICRC Opinion Paper* (2008). *See also* Common Article 2, Geneva Conventions I – IV, and Article 1(4) Additional Protocol I.

83 *See* 'How is the Term 'Armed Conflict' Defined in International Humanitarian Law'. *See also* Common Article 3, Geneva Conventions I – IV and Article 1(1) Additional Protocol II. Additional Protocol II, which 'develops and supplements' Common Article 3 'without modifying its existing conditions of application' presents a more restrictive definition of non-international armed conflict.

84 The International Criminal Tribunal for the Former Yugoslavia has used the criteria of 'protracted armed violence' among 'organized armed groups' to determine the existence of a non-international armed conflict. *The Prosecutor* v. *Dusko Tadic* aka Dule, (*Decision on the Defence Motion on Jurisdiction*) [1995] IT-94-1, International Criminal Tribunal for the Former Yugoslavia, para. 70.

5.3 Type of Armed Conflict

More generally, the relevant paradigm – international armed conflict or non-international armed conflict – determines the applicable law. In terms of the rules regulating the conduct of hostilities, the qualification may not make an important difference in practice, as many of the treaty rules applicable in international armed conflict also apply in non-international armed conflict as a matter of customary law. However, the applicable paradigm may have important implications for the status and treatment of people deprived of their freedom and for the relevance of the framework of the law of occupation.[85] There is generally agreement that when a force deployed by the UN or another IO takes action against the armed forces of a State, the law of international armed conflict applies.[86] However, this issue remains unsettled when such a force takes action against an organised armed group.

One view maintains that the law of international armed conflict should govern such situations.[87] It emphasises that UN operations are international in nature; they are set up and carried out by a subject of international law whose actions are exclusively governed by international law and are comprised of personnel from different countries. Applying the law of international armed conflict would avoid the situation where the UN force would be required to provide different standards of treatment to different adversaries.[88] Moreover, applying the higher standards of the law of international armed conflict would be consistent with the UN's commitment to international law and social principles.[89] Similar arguments could be made regarding the forces of other regional organisations.

Another view asserts that the rules of non-international armed conflict should apply to the relationship between the international force and an organised armed group, stressing the necessity of looking into each bilateral belligerent relationship to determine applicable law.[90] It advocates applying the same criteria traditionally used for qualifying a foreign intervention by a State. In practice, applying the law of non-international armed conflict would hold the UN force and the government to the same rules – avoiding the situation where the same individual would benefit

85 *Kolb* (n 71) 61.

86 *Faite and Labbé Grenier* (n 59) 11.

87 *See David* (n 35) 146. This has traditionally been the majority position.

88 *Kolb* (n 71) 57 – 58.

89 *Faite and Labbé Grenier* (n 59) 63.

90 Ibid. 63 – 64. This is the approach currently taken by the ICRC. Hence, the ICRC has qualified the conflict in Afghanistan after June 2002 as non-international – albeit with an international component in the form of a foreign military presence on one side. Consequently, the law of non-international armed conflict governs the hostilities between NATO and coalition forces and different armed groups in the ICRC's view. *See* 'International Humanitarian Law and the Challenges of Contemporary Armed Conflict' Document prepared for the 30th International Conference of the Red Cross and Red Crescent (October 2007) 7.

from different standards of treatment at the hands of the UN force and at the hands of the government.[91]

Practice is inconclusive on this issue. Although the 1994 Convention on the Safety of the United Nations and Associated Personnel provides that 'the law of international armed conflict' would apply to 'a United Nations operation authorized by the Security Council as an enforcement action under Chapter VII', the precise meaning and scope of this provision is unclear.[92] The Secretary-General's 1999 Bulletin generally draws upon the law of international armed conflict in identifying the rules applicable to UN forces, but it does not purport to qualify situations in which the UN is involved as international armed conflict.[93] Over the years, the UN itself has qualified its involvement differently in different contexts. In the Congo in the 1960s, for example, it seemingly considered itself to be bound by the law of international armed conflict. By contrast, in Somalia in the 1990s, it did not acknowledge being a party to an international armed conflict; the law of non-international armed conflict applied.[94]

5.4 Temporal and Geographical Scope of the Armed Conflict

There is a risk that the rules regarding the temporal and geographical scope of application of IHL could be restrictively interpreted in the context of peace operations. The UN Secretary-General's 1999 Bulletin on the Observance of International Humanitarian Law by United Nations Forces could in fact lend support to arguments attempting to limit the applicability of IHL to the specific time and place of hostilities involving UN forces. It provides that the rules of IHL 'are applicable to United Nations forces when in situations of armed conflict they are actively engaged as combatants, to the extent and for the duration of their engagement.'[95] This wording could suggest that armed conflicts involving UN personnel can be intermittent, with UN forces engaged as combatants one moment and as non-combatants the next.[96] Yet such an interpretation would be inconsistent with the rules of IHL as developed in treaty law and confirmed in international jurisprudence.[97]

---

91 *Kolb, Porretto and Vité* (n 33) 184 – 185.

92 Article 2(2) Convention on the Safety of United Nations and Associated Personnel.

93 *Faite and Labbé Grenier* (n 59) 11.

94 *Greenwood* (n 33) 26; *see also Faite and Labbé Grenier* (n 59) 65 – 66 and *Kolb, Porretto and Vité* (n 33) 187 – 188.

95 *ST/SGB/1999/13* (n 51) section 1.1.

96 *Zwanenburg* (n 10) 190.

97 The limiting language 'to the extent and for the duration of their engagement' is similar to the standard circumscribing a civilian's loss of protection against attack for directly participating in hostilities. IHL provides that civilians are protected against attack unless and for such time as they take a direct part in hostilities. Jean-Marie Henckaerts and Louise Doswald-Beck, *Customary International Humanitarian Law Rules* (Vol. 1, Cambridge University Press, Cambridge, 2005) 19. *See also*, Article 51(3) Additional Protocol I and Article 13(3) Additional Protocol *II*. Yet when UN forces are engaged in armed conflict, it would be inappropriate to assimilate them to civilians. In such situa-

IHL generally applies for the duration of an armed conflict. It begins to apply as soon as armed conflict arises.[98] The end of its application is more difficult to pinpoint. Today's conflicts rarely end in a decisive victory for one side and the re-establishment of a genuine peace; often they result in fragile cease-fires, continue at a lower intensity or are frozen by an outside intervention. In addition, the IHL treaties use rather vague terms to define the end of application of IHL.[99] For international armed conflicts, the Geneva Conventions and Additional Protocol I fix the end of their application at 'the general close of military operations.'[100] For situations of occupation, Geneva Convention IV generally defines its end of application as 'one year after the general close of military operations' while Additional Protocol I extends the applicability of IHL until 'the termination of the occupation'.[101] For non-international armed conflicts covered by Additional Protocol II, IHL applies until 'the end of armed conflict'.[102] The application of IHL may extend beyond such timeframes for persons deprived of their liberty, however, as the law continues to apply until they are released and, where relevant, repatriated and re-established.[103] Regarding the temporal scope of application of IHL, the International Criminal Tribunal for the Former Yugoslavia (ICTY) has determined that it extends beyond the actual hostilities.[104]

Moreover, the application of IHL is not restricted to the vicinity of the actual hostilities. Although the 1949 Geneva Conventions and their Additional Protocols of 1977 make no explicit reference to their geographical scope of application, multiple provisions suggest that they apply to the entire territory of the parties to the conflict.[105] In addressing this issue, the ICTY has determined that 'international

---

tions, they are conducting hostilities on behalf of a party to an armed conflict as members of its armed forces.

98 *E.g.* Article 6(1) Geneva Convention IV (providing that the Convention applies 'from the outset of any conflict or occupation') and Article 3(b) Additional Protocol I (providing that the Geneva Conventions and Additional Protocol I apply 'from the beginning of any situation referred to in Article 1').

99 Marco Sassòli and Antoine A. Bouvier, *How Does Law Protect in War?* (Vol. 1, ICRC, Geneva, 2006) 116.

100 Article 6(2) Geneva Convention IV and Article 3(b) Additional Protocol I.

101 Article 6(3) Geneva Convention IV and Article 3(b) Additional Protocol I.

102 Article 2(2) Additional Protocol II.

103 Article 5 Geneva Convention III, Article 6(4) Geneva Convention IV, Article 3(b) Additional Protocol I. and Article 2(2) Additional Protocol II.

104 *Tadic* (n 84) para. 69. The Court noted that '[i]nternational humanitarian law applies from the initiation of such armed conflicts and extends beyond the cessation of hostilities until a general conclusion of peace is reached; or, in the case of internal conflicts, a peaceful settlement is achieved.' Ibid. para. 70.

105 For example, in the context of international armed conflict, Article 6(2) of Geneva Convention IV and Article 3(b) of Additional Protocol I refer to 'the territory of Parties to the conflict' when articulating when their application ends. In the context of non-international armed conflict, Common Article 3 to Geneva Conventions I – IV extends protection to '[p]ersons taking no active part in the hostilities' while Article

humanitarian law continues to apply in the whole territory of the warring States or, in the case of internal conflicts, the whole territory under the control of a party, whether or not actual combat takes place there.'[106] Thus, for IHL to apply to a particular act, there must be a connection between it and the armed conflict, regardless of where on the territory of a party to the conflict it occurs.

5.5 Relevance of the Law of Occupation

A number of challenges have emerged in relation to the applicability of the law of occupation to peace operations, particularly those that involve the international administration of a territory.[107] In contexts such as Timor Leste and Kosovo, the UN has assumed far-ranging governance and institution-building functions.[108] In the case of Timor Leste, the UN was tasked with typical peacekeeping functions as well, taking over related responsibilities from an Australian-led multinational force. In Kosovo, by contrast, NATO has assumed a range of parallel military functions. There are conflicting opinions as to whether the law of occupation provides a relevant legal framework in such situations. Arguments underscoring the law's pertinence point to the factual similarities between classic situations of military occupation and certain operations fielded by the UN and other IOs. They assert that the material conditions for the law's applicability could be fulfilled in certain circumstances in line with strict *jus in bello* criteria. Counter-arguments claim that the conditions for applying the law of occupation are not fulfilled and bring in *jus ad bellum* considerations to stress the difficulty of assimilating the UN to an occupying force in light of the mission's legitimacy, mandate and mode of functioning.[109] As with the applicability of IHL generally, the applicability of the law of occupation is a question of fact. It is therefore necessary to analyse the situation on the ground in each concrete instance in order to determine the applicability of IHL, *de jure* or *de facto*.

Conceived as a temporary legal framework designed to preserve the *status quo ante*, the law of occupation comes into effect whenever a territory falls under enemy control. The 1907 Hague Regulations provide:

2(1) of Additional Protocol II provides that the Protocol shall be applied 'to all persons affected by an armed conflict as defined in Article 1' without geographical limitations.

106 *Tadic* (n 84) para. 70. This approach has been followed in subsequent decisions of the ICTY and the International Criminal Tribunal for Rwanda. *E.g. The Prosecutor* v. *Jean-Paul Akayesu (Judgment)* [1998] ICTR-96-4-T, International Criminal Tribunal for Rwanda paras 635 – 636.

107 In 2007, the ICRC initiated a study on occupation and other forms of administration of foreign territory. This study, aimed at clarifying related legal issues, will also cover the challenges raised by the applicability of occupation law to peace forces and to the UN administration of foreign territory. *Kellenberger* (n 60).

108 In Kosovo, OSCE and EU activities are subsumed within the UNMIK framework.

109 *See* Sylvain Vité, 'L'applicabilité du droit international de l'occupation militaire aux activités des organisations internationales' (2004) 86 *International Review of the Red Cross*, No. 853, 19 – 20. Such arguments mirror the arguments made more generally for denying the *ratione materiae* applicability of IHL to peace operations.

> Territory is considered occupied when it is actually placed under the authority of the hostile army. The occupation extends only to the territory where such authority has been established and can be exercised.[110]

The occupying power is prohibited from bringing about changes in the territory's institutions or government that would render the law of occupation inapplicable.[111] Moreover, during the period of occupation, the occupying power must ensure the continuity of the legal system; penal laws remain in force unless they threaten the occupying power's security or the application of IHL, with local courts continuing to function. More generally, the occupying power can only make 'essential' changes to the law in order to fulfil its IHL obligations, guarantee the territory's administration, and to ensure its security.[112] Such situations constitute international armed conflicts.

The *de jure* applicability of the law of occupation to operations conducted by the UN and other IOs revolves around the issue of the consent of the host State. Consensual operations, whether established under Chapter VI or Chapter VII of the UN Charter, do not square with the identification of the occupying power as the 'hostile army'. Accordingly, the law of occupation is not applicable to situations in which an international force exercises effective control over a territory with the consent of the government of that territory.[113] Conversely, the law of occupation may be a relevant legal framework in situations where the host State has not given its consent the operation, or its consent was coerced.[114] In both Timor Leste and Kosovo, different issues arose with regard to the consent given.[115]

110 Article 42 Hague Regulations Respecting the Laws and Customs of War on Land (18 October 1907). Article 2(2) of Geneva Convention IV specifies that the Convention applies to all situations of occupation, 'even if the said occupation meets with no armed resistance.'

111 Article 47 Geneva Convention IV.

112 Article 64 Geneva Convention IV. Article 43 of the 1907 Hague Regulations provide that the occupying power is tasked with restoring public order and safety and is obliged to respect the laws in force 'unless absolutely prevented.' *See Vité* (n 109) 16 – 18 for a discussion of the scope of this provision and Article 64 of Geneva Convention IV. *See also* Adam Roberts, 'Transformative Military Occupation: Applying the Laws of War and Human Rights' (2006) 100 *American Journal of International Law,* No. 3, 587 – 588.

113 Of course, it may become necessary to re-evaluate the host government's consent as the situation on the ground evolves. A government could always revoke its consent to the UN operation, for example. *See further* Tristan Ferraro, 'The Applicability of the Law of Occupation to Peace Forces' in Gian Luca Beruto (ed), *International Humanitarian Law, Human Rights and Peace Operations: Proceedings of the 31st Round Table on Current Issues of International Humanitarian Law* (Institute of Humanitarian Law, Sanremo, 2009) 123 – 128.

114 A lack of consent in a context with no effective government can be assimilated to a refusal of consent.

115 Indonesia's consent to the international presence in Timor Leste has been challenged on the grounds that as an occupying power, it did not have the authority to consent. Under the circumstances, the question of whether the Timorese people consented to the deployment of the international force was never asked. *See* Bertrand Levrat, 'Le

Beyond the issue of consent, it is difficult to reconcile certain provisions of the law of occupation with the particular nature of international territorial administrations. In reality, such situations aim to overcome the *status quo*, not to maintain it.[116] Accordingly, in both Timor Leste and Kosovo, the UN operations surpassed the strict framework of the law of occupation through the transformative authority they exercised.[117] The related implications – some of which blur the distinction between *jus in* bello and *jus ad* bellum – are unclear. One possibility would be to consider that such regimes run counter to the law of occupation and should be forbidden. To the extent that the UN Security Council can supersede the application of the law of occupation under Article 103 of the UN Charter and transform the institutional and legal status of a particular territory, however, this does not seem like a viable option.[118] Under such circumstances, it might be possible to conceive of the legal regime applicable to transitional administrations as an adaptation of the law of occupation. This would leave open the possibility that the law of occupation is initially applicable in such situations, but that it is replaced by a transitional administration regime, based on a Security Council resolution.[119]

The UN has not acknowledged the *de jure* applicability of the law of occupation to peace operations under its command and control. In practice, it has never

---

droit international humanitaire au Timor oriental: entre théorie et pratique' (2001) *International Review of the Red Cross*, No. 841, 97. Concerning Kosovo, although the Federal Republic of Yugoslavia and Serbia signed an agreement consenting to KFOR's presence in the midst of the NATO air strikes, this was a mere formality. Article 52 of the Vienna Convention on the Law of Treaties, which provides that 'a treaty is void if its conclusion has been procured by the threat or use of force in violation of the principles of international law embodied in the Charter of the United Nations', is potentially relevant in this context. *See* John Cerone, 'Minding the Gap: Outlining KFOR Accountability in Post-Conflict Kosovo' (2001) 12 *European Journal of International Law*, No. 3, 484.

116 Steven R. Ratner, 'Foreign Occupation and International Territorial Administration: The Challenges of Convergence' (2005) 16 *European Journal of International Law*, No. 4, 700.

117 'Exercis[ing] all legislative and executive authority, including the administration of justice' figured among the responsibilities accorded to UNTAET in the case of Timor Leste. *UNSC Res. 1272* (25 October 1999). In the case of Kosovo, the UN Security Council tasked UNMIK with '[o]rganizing and overseeing the development of provisional institutions for democratic and autonomous self-government pending a political settlement, including the holding of elections.' *UNSC Res. 1244* (10 June 1999).

118 *See Vité* (n 109) 25 – 27. *See also Faite and Labbé Grenier* (n 59) 15. At the same time, however, it is questionable whether the UN Security Council could institute a regime that adopts a lower standard of protection than that provided in the rules of IHL. *Faite and Labbé Grenier* (n 59) 76.

119 *Vité* (n 109) 27 – 29. Christopher Greenwood notes: 'It is perfectly possible that the United Nations itself...could occupy part or all of the territory of an adversary in the course of an international armed conflict. In such a case, the law of belligerent occupation would apply but only unless and until the Security Council used its Chapter VII powers to impose a different regime as part of the measures which it considered necessary for the restoration of peace and security.' *Greenwood* (n 33) 28.

applied the IHL rules *de jure*, even in situations where the criteria for its applicability were arguably met.[120] In addition, the UN Secretary-General's 1999 Bulletin on the Observance of International Humanitarian Law by United Nations Forces does not refer to the law of occupation, suggesting that it may not consider it to be a relevant legal framework for peace operations.[121] Moreover, Security Council resolutions authorising the deployment of UN forces do not refer to the law of occupation.[122]

Barring the *de jure* applicability of the law of occupation to peace operations conducted by the UN and other IOs, it is necessary to consider the law's *de facto* application. At the outset of a complex peace operation, troops may find themselves in a situation akin to occupation, carrying out duties typical of an occupying power. In such situations the law of occupation could be applicable by analogy, providing a relevant and familiar yardstick.[123] Similarly, for international missions involving the administration of a territory, relevant IHL rules could offer a normative framework for the maintenance of public order.[124] Thus, for example, the law of occupation rules related to the treatment of detainees, interactions with local authorities and the treatment of property could provide useful guidance.[125]

6. Content of the IHL Obligations of the UN and Other International Organisations

In the final analysis, issues related to the applicability of the rules of IHL *ratione personae* and *ratione materiae* to peace operations circumscribe its content. The UN and other IOs are unquestionably bound by the customary rules of IHL provided the conditions for its applicability are met.[126] Yet such organisations do not have the capacity to implement those IHL rules that imply the existence of a State structure (i.e. provisions presupposing territorial control or the existence of judi-

120 Michael J. Kelly, *Restoring and Maintaining Order in Complex Peace Operations*, (Kluwer, The Hague, 1999) 178.

121 Sylvain Vité notes that a number of rules contained in the Bulletin would nevertheless be relevant in situations of occupation *Vité* (n 109) 22.

122 Ferraro (n 113) 132.

123 *Faite and Labbé Grenier* (n 59) 77.

124 *Vité* (n 109) 29. Marco Sassòli asserts that the UN has an interest in referring to the *de* facto applicability of law of occupation because it is a recognised and consistent legal framework that is applicable independent of *jus ad bellum* justifications for an intervention and provides practical solutions to the problems that UN and other international forces face on the ground. He also notes that denying the applicability of IHL to UN forces would create a negative 'spillover effect' regarding its relevance for operations carried out by other international organisations. *Faite and Labbé Grenier* (n 59) 24.

125 Marten Zwanenburg, 'Pieces of the Puzzle: Peace Operations, Occupation and the Use of Force' (2006) 45 *Revue de droit militaire et de droit de la guerre* 244. Zwanenburg notes that the law of occupation provides less clear guidelines on the use of force, due to its general nature.

126 In addition States party to the Geneva Conventions and Additional Protocol I are obliged to 'respect and ensure respect for' the law in all circumstances.

cial mechanisms).[127] This reality affects the content of applicable rules as well as the modalities of the law's application.[128] Beyond these issues, the qualification of a particular situation – as international armed conflict or non-international armed conflict – may affect the content of applicable law. As noted previously, this distinction is minimized to the extent that many rules of customary IHL are applicable in both international and non-international armed conflicts.[129] However, it may nevertheless have implications with regard to the status and treatment of persons deprived of their liberty and the relevance of the law of occupation, in particular. It is beyond the scope of this chapter to identify and analyse all of the rules of IHL applicable to UN and other IOs undertaking peace operations; this section will merely highlight some of their core protection and conduct of hostilities obligations.

The UN Secretary-General's Bulletin purports to set out the 'fundamental principles and rules' applicable to forces under UN command and control. It identifies five categories of 'principles and rules': [1] protection of the civilian population; [2] means and methods of combat; [3] treatment of civilians and persons *hors de combat*; [4] treatment of detained persons; and [5] protection of wounded, sick and medical and relief personnel.[130] Some of the Bulletin's content reflects customary rules of IHL. Regarding the protection of persons not or no longer taking a direct part in hostilities, it essentially restates the general protection standards provided in IHL. In terms of the conduct of hostilities, it includes virtually all of the core rules of customary law applicable in both international and non-international armed conflict.

However, the Bulletin's accuracy as a pure restatement of the law is questionable. Because it draws largely from the law applicable in international armed conflicts, the standards it sets do not mirror the rules applicable in non-international armed conflicts in some instances. This is most striking with regard to the content of the rules on treatment of detained persons; the Bulletin provides that detainees 'shall be treated in accordance with the relevant provisions of the Third Geneva Convention of 1949, as may be applicable to them *mutatis mutandis*.'[131] Beyond the international armed conflict – non-international armed conflict variance, the content of the 'prin-

127 *See Ferraro* (n 113) 132. It is important to note that the UN and other international organisations can apply most IHL rules without difficulty. Moreover, even those that cannot be strictly applied may be modified and applied by analogy. Thus, for example, the UN could transfer certain obligations to troop-contributing countries, *Kolb* (n 71) 65 – 66; *Greenwood* (n 33) 15 – 16.

128 *Kolb* (n 71) 65; *Greenwood* (n 33) 15. Robert Kolb argues that those IHL rules linked to humanitarian protections in armed conflict should be applicable with minimal modifications. *Kolb* (n 71) 68.

129 Of the 161 IHL rules identified in the ICRC's study on customary IHL, 142 are applicable in both international and non-internal armed conflicts. *See* Jean-Marie Henckaerts 'Study on Customary International Humanitarian Law: A Contribution to the Understanding and Respect for the Rule of Law in Armed Conflict' (2005) 87 *International Review of the Red Cross*, No. 857, 198 – 212.

130 *ST/SGB/1999/13* (n 51) sections 5 – 9.

131 Ibid. section 8. It is significant that the text refers to Geneva Convention III as opposed to Geneva Convention IV. *Ryniker* (n 50) 802.

ciples and rules' identified goes beyond norms of customary IHL in places.[132] In addition, certain criticisms have been raised as to the content of the rules identified. For example, Section 5 provides that 'military installations and equipment of peacekeeping operations, as such, shall not be considered as military objectives'.[133] However, to the extent that a UN force takes part in an armed conflict, its installations do in fact become military objectives.[134] Moreover, as mentioned previously, the Bulletin does not refer to the law of occupation, although it may be a relevant legal framework for peace operations. It is thus necessary to look beyond the Secretary-General's Bulletin to ascertain the rules of IHL applicable to peace operations.

7. Conclusions

International humanitarian law is potentially applicable to peace operations conducted by the UN and other IOs. The law's *ratione personae* applicability to the UN and regional organisations with a peace and security remit is no longer seriously challenged. Violations of the law can be attributed to them to the extent that they exercise effective control over the conduct in question. Moreover, when peace operations are involved in armed conflict, IHL becomes applicable to them *ratione materiae*. In such situations, troops are obliged to respect the customary rules of IHL, as adapted to fit the peace operation mould. At the end of the day, *jus ad bellum* arguments related to an operation's mandate and legitimacy are not relevant for assessing whether the rules of IHL are applicable. The fact that there are a number of unresolved issues related to the how the law should be applied in such circumstances should not prevent its application. This said, there is a need to develop a coherent framework going beyond the rules of IHL for addressing the range of challenges posed by today's complex and multifaceted operations. IHL should not be considered and applied in a vacuum.

132 *See Shraga* (n 45) 409. *See generally Henckaerts and Doswald-Beck* (n 97).

133 *ST/SGB/1999/13* (n 51) section 5.

134 *Ryniker* (n 50) 801; *see also Benvenuti* (n 53) 363 – 364.

Chapter 4

A Single Standard for Coalitions: Lowest Common Denominator or Highest Standard?

*Susan C. Breau**

1. Introduction

The legal issue for consideration in this chapter is the applicable International Humanitarian Law (IHL) for coalition actions. These are actions conducted not under the auspices of the United Nations (UN) Security Council (discussed in the chapter by Katie Sams) but rather those actions justified by other legal grounds such as the intervention by NATO in the Federal Republic of Yugoslavia concerning Kosovo (Operation Allied Force) and the coalition actions in Afghanistan in 2001 (Operation Enduring Freedom) and Iraq in 2003 (Operation Iraqi Freedom). Although in the second two there are certainly partial and disputed elements of Security Council authorisation, for the purpose of this analysis the focus will be on wars fought by alliances/coalitions of States, which is a long-standing historical tradition.[1] These three armed conflicts are excellent case studies on the applicability of treaty and customary IHL to various members of a coalition. The general question to be considered in this chapter is to determine which rules of IHL do different members of coalitions follow when they may be bound by different treaty obligations – is there a common standard? As Stein argues:

> Today's coalitions 'inter-operate' so closely that it may be difficult, if not impossible, for adversaries and outsiders, such as the International Committee of the Red Cross (ICRC) that seek to monitor the observance of obligations under international humanitarian law, to identify who did what and to whom.[2]

* My gratitude to Mr. Rory Grant, student at the School of Law at the University of Surrey, for his brilliant research assistance on this chapter.

1 *See* Nicholas Rostow, 'Introduction to a special section on Coalition Operations' (2003) 78 *Int'l L. Stud. Ser. US Naval War Col.* 313.

2 T. Stein, 'Coalition Warfare and Differing Legal Obligations' (2003) 78 *Int'l L. Stud. Ser. US Naval War Col.* 315.

M. Odello and R. Piotrowicz (eds.), International Military Missions and International Law.
2011 Koninklijke Brill NV. Printed in The Netherlands. ISBN *978 9004 17437 5. pp. 73–97.*

A major issue in coalition actions is the variation in ratifications of Additional Protocol I (AP I) of 1977 to the Geneva Conventions of 1949.[3] This is the case in any coalition action involving the United States which has not adopted this treaty – the three case studies in this chapter all involved the United States. This chapter also considers whether as a result of the release by the International Committee of the Red Cross (hereafter ICRC) of the Customary IHL Study,[4] it can be confirmed that many of the provisions of AP I are arguably confirmed as part of the corpus of IHL. This author was fortunate to be part of a project that studied the methodology of the ICRC Study and a collection published of a scholarly examination of most the rules confirmed the customary status of many of the rules contained in the Study.[5] Yet a careful examination of these rules confirm that even if they are established to be binding on all members of a coalition, they do not resolve some of the controversies over targeting that have existed in all three operations.

But the final question to be reviewed throughout this chapter, and a focus of academic debate, is: if indeed the rules, treaty provisions or the interpretation of those provisions do differ, what is the law applicable to the coalition - the lowest common denominator or the highest standard? This requires specific reference to the three operations undertaken by coalitions in the recent past to determine how the rules of IHL were applied and reference to the academic debate on this issue. This topic alone could form the subject of a major study on these three major and recent armed conflicts and this chapter can only begin this discussion.

This chapter will firstly set out the major rules of armed conflict that are applicable. Secondly, it will review the impact of the customary international law study and determine if there are rules that remain uncertain. Thirdly, it will review the specific three operations in Kosovo, Afghanistan and Iraq and the academic commentary on those operations, to determine whether coalitions are bound by the lowest common denominator or the highest standards in IHL.

2. The Rules of Armed Conflict Applicable in Coalition Operations

On 21 August 2008, the ICRC announced universal acceptance of the Geneva Conventions of 1949 with the accessions received from the Republic of Nauru and the Republic of Montenegro.[6] The four Conventions on the wounded and sick armed forces on land and at sea, on prisoners of war, and on civilians who find themselves in a situation of armed conflict, constitute perhaps the most important body of IHL.

3 1977 Protocol Additional to the Geneva Conventions of 12 August 1949, and Relating to the Protection of Victims of International Armed Conflicts (1977 Additional Protocol I) (Geneva, 8 June 1977, in force 7 December 1978), 1125 UNTS 3.

4 J. M. Henckaerts and L. Doswald-Beck, *Customary International Humanitarian Law* (2 volumes) (ICRC and CUP, Cambridge, 2005).

5 E. Wilmshurst and S. Breau (eds), *Perspectives on the ICRC Study on Customary International Humanitarian Law* (CUP, Cambridge, 2007).

6 News release found at <www.icrc.org/Web/Eng/siteengo.nsf/htmlall/geneva-conventions-news-210806> (accessed 4 July 2009).

The difficulty with these Conventions is that in some respects there are major omissions, not thought critical at the end of the Second World War. These omissions were those involved particularly with the law of targeting. The cardinal principles of humanitarian law, the rules of necessity, distinction and proportionality, were not codified in treaty law until almost 30 years later in AP I of 1977, drafted in the wake of targeting controversies in the Vietnam War.[7]

The 1977 AP I states in its title an important limitation; that it is 'Relating to the Protection of Victims of International Armed Conflicts', and thus limits its applicability to international armed conflicts. However, when a coalition embarks on a military operation, it invariably results in an international armed conflict – although the continuing operations in Iraq and Afghanistan, after the initial invasion, and after the installation of new governments, are said to be non-international armed conflicts, but one could take issue with this characterisation.[8] This treaty sets out the key targeting principles which govern how the signatories to the treaty can conduct their military operations. The key principle of distinction requires a belligerent to distinguish between civilian and military objectives and between civilians and combatants. Article 48 of AP I codifies the basic rule of distinction:

> In order to ensure respect for and protection of the civilian population and civilian objects, the Parties to the conflict shall at all times distinguish between the civilian population and combatants and between civilian objects and military objectives and accordingly shall direct their operations only against military objectives.

The concept of total war has been abolished by this provision. Article 51 (2) of AP I prohibits 'acts or threats of violence the primary purpose of which is to spread terror among the civilian population'. In paragraphs 4 and 5 of the same article, area bombardment is outlawed, which was defined as 'an attack by bombardment by any methods or means which treats as a single military objective a number of clearly separated and distinct military objectives in a city, town, (or) village'.

The second and third critical concepts are the rules of necessity and proportionality, which are intertwined in the treaty provisions. It means that in warfare, 'a belligerent may apply only that amount and kind of force necessary to defeat the enemy'.[9] The rule implies that the enemy should be defeated with a minimum loss of life or property. The use of any kind of force not required for the defeat of the enemy is prohibited. An important limitation is that even if a target is a military objective, it should be avoided if it might cause excessive civilian casualties. Article 52 (2) of AP I defines a military objective, and there were two important elements: the object must make 'an effective contribution to military action', and its elimination must offer a

7 *1977 Additional Protocol I* (n 3).

8 Space in this chapter does not permit this analysis which is not essential as many of the subsequent customary rules discussed apply in non-international armed conflict.

9 C. Greenwood, 'Historical Development and Legal Basis' in D. Fleck (ed), *The Handbook of Humanitarian Law in Armed Conflict* (OUP, Oxford, 1995) 30.

'definite military advantage'.[10] Attacks on individual civilians and on the civilian population are prohibited, but not attacks on military objectives that might have civilians in them or close by. Civilians who are killed are categorised as 'collateral damage'. This is defined in the *US Naval Handbook* under military necessity, stating that:

> While the principle does recognize that some amount of collateral damage and incidental injury to civilians and civilian objects may occur in an attack upon a legitimate military objective, it does not excuse the wanton destruction of life and property disproportionate to the military advantage to be gained from the attack. [11]

Article 55 specifies that targets indispensable to the survival of the civilian population are not to be attacked, such as agricultural areas, drinking water installations and irrigation works.

One of the most important aspects of targeting is the choice of a military objective. This is made using a two-pronged test. The first prong in Article 52 (2) lists four conditions: nature, location, purpose and use. If the nature, location, purpose and use of the objective make a contribution to the military action, then the target is a military objective. The second prong, set out in Article 52 (2), is whether the total or partial destruction, capture or neutralisation of the object in the circumstances ruling at the time offers a definite military advantage.[12] This section combines both an objective and subjective element. It is an objective decision as to whether the target contributes effectively to military operations and it is a subjective decision as to whether destroying the target constitutes a military advantage to the attacking state.[13] This is an extremely difficult and complex process for the military lawyer coupled with the duty to assess the weapons systems and the delivery systems used in attacking the target.

The selection of military objectives involves the other key principle of proportionality set out in Articles 51(5) (b) and 57(2) (b) of AP I, which prohibits military acts where civilian casualties outweigh the military gain. A balance has to be struck between the importance of the military objective and the 'collateral damage', the civilian casualties that might result. There might be large numbers of civilians working in the military objective (there are always large numbers of civilians working on military bases) or civilians could be used as shields (as in the Gulf War and on the bridges during Kosovo). It has been argued that a munitions factory would be such an important military objective that even though there might be a large number of

---

10 F. Kalshoven, *Constraints on the Waging of War* (ICRC, Martinus Nijhoff Publishers, Dordrecht, 1987) 89.

11 U.S. Navy, U.S. Marine Corps, U.S. Coast Guard, *The Commander's Handbook on the Law of Naval Operation* (Department of the Navy, 2007) para. 6.2.6.4.2 'Military Necessity'.

12 H.B. Robertson, 'The Principle of the Military Objective in the Law of Armed Conflict' in M. Schmitt (ed), *International Law Studies Volume 72* (Naval War College, Newport, R.I, 1998) 208-211.

13 S. Oeter, 'Methods and Means of Combat' in D. Fleck (ed), *The Handbook of Humanitarian Law* (n 9) 156-158.

civilian casualties caused by the blowing up of the factory it is still in compliance with IHL.[14] The ICRC commentary on AP I disagreed, stating:

> The idea has also been put forward that even if they are very high, civilian losses and damages may be justified if the military advantage at stake is of great importance. This idea is contrary to the fundamental rules of the Protocol...The Protocol does not provide any justification for attacks which cause extensive civilian losses and damages. Incidental losses and damages should never be extensive.[15]

As none of these detailed considerations are contained in the four Geneva Conventions, the issue of the applicability of these provisions to coalition operations is critical. It seems clear that AP I is a higher standard due to the specificity and codification of primary rules of targeting and respect for the rights of civilians.

Furthermore, there are a number of other conventions that deal with IHL that are not universally ratified. In his assessment of the Kosovo operation, Stein argues that Protocol I may not be the biggest problem.[16] There are other treaties that are not universally ratified including the 1980 UN Conventional Weapons Convention and its Protocols and the 1997 Ottawa Convention on Anti-personnel mines.[17] The new Convention on Cluster Munitions, will cause even more controversy and the United States has indicated its intention not to be bound by this Convention.[18] Therefore, in addition to potential serious disagreements over targeting, there may be differing opinions on the use of such weapons as land mines, or cluster munitions.

International law is not only composed of treaty law. An equally important element in determining the applicability of the law to coalition operations is to determine which rules of customary international law are relevant. One body of law accepted to be customary is the Hague Regulations of 1907.[19] However, there are also certain principles accepted to be customary that are similar to those set out in AP I. The *Nuclear Weapons* Advisory Opinion has confirmed the customary status of cardinal rules of humanitarian law and included in the judgment is a crucial statement:

---

14 A.P.V. Rogers, *Law on the Battlefield* (Manchester University Press, Manchester, 1996) 14-19.

15 Y. Sandoz, C. Swinarski and B. Zimmerman (eds), *Commentary on the Additional Protocols of 8 June 1977* (ICRC, Martinus Nijhoff Publishers, Geneva, 1987) para. 1980.

16 *Stein* (n 2) 316.

17 United Nations Convention on the Prohibitions or Restrictions on the Use of Certain Conventional Weapons Which May Be Deemed to be Excessively Injurious or to have Indiscriminate Effects, Geneva, 1342 UNTS 168 and Convention on the Prohibition of the Use, Stockpiling, Production and Transfer of Anti-Personnel Mines and on their Destruction 2056 UNTS 211.

18 Convention on Cluster Munitions, Adopted at Dublin 30 May 2008 – entered into force on 1 August 2010.

19 Convention (IV) Respecting the Laws and Customs of Wars on Land and its Annex: Regulations Concerning the Laws and Customs of War on Land The Hague (18 October 1907) (1910) UKTS 10.

> The cardinal principles contained in the texts constituting the fabric of humanitarian law are the following. The first is aimed at the protection of the civilian population and civilian objects and establishes the distinction between combatants and non-combatants; States must never make civilians the object of attack and must consequently never use weapons that are incapable of distinguishing between civilian and military targets. According to the second principle, it is prohibited to cause unnecessary suffering to combatants: it is accordingly prohibited to use weapons causing them such harm or uselessly aggravating their suffering. In application of that second principle, States do not have unlimited freedom of choice of means in the weapons they use...[20]

These fundamental rules are to be observed by all States whether or not they have ratified the conventions that contain them, because they constitute intransgressible principles of international customary law.

Although this is an important statement on the customary status of customary IHL, it does not confirm the customary nature of the specific rules of targeting discussed above. This was only accomplished by an important initiative of the ICRC to which we now turn.

3. The Customary International Law Study

As a result of a reduced number of treaty ratifications for Additional Protocols I and II, the 26th International Conference of the ICRC, held in 1995, gave the ICRC the mandate to conduct a survey of the customary rules of IHL applicable in both international and non-international armed conflict.[21] In 2005 the ICRC published its monumental two-volume work which reviewed the extent to which the treaty rules of IHL had the force of customary international law and proposed 161 rules of customary IHL, many of which, applicable in international and non-international armed conflict. ICRC President Jakob Kellenberger stated that the Study captured the clearest possible 'photograph' of that law.[22]

These rules are not without controversy and certainly some American experts have had problems with various rules.[23] However, a study conducted by United Kingdom and other internationally recognised IHL experts, in spite of some substantial criticism of the methodology of the *Study*, found that the majority of rules were indeed customary in both international and non-international armed conflict.[24]

---

20 *Legality of the Threat or Use of Nuclear Weapons* (Advisory Opinion), ICJ Rep. 226 [1996)] para. 78, *see also* paras. 75-82.

21 Resolutions of the 26th International Conference of the ICRC at <www.icrc.org/web/eng/siteengo.nsf/html/57JMVH> (accessed 4 July 2009).

22 *'Foreword' by Dr. Jakob Kellenberger* in *Henckaerts and Doswald-Beck* (n 4) xi.

23 J. B. Bellinger III and W. J. Haynes II, 'A US government response to the International Committee of the Red Cross study Customary International Humanitarian Law' (2007) 866 *IRRC* 443.

24 *Wilmshurst and Breau* (n 5).

Although the ICRC Study and the analysis in *Perspectives on the ICRC Study on Customary IHL* concerned most of the 161 customary rules proposed there are two areas of special importance in recent coalition operations, the law of targeting and fundamental guarantees as framed in Article 75 of AP I. It is these two areas that will be reviewed here.

Firstly, Schmitt, in his study of the rules of targeting, although expressing some reservation about methodology, confirmed that most of the rules were of customary status.[25] The rules although worded slightly differently from the AP I provisions discussed above, were substantially similar. Due to the importance of these rules to targeting issues in coalition operations they are cited in this chapter in full and included in the following is the reaction to them by Schmitt a noted expert in targeting matters, in the chapter in *Perspectives*. The Rules are:

3.1 The Principle of Distinction

3.1.1 Distinction between Civilians and Combatants:

Rule 1. The parties to the conflict must at all times distinguish between civilians and combatants. Attacks may only be directed against combatants. Attacks must not be directed against civilians [IAC/NIAC].[26]
- Confirmed as 'unquestionably' customary by Schmitt.[27]

Rule 2. Acts or threats of violence the primary purpose of which is to spread terror among the civilian population are prohibited [IAC/NIAC].
- Confirmed as generally accepted as customary by Schmitt.[28]

Rule 6. Civilians are protected against attack, unless and for such time as they take a direct part in hostilities [IAC/NIAC].
- Schmitt took issue with the definition of civilian in the commentary to the rule and with the definition of what constituted direct participation. He applauds the commentary that states that a 'clear and uniform definition of direct participation in hostilities has not been developed in state practice'.[29]

3.1.2 Distinction between Civilian Objects and Military Objectives

Rule 7. The parties to the conflict must at all times distinguish between civilian objects and military objectives. Attacks may only be directed against military objectives. Attacks must not be directed against civilian objects [IAC/NIAC].

25 M. Schmitt, 'The Law of Targeting' Chapter 6 in Ibid. 131-168.

26 The Initials IAC constitute International Armed Conflict, and the initials NIAC Non-International Armed Conflict.

27 *Schmitt* (n 25) 136.

28 Ibid. 139.

29 Ibid. 141, and *Henckaerts and Doswald-Beck* (n 4) 22.

- Schmitt agrees that this is a 'cardinal principle' of IHL as argued in the *Nuclear Weapons* Advisory Opinion.[30]

Rule 8. In so far as objects are concerned, military objectives are limited to those objects which by their nature, location, purpose or use make an effective contribution to military action and whose partial or total destruction, capture or neutralization, in the circumstances ruling at the time, offers a definite military advantage [IAC/NIAC].

- This provision is virtually identical to AP I Article 52 (2). Schmitt confirms that this formula for identifying a military objective is 'universally accepted'. However, as Schmitt reveals in his commentary, it is this rule of targeting that causes the most difficulty in coalition operations and which is highlighted in the case studies below. It is not in the language of the rule itself but the modality of interpretation. Schmitt states:

> The dominant controversy surrounding qualification as a military objective is the US notion of 'war-sustaining.' In the *Commander's Handbook*, the United States defines military objectives as 'combatants and those objects which, by their nature, location, purpose, or use, effectively contribute to the enemy's war-fighting or war-sustaining capability and whose total or partial destruction, capture, or neutralization would constitute a definite military advantage to the attacker under the circumstances at the time of the attack.' It notes that '[e]conomic targets of the enemy that indirectly but effectively support and sustain the enemy's war-fighting capability may also be attacked.'[31] Footnotes characterize this as 'a statement of customary law,' using the example of cotton export revenues funding the Confederate war effort during the US Civil War.[32] The contemporary illustration would be reliance on a single export, such as oil.[33]

Rule 9. Civilian objects are all objects that are not military objectives [IAC/NIAC].

- Not commented upon by Schmitt but self-evidently customary as it follows naturally from Rule 8.

---

30 *Legality of the Threat or Use of Nuclear Weapons* (n 20) ICJ Rep. 66 para.78; *Schmitt* (n 25) 145.

31 US Navy, Marine Corps, Coast Guard, *The Commander's Handbook on the Law of Naval Operations*, NWP 1-14M, MCWP 5-2.1, COMDTPUB P5800.7 (1995) paras. 8.1.1, reprinted in its annotated version as (1999) 73 *US Naval War College International Law Studies* (hereinafter known as *Commander's Handbook*).

32 Ibid. para. 8.1.1, fns. 10 & 11, citing General Counsel, Department of Defense, letter of 22 Sept. 1972, reprinted in (1973) 67 *AJIL* 123-24. US joint doctrine reinforces this approach by providing that '[c]ivilian objects consist of all civilian property and activities other than those used to support or sustain the adversary's warfighting capability'. Joint Chiefs of Staff, Joint Doctrine for Targeting, Joint Publication 3-60 (17 Jan. 2002) para. A-2. The term 'war sustaining' also appears in the Instructions for the US Military Commission at Guantanamo, Department of Defense, Military Commission Instruction No. 2, Crimes and Elements for Trials by Military Commission (30 Apr. 2003) para. 5D (footnote taken from *Schmitt* (n 25) 148.

33 *Schmitt* (n 25) 148.

Rule 10. Civilian objects are protected against attack, unless and for such time as they are military objectives [IAC/NIAC].

– This rule is not identical to the provision in AP I and contains an omission argued by Schmitt to be correct; the rule does not include AP I Article 52 (3) which states:

> In case of doubt whether an object which is normally dedicated to civilian purposes, such as a place of worship, a house or other dwelling or a school, is being used to make an effective contribution to military action, it shall be presumed not to be so used.

Schmitt applauds the *Study* for this omission as he would not confirm this part of the rule as customary; however, it might cause difficulty in coalition operations.[34]

3.1.3 Indiscriminate Attacks:

Rule 11. Indiscriminate attacks are prohibited [IAC/NIAC].

Rule 12. Indiscriminate attacks are those:
(a) which are not directed at a specific military objective;
(b) which employ a method or means of combat which cannot be directed at a specific military objective; or
(c) which employ a method or means of combat the effects of which cannot be limited as required by IHL; and consequently, in each such case, are of a nature to strike military objectives and civilians or civilian objects without distinction [IAC/NIAC].

– This rule again is identical to AP I Article 51 (4). Schmitt confirms that 'there is no doubt that Rules 11 and 12 reflect the customary textual expressions of that norm'.[35]

Rule 13. Attacks by bombardment by any method or means which treats as a single military objective a number of clearly separated and distinct military objectives located in a city, town, village or other area containing a similar concentration of civilians or civilian objects are prohibited [IAC/NIAC].

– This rule 'replicates' the formula provided in Article 51(5) of AP I and according to Schmitt is an 'accepted textual articulation of the customary norm'.

3.1.4 Proportionality in Attack:

Rule 14. Launching an attack which may be expected to cause incidental loss of civilian life, injury to civilians, damage to civilian objects, or a combination thereof, which would be excessive in relation to the concrete and direct military advantage anticipated, is prohibited [IAC/NIAC].

34 Ibid. 150-151.

35 Ibid. 152.

- Schmitt states that the text of Rule 14 is 'fundamental' but disagrees with some of the commentary provided with this rule. However, this rule is a customary rule statement of proportionality almost identical to AP I, Article 51 (5) and Article 57 (2).[36]

3.1.5 Precautions in Attack:

Rule 15. In the conduct of military operations, constant care must be taken to spare the civilian population, civilians and civilian objects. All feasible precautions must be taken to avoid, and in any event to minimize, incidental loss of civilian life, injury to civilians and damage to civilian objects [IAC/NIAC].

Rule 16. Each party to the conflict must do everything feasible to verify that targets are military objectives [IAC/NIAC].

Rule 17. Each party to the conflict must take all feasible precautions in the choice of means and methods of warfare with a view to avoiding, and in any event to minimizing, incidental loss of civilian life, injury to civilians and damage to civilian objects [IAC/NIAC].

Rule 18. Each party to the conflict must do everything feasible to assess whether the attack may be expected to cause incidental loss of civilian life, injury to civilians, damage to civilian objects, or a combination thereof, which would be excessive in relation to the concrete and direct military advantage anticipated [IAC/NIAC].

Rule 19. Each party to the conflict must do everything feasible to cancel or suspend an attack if it becomes apparent that the target is not a military objective or that the attack may be expected to cause incidental loss of civilian life, injury to civilians, damage to civilian objects, or a combination thereof, which would be excessive in relation to the concrete and direct military advantage anticipated [IAC/NIAC].

- Schmitt examines these rules as a group. These rules are a lot less extensive than the precautionary provisions in Article 57 (2) and Schmitt argues that they constitute a 'marked improvement over the unwieldy Article 57'. However, the rules do contain the essence of the obligation to take 'all feasible precautions' and he agrees that this formulation is customary.[37]

Rule 20. Each party to the conflict must give effective advance warning of attacks which may affect the civilian population, unless circumstances do not permit [IAC/NIAC].

- This rule derives not only from AP I, Article 57 (2) but from Article 26 of the Hague Regulations of 1907. Schmitt confirms that the ICJ in both the Advisory Opinion on the *Legal Consequences of the Construction of a Wall in the Occupied*

36 Ibid. 156-161.

37 Ibid. 162-165.

Palestinian Territory and the *Nuclear Weapons* Advisory Opinion characterised the Hague Regulations as customary.[38]

Rule 21. When a choice is possible between several military objectives for obtaining a similar military advantage, the objective to be selected must be that the attack on which may be expected to cause the least danger to civilian lives and to civilian objects [IAC/arguably NIAC].

- This is the one rule based on Article 57 (3) of AP I that Schmitt argues that, given the US objection to the provision, it would be 'difficult to imagine how the Rule could constitute customary international law unless the US position has changed'. This is based on Schmitt's assertion of the US as being the world's most dominant military power. One could take issue with this assertion in that the objection of one State, according to the *Nicaragua* decision, cannot prevent a rule of customary law rule from emerging. However, Schmitt rightly cites the *North Sea Continental Shelf* case as standing for the proposition that specially affected States might have more influence on the development of customary international law.[39]

There is further evidence from the United States standpoint on the customary nature of these rules of targeting. The latest U.S. Navy, U.S. Marine Corps, U.S. Coast Guard, *The Commander's Handbook on the Law of Naval Operations,* in its Chapter 8, 'The Law of Targeting' enumerates in a similar fashion those customary rules of targeting which are remarkably similar to AP I, except for one significant variation that reflects the United States' position. Amongst the definition of 'military objective' is the phrase 'war-fighting or war-sustaining capability',[40] which had been in its earlier 1995 Manual and highlighted by Schmitt under Rule 8. This is not part of the definition of 'military objective' in either the customary rule or AP I and as we will see in our case studies this expansion of a notion of military objective has been the major difficulty in coalition operations.

Besides these critical rules on targeting there is another very important provision in AP I that introduces an element of consideration of human rights to IHL; Article 75, Fundamental Guarantees:

> 1. In so far as they are affected by a situation referred to in Article 1 of this Protocol, persons who are in the power of a Party to the conflict and who do not benefit from more favourable treatment under the Conventions or under this Protocol shall be treated humanely in all circumstances and shall enjoy, as a minimum, the protection provided by this Article without any adverse distinc-

38 *Legal Consequences of the Construction of a Wall in the Occupied Palestinian Territory* (Advisory Opinion) [2004] ICJ Rep, para. 89; *Nuclear Weapons* (n 20) para. 79; *Schmitt* (n 25) 165-166.

39 *North Sea Continental Shelf (Federal Republic of Germany/Denmark; Federal Republic of Germany/Netherlands)* ICJ Rep 3 [1969]; *Schmitt* (n 25) 167-168.

40 U.S. Navy, U.S. Marine Corps, U.S. Coast Guard, *The Commander's Handbook on the Law of Naval Operations* (Department of the Navy 2007) *see* Chapter 8 particularly 8.2 *see also* Chapter 5.

tion based upon race, colour, sex, language, religion or belief, political or other opinion, national or social origin, wealth, birth or other status, or on any other similar criteria. Each Party shall respect the person, honour, convictions and religious practices of all such persons.

2. The following acts are and shall remain prohibited at any time and in any place whatsoever, whether committed by civilian or by military agents:
   (a) Violence to the life, health, or physical or mental well-being of persons, in particular:
      (i) Murder;
      (ii) Torture of all kinds, whether physical or mental;
      (iii) Corporal punishment ; and
      (iv) Mutilation;
   (b) Outrages upon personal dignity, in particular humiliating and degrading treatment, enforced prostitution and any form of indecent assault;
   (c) The taking of hostages;
   (d) Collective punishments; and
   (e) Threats to commit any of the foregoing acts.[41]

The rules resulting from this provision were examined by a noted humanitarian law and human rights expert Françoise Hampson, who had difficulty with the methodology employed in the Study to support the rules developed from this provision, particularly the extensive use of human rights law without setting the proper territorial applicability.[42] Unlike Schmitt, she fails to give her clear support to the customary nature of all of these rules which are set out here as follows:

Rule 87
Civilians and persons *hors de combat* must be treated humanely.

Rule 88
Adverse distinction in the application of IHL based on race, colour, sex, language, religion or belief, political or other opinion, national or social origin, wealth, birth or other status or on any other similar criteria is prohibited.

Rule 89
Murder is prohibited.

Rule 90
Torture, cruel or inhuman treatment and outrages upon personal dignity, in particular humiliating and degrading treatment, are prohibited.

Rule 91
Corporal punishment is prohibited.

---

41 *1977 Additional Protocol I* (n 3) Article 75.

42 *Hampson* in *Wilmshurst and Breau* (n 5) 282-301.

Rule 92
Mutilation, medical or scientific experiments or any other medical procedure not indicated by the state of health of the person concerned and not consistent with generally accepted medical standards are prohibited.

Rule 93
Rape and other forms of sexual violence are prohibited.

Rule 94
Slavery and the slave trade in all their forms are prohibited.

Rule 95
Uncompensated or abusive forced labour is prohibited.

Rule 96
The taking of hostages is prohibited.

Rule 97
The use of human shields is prohibited.

Rule 98
Enforced disappearance is prohibited.

Rule 99
Arbitrary deprivation of liberty is prohibited.

Rule 100
No one may be convicted or sentenced, except pursuant to a fair trial affording all essential judicial guarantees.

Rule 101
No one may be accused or convicted of a criminal offence on account of any act or omission which did not constitute a criminal offence under national or international law at the time it was committed; nor may a heavier penalty be imposed than that which was applicable at the time the criminal offence was committed.

Rule 102
No one may be convicted of an offence except on the basis of individual criminal responsibility.

Rule 103
Collective punishments are prohibited.

Rule 104
The convictions and religious practices of civilians and persons *hors de combat* must be respected.

Rule 105
Family life must be respected as far as possible.

However, if one turns to the *Study* and its commentary, this author would assert that the support of these rules as customary in almost all circumstances, whether the territory is controlled by an occupying force or not, could be ascertained due to the long-standing condemnation of these practices in the wars of the 20th century as confirmed in the case law of the International Military Tribunals for Germany and Japan.[43] The issue of enforceability of human rights norms certainly exists for those territories not controlled by an occupying force, but it has long been rules of armed conflict that even in the heat of battle civilians are to be respected and protected as far as possible.[44] These rules are particularly pertinent in the last two of the coalition operations examined here in the so-called 'Global War on Terror' and the establishment of detention centres such as Guantanamo Bay and the use of rendition to countries that might practice torture. As a result, these rules have never been so relevant.

As can be seen from this analysis, many of the fundamental rules applicable to any coalition operation bind all members of the coalition by virtue of the customary nature of the rules. One can argue that these rules are clearly not the lowest common denominator which would be to argue the applicability of The Hague Regulations of 1907 or Geneva Conventions of 1949. They are very similar to the provisions of AP I, which could be argued to be the higher standard of conduct for coalitions.

In spite of the unquestioned customary status of these rules, there have been problems in application in various armed conflicts initiated by groups of States, particularly in the definition of a military objective and, in the last two examples, in the application of fundamental guarantees.

4. Case Studies of Coalition Actions

4.1 Kosovo 1999[45]

The extensive material on the NATO air war with the Federal Republic of Yugoslavia over Kosovo enables the analyst to examine the legal issues surrounding the applicability of treaty law. All of the parties to the conflict except for the United States

---

43 *Henckaerts and Doswald-Beck* (n 4) 299-383; *see generally* International Military Tribunal (Nuremberg) Judgment and Sentences, reprinted in (1947) 41 *AJIL* 172.

44 *R (on the application of Al-Skeini) v. Secretary of State for Defence* [2007] UKHL 26, Judgment 13 June 2007 for a discussion of extra-territoriality and human rights law, the House of Lords holding that the only victim with a human rights claim was in actual British custody.

45 Most of this section on Kosovo is taken from S. Breau, *Humanitarian Intervention: The United Nations and Collective Responsibility* (Cameron May, London, 2005) Chapter 9.

and France were parties to AP I.[46] The United States conducted its campaign in concert with the other NATO powers bound by the Protocol and some of its key provisions were part of customary international law and applied to the United States as well.[47] The reality of the coalition exercise was that the United States was largely constrained in its actions by AP I.[48] However, as expected from the analysis of the customary law above, there was a fundamental philosophical difference between the United States and some of the other participants in the Kosovo conflict over the choice of targets in the context of what constituted a military objective.

The controversy in the Kosovo conflict involved two aspects of the choice of military objectives: the expansion of the definition by the US, and the targeting of 'dual-use' facilities. The United States, in the 1995 *Navy/Marine Corps/Coast Guard Manual,* defined military objectives in a manner possibly at odds with AP I. The manual indicated that those objects which contributed to the enemy's 'war-fighting or war-sustaining capability' would be military objectives.[49] This broadened the definition and led to disagreements between States as to what constituted military objectives.[50] Objects that contributed to the enemy's war fighting and war-sustaining capabilities could also be 'dual-use' objects. They could be used for both civilian and military purposes, such as factories, oil refineries, power plants and communications facilities.[51] There would naturally be many civilians present in these locations.[52] The American position was that the definition of a military objective in AP I was focused too narrowly on definite military advantage and paid too little attention to war sustaining capability, which included economic targets.[53]

This very controversial campaign resulted in various complaints and allegations that were submitted to the Prosecutor's Office of the International Criminal Tribunal for Yugoslavia, including allegations that NATO personnel and leaders may have committed crimes falling within the jurisdiction of the Tribunal during the NATO air campaign. The documents received were from a number of sources including academics, lawyers on behalf of the Federal Republic of Yugoslavia, and reports from

46 France became a party to Additional Protocol I as of 11 April 2001.

47 C. Greenwood, 'Customary International Law and the First Geneva Protocol of 1977 in the Gulf Conflict' in P. Rowe (ed), *The Gulf War 1990-1991 in International and English Law* (Routledge, New York, 1993) 63-88, as to which provisions of AP I are part of customary international law.

48 M. Schmitt, 'The Law of Armed Conflict as Soft Power' in M. Schmitt (ed), *International Law Studies Volume 75* (Naval War College, Newport, R.I. 2000) 459.

49 U.S. Navy, U.S. Marine Corps, U.S. Coast Guard, *The Commander's Handbook on the Law of Naval Operations* (Department of the Navy, 1995)

50 M. Ignatieff, *Virtual War: Kosovo and Beyond* (Chatto and Windus, London, 2000) 206.

51 J. Burger, 'International Humanitarian Law and the Kosovo Crisis: Lessons Learned or to be Learned' (2000) 837 *IRRC* 129.

52 M. Schmitt, 'Bellum Americanum: The U.S. View of Twenty-First Century War and Its Possible Implications for the Law of Armed Conflict' in M. Schmitt and L. Green (eds), *International Law Studies Volume 71* (Naval War College, Newport, R.I. 1998) 399-400 for discussion of the greater use of civilians in military facilities.

53 H. Parks, 'Air War and the Law of War' (1990) 32 *Air Force Law Review* 135-145.

human rights organisations, especially an influential Amnesty International Report.[54] The Prosecutor's committee was established on 14 May 1999 and its mandate was to advise the Prosecutor as to whether there was sufficient basis to initiate an investigation. In examining five of the controversial targets, the report recommended in each case that an investigation was not necessary and that IHL had not been violated. Nevertheless, the controversial targets below have been discussed in various articles, media reports, as well as General Wesley Clark's book on the campaign.[55] These targets revealed the difficulty in assessing military objectives based both on the lack of clarity in AP I and the American effort to expand the definition.

The first very controversial decision was the choice of the Yugoslav power grid as a target. The bombing not only disabled the air-defence radar stations but also hospitals, babies' incubators and water-pumping stations. Ignatieff alleges that British pilots took no part in this operation because of the potential violation of AP I.[56] It was the most effective strike of the war as hitting the civilians depleted the Milosevic regime's support.[57] This target illustrated the problem of distinguishing between military power supplies and civilian energy installations.[58] The fact is that both would be merged in the same power source. This issue was also present during the Gulf War, when the integrated national electricity grid was treated as a lawful target. The same legal issue was present as Article 52(2) did not specify 'dual use' targets. Greenwood argued that the question should be whether the power grid was making 'an effective contribution to military action, such that its destruction or neutralisation offered a definite military advantage'.[59] On the other hand, Ignatieff argued that the dual use targets, as were the television station, power grid and bridges, blurred the distinction between military and civilian objectives. He declared that 'there is no guarantee that war directed at the nervous system of a society will be any less savage than war directed only at its troops'.[60] The principle of proportionality would seem to dictate that if it were established that many civilian casualties resulted then they would have to be balanced against the military advantage. The actual attack in this case resulted in almost non-existent civilian casualties but surely the military commander has to assess the potential casualties involved in crippling the power system to hospitals and homes.[61] However, this is an area that has not been explored at any length and it has

54 ICTY, Office of the Prosecutor, 'Final Report to the Prosecutor by the Committee Established to Review the NATO Bombing Campaign against the Federal Republic of Yugoslavia' at <www.un.org/icty/pressreal/nato061300.htm> (accessed 4 July 2009). *See also* P. Benvenuti, 'The ICTY Prosecutor and the Review of the NATO Bombing Campaign against the Federal Republic of Yugoslavia' (2001) 12 *EJIL* 503.

55 W. Clark, *Waging Modern War* (Public Affairs Books, New York, 2001) *see* Chapter Nine 'Apaches and Targets' for General Clark's views on the targeting controversy, 221-242.

56 *Ignatieff* (n 50) 207.

57 Ibid. 108.

58 *Oeter* (n 13) 161.

59 *Greenwood* (n 47) 73.

60 *Ignatieff* (n 50) 170.

61 *Hampson* in *Rowe* (n 47) 100, the number of casualties that resulted from the power grid

to be accepted that the power supply to an army is an essential target if a military campaign is to be successful.

The second controversial target was the bombing of the Serbian Television Centre, which left fifteen civilians dead. The justification by NATO was that the TV centre was the centre of propaganda for the Milosevic regime and it was used for military relays. The British lawyers argued that the Geneva Conventions prohibited the targeting of journalists and television stations, but the Americans argued that the propaganda broadcasted by the station made it a military target.[62] In addition, the practice of 'Operation Desert Storm' during the Gulf War was to destroy the total network of telecommunications in order to paralyse the command and control structures of the Iraqis.[63] It should be noted that the ICRC's 1956 list of permissible targets included lines and means of communication, broadcasting and televisions stations, in so far as they were of fundamental military importance.[64] The Prosecutor's report concluded that if the attack was aimed at disrupting the FRY Command, Control and Communications network, it was legally acceptable. However, if the attack was aimed at securing equal time for Western broadcasts or because the station was part of the propaganda machinery then the legality of the attack was debatable.[65] The report concluded that an investigation into this incident was not warranted, as it seemed to be part of an integrated attack on command and control facilities. The statements reported by various political leaders do reveal that the target was not chosen simply as a communication target and that the propaganda factor was certainly present. Again, the media is a critical tool of modern warfare as demonstrated by Nazi propaganda and the propaganda in Rwanda, particularly by Radio Milles Collines.

The third category of controversial targets was the factories and trade and industry targets, also bombed in the NATO campaign. Military objectives are defined by AP I as 'those which by their location, nature, purpose or use make an effective contributions to military action, and whose total or partial destruction, capture or neutralisation, in the circumstances ruling at the time, offers a definite military advantage'.[66] To Rogers, a civilian object containing military personnel or items of military significance can be considered a military objective.[67] He also includes factories 'producing or developing military supplies and other supplies or military value, including metallurgical, engineering and chemical industries supporting the war effort'.[68] However, Rogers cautions that economic targets must make an effective contribution to military action and their destruction must offer a definite military

failure is not known.

62 *Ignatieff* (n 50) 149 and 194.

63 *Oeter* (n 13) 161 (note that this list was prior to AP I).

64 Ibid. 160.

65 *ICTY Final Report* (n 54) 23.

66 Article 52(7).

67 (A.P.V. Rogers, *Law on the Battlefield* (Manchester University Press, Manchester, 1996) 36.

68 Ibid. 37.

advantage so that it excludes the general industrial and agricultural potential of the enemy.[69] The issue of economic warfare is still replete with uncertainty. If the notion is that any industry fundamental to the war effort is to be a target, it means that almost all industry and trade areas are targets in a highly developed industrial society.[70] This is a serious problem in choice of targets that has not yet been resolved and continues in our other two case studies.

There was a fourth area of disagreement between the NATO powers that was not mentioned in the Prosecutor's report and that was the targeting of the bridges over the Danube. It is alleged that the French government refused to take part in strikes against Belgrade bridges and did manage to persuade the allies not to destroy them all.[71] Once again, although not a factory, clearly the bridges would be an important part of the military campaign being a vital part of the transportation network of Serbia. However, they also represented a clearly civilian link between parts of cities. They also may have had cultural significance. This was also an issue during the Gulf War, and the same test as for the power grid should have been employed. Each bridge should have been assessed on the basis of offering a distinct military advantage. This information is not available to this writer but the process should have been the same as for other 'dual-use' objects.[72]

The critics incorrectly argue that these targets were of no military value, such as non-military related factories, oil refineries, power stations, water supplies or the Serbian Television Building. However, as Lowe argues, contemporary warfare 'admits of no clear distinction between civilian and military targets'.[73] The industrial targets mentioned in the complaint to the Prosecutor could clearly be 'dual-purpose' and could be used in the manufacturing of equipment for the armed forces. However, as an investigation was not ordered, the issue of whether 'dual-use' targets and targets that sustained the conflict were military objectives has not been satisfactorily resolved.

The question then, is whether in the two subsequent operations there was a movement toward resolution of the targeting issues of 'war-fighting or war-sustaining capability' and so called 'dual-purpose' targets.

4.2 Afghanistan 2001

The war in Afghanistan, which is ongoing, has not attracted the same in depth analysis of compliance to IHL as Kosovo. Notwithstanding this fact there have been a number of substantial criticisms of the coalition action and a proposal by one commentator concerning the highest standard of conduct. In a contribution to the book *US Hegemony and the Foundations of International Law*, Daniel Thürer stated

---

69 Ibid. 41.

70 *Oeter* (n 13) 161.

71 *Ignatieff* (n 50) 207.

72 *Greenwood* (n 47) 74-75.

73 V. Lowe, 'International Legal Issues Arising in the Kosovo Crisis' in S. Yee and W. Tieya (eds), *International Law in the Post-Cold War World, Essays in Memory of Li Haopei* (Routledge, London, 2001) 286.

that obvious that the United States and Afghanistan were both bound by the four Geneva Conventions and not the two Additional Protocols but importantly asserted that '[t]he principles and rules of existing customary law are, however reflected in the Protocols and of universal binding force.'[74] The rules that are binding according in the conflict with the Taliban are:

> that the parties are to make a clear distinction between military objectives and combatants on the one hand and civilians and property on the other; that the targeting of civilians and their property is prohibited and that the parties are obliged to limit, as much as possible, collateral damage inflicted on civilians or property in their attacks on military objectives; that acts aimed at spreading terror among civilians are prohibited; and that protection should be given to persons who do not participate or no longer participate in hostilities, for instance civilians, wounded combatants and prisoners of war. This protection also includes rules that prohibit the abuse and harm of these persons.

It is evident that these are precisely the primary customary rules derived from provisions in AP I, including the fundamental guarantees in Article 75. It is this standard by which the action in Afghanistan can be assessed. As with the controversy over targeting in Kosovo, there have been substantial criticisms concerning compliance to the obligations contained above.

Dorronsoro argues that the war in Afghanistan has marked 'a new phase in practices condemned by the international community' which he enumerates as the poor treatment and in some cases torture of prisoners; the refusal to recognise the legal status of combatants; the creation of detention camps such as Guantanamo Bay; the transfer of detained to countries that practice torture; and 'the execution of military operations with little regard for the well-being of civilians'.[75] This reveals that for one partner in the coalition compliance with the customary rules of fundamental guarantees was not present.

This controversy over fundamental guarantees in Afghanistan and continued into Iraq was the issue of the so called 'unlawful combatant' and the use of so called 'conditioning techniques' amounting in some cases to torture. Garraway commented on this debate in his article "England Does Not Love Coalitions' – Does Anything Change?' He stated:

> It is interesting in reading the so-called 'Torture Memos,' to find the almost complete lack of reference to Additional Protocol I. It is as if it has been wiped out of the memory bank. It is no longer even clear whether the United States accepts such

74 D. Thürer, 'Comments on Chapters 7 and 8' in M. Byers and G. Nolte, *US Hegemony and the Foundations of International Law* (CUP, Cambridge, 2003) 281.

75 G. Dorronsoro, 'Afghanistan, The War on Terror and Humanitarian Law' in V. Lowe, A. Roberts, J. Welsh and D. Zaum (eds), *The United Nations Security Council and War* (OUP, Oxford, 2008) 464.

> key provisions as Article 75 on Fundamental Guarantees. . . . This lack of legal clarity causes acute problems for Allies seeking to work alongside the United States.[76]

There was also substantial criticism of the targeting given in a report of the Afghanistan Independent Human Rights Commission which amongst other examples cited an aerial bombardment in the Kapisa province on 4 March 2007 where international and national forces initiated air and artillery attacks against a residential compound in Jabar village. A US military spokesman argued that there were two men suspected on insurgent activities who had been firing their weapons at a nearby military base but the bombing resulted in the death of nine civilians including two pregnant women and children and the injury of five more. The report concluded based on the customary targeting principles that 'it is clear that even if the accusations against him (an alleged insurgent) were accurate he was of very limited importance and the military advantage of his possible elimination cannot justify the collateral killing of nine innocent civilians.' The report alleged that this attack was carried out with excessive force and constituted a violation of IHL.[77]

It seems clear then, that the targeting controversies continued in Afghanistan. One target that was especially controversial was an attack on Al-Jazeera. In 2001 a US missile destroyed the offices of the television outlet in Kabul. [78] The US Military denied that they had targeting this outlet but the media has reported strong suspicions of deliberate targeting.[79] In an almost unbelievable coincidence Al-Jazeera was also bombed in its Baghdad on 8 April 2003, Reporters without Borders expressed outrage at the attack that killed one of its journalists, cameraman Tarek Ayoub, and wounded another.[80] Ken Watkin discusses the Canadian perspective on the coalition operations in Afghanistan. Watkin reveals that:

> Since October 24, 2001 when Canada acted 'in the exercise of the inherent right of individual and collective self defence in accordance with Article 51' of the United Nations Charter in response to the armed attacks on the United States, Canada has

---

76 C. Garraway, '"England Does Not Love Coalitions" – Does Anything Change?' in A.M. Helm (ed), *The Law of War in the 21st Century: Weaponry and the Use of Force* (Vol. 82, US Naval War College International Law Studies, 2006) 233, 238.

77 Afghanistan Independent Human Rights Commission Report, 'Violations of International Humanitarian Law in Afghanistan: Practices of Concern and Example Cases', available at: <www.aihrc.org.af/IHL_practices_and_examples_final_Coalition_Violation.pdf> (accessed 4 July 2009).

78 M. Wells, 'How Smart was this Bomb', The Guardian (London, 19 November 2001) <www.guardian.co.uk/media/2001/nov/19/mondaymediasection.afghanistan> (accessed 5 July 2009).

79 Ibid.

80 'Reporters without borders outraged at bombing of Al-Jazeera office in Baghdad' (8 April 2003) <www.rsf.org/Reporters-Without-Borders-outraged.html> (accessed 5 July 2009).

> been a steadfast participant in conducting military operations against the threats posed by Al Qaeda and the Taliban.[81]

Watkin acknowledges that there are differences in coalition operations. He points out that Canada is a party to the 1997 Ottawa Convention on anti-personnel mines which prohibits the use, development, production, stockpiling, retention or transfer of anti-personnel mines, as well as assisting, encouraging or inducing such activities. However, he indicated that Canadian troops could participate with a state such as the United States, a non-party state, provided that Canadian troops not use anti-personnel mines and cannot request, directly or indirectly, the protection of those mines.[82]

As with the Kosovo operation, Watkin again mentions the continuing targeting controversy concerning military objective. [83] He asserts:

> ... the US interpretation of 'military objective,' to the extent that it includes an enemy's 'war sustaining capability,' is broader than that of most States, including Canada. However, it should also be noted that Canada entered a reservation to AP I that states, '[T]he military advantage anticipated from an attack is intended to refer to the advantage anticipated from the attack considered as a whole and not from isolated or particular parts of the attack.' From a Canadian perspective, targets would not be limited to military forces and could include strategic targets such as rail yards, electric power grids, oil refineries, lines of communication, bridges and supply routes. To the extent, however, that the US wording would include attacks on exports that may be the source of financial resources for a belligerent, it could very well present, as Professor Dinstein has noted, 'a slippery slope' in which every economic activity might be considered as indirectly sustaining the war effort.[84]

He also significantly agrees with Garraway specifically mentioning Article 85 by stating that 'Canada has accepted the application of human-rights based norms regarding the treatment of detainees reflected in Common Article 3 of the Geneva Conventions and Article 75 of Additional Protocol I (which itself reflects the ICCPR norms)'.[85]

Helen Duffy in her book, *The War on Terror and the Framework of International Law,* examined issues of IHL in the coalition campaign in Afghanistan. She highlighted the bombardment on 11 October 2001 by American forces of the Afghan radio station justified by US Defense Secretary Rumsfeld on the basis that the radio station was 'the propaganda machine of the opposing forces'. She pointed out that there was criticism by Amnesty International of targeting civilian radio and televi-

81 K. Watkin, 'Coalition Operations: A Canadian Perspective' (2008) 84 *Int'l L. Stud.* 253.

82 Ibid. 254.

83 Ibid. 255.

84 Ibid; *see also* Y. Dinstein, *The Conduct of Hostilities under the Law of International Armed Conflict* (CUP, Cambridge, 2004) 87 for his discussion of the 'slippery slope'.

85 Ibid. 257.

sion stations.[86] She also cited aerial bombardment that resulted in civilian casualties including 30 fatalities at a wedding party in Uruzgan, 25 deaths at Chaskar village, 23 deaths in Thori village and 25-35 fatalities in Chowkar-Karex villages. She questions the proportionality calculations in these circumstances even if these persons were near legitimate military targets.[87]

If anything the controversy over the highest applicable standard or the lowest common denominator intensified with the Afghanistan conflict both in the definition of military objective and in the lack of consideration of the importance of the fundamental guarantees established in Article 75 of AP I also confirmed to be customary. There seemed to be a substantial divide emerging between the United States policy and those of the rest of the coalition partners which continued into the war in Iraq.

4.3 Iraq 2003

According to coalition officers involved in the war in Iraq in 2003, the use of AP I standards for targeting may well have been resolved. Neil Brown a Naval Legal Officer states:

> Nevertheless, in 2003 as a matter of practice it is arguable that the definition of a military objective and the principles of distinction and proportionality, even the use of precautions in attack, as they are set out in AP I,6 were generally applied by all coalition forces. Put simply, if asked whether as a matter of practice AP I differences were significant in the early part of 2003, I would have to say that on the whole they were not.[88]

Brown goes on to state that the Iraq operation represented a straightforward application of customary international law as reflected in AP I.[89]

In spite of Brown's assurances there are certainly controversies in targeting in Iraq that have attracted the attention of Non-governmental Organisations such as Human Rights Watch and Amnesty International. In 'Off Target: The Conduct of War and Civilian Casualties in Iraq', a report released by Human Rights Watch, there was a specific reference to dual use targets:

> Dual-use facilities are those that can have both a military and civilian application. In Iraq, the United States and United Kingdom considered electrical power, media, and telecommunications installations dual use and attacked examples of each. In some instances, however, it was not clear to Human Rights Watch why Coalition

86 H. Duffy, *The War on Terror and the Framework of International Law'* (CUP, Cambridge, 2005) 260 *see also* Amnesty International, 'Afghanistan: Accountability for Civilian Deaths' New Release (26 October 2001) AI Index: ASA/11/022/2001.

87 Ibid. 261.

88 N. Brown, 'Issues Arising from Coalition Operations: An Operational Lawyer's Perspective' in Carsten MD (ed), *International Law and Military Operations* (84 International Law Studies Series, Naval War College, 2008) 225.

89 Ibid.

> forces characterized certain installations in that way. A dual-use object may be a legitimate military target because it makes an 'effective contribution to military action' and its destruction offers 'a definite military advantage.' Yet the harm to the civilian population in its destruction may be disproportionate to the expected 'concrete and direct military advantage,' rendering an attack impermissible. [90]

McConachie, an Australian naval officer, also expresses reservations concerning the coalition operation in Iraq.[91] She argues that legal interoperability is essential in coalition operations but it is difficult to achieve. She discusses in particular the fact that Australia is a party to the prohibition against land mines in the Ottawa Convention and in the Iraq War 'air-refueling aircraft in Iraq in 2003 were ordered not to refuel any US airframe that was fitted with air-delivered anti-personnel mines, such as the scatterable, mixed-munitions GATORS system'.[92] She also discussed a red card system that enable Australian forces to not to strike a target that they deemed unlawful under AP I, targets which could include the dual use targets.[93]

Garraway, in his contribution on a general examination of coalition operations in a conference at the US Naval War College, highlights the key question: [W]hat is the US definition of a military objective?[94] As seen above, once again US forces bombed a media outlet and human rights organisations have complained about many other targets too numerous to be discussed here.[95] Brown may be overly optimistic that the AP I controversy is resolved.

The controversy with regard to AP I and human rights guarantees continued on from the Afghanistan War and one need not repeat here the sorry details of the abuse of detainees in Abu Ghraib, nor the continued use of Guantanamo Bay nor the rendition of suspects, all clearly outside of the customary rules of protection of civilians. This will be further discussed and debated as such items as torture memos and many cases of financial compensation for detainees are finally released to the public.

5. Conclusion

The three coalition operations here certainly reveal difficulties over two main areas of IHL, the definition of a military objective and the fundamental guarantees for civilians in an armed conflict. If one takes the position of human rights organisations one might argue that the lowest common denominator prevails but this is certainly not the point of view of many of the commentators who have had actual experience of coalition operations. These commentators also point out the fact that by and large

90 Human Rights Watch, 'Off Target: The Conduct of War and Civilian Casualties in Iraq' <www.hrw.org/reports/2003/usa1203/usa1203.pdf> (accessed 4 July 2009).

91 V. McConachie, 'Coalition Operations: A Compromise or an Accommodation?' in Carsten MD (ed), *International Law and Military Operations* (84 Naval War College International Law Studies Series, 2008) 235.

92 Ibid. 245.

93 Ibid.

94 *Garraway* (n 76) 238.

95 *Human Rights Watch* (n 90).

coalition operations are conducted according to the rules in AP I and the rules of customary international law.

The lack of respect for fundamental guarantees was not confusion over the highest standard but a blatant disregard for the rules that existed. The one area that needs further clarification is the US definition of military objective which does not dispute the distinction rule but rather takes an overbroad version of objective to include 'war sustaining'. One hopeful aspect of this debate is the position of other coalition partners that seem in these operations to 'red card' those targets that in their view do not represent a military objective according to AP I.

On a careful analysis this author agrees with the position in Stein's work on this topic that in coalition operations the maximum standard prevails.[96] Schmitt makes a cogent argument for the highest standard to apply in coalition operations. He states:

> Law can even shape war for those not party to a particular normative standard. For instance, Additional Protocol I, which the United States has not ratified, prohibits most attacks on dams, dikes, and nuclear electrical generating stations. Despite U.S. opposition to this particular provision, there have been no U.S. attacks on any of these target sets since the Vietnam War; should it conduct such an attack it would be condemned, for many will miss the fine distinction between a customary norm of international law, which binds all States and a treaty norm, which obligates only parties to comply. Apprehension over condemnation certainly influences the policy choice of whether to engage in such strikes. This de facto effect of law on non-Party States action can only expand as military operations become increasingly multilateral in composition, thereby frequently allying States with disparate legal obligations. In must such cases, the greatest common normative denominator will apply. For instance, it would be hard to imagine, e.g. U.S. forces in a coalition intentionally conducting an operation that would violate Protocol I, but no other legal regime if any significant coalition partners were parties to the treaty. The realities of coalition-building and maintenance would simply not allow it.[97]

96 *Stein* (n 2) 335.

97 M. Schmitt, 'The Law of Armed Conflict as Soft Power: Optimizing Strategic Choice' in M. Schmitt (ed), *International Law Across the Spectrum of Conflict: Essays in Honour of Professor L.C. Green on the Occasion of his Eightieth Birthday* (Vol. 75, US Naval War College, Newport, R.I., 2000) 459.

Schmitt gets very close to the reason necessary for the highest common standard. It can be argued that the development of customary humanitarian law, more than anything else had contributed to rules of armed conflict, of the highest standard, than can apply across coalitions. There will remain unresolved disputes over the interpretation over military objectives, but provided the other members of the coalition refuse to participate in these missions, chances are excellent that the highest standard over the total military campaign will prevail.

Chapter 5

Human Rights Law and Peacekeeping Operations

*Noëlle Quénivet**

1. Introduction

In the past two decades the United Nations (UN) has deployed personnel, both military and civilian, to maintain peace and security, to promote human rights, democracy and the rule of law as well as to protect populations from human rights violations. This use of multifaceted and complex operations is now a widely accepted mechanism established by the UN to restore, maintain and cement peace and security in areas such as Kosovo, Sudan, Haiti and Afghanistan.[1] Still, the mechanism is not without flaws. One of the recent criticisms raised regards widespread and regular violations of human rights by personnel deployed in such missions. The apparent total immunity granted to peacekeepers accentuates the feeling of resentment towards those who have been sent to assist the local population. Moreover, these violations endanger the very tasks of UN peace missions as they 'undermine the realisation and growth of human rights, as well as the potential success of each peace operation'.[2]

At the international level this concern is increasingly tackled via international criminal law.[3] Yet the prosecution of violations that fall within the purview of crimes

* The author is particularly grateful to Sabine Hassler, Boris Kondoch, Karen Oliveira da Costa and Jan Wetzel for their valuable comments. The last changes were made in September 2009.

1 *See* Chapter 1 in this book.

2 Rachel Opie, 'Human Rights Violations by Peacekeepers: Finding a Framework for Attribution of International Responsibility' [2006] *NZ Law Review* 1, 3. *See also* Florian Hoffmann and Frédéric Mégret, 'Fostering Human Rights Accountability: An Ombudsperson for the United Nations?' (2005) 11 *Global Governance* 43, 49.

3 *See e.g.* Noëlle Quénivet, 'The Role of the International Criminal Court in the Prosecution of Sexual Offences Committed by Peacekeepers' in Roberta Arnold (ed.), *Law Enforcement within the Framework of PSO* (Brill, Leiden 2008) 399-431. Moreover, much discussion is devoted as to which State is able and bound to prosecute individuals who have committed crimes. *See* UNCHR, 'Administration of Justice, Rule of Law and Democracy: Working Paper on the Accountability of International Personnel Taking Part in Peace Support Operations' (7 July 2005) UN Doc. E/CN.4/Sub.2/2005/42, paras 7; 15-25. Noëlle Quénivet, 'The Dissonance between the United Nations Zero-tolerance Policy and the Criminalisation of Sexual Offences on the International Level' (2007) 7.4 *Int C L R* 657-676.

M. Odello and R. Piotrowicz (eds.), International Military Missions and International Law.
2011 Koninklijke Brill NV. Printed in The Netherlands. ISBN *978 9004 17437 5. pp. 99-143.*

against humanity, war crimes or genocide overshadows the commission of other violations of human rights, for the aim of international criminal law is to prosecute those who have committed the most serious crimes,[4] or are responsible for the commission of such crimes.[5] The importance of applying human rights law to peacekeeping operations must therefore be recognised all the more, as their applicability is not only a theoretical question.[6] Members of peacekeeping operations have on numerous occasions been 'accused of human rights abuses ranging from disproportionate use of weapons to torture and involvement in prostitution'.[7] For example, following the peacekeeping mission in Somalia in 1994, several reports written by the governments of contributing troops pointed to serious violations of human rights law.[8] More recently the UN has admitted that peacekeepers have engaged in a variety of sexual offences.[9]

Human rights law is traditionally enforced through State responsibility, which consists of an objective element: the breach of a norm of international law; and a subjective one: the breach is imputable[10] to the *State*.[11] The primary rules of State

4 *See* Article 1 of the ICTY Statute (Statute of the International Criminal Tribunal for the Former Yugoslavia, *UNSC Res. 827* (25 May 1993) UN Doc. S/RES/827) and Article 1 of the Statute of the ICC (Rome Statute of the International Criminal Court (adopted 17 July 1998, entered into force 1 July 2002) 2187 UNTS 3.

5 *See* Article 1 of the Statute of the Special Court for Sierra Leone (Statute of the Special Court for Sierra Leone, *UNSC Res. 1315* (14 August 2000) UN Doc. S/RES/1315).

6 'That peace-keeping forces violate human rights is not a merely hypothetical situation'. Council of Europe, Parliamentary Assembly, 'Areas where the European Convention on Human Rights Cannot Be Implemented' (11 March 2003) Doc 9730, para 50. *See also* Chapter 2 in this book.

7 Boris Kondoch, 'Human Rights Law and UN Peace Operations in Post Conflict Situations' in Nigel White and Dirk Klaasen (eds), *The UN, Human Rights and Post-Conflict Situations* (Manchester University Press, Manchester, 2005). *See also Hoffmann and Mégret* (2005) (n 2) 44-45.

8 *See* report drafted by Canada ('Commission of Inquiry into the Deployment of Canadian Forces to Somalia, Dishonoured Legacy: The Lessons of the Somalia Affair, Report of the Commission of Inquiry into the Deployment of Canadian Forces to Somalia' (Public Works and Government Services Canada - Publishing, Ottawa, June 1997)) and by Italy (as presented and analysed in Natalio Lupi, 'Report by the Enquiry Commission on the Behaviour of Italian Peacekeeping Troops in Somalia' (1998) 1 *YIHL* 375).

9 Report of the Secretary-General, 'Investigation by the Office of Internal Oversight Services into Allegations of Sexual Exploitation and Abuse in the United Nations Organization Mission in the Democratic Republic of the Congo' (5 January 2005) UN Doc. A/59/661. Report of the Secretary-General, '17th Report of the Secretary-General on the United Nations Organization Mission in the Democratic Republic of the Congo' (15 March 2005) UN Doc. S/2005/167.

10 'Imputability is the legal fiction which assimilates the actions or omissions of State officials to the State itself and which renders the State liable for damage resulting to the property or person of an alien'. Malcolm Shaw, *International Law* (Cambridge University Press, Cambridge, 2003) 701.

11 *See* Article 2 ILC Draft on Responsibility of States for Internationally Wrongful Acts,

responsibility define the content of the obligation, while the secondary rules identify the general conditions under which States are considered liable for acting in violation of an international norm.[12] It is well established that international organisations (IOs) can also incur international responsibility.[13] In the context of IMM, the primary rules are spelled out in treaties and customary international law relating to human rights.[14] As the question of imputability is discussed in Chapter 8,[15] this chapter is confined to aspects of international law relating to States' and IOs' obligations to ensure compliance by peacekeeping personnel with international human rights norms - the objective element of State responsibility. In the context of peacekeeping operations the applicability of human rights law is not as straightforward as it may appear *prima facie*. Questions such as the extra-territorial application of human rights law treaties and the difficult enforcement of customary human rights law more generally should not be overlooked.

Moreover, concerning the applicability of human rights law to peacekeeping forces via IOs, the issue arises as to whether acts carried out during peacekeeping missions can be attributed to IOs. Peacekeeping missions are usually established by the Security Council (and occasionally by the General Assembly), and are under the authority of the Secretary-General. Accordingly, UN peacekeeping troops are considered as subsidiary organs of the UN.[16] Thus, if it is proven that the IO is obligated to apply human rights law, then peacekeeping troops, as agents of the organisation, would also be obliged to respect such rules.[17] The crux is therefore to show that IOs and, more particularly, the UN, are bound by human rights law either via treaty or customary law. That being said, a plethora of mission-specific instruments, most of which are not legally binding, have been generated by various IOs involved in peacekeeping missions.

This contribution deals only with military and police forces because the complexity of the various statuses of personnel involved in peacekeeping operations is such that they cannot all be addressed in one chapter.[18] Moreover the focus is on

---

annex to *UNGA Res. 56/83* (12 December 2001) and corrected by document UN Doc. A/56/49(Vol. I)/Corr.4.

12 Ibid. (General Commentary on the ILC Draft on State Responsibility) para 1.

13 'The responsibility of international organizations has not been as extensively studied as state responsibility, but a broad consensus seems to surround the proposition that the rules of state responsibility should constitute, mutatis mutandis, the law of responsibility of international organizations'. Carla Bongiorno, 'A Culture of Impunity: Applying International Human Rights Law to the United Nations in East Timor' (2002) 33 *Colum Hum Rts L Rev* 623, 644.

14 The issue whether responsibility arises from a violation of a treaty obligation or of a general obligation owed towards all States is not addressed here.

15 *See also* Aurel Sari, 'Jurisdiction and International Responsibility in Peace Support Operations: The Behrami and Saramati cases' (2008) 8 *H R L Rev* 151-170.

16 Marten Zwanenburg, 'Compromise or Commitment: Human Rights and International Humanitarian Law Obligations for UN Peace Forces' (1998) 11 *LJIL* 229, 231.

17 Ibid. 232.

18 For an explanation of the various statuses, *see e.g.* Noëlle Quénivet, 'The Role of the

peacekeeping and peace enforcement rather than on observer missions, as the former are more likely to involve the use of force and hence more likely to result in human rights violations. Against this backdrop, peacekeeping is defined as 'the deployment of a United Nations presence in the field, hitherto with the consent of all the parties concerned, normally invoking United Nations military and/or police personnel and frequently civilians as well'.[19]

After exploring the applicability of human rights treaties to States and IOs in peacekeeping missions, this chapter examines the applicability of other sources of public international law such as customary law and general principles of law. It then focuses on mission-specific rules issued by the UN when engaged in peacekeeping missions. This chapter argues that while there is a wealth of human rights instruments binding upon States and IOs, it would be best if, for the sake of clarity and consistency, the UN would issue a single instrument listing all its human rights obligations when engaged in peacekeeping operations.

2. Applicability of Treaty Law to Peacekeeping Operations

The great majority of contributing States to peacekeeping missions are parties to key international human rights treaties such as the International Covenant on Civil and Political Rights (with the exceptions of Pakistan and Indonesia that are troop-contributing nations)[20] and the Convention Against Torture.[21] In addition, many are also parties to regional human rights instruments such as the European Convention on Human Rights and Fundamental Freedoms,[22] the American Convention on Human Rights,[23] and the African Charter on Human and Peoples' Rights.[24] Conversely, IOs cannot be parties to these legal instruments.[25]

International Criminal Court in the Prosecution of Sexual Offences Committed by Peacekeepers' in *Arnold* (n 3) 399-431.

19 Boutros Boutros-Ghali, 'An Agenda for Peace: Preventative Diplomacy, Peacemaking and Peace-keeping' (17 June 1992) UN Doc. A/47/277, S/2411, para 20.

20 International Covenant on Civil and Political Rights (adopted 16 December 1966, entered into force 23 March 1976) 999 UNTS 171 (ICCPR).

21 Convention Against Torture and Other Cruel, Inhuman or Degrading Treatment or Punishment (adopted 10 December 1984, entered into force 26 June 1987) 1465 UNTS 85 (CAT).

22 European Convention for the Protection of Human Rights and Fundamental Freedoms (adopted 4 November 1950, entered into force 3 September 1953) 213 UNTS 221 (ECHR).

23 American Convention on Human Rights (adopted 22 November 1969, entered into force 18 July 1978) 1144 UNTS 123. *See also* the non-binding American Declaration of the Rights and Duties of Man (2 May 1948) OAS Res. XXX.

24 African Charter on Human and Peoples' Rights (adopted 26 June 1981, entered into force 21 October 1986) OAU Doc CAB/LEG/67/3 Rev. 5.

25 A potential exception is the accession of the European Union to the ECHR. Article 17 of Protocol 14 provides: 'Article 59 of the Convention shall be amended as follows: 1. A new paragraph 2 shall be inserted which shall read as follows: 2. The European Union

In the case of the applicability of human rights treaties to States involved in peacekeeping operations the focus is on jurisdiction,[26] as this determines the scope of the parties' obligations and is a prerequisite to the consideration of State responsibility.[27] In contrast, in the context of the applicability of such treaties to IOs, the issue is whether IOs are bound by human rights treaties.

2.1. Applicability of Treaty Law to States: Extra-Territorial Application of Human Rights Law

That States are compelled to respect human rights obligations set out in treaties beyond their territorial borders is not a new notion. Still, the increasing number of military missions abroad, whether for peaceful or for more belligerent purposes, calls for a review of the provisions relating to jurisdiction in human rights treaties and the jurisprudence produced by the bodies implementing them. In essence, the question of the binding nature of treaties upon States focuses on the different sets of criteria laid down by human rights mechanisms to assert the State's exercise of jurisdiction[28] abroad, i.e. the extra-territorial applicability of treaties.

By and large, while the Human Rights Committee (HRC) has readily recognised the application of its founding treaty extra-territorially, the European Court of Human Rights (ECtHR) has been more reticent in this regard, sending mixed and even contradictory signals. Yet its jurisprudence is probably the most pertinent inasmuch as a host of the factual situations examined by the court relate to occupation, a state that 'bear[s] broad similarities with the legal status of complex peace operations'.[29]

---

may accede to this Convention' Protocol No. 14 to the Convention for the Protection of Human Rights and Fundamental Freedoms, amending the Control System of the Convention (adopted 13 May 2004 but not yet entered into force) ETS No. 194.

26 'The question of jurisdiction relates to a breach of an international obligation'. Morten Peschardt Pedersen, 'Territorial Jurisdiction in Article 1 of the European Convention on Human Rights' (2004) 73 *Nord J Intl L* 279, 303. *See also Council of Europe, Parliamentary Assembly* (n 6) paras 17-18. For a contrary view, *see* Alexander Orakhelashvili, 'Restrictive Interpretation of Human Rights Treaties in the Recent Jurisprudence of the European Court of Human Rights' (2003) 14 *EJIL* 529-568.

27 Sonia Parayre, 'Beyond International Humanitarian Law: Aspects of the Applicability of International Human Rights Law' in Alexandre Faite and Jérémie Labbé Grenier (eds), *Expert Meeting on Multinational Peace Operations. Applicability of International Humanitarian Law and International Human Rights Law to UN Mandated Forces* (ICRC, Geneva, 2003) 45.

28 'Jurisdiction involves the assertion or exercise of legal authority, actual or purported, over persons owing some form of allegiance to that state or brought within that state's control'. Stefka Kavaldjieva, 'Jurisdiction of the European Court of Human Rights: Exorbitance in Reverse? Can, and Should, an Iraqi Victim of Human Rights Abuses Inflicted by U.K. Troops have a Remedy in U.K. Courts under the European Convention of Human Rights' (2006) 37 *GJIL* 507, 511.

29 *Opie* (n 2) 11.

2.1.1. The International Covenant on Civil and Political Rights

According to Article 2(1) ICCPR, each party is obliged to respect and ensure human rights 'to all individuals within its territory and subject to its jurisdiction'. A literal reading of this provision unequivocally indicates that the individual must be subject to the jurisdiction of the State and, additionally, present on the territory of the State.[30] The drafters used a conjunctive 'and' instead of a disjunctive 'or'. Therefore, the State is only obligated towards those individuals who are present on its territory. However, there is substantial support for another view: that the drafters did not intend such a restrictive interpretation,[31] that Article 5(1) ICCPR[32] permits a broader interpretation, and that the Optional Protocol to the ICCPR does not include any territorial limitation to the HRC receiving individual communications;[33] therefore, the sentence has to be read in a disjunctive manner.[34]

30 Michael Dennis, 'Applying Human Rights Law and Humanitarian Law in the Extra-territorial War against Terrorism: Too Little, Too Much, or Just Rights?: Application of Human Rights Treaties Extra-territorially to Detention of Combatants and Security Internees: Fuzzy Thinking All Around?' (2006) 12 *ILSA J Intl L* 459, 464.

31 *See* opinions of Theodor Meron, 'Agora: The 1994 US Action in Haiti: Extra-territoriality of Human Rights Treaties' (1995) 89 *AJIL* 78, 78-80; Rick Lawson, 'The Concept of Jurisdiction and Extra-territorial Acts of State' in Gérard Kreijen and others (eds), *State, Sovereignty, and International Governance* (New York University Press, New York, 2002) 283-284. For a contrary opinion, Ibid. 466.

32 Article 5(1) reads 'Nothing in the present Covenant may be interpreted as implying for any State, group or person any right to engage in any activity or perform any act aimed at the destruction of any of the rights and freedoms recognised herein or at their limitation to a greater extent than is provided for in the present Covenant'. *ICCPR* (n 20).

33 *See* Article 1 of the Optional Protocol to the ICCPR (Ibid.). *See also* the interpretation made by the HRC in the *Lopez Burgos v. Uruguay* case: '[T]he reference [to 'individuals subject to its jurisdiction' in article 1 of the Optional Protocol] is not to the place where the violation occurred but rather to the relationship between the individual and the State in relation to a violation of any of the rights set forth in the Covenant, wherever they occurred'. *Lopez Burgos v. Uruguay*, Communication No. 52/1979 (29 July 1981) UN Doc. CCPR/C/OP/1, para 12.2.

34 *See* in particular Thomas Buergenthal, 'To Respect and Ensure: State Obligations and Permissible Derogations' in Louis Henkin (ed), *The International Bill of Rights: The Convention on Civil and Political Rights* (Columbia University Press, New York, 1981) 72-77; René Provost, *International Human Rights and Humanitarian Law* (Cambridge University Press, Cambridge, 2002) 22.

In spite of this, some States[35] and commentators[36] have vehemently opposed this interpretation of the jurisdictional scope of the ICCPR. Their main backing, besides a literal interpretation of the jurisdictional clause, is the *travaux préparatoires*[37] which indicate the drafters' lack of intention to bind States in their activities abroad.[38] Scholars also point out that when operating abroad States do not issue a derogation notice, thereby evidencing their opposition to a broad interpretation of the jurisdictional clause.[39] The HRC has outwardly rejected these comments, stating that, provided some conditions were fulfilled, States were bound by ICCPR provisions abroad. In *Lopez Burgos v. Uruguay*, the HRC acknowledged that Uruguay could be held to be in violation of the ICCPR even though the acts were committed by Uruguayan agents on foreign soil.[40] In the opinion of the HRC:

> [i]t would be unconscionable to so interpret the responsibility under article 2 of the Covenant as to permit a State Party to perpetrate violations of the Covenant on the territory of another state, which violations it could not perpetrate on its own territory.[41]

---

35 United States: 'The United States has maintained consistently that the Covenant does not apply outside the United States or its special maritime and territorial jurisdiction, and that it does not apply to operations of the military during an international armed conflict'. US Department of Defence, 'Working Group Report on Detainee Interrogations in the Global War on Terrorism; Assessment of Legal, Historical, Policy, and Operational Considerations' (6 March 2003). *See also* US Department of State, 'United States Second and Third Report Concerning the International Covenant on Civil and Political Rights' (21 October 2005) <www.state.gov/g/drl/rls/55504.htm> (accessed 6 July 2009); Israel: 'Israel has consistently maintained that the Covenant does not apply to areas that are not subject to its sovereign territory and jurisdiction. This position is based on the well-established distinction between human rights and humanitarian law under international law'. HRC, 'State Periodic Report: Israel' (4 December 2002) UN Doc. CCPR/C/ISR/2001/2, para 8.

36 *See e.g.* Christian Tomuschat, *Human Rights: Between Idealism and Realism* (Oxford University Press, Oxford, 2003) 110.

37 It is recorded that the formula was suggested by Eleanor Roosevelt to avoid application in relation to people in occupied territories. 'Summary Record of the 138th Meeting, UN ESCOR Hum Rts Comm' (1950) UN Doc. E/CN.4/SR.138.

38 Michael Dennis and Andre Surena, 'Application of the International Covenant on Civil and Political Rights in Times of Armed Conflict and Military Occupation: The Gap between Legal Theory and State Practice' (2008) 6 *EHRLR* 714; *Dennis* (n 30) 459; *See* in contrast John Cerone, 'Peace Operations and the Complementarity of Human Rights Law and International Humanitarian Law' in *International Institute of Humanitarian Law and International Committee of the Red Cross, Proceedings of the XXXIst San Remo Round Table 'International Humanitarian Law and Human Rights in Peace Operations'* (International Institute of Humanitarian Law and International Committee of the Red Cross, San Remo, 2008) 124.

39 *Dennis* (n 30) 459.

40 *Lopez Burgos* (n 33).

41 *Lopez Burgos* (n 33) para 12.3.

This finding, which mostly relates to persons falling within State power, was confirmed in the case *Lilian Celiberti de Casariego v. Uruguay*.[42] Both cases reveal that when State agents are in control of individuals abroad they must comply with the ICCPR. Arguably, this line of reasoning allows for the conclusion that, in peacekeeping context, the human rights of individuals under the authority of peacekeepers are to be safeguarded by the State whose contingents are involved in peacekeeping missions.

Under the reporting mechanism of the ICCPR, the HRC has declared that a State must also apply human rights law standards whenever it is in effective control of part of a foreign territory. It has, for example, criticised Israel for failing to provide information about the implementation of human rights law in territories under Israeli control[43] and Iraq for failing to address the events that took place during its occupation of Kuwait.[44] The HRC has also expressed concerns regarding the behaviour of Belgian peacekeeping troops operating in Somalia,[45] and the fact that as of 2001, six years after the fall of Srebrenica, the Netherlands had not yet undertaken any investigation with regards to the involvement of its armed forces.[46] Although in the first instance the HRC did not ascertain whether the ICCPR was breached, in the latter instance it noted the States' obligations under Articles 2 and 6 ICCPR during peacekeeping missions.

Jurisdiction is not linked to the legality of the act in terms of international law: it reflects a factual notion.[47] For instance, in the *Lopez Burgos* case, the HRC said that it did not matter whether the State on whose territory the violations were committed had acquiesced in the presence of the agents of the violating State or whether it had opposed it.[48] In the context of peacekeeping operations, it means that States are obliged to apply human rights law standards to the full range of peacekeeping missions, i.e. from traditional peacekeeping that is predicated on consent[49] to peace enforcement.

42 *Lilian Celiberti de Casariego v. Uruguay*, Communication No. 56/1979 (29 July 1981) UN Doc. CCPR/C/OP/1.

43 HRC, 'Concluding Observations' (4 July 1998) UN Doc. CCPR/C/79/Add. 93, para 10.

44 HRC, 'Report to the UN General Assembly' (10 October 1991) UN Doc. A/46/40, para 652.

45 HRC, 'Concluding Observations (Belgium)' (19 November 1998) UN Doc. CCPR/C/79/Add.99, para 14.

46 HRC, 'Concluding Observations (The Netherlands)' (27 August 2001) UN Doc. CCPR/CO/72/NET, para 8.

47 Ralph Wilde, 'Triggering State Obligations Extraterritorially: The Spatial Test in Certain Human Rights Treaties' in Roberta Arnold and Noëlle Quénivet (eds), *International Humanitarian Law and Human Rights Law. Towards a New Merger in International Law* (Martinus Nijhoff Publishers, Leiden, 2008) 142.

48 *Lopez Burgos* (n 33) para 12.3.

49 On the issue of consent and peacekeeping operations, *see* discussions in Alexander Orakhelashvili, 'The Legal Basis of the United Nations Peace-keeping Operations' (2003) 43 *Va J Intl L* 485, 518-520 and David Wippman, 'Military Intervention, Regional Organizations, and the Host-state Consent' (1996) 7 *Duke J Comp & Intl L* 209-239.

In sum, as declared by the HRC in General Comment No 31:

> [a] State party must respect and ensure the rights laid down in the Covenant to anyone within the power and effective control of that State Party, even if not situated within the territory of the State Party … regardless of the circumstances in which such power or effective control was obtained, such as forces constituting a national contingent of a State Party assigned to an international peace-keeping or peace-enforcement operation.[50]

In light of these cases and comments, there is no doubt that States are bound by the ICCPR when deploying troops in peacekeeping missions, provided these troops are in control of the area or wield authority over specific individuals.

2.1.2. The European Convention on Human Rights (ECHR)

The scope of the obligations under the ECHR is also framed in jurisdictional terms.[51] However, in contrast to the ICCPR, Article 1 ECHR obliges States to secure human rights to those individuals within their jurisdiction. There is no mention of territory. Accordingly, it is possible to apply the ECHR beyond the territory of the parties. Indeed, while jurisdiction is primarily territorial, it is not exclusively so.[52] Unfortunately, the *travaux préparatoires* relating to the choice of the words used in Article 1 ECHR are not exhaustive enough to permit a historical interpretation.[53] It must be noted that, as the Court has asserted, the ECHR, being a 'living instrument',[54] must be interpreted in the light of present-day conditions and situations. Furthermore, a contextual interpretation taking into consideration Article 17 allows for a broad interpretation.[55] An object and purpose interpretation has indisputably led the Court to accept the extra-territorial application of the Convention.

50 HRC, 'General Comment No. 31 on Article 2 of the Covenant: The Nature of the General Legal Obligations Imposed on States Parties to the Covenant' (21 April 2004) UN Doc. CCPR/C/74/CRP.4/Rev.6, para 10.

51 *Parayre* (n 27) 45.

52 *Legal Consequences of the Construction of a Wall in Occupied Palestine*, Advisory Opinion [2004] ICJ Rep 136, para 109.

53 *See* discussion in *Peschardt Pedersen* (n 26) 281-283.

54 *Selmouni v. France* (App no 25803/94) (2000) 29 *EHRR* 403, para 101.

55 The European Commission on Human Rights noted specifically: 'The operation of the Convention in the occupied part of Cyprus would become ineffective if one accepted [Turkey's] submission that alleged violations of the Convention in that area could not be examined by the Commission. It followed from Article 17 that the Convention did not allow such a vacuum in the protection of its rights and freedoms'. *Cyprus v. Turkey* (App nos 6780/74 and 6950/75) ECHR (26 May 1975). Article 17 ECHR reads as follows 'Nothing in this Convention may be interpreted as implying for any State, group or person any right to engage in any activity or perform any act aimed at the destruction on any of the rights and freedoms set forth herein or at their limitation to a greater extent than is provided for in the Convention'.

It would be inconceivable to permit States to indulge in human rights violations abroad when analogous acts committed at home are clearly prohibited.[56] The Court has accepted that there are three distinct exceptional cases when the Convention is applicable abroad: jurisdiction based on authority over individuals, jurisdiction based on effective control over territory and 'diplomatic' protection.[57]

2.1.2.1. Jurisdiction Based on Authority over Individuals

The implementation bodies of the ECHR, both the Commission and the Court, have long conceded the extra-territorial applicability of the Convention where State agents are responsible for convention-incompatible acts or omissions that affect persons outside the State's territory.[58] The decisive factor is the State's ability to control the individual.[59] In several cases it has been decided that the Convention applies from the moment a person is handed over to the authorities of a State party even if the transfer occurs abroad.[60] The salient point, as clarified in the *Öcalan* judgment, is that a person is under the 'authority and control' of a State party to the Convention.[61] British courts have adopted this jurisprudence in the *Al-Skeini* case, accepting that the death of a detainee fell within the State's extra-territorial jurisdiction.[62] This type of extra-territorial applicability of the Convention is frequently described as being linked to 'personal jurisdiction'[63] and is predominantly applicable in a custodial environment.[64]

---

56 *Opie* (n 2) 21.

57 *Al-Saadoon and Mufdhi v. UK* (App no 61498/08) ECHR (30 June 2009) para 85.

58 *X v. Federal Republic of Germany* (App no 1611/12), ECHR (25 September 1965). The Court clarified that '[t]he term 'jurisdiction' is not limited to the national territory of the High Contracting Parties; their responsibility can be involved because of acts of their authorities producing effects outside their own territory'. *Drozd and Janousek v. France and Spain* (App no 12747/87) (1992) 14 *EHRR* 745, para 91.

59 Kerem Altiparmak, 'Bankovic: An Obstacle to the Application of the European Convention on Human Rights in Iraq' (2004) 9 *JCSL* 213, 218.

60 *See e.g. Freda v. Italy* (App no 8916/80) [1980] 21 DR 250; *Reinette v. France* (App no 14009/88) [1989] 63 DR 189; *Sánchez-Ramirez v. France* (App no 28780/95) [1996] 86-A DR 155; *Öcalan v.Turkey* (App no 46221/99) ECHR (14 December 2000) (admissibility).

61 Ibid. (*Öcalan*).

62 *R (on the application of Al-Skeini and others) v. Secretary of State for Defence* [2004] EWHC 2911 (Admin) para 61. Unfortunately the reasoning of the Court is flawed inasmuch as it links personal jurisdiction to the exceptional exercise of jurisdiction abroad based on embassies, vessels and aircrafts. It must also be added that US Courts have also adopted this type of extra-territorial jurisdiction. *See Rasul v. Bush*, 542 U.S. 466 (2004) and *Omar et al. v. Secretary of the United States Army et al.*, 479 F. 3d 1 (D.C. Cir. [2007]). On a domestic level, this test is sometimes referred to as 'effective military control of the person'. *See Amnesty International Canada and British Columbia Civil Liberties Association v. Chief of the Defence Staff for the Canadian Forces, Minister of National Defence and Attorney General of Canada* [2008] FC 336, 12 March 2008, para 201.

63 Philip Leach, 'The British Military in Iraq – The Applicability of the Espace Juridique Doctrine under the European Convention on Human Rights' (2005) 1 *PL* 448.

64 Counsel Greenwood expressed that 'a prisoner is the archetypal example of someone who comes within the jurisdiction of the detaining State which exercises the most

That when making arrests abroad,[65] State agents must abide by the ECHR is of utmost significance in the context of peacekeeping operations. Indeed, for instance, '[w]hen UNMIK Police arrest and detain individuals, they assert effective control over those persons, bringing them temporarily within their State's jurisdiction'.[66] Therefore, if it can be demonstrated that peacekeeping forces are in control of a particular individual, then they must observe human rights law.[67] States are however 'not required to secure the entire range of substantive rights set out in the Convention, but rather to respect the individual's rights "to the extent that [they] exercise authority over such persons"'.[68] This means that States must at least ensure that the individual can challenge the lawfulness of his/her detention as no-one can be deprived of his/her liberty without a clear legal basis.[69] The right to effective judicial review and the right to be heard must be guaranteed. Regrettably, UN police forces in Kosovo 'have been accused of authoritarian behaviour[70] and of ignoring the decisions of courts',[71] thereby, if proven, breaching the provisions of the ECHR.[72]

---

extreme type of control over him'. Verbatim record of the hearing held in Bankovic (24 October 2001) as cited in Michael O'Boyle, 'The European Convention on Human Rights and Extraterritorial Jurisdiction: A Comment on "Life after Bankovic"'in Fons Coomans and Menno Kamminga (eds), *Extraterritorial Application of Human Rights Treaties* (Intersentia, Antwerp, 2004) 139.

65 For an overview of the operations in which peacekeeping troops have detained individuals, *see* Bruce Oswald, 'The Treatment of Detainees by Peacekeepers: Applying Principles and Standards at the Point of Detention' in *Arnold* (n 3) 197.

66 *Opie* (n 2) 30.

67 Unfortunately, if the individual is not deemed to be under the control of the peacekeeping forces, he/she does not benefit from the rights enshrined in the ECHR.

68 *Council of Europe, Parliamentary Assembly* (n 6) para 42. *See also Opie* (n 2) 30; *Cerone* (n 38) 122-123.

69 *See* in particular *Articles 6 and 13 ECHR* (n 22) and the jurisprudence of the ECHR in e.g. *Aksoy v. Turkey* (App no 100/1995/606/694) (1996) 23 *EHRR* 553.

70 A form of 'authoritarian behaviour' is the executive detention of individuals without judicial oversight. *See e.g. Saramati v. France, Germany and Norway* (App no 78166/01) ECHR (2 May 2007) (admissibility); David Marshall and Shelley Inglis, 'The Disempowerment of Human Rights-based Justice in the United Nations Mission in Kosovo' (2003) 16 *Harv Hum Rts J* 95, 103; 113-114; 142.

71 *Hoffmann and Mégret* (2005) (n 2) 45; *See also* Human Rights Watch, *Better Late than Never: Enhancing the Accountability of International Institutions in Kosovo*, No. 2, June 2007, 25-26; Ibid. (*Marshall and Inglis*) 103; 113-114.

72 This is only the case if the States whose contingents committed these violations are State parties to the ECHR. *See* discussion in Federico Sperotto, *The International Security Presence in Kosovo and the Protection of Human Rights* (Human Rights and Human Welfare Working Papers No 48, 24 May 2008) 7-8.

2.1.2.2. Jurisdiction Based on Control over Territory

Relying on the rules of occupation, this was extended in *Cyprus v. Turkey* to include military acts,[73] an interpretation confirmed in subsequent jurisprudence.[74] The seminal *Loizidou v. Turkey* case stated that:

> the responsibility of a Contracting Party may also arise when as a consequence of military action – whether lawful or unlawful – it exercises effective control of an area outside its national territory. The obligation to secure, in such an area, the rights and freedoms set out in the Convention derives from the fact of such control whether it be exercised directly, through its armed forces, or though a subordinate local administration.[75]

In the merits decision regarding *Loizidou*, the Court used the expression 'effective overall control'[76] and justified its decision to apply the ECHR on the basis that the legitimate government did not exercise effective overall control,[77] that the large number of Turkish troops stationed on the island proved that Turkey was in effective control of the island,[78] that the Turkish Republic of Northern Cyprus was neither an integral part of Cyprus nor a State,[79] and that since Cyprus was a party to the ECHR, Northern Cypriots should not be denied the rights provided for in the Convention. Analogous factors were drawn upon by the Court in the *Ilascu* case.[80] Based on this, it is contended that whenever contingents involved in peacekeeping missions are in effective control of a certain area, the State to which theses forces belong must ensure that their actions conform to the norms spelled out in the ECHR.[81]

The concept of 'effective control' was later restricted in the *Bankovic* case.[82] Outwardly, one of the main criteria for denying the applicability of the ECHR was that NATO was 'only' in control of the air[83] and had no ground forces involved in

73 *Cyprus v. Turkey* (App no 8007/77) [1978] 13 DR 146.

74 *See e.g. Chrysostomos, Papachrysostomou and Loizidou v. Turkey* (App nos 15299/89, 15300/89 and 15318/89) [1991] 68 DR 228; *Cyprus v. Turkey* (App no 25781/94) (1997) 23 *EHRR* 244.

75 *Loizidou v. Turkey* (App no 15318/89) (1995) 20 *EHRR* 99, para 62.

76 *Loizidou v. Turkey* (App no 15318/89) (1996) 23 *EHRR* 513, para 52.

77 Ibid. para 50.

78 Ibid. para 56.

79 Ibid. para 56.

80 *See* discussion in *Kavaldjieva* (n 28) 516-517. For a contrary view, *see* Michael Bothe, 'Die Anwendung der Europäischen Menschenrechtskonvention in bewaffneten Konflikten – eine Überforderung?' (2005) 65 *ZaöRV* 615, 618.

81 *Kavaldjieva* (n 28) 523; *Opie* (n 2) 17.

82 *Bankovic et al. v. Belgium et al.* (App no 52207/99) ECHR (12 December 2001) (Admissibility).

83 Altiparmak notes that '[t]he ECrtHR's approach leads to the conclusion that prohibitions concerning traditional means of warfare do not apply to modern means of warfare unless the warring parties exercise effective authority over its opponent's territory. However, armies of the powerful states cause most of their damage, before they effec-

military actions. The Court seems to understand 'effective control' as related to control of the land and the 'use of precision-targeted air strikes does not amount to such control'.[84] Such reasoning arguably contradicts international law, for territory is understood as encompassing land, sea, and air.[85] Yet, previous ECHR cases predominantly related to occupation and the ability of a State to exercise public powers on the territory of another State,[86] which is obviously not the case in air strikes.[87] In other words, the Court is showing consistency in its jurisprudence. Moreover, although *Bankovic* has been severely criticised and dismissed as unsound by some commentators[88] while others have declared that not too much weight should be given to the reasoning,[89] national courts have relied heavily upon it.[90] Hence, the restrictive interpretation adopted by the Court should not be so readily discounted. Applying *Bankovic* to peacekeeping missions does not present any hurdles, for peacekeeping missions overwhelmingly take place on the ground. Hence, whenever such forces are in effective control of the territory (akin to occupation) the States whose contingents are on the ground have to abide by the ECHR.[91]

Whilst the 'effective control' doctrine appears to be established in ECHR jurisprudence, albeit interpreted in different ways, the Court introduced in the *Ilascu* case the concept of 'decisive influence'[92] and in the *Issa* case[93] that of 'temporary effective overall control'. Undeniably, these notions go well beyond the strict 'effective control'

tively control the territory of the state against which they organise their attacks. The ECrtHR's approach in the Bankovic case may create an inequality in favour of powerful states and encourage aerial bombardment before invasion'. *Altiparmak* (n 59) 219.

84 Tarik Abdel-Monem, 'How Far Do the Lawless Areas of Europe Extend? Extraterritorial Application of the European Convention on Human Rights' (2005) 14.2 *J Transnat'l L & Pol'y* 159, 196.

85 Ian Brownlie, *Principles of Public International Law* (6th ed. Oxford University Press, Oxford, 2003) 105.

86 Miltner explains that according to the Bankovic jurisprudence, 'the control must additionally involve an exercise of public powers normally to be exercised by that Government'. Barbara Miltner, 'Extraterritorial Jurisdiction under the European Convention on Human Rights: An Expansion under Isaak v Turkey?' (2007) 2 *EHRLR* 172, 176.

87 *Peschardt Pedersen* (n 26) 302; *Leach* (n 63) 3.

88 *See e.g. Miltner* (n 86).

89 'Working Session III: Beyond International Humanitarian Law: Aspects of the Applicability of International Human Rights Law' in *Faite and Labbe Grenier* (n 27) 18-19.

90 In Germany: Higher Regional Court at Cologne (Oberlandesgericht) Judgment (28 July 2005) Case no 7 U 8/04 *and* District Court at Bonn, Judgment (10 December 2003) Case no 1 O 361/02; in the UK: *Al-Skeini et al. v. Secretary of State for Defence*, [2007] UKHL 26, para 68; In Canada: *Amnesty International Canada* (n 62) para 215; In the Netherlands: Dutch Supreme Court, HR (29 September 2002) NJ 2003, 35.

91 Unfortunately, if peacekeeping forces have control over air and sea only, it seems impossible to rely on the *Bankovic* jurisprudence.

92 *Ilascu et al. v. Moldova and Russia* (App no 48787/99) (2005) 40 *EHRR* 46, para 392.

93 *Issa and Others v. Turkey* (App no 31821/96) (2004) 41 *EHRR* 567, para 74.

test spelled out by the Court. Even its most lenient interpretations do not encompass mere influence,[94] albeit a closer examination at the *Ilascu* judgment reveals that what determines effectiveness is in fact 'the degree to which the area is dependent on the contracting State for its subsistence'.[95] The *Ilascu* case is of particular interest. Indeed, what is remarkable is that the Russian troops stationed in Transdniestr are so-called peacekeeping forces and thus the case-law could readily be exploited to assert that States sending peacekeeping troops abroad have to adhere to the ECHR. In this instance the Russian troops controlled a subordinate local administration (the separatist regime in Tiraspol), a situation similar to certain peacekeeping operations where the UN via a local administration is governing a certain area. The 'temporary effective overall control' test provides unquestionably another broad interpretation,[96] because it only requires 'overall control of the area' rather than 'detailed control over the policies and actions of the authorities in the area'[97] and, unlike in prior cases relating to occupation, it allows for control to be exercised for a limited span of time.[98] Nevertheless, the Court clearly spelled out a two-tiered factual test: the jurisdictional control must be proven and this must be done beyond reasonable doubt.[99] As Mantouvalou emphasises, '[m]ilitary action, then, may constitute temporary exercise of jurisdiction'.[100] In other words, those States whose peacekeeping troops are carrying out a specific mission in a particular area may be held to be in breach of the ECHR.[101]

It is contended that the doctrine of 'effective control' developed by the ECtHR aimed to avoid a vacuum in human rights protection in territories the inhabitants of

94 Some authors agree that 'the 'decisive influence' test is troubling'. Terje Einarsen, Mark Gibney and Erik Roxstrom, 'The NATO Bombing Case (*Bankovic et al. v. Belgium et al.*) and the Limits of Western Human Rights Protection' (2005) 23.1 *B U Intl L J* 55, 126.

95 Joanne Williams, 'Al Skeini: A Flawed Interpretation of Bankovic' (2005) 23.4 *Wis Intl L J* 687, 705.

96 *See* comments by Jérémie Labbé Grenier, 'Extra-territorial Applicability of Human Rights Treaty Obligations to United Nations-mandated Forces' in *Faite and Labbé Grenier* (n 27) 79, 81.

97 *Issa* (n 93) para 70. It must be noted that the expression of 'detailed control' was already used in *Loizidou* (1996) (n 76). *See also* discussion in *Amnesty International Canada* (n 62) paras 227-235.

98 For a discussion on the *Issa* case, *see* Nuala Mole, 'Issa v. Turkey: Delineating the Extra Territorial Effect of the European Convention on Human Rights?' (2005) 10 *EHRLR* 86-91.

99 *Issa* (n 93). For a discussion on this issue, *see* Tarik Abdel-Monem, 'The Long Arm of the European Convention on Human Rights and the Recent Development of Issa v. Turkey' (2005) 12 *Human Rights Brief* 9-11.

100 Virginia Mantouvalou, 'Extending Judicial Control in International Law: Human Rights Treaties and Extra-territoriality' (2005) 9 *IJHR* 147, 153.

101 This situation is however fraught with practical difficulties in cases operations are carried out by a mixture of contingents that belong to States parties and non-parties to the ECHR.

which would have benefited from the protection offered by the Convention.[102] The ECtHR formally enunciated the 'European legal space' doctrine in the *Bankovic* case whereby it maintained that, owing to its European character, the Convention could only apply within the European legal space.[103] As Serbia-Montenegro did not belong to the Council of Europe (CoE), the Convention did not apply to the military actions carried out by NATO against that State. Although this approach was seriously slated by legal commentators,[104] notably because it transforms the ECHR into a convention on European human rights[105] and because it runs counter to the jurisprudence of the Court by limiting the Convention to a pure reciprocity of rights and obligations,[106] it was nevertheless adopted in the UK in the *Al-Skeini* case.[107] In spite of this, a wide application of the Convention might be possible. Some scholars aptly note that the Court 'described [its] jurisdiction as operating in an "essentially" regional context, and "notably" in the contracting States' legal space'.[108] The use of the words 'essentially' and 'notably' may explain why, in ensuing jurisprudence, the Court accepted the applicability of the Convention outside the territory of the implicated States and in areas that were not covered by the Convention. For example, in *Issa*

---

102 *Cyprus v. Turkey* (App no 25781/94) (2001) 35 EHHR 30, para 78; *Issa* (n 93) para 57. However, the Court did not refer to this doctrine in the *Loizidou* case ((1996) (n 76)). *See also* Andreas Laursen, 'NATO, the War over Kosovo, and the ICTY Investigation' (2002) 17 *Am U Intl L Rev* 765; *Peschardt Pedersen* (n 26) 297.

103 'The Convention is a multi-lateral treaty operating, subject to Article 56 of the Convention, in an essentially regional context and notably in the legal space (*espace juridique*) of the Contracting States. The FRY clearly does not fall within this legal space. The Convention was not designed to be applied throughout the world, even in respect of the conduct of Contracting States. Accordingly, the desirability of avoiding a gap or vacuum in human rights' protection has so far been relied on by the Court in favour of establishing jurisdiction only when the territory in question was one that, but for the specific circumstances, would normally be covered by the Convention'. *Bankovic* (n 82) para 80. *See also Council of Europe, Parliamentary Assembly* (n 6) para 11. For a discussion on the European legal space, *see* Malcolm Evans, 'State Responsibility and the European Convention on Human Rights: Role and Realm' in Malgosia Fitzmaurice and Danesh Sarooshi (eds), *Issues of State Responsibility before International Judicial Institutions* (Hart Publishing, Oxford, 2004) 153; Ralph Wilde, 'The 'Legal Space' or 'Espace juridique' of the European Convention on Human Rights: Is it Relevant to Extraterritorial State Action?' (2005) 10 *EHRLR* 115.

104 Matthew Happold, 'Bankovic v. Belgium and the Territorial Scope of the European Convention on Human Rights' (2003) 3 *H R L Rev* 88.

105 *Kavaldjieva* (n 28) 522. *See also Einarsen, Gibney and Roxstrom* (n 94) 93-94. Altiparmak also contends that '[t]he ECHR is not a citizen's rights treaty, but a human rights treaty that requires the protection of human rights of all people that fall within the jurisdiction of contracting states regardless of the nationality of the person'. *Altiparmak* (n 59) 243.

106 *See e.g. Ireland v. United Kingdom* (App no 5310/71) (1978) 2 *EHRR* 25, paras 90-91. For a discussion, *see Orakhelashvili* (n 26) 548-550.

107 *Al-Skeini et al. v. Secretary of State for Defence*, [2007] UKHL 26, para 109.

108 *Leach* (n 63) 2 (Emphasis added) *See also* discussion in *Wilde* (2005) (n 103) 116-117.

v. Turkey the Court accepted the possibility that the ECHR would apply in Iraq.[109] If one follows the current jurisprudence, which in fact reflects that of the HRC in terms of justification, then the ECHR would be applicable in peacekeeping operations. However, if one follows the *Al-Skeini* precedents, States whose contingents are involved in peacekeeping operations outside the territory of the Contracting Parties to the ECHR may not be held responsible for violations of human rights committed by their troops.

In the *Loizidou*[110] and *Cyprus* cases[111] the Court clearly affirmed that the lawfulness or not of the military intervention has no bearing on the fact that a State must respect and protect human rights. The illegality of Turkey's exercise of power did not affect its human rights obligations on the territory of Northern Cyprus.[112] As peacekeeping missions are established by the UN Security Council (and occasionally the UN General Assembly) in pursuance of Chapter VI or VII UN Chapter, they are deemed lawful.[113]

However, in *Bankovic* the Court retreated from its earlier standpoint[114] asserting that these were only exceptional cases[115] and thereby implying that jurisdiction could only be established '[t]hrough the consent, invitation or acquiescence of the Government of that territory [and the intervening state] exercises all or some of the public powers normally to be exercised by that Government'.[116] Applied to peacekeeping operations, this means that *prima facie* the State whose contingents are involved in peacekeeping missions having obtained the consent of the host State are bound to apply human rights law abroad.

However, two problems need to be highlighted. First, should peacekeepers become enmeshed in the conflict and use force in contravention of the mandate, one may ask whether the yardstick for assessing the applicability of the ECHR would be

---

109 'Accordingly, there is sufficient factual basis for holding that, at the relevant time, the victims were within that specific area, it would follow logically that they were within the jurisdiction of Turkey (and not that of Iraq, which is not a Contracting State and clearly does not fall within the legal space (espace juridique) of the Contracting States (*see* the above-cited *Banković* decision, 80)'. *Issa* (n 93) para 74. The Court reasoned that 'Art 1 of the Convention cannot be interpreted so as to allow a State party to perpetrate violations of the Convention on the territory of another State, which it could not perpetrate on its own territory'. para 71.

110 *Loizidou* (1996) (n 76) para 62.

111 *Cyprus* (2001) (n 102) para 71.

112 *Einarsen, Gibney and Roxstrom* (n 94) 89.

113 There seems to be a presumption that the Security Council's actions are *per se* lawful. *See* discussion in Alan Boyle and Christine Chinkin, *The Making of International Law* (Oxford University Press, Oxford, 2007) 230-231.

114 For a critique of this position, *see* Martin Scheinin, 'Extraterritorial Effect of the International Covenant on Civil and Political Rights' in *Coomans and Kamminga* (n 64) 79-80.

115 *Bankovic* (n 82) para 67. As Williams correctly asserts, 'Bankovic is the first case in which extraterritorial jurisdiction ... was held to be 'exceptional''; *Williams* (n 95) 692.

116 *Bankovic* (n 82) para 71.

the mandate (based on the territorial State's consent) or the situation on the ground. Having regard to its jurisprudence that takes a pragmatic approach to legal issues, it is submitted that the Court would not confine its analysis to the mandate but would also examine the situation on the ground.[117] Second, classical peacekeeping operations do not usually entail the 'exercise [of] all or some of the public powers normally to be exercised by [a] Government'.[118] Moreover, even in cases where such public powers are exercised, they are exercised by the UN and not the individual home States. This seems to argue against the applicability of the ECHR to most peacekeeping missions.

A further problematic situation relates to peace-enforcement missions as they do not fall within the categories of missions deployed following the 'invitation' of the affected State(s).[119] In this case it might be argued that as States have ratified the UN Charter they have *generally* consented to the binding effect of Chapter VII resolutions and, hence, consented to the imposition of Chapter VII resolutions against them.[120] Therefore the ECHR would be applicable to such operations. On the other hand, it might also be argued that the affected State has not consented to the specific Security Council resolution, in which case the ECHR would not be applicable. This stance is however more difficult to buttress because it is neither 'possible for states to opt out of binding UNSC resolutions, nor to formulate reservations'.[121]

Indubitably, using the *Bankovic* precedent to gauge the applicability of the ECHR to peacekeeping missions lends credence to the claim that such missions may not bound by human rights provisions enshrined in the said treaty. However, more recently the Court has reversed to its previous jurisprudence, upholding that the 'effective control over an area' exception with regards to the applicability of the Convention does not hinge upon the lawfulness of the State's actions but rather on their context and *de facto* effects.[122]

---

117 For instance, in the *Al-Saadoon* case, the ECHR examined the *de facto* and *de jure* control exercised by the United Kingdom. *Al-Saadoon* (n 57) para 88.

118 *Bankovic* (n 82) para 71.

119 As Malone aptly describes, peacekeeping and peace-enforcement are 'two types of operations [that] were, in fact, fundamentally different, one requiring consent and impartiality, the other requiring international personnel to confront one or several belligerent groups …'. David Malone, 'The Security Council in the Post-Cold War Era: A Study in the Creative Interpretation of the U.N. Charter' (2003) 35 *N Y U J Intl L & Pol'y* 487, 492.

120 Klabbers states that there are three theories (of treaty-analogy, delegation, and legislation) that may help understanding why States are bound by law-making instruments adopted outside constitutionally controlled conditions. Jan Klabbers, *An Introduction to International Institutional Law* (2nd ed. Cambridge University Press, Cambridge, 2009) 184-188.

121 *Boyle and Chinkin* (n 113) 233. Sarooshi adds that the 'UN Security Council does not require the consent of States to exercise its Chapter VII powers'. Dan Sarooshi, *International Organizations and their Exercise of Sovereign Powers* (Oxford University Press, Oxford, 2007) 25.

122 *Issa* (n 93) paras 69 and 71; *El Mahi and Others v. Denmark* (App no 5853/06) ECHR (11 December) 2006.

2.1.2.3. The 'Diplomatic' Exception

A further ground for extra-territorial jurisdiction spelled out by the ECtHR on several occasions relates to situations where 'customary international law and treaty provisions have recognized the extra-territorial exercise of jurisdiction by the relevant state'.[123] Illustrative examples provided by the Court are 'cases involving the activities of its diplomatic or consular agents abroad and on board craft and vessels registered in, or flying the flag of, that state'.[124] Such examples are the reason why this exception to the territorial applicability of the Convention is termed 'diplomatic exception'.

Although it is repeatedly overlooked in legal literature since the focus is on the extension of jurisdiction to territory and persons abroad, it might be of relevance with regards to peacekeeping mission operations. Indeed, reliance on this ground for jurisdiction might be an avenue to avert the non-applicability of the ECHR to peacekeeping. It might be contended that Chapter VII UN Charter contains provisions that recognise the extra-territorial exercise of jurisdiction by States inasmuch as it authorises the Security Council (SC) to take measures deemed necessary, e.g. authorise States to use force abroad which, in turn, can be interpreted as entitling States to exercise jurisdiction abroad. Bearing in mind that '[d]irect State control over its own troops in the context of a collective military operation equates to the exercise of jurisdiction over the territory covering the theatre of operations, and over its resident population',[125] authorisation given to States to use force automatically leads to an authorisation to wield jurisdiction. In case this argument falls short, then the ECHR cannot be applied abroad and the only applicable law in peace-enforcement missions would be IHL.

In sum, it emerges from the ECtHR jurisprudence, that the ECtHR is dealing with situations on a case-by-case basis and is not making *obiter dicta* that are applicable across the board. Unfortunately, the conclusion seems to be that there is no clear-cut position on the issue.

2.1.3. Summary: The Two Situations in which Human Rights Treaties Are Applicable to Peacekeeping Operations

The International Court of Justice (ICJ) has confirmed the view that human rights treaties are applicable abroad. It determined in the Advisory Opinion on *The Wall*,[126] and subsequently in the contentious case *Democratic Republic of Congo v. Uganda*, that 'international human rights instruments are applicable in respect of acts done by a State in the exercise of its jurisdiction outside its own territory, particularly in occupied territory'.[127] The obligation to comply with human rights provisions is only

123 *Bankovic* (n 82) para 73.

124 *Bankovic* (n 82) para 73.

125 Gabriele Porretto and Sylvain Vité, *The Application of International Humanitarian Law and Human Rights Law to International Organisations* (Research Paper Series No. 1, CUDIH, Geneva, 2006) 78.

126 *Legal Consequences on the Construction of a Wall in the Occupied Palestinian Territory* (n 52) paras 107-113.

127 *Armed Activities on the Territory of the Congo* (*Democratic Republic of Congo v. Uganda*),

constrained by the condition that the actions must have been carried out in relation to individuals within the power, effective control or authority of a State. Moreover the applicability of human rights law as encapsulated in treaties does not hinge upon the acquiescence of the territorial State. Also it is not circumscribed to situations of occupations as the ICJ employs the adverb 'particularly', thereby illustrating its statement by reference to a specific situation. As McCorquodale and Simons explain:

> [i]n reaching this conclusion, the ICJ is determining that the obligation of all states (and not only occupying powers) under all international human rights instruments (to which a state is a party) ... are applicable in relation to the acts of a state outside its territory.[128]

Consequently, if it can be proven that a national contingent of a peacekeeping mission is in effective control of an area or a person, then this contingent must observe human rights law.

Thus, States are obliged to apply the provisions of human rights law treaties if their agents, be they armed or police forces, are directly in contact with an individual and are in full control of the person, e.g. detaining the individual. A second common criterion that is well-established in the jurisprudence of many human rights bodies is that the State must apply treaty law whenever it is in effective control of part of territory.[129] As Wilde intelligently summarises: '[e]xtraterritorial jurisdiction subsists when the State exercises control or authority over either territory – what might be termed the spatial basis for jurisdiction – or individuals – what might be termed the personal basis for jurisdiction'.[130] In these two cases, it is clear that States must comply with human rights law (as enshrined in treaties) when their troops are sent to peacekeeping missions.

2.2. *Applicability of Treaty Law to International Organisations*

The applicability of human rights treaties to IOs is an extremely controversial topic since they are unlikely to be a party to them. Indeed most human rights treaties,

Merits [2005] ICJ Rep 116, para 216. The ICJ also specifically explained that the Convention on the Elimination of All Forms of Racial Discrimination is also applicable abroad. *Application of the International Convention on the Elimination of All Forms of Racial Discrimination* (*Georgia v. Russian Federation*) Order (15 October 2008) para 109.

128 Robert McCorquodale and Penelope Simons, 'Responsibility beyond Borders: State Responsibility for Extraterritorial Violations by Corporations of International Human Rights Law' (2007) 70 *MLR* 598, 605.

129 'Working Session III: Beyond International Humanitarian Law: Aspects of the Applicability of International Human Rights Law' in *Faite and Labbé Grenier* (n 27) 19. For a contrary opinion, *see Amnesty International Canada* (n 62) para 332.

130 *Wilde* (2005) (n 103) 115-116.

such as the ICCPR,[131] the ICESCR[132] and the ECHR[133] stipulate that only States can ratify them. As a consequence, IOs cannot be directly bound by them.[134] However, treaties may affect IOs indirectly, because they codify human rights norms and their content may have been subsequently become accepted as part of customary international law which is applicable to IOs.,[135] an issue discussed below.

Owing to the fact that the UN has been responsible for the adoption of countless human rights treaties, one may consider applying these conventions to it. It is claimed that since the UN Charter contains several provisions relating to human rights, they are applicable to UN peacekeeping operations.[136] Indeed, the preamble, Articles 1(3), 13 and 55(c) all speak of human rights. On this basis, some authors insist that the '[a]pplication of human rights standards in peace support operations is part of the UN commitment and is embodied in the UN Charter'[137] and that 'it is clear that UN peace operations should strictly observe human rights as the promotion of human rights is one of the purposes and principles of the UN'.[138] However, as Mégret and Hoffmann comment, this argument is 'without any added juridical *finesse*'.[139] As a literal interpretation of these provisions indicates, the duty to abide by human rights law is imposed upon States rather than upon the UN. The peoples of the UN are 'determined to reaffirm faith in fundamental human rights,'[140] the purpose of the UN is '[t]o achieve international co-operation ... in promoting and encouraging respect for human rights and for fundamental freedoms for all;'[141] and the UN shall promote 'universal respect for, and observance of, human rights and fundamental freedoms for all'. None of these statements obliges the UN to conform to human rights law; rather, it obliges States to do so and the UN merely to promote[142] human

131 *ICCPR* (n 20).

132 International Covenant on Economic, Social and Cultural Rights (adopted 16 December 1966, entered into force 3 January 1976) 993 UNTS 3.

133 *ECHR* (n 22).

134 Frédéric Mégret and Florian Hoffmann, 'The UN as a Human Rights Violator? Some Reflections on the United Nations Changing Human Rights Responsibilities' (2003) 25 *Hum Rts Q* 314, 316.

135 *See* discussion in Javaid Rehman, *International Human Rights Law. A Practical Approach* (Longman, Harlow, 2003) 20.

136 David B Hodgkinson and others, 'Human Rights Training to Law Enforcement Agents: A Key to PSO Success' in *Arnold* (n 3) 311; *Kondoch* (n 7).

137 Ibid. (*Hodgkinson and others*) 313. *See also* more generally Zenon Stavrinides, 'Human Rights Obligations under the United Nations Charter' (1999) 3 *IJHR* 38, 40.

138 *Kondoch* (n 7).

139 *Mégret and Hoffmann* (2003) (n 134) 317.

140 Preamble, UN Charter, 24 October 1945, 1 UNTS XVI.

141 Ibid. (Article 1).

142 Mégret and Hoffmann define 'promotion' and 'encouragement' as 'efforts at raising public awareness as to the right and procedures for asserting and protecting human rights'. *Mégret and Hoffmann* (2003) (n 134) 319.

rights.[143] The UN is manifestly not the addressee of these obligations.[144] Moreover, while the Charter bestows the UN with the power to promote and encourage compliance with human rights norms, it leaves it up to States to ensure the protection of such rights. Nonetheless, as pointed out by several authors, it is difficult to imagine that an organisation whose aim is to promote human rights law and assist States in their endeavours to respect such norms can claim not to be bound by human rights law on the basis that it is not so provided in its founding document.[145] *De lege ferenda*, the UN is bound by human rights law or as Arbour states '[i]f only as a matter of sound policy, I would suggest that the UN should ensure that its own operations and processes subscribe to the same standards of rights protection which are applicable to individual states'.[146] That being said, the issue remains that in terms of positive law the UN is not bound by human rights treaties.

Another way to bind the UN to human rights obligations is to view its founding documents as a constitution, especially if one accepts that a constitution reflects a set of core values and belief system binding upon the institutions it creates.[147] The question arises whether human rights law can be viewed as part of the UN 'constitution', taking into account that the UN Charter is by and large viewed as the core constitutional document.[148] Experts, such as Dupuy, contend that the UN Charter, taken in conjunction with the Universal Declaration of Human Rights (UDHR)[149]

143 '[I]n the Charter, a clear distinction is drawn between the promotion and encouragement of respect for human rights, and the actual protection of these rights. The one is entrusted to the United Nations. The other remains the prerogative of each Member state'. Georg Schwarzenberger, *Power Politics: A Study of World Society* (3rd ed., MacMillan, London, 1964) 462. Some authors even argue that '[t]he U.N. Charter does not create any immediate or binding obligation upon ... its members to protect human rights'. *Bongiorno* (n 13) 633.

144 *Porretto and Vité* (n 125) 47.

145 Robert Kolb, Gabriele Porretto & Sylvain Vité, *L'articulation des règles de droit international humanitaire et de droits de l'homme applicables aux forces internationales et aux administrations civiles internationales transitoires* (CUDIH, Geneva, 2003) 138; Lindsey Cameron, *Accountability of International Organisations Engaged in the Administration of Territory* (Dissertation, CUDIH, Geneva, 2006) 42; *Marshall and Inglis* (n 70) 104.

146 Louise Arbour, *Address at the Opening of the Judicial Year 2008 of the European Court of Human Rights* (25 January 2008) available at: <www.echr.coe.int/NR/rdonlyres/2A9BAFB0-181F-4484-A525-561EFFE08B32/0/Ouverture_Annee_Judiciaire_Louise_Arbour.pdf> (accessed 25 August 2009).

147 For a definition of a constitution, *see* Pierre Marie Dupuy, 'The Constitutional Dimension of the Charter of the United Nations Revisited' (1997) 1 *Max Planck Yb UN L* 1, 3.

148 Bardo Fassbender, 'The Meaning of International Constitutional Law' in Ronald MacDonald and Douglas Johnston (eds), *Towards World Constitutionalism: Issues in the Legal Ordering of the World Community* (Martinus Nijhoff Publishers, Leiden, 2005) 848; Christian Tomuschat (ed), *The United Nations at Age Fifty. A Legal Perspective* (Kluwer Law International, The Hague, 1995) ix.

149 Universal Declaration of Human Rights, *UNGA Res. 217 A* (III) (10 December 1948) UN Doc. A/810.

and the human rights Covenants, are applicable to UN peace operations because these instruments stem from the constitution of the UN.[150] This is based on the premise that the UDHR 'could be considered as an authoritative interpretation of the Charter'.[151] Other authors are more oblique as they view only certain human rights to pertain to the UN constitution. For example, Kadelbach refers to the core elements of the human rights conventions.[152] If, for the sake of the argument, it is agreed that human rights norms are fundamental and that '[t]he most fundamental norms might represent global constitutional law',[153] then it may be claimed that human rights norms, as spelled out in various UN instruments, constitute the basis of a UN constitutional legal system. Kondoch straightforwardly rejects this proposition on the basis that none of the aforementioned instruments 'were conceptualised by the UN or by member States to become together with the UN Charter the constitution of the organisation'.[154] This is certainly a sound position as the UN, albeit a 'supreme type of international organisation having legal personality that is in certain aspects superior to nation states',[155] was not designed to be a supranational IO[156] and the Charter cannot be viewed as a comprehensive constitutional document that codifies the scope and powers of all its bodies.[157]

A further step is to argue that human rights treaties are World Order Treaties, i.e. *traités-lois* which create an objective international legal order that binds all subjects of international law. Moreover, such treaties embody 'collective obligations serving global community interests which transcend the individual interest of the state parties',[158] thereby creating universal legal norms. In particular, De Wet stresses that the 'collective interest nature of [human rights obligations] gives the international community as a whole an interest in their performance and reflects that they amount to more than mere "bundles of bilateral obligations".'[159] This is compounded

150 *Dupuy* (n 147).

151 Comment made by René Cassin, as cited in *Rehman* (n 135) 58.

152 Stefan Kadelbach, 'Jus Cogens, Obligations Erga Omnes and other Rules – The Identification of Fundamental Norms' in Christian Tomuschat and Jean-Marc Thouvenin (eds), *The Fundamental Rules of the International Legal Order: Jus Cogens and Obligations Erga Omnes* (Martinus Nijhoff Publishers, Leiden, 2006) 27.

153 Anne Peters, 'Compensatory Constitutionalism: The Function and Potential of Fundamental International Norms and Structures' (2006) 19 *LJIL* 579, 586.

154 *Kondoch* (n 7).

155 Nigel D White, *Law of International Organisations* (Manchester University Press, Manchester, 1996) 47.

156 For a definition of a supranational international organisation, *see* Henry Schermers, *International Institutional Law* (2nd ed. Martinus Nijhoff Publishers, The Hague, 1980) 29-30.

157 Anne Peters, 'Global Constitutionalism Revisited' (2005) 11 *International Legal Theory* 39, 43-44.

158 Ibid. 51-52.

159 Erika de Wet, 'The Emergence of International and Regional Value Systems as a Manifestation of the Emerging International Constitutional Order' (2006) 19 *LJIL* 611, 617.

by the precept of the universality of human rights emphasised in several human rights treaties such as the ECHR.[160]

A further way to compel the UN to adhere to human rights standards is to do so indirectly by way of its members in a type of 'functional treaty succession by international organizations to the position of their member states',[161] bearing in mind States' legal duty to respect human rights. This theory, derived from the German legal system and known as *Funktionsnachfolge*, albeit in the context of State succession, is an auxiliary construction to ensure that while a solution is being achieved the interests of a particular group of individuals or States are preserved. Applied to IOs (the European Union amongst others),[162] it prescribes that by taking over certain functions from its Member States the UN participates in their obligations under international law. In other words, the UN is substituting its member States in the performance of certain acts and is, consequently, constrained by these standards, as the ICJ stressed in the *Reparation* Advisory Opinion.[163] The basic and correlated tenet is that it would not be acceptable if States would be able to avoid their own duties by claiming that another institution is in charge.[164] Nevertheless, although this theory is not firmly grounded in international law, being neither enshrined in any treaty nor considered as customary law, it remains a possible legal option to bind the UN to human rights treaties.[165] This theory, however, is only applicable where national contingents are engaged in peacekeeping operations.[166] In other words, this theory could only be applied in cases where the State is sending individuals who can be considered as its agents for the purposes of State responsibility.

160 *See* Preamble of the ECHR (n 22).

161 August Reinisch, 'Securing the Accountability of International Organizations' (2001) 7 *Global Governance* 143.

162 Waldemar Hummer, 'Untergang, 'Entkernung' und Funktionsnachfolge Internationaler Organisationen – dargestellt am Beispiel der EGKS und der WEU' in Franz Zehetner (ed), *Festschrift für Hans-Ernst Folz* (Neuer Wissenschaftlicher Verlag, Vienna, 2003) 117-144; Robert Uerpmann, *International Law as an Element of European Constitutional Law: International Supplementary Constitutions* (Jean Monnet Working Paper 9/03, Max Planck Institute for Comparative Public Law and International Law, Heidelberg, 2003).

163 *Reparation for Injuries Suffered in the Service of the United Nations*, Advisory Opinion [1949] ICJ Rep 174.

164 '... the four States, in forming the AOI, did not intend wholly to disappear behind it, but rather to participate in the AOI as "members with liability" ...'. *Westland Helicopters Ltd. v. Arab Organization for Industrialization, United Arab Emirates, Kingdom of Saudi Arabia, State of Qatar, Arab Republic of Egypt and Arab British Helicopter Company*, 5 [1984] 80 *ILR* 600.

165 *Kolb, Porretto and Vité* (n 145) 127. In this case one still needs to remember the above discussion on the extra-territorial applicability of human rights treaties.

166 Indeed, where individuals are contracted by international organisations to carry out specific tasks in peacekeeping missions, it is not possible to maintain that such persons are acting on behalf of their States of nationality and thereby exercising the jurisdiction of these States. *Cameron* (n 145) 39.

A softer method that may 'bind', though only morally, IOs to human rights treaties, is to encourage cooperation between peacekeeping missions and human rights bodies. In this scenario, applicability is primarily reached by enabling supervisory mechanisms to review the activities of peacekeeping missions.[167] Though not legally enforceable, as the UN cannot become a party to these instruments, such a mechanism still allows some 'imposition' of human rights norms upon peacekeeping missions. For instance, the HRC in its comment upon the report submitted by Serbia 'encourage[d] UNMIK, in cooperation with the Provisional Institutions of Self-Government (PISG), to provide, without prejudice to the legal status of Kosovo, a report on the situation of human rights in Kosovo since June 1999'.[168] As Mansson stresses, '[f]or the first time in the history of the UN human rights treaty body system, the UN responded to its own supervisory body on how it has succeeded in ensuring the enjoyment of the universal rights drafted and proclaimed by the UN itself'.[169] Reports and comments were submitted by UNMIK in 2006 and 2008,[170] thereby demonstrating that it took the ICCPR mechanism seriously.[171]

In another case the CoE managed to conclude with UNMIK and NATO agreements 'providing an application *mutatis mutandis* of the conventions to the international organizations concerned, including, whenever possible and appropriate, the aspects of reporting or the ways in which control mechanisms could apply'.[172] The two agreements pertain to the application of the European Convention for the Prevention of Torture and Inhuman or Degrading Treatment or Punishment[173] and the Framework Convention for the Protection of National Minorities.[174] The former clearly spells out that the existence of such a document does not signify that UNMIK is a party to the European Convention for the Prevention of Torture and that it aims at 'promoting technical cooperation ... and facilitating the functions

167 As Parayre states, 'roughly speaking, there are at least two approaches to the notion of "applicability" of human rights treaties, according to whether it concerns the treaty itself or its effective implementation and supervision by an international supervisory mechanism'. *Parayre* (n 27) 43.

168 HRC, 'Concluding Observations of the Human Rights Committee: Serbia' (12 August 2004) UN Doc. CCPR/CO/81/SEMO.

169 Katarina Mansson, 'Book Review: The UN, Human Rights and Post-conflict Situations, Edited by Nigel D. White and Dirk Klaasen' (2006) 17 *EJIL* 1033, 1033.

170 HRC, 'Report Submitted by the United Nations Interim Administration Mission in Kosovo to the Human Rights Committee on the Human Rights Situation in Kosovo since 1999' (13 March 2006) UN Doc. CCPR/C/UNK/1; HRC, 'Comments by the United Nations Interim Administration Mission in Kosovo (UNMIK) on the Concluding Observations of the Human Rights Committee' (CCPR/C/UNK/CO/1) (1 April 2008) UN Doc. CCPR/C/UNK/CO/1/Add.1.

171 It must be noted that the 2008 'Comments' contains 284 paragraphs!

172 *Parayre* (n 27) 47.

173 European Convention for the Prevention of Torture and Inhuman or Degrading Treatment or Punishment (26 November 1987) ETS No. 126.

174 Framework Convention for the Protection of National Minorities (1 February 1995) ETS No. 157.

of the European Committee ...'[175] Comparable wording is used in the latter agreement.[176] Still, this is a first step towards 'binding' the UN to human rights treaties. One of the reasons adduced for UNMIK acceptance is that the reports and recommendations released by both implementing mechanisms are not legally binding.[177] A further step would be to convince IOs to adhere *ad hoc,* in the framework of specific operations, to certain human rights treaties.[178]

Overall, there is a wide range of sound arguments to explain why the UN may be bound by human rights treaties in peacekeeping operations, especially if a broad or de *lege ferenda* interpretation is adopted.

3. Applicability of Other Sources of International Law to Peacekeeping Operations

A second sub-question explored in this part is the customary nature of human rights law and how it binds both States and IOs, thereby establishing obligations for States that have not ratified the major international human rights instruments, and maybe for IOs, which cannot become parties to them, as well. Additionally, other sources of public international law, such as general principles of international law, and the concept of *jus cogens* will be explored.

3.1. Applicability of Customary Law to Peacekeeping Operations

Customary human rights law is comprised of two components that must be conjunctly fulfilled: a pattern of practice or behaviour and the acceptance of such practice/behaviour as a legal obligation.[179] Accordingly, customary human rights law may exist and apply independently of treaty law, even in cases where they cover congruent subject matters and prescribe the same rules.[180]

---

175 Agreement between the United Nations Interim Administration Mission in Kosovo and the Council of Europe on Technical Arrangements Related to the European Convention for the Prevention of Torture and Inhuman or Degrading Treatment or Punishment, available at: <www.cpt.coe.int/documents/scg/2004-08-23-eng.htm> (accessed 18 September 2009) preambular paragraphs.

176 European Commission for Democracy through Law, 'Opinion on Human Rights in Kosovo: Possible Establishment of Review Mechanisms', Opinion No. 280/2004 (11 October 2004) CDL-AD (2004) 033, para 82.

177 Ibid. para 85.

178 *Porretto and Vité* (n 125) 43.

179 *See generally Lotus* case (Merits) PCIJ Rep Series A No 10; Article 38 ICJ Statute, Statute of the International Court of Justice (26 June 1945) 59 Stat. 1055, 1060 (1945). For a discussion on the elements of customary international human rights law, *see* Theodor Meron, *Human Rights and Humanitarian Norms as Customary Law* (Clarendon Press, Oxford, 1989) and Jordan Paust, 'The Complex Nature, Sources and Evidences of Customary Human Rights' (1995) 25 *Ga J Intl & Comp L* 147, 148.

180 *Case Concerning Military and Paramilitary Activities in and against Nicaragua* (*Nicaragua v. USA*) Merits [1986] ICJ Rep 14, para 179.

3.1.1. Applicability of Customary International Law to States and IOs

Undoubtedly States are bound by customary human rights norms, for customary international law is one of the three chief sources of international law.[181] This is of paramount significance considering that many States have not signed and/or ratified relevant human rights treaties.[182] It is widely agreed that States, whose contingents are involved in peacekeeping operations, must observe human rights norms as enshrined in customary international law.[183]

The situation with regards to the applicability of customary law to IOs is more complex. Some legal scholars argue that international customary law is automatically applicable to all subjects of international law, including IOs 'with the capacity to bear rights and obligations at the international level'.[184] The paucity and doubtful legal validity of arguments buttressing this standpoint must however be stressed.[185]

Another set of scholars, on the other hand, contends that only certain norms of customary nature are applicable to IOs. As Klabbers notes, it is difficult to explain 'why an organization would be legally bound (as opposed to morally bound) to respect certain rules'.[186] According to the proponents of this viewpoint, the substance of a customary rule indicates to which international law subjects the rule is addressed.[187] As human rights are meant to place restraints on the exercise of State power towards individuals under their jurisdiction, customary human rights are not *ipso facto* binding upon IOs that are not in direct contact with human beings. In particular, relying on the doctrine of consent, it is argued that customary law emerges as practice between subjects of international law and cannot be imposed on those subjects that did not take part in its formation.[188]

However, a certain number of avenues can be used to elicit support for the view that customary law and, more specifically, customary human rights law is applicable to IOs, i.e. the UN.

First, the UN Charter specifies in Article 1(1) that one of the purposes of the UN is 'to maintain international peace and security ... in conformity with the principles of justice and international law'.[189] Combined with the UN obligation to promote 'universal respect for ... human rights and fundamental freedoms',[190] this suggests

181 Article 38 ICJ Statute (n 179).

182 *Bongiorno* (n 13) 638.

183 *Hodgkinson and others* (n 136) 317. Andrew Clapham, *Human Rights Obligations of Non-State Actors* (Oxford University Press, Oxford, 2006) 109-110.

184 Ibid. (*Clapham*) 109.

185 For example, Clapham refers to a resolution adopted by the Institut de Droit International in 1999 and to various UN training manuals. *Clapham* (n 183) 111.

186 *Klabbers* (2009) (n 120) 284.

187 *See* discussion in Albert Bleckmann, 'Zur Verbindlichkeit des allgemeinen Völkerrechts für internationale Organisationen' (1977) 37 *ZaöVR* 107, 110-113.

188 Ibid. 110.

189 *UN Charter* (n 140).

190 Article 55(b) *UN Charter* (n 140).

that the UN is bound by virtue of its own founding treaty to conform to international human rights standards,[191] which are likely to be enshrined in customary law as the UN cannot become a party to a human rights treaty.

Second, as IOs find their roots in international law,[192] they are required to accept the totality of its norms. As subjects of international law, 'international organizations are bound by any obligations incumbent upon them under general rules of international law'.[193] That being said, this still does not explain what these obligations are and whether they relate to human rights law. Nonetheless, authors such as Porretto and Vité have argued that 'an organization conducting activities relating *ratione materiae* to the sphere of application of customary human rights rules cannot avoid observing them',[194] hitherto combining this theory with that of functionalism.

Third, the same authors submit that when IOs are undertaking tasks that are usually entrusted to States, they are bound by the same rules. In this case 'the organization becomes an addressee of the rights and obligations deriving from international human rights norms'.[195]

Fourth, the theory of *Funktionsnachfolge*, developed earlier in this Chapter, can also be exploited with regards to the applicability of customary law to IOs.[196]

Fifth, and related to the previous argument, it might be contended that these organisations are also bound by rules enshrined in international customary law[197] to the extent that the IO is acting in a field related to its purpose and function and human rights norms are of customary nature.[198] Its legal personality is functional in the sense that it hinges upon its functions and purposes, which are 'specified or implied in its constituent documents and developed in practice'.[199] Since the key functions of the UN are the maintenance of international peace and security and the promotion and protection of human rights, it is submitted that, based on the principle of functional legal personality, the UN is obliged to respect human rights law.[200]

---

191 Jennifer Murray, 'Who Will Police the Peace-builders? The Failure to Establish Accountability for the Participation of United Nations Civilian Police in the Trafficking of Women in Post-conflict Bosnia and Herzegovina' (2003) 34 *Colum Hum Rts L Rev* 475, 519.

192 *Bongiorno* (n 13) 641; Henry Schermers and Niels Blokker, *International Institutional Law: Unity within Diversity* (3rd ed. Kluwer Law International, The Hague, 1995) 983-984.

193 *Interpretation of the Agreement of 25 March 1951 between the WHO and Egypt,* Advisory Opinion [1980] ICJ Rep 73.

194 *Porretto and Vité* (n 125) 46.

195 *Porretto and Vité* (n 125) 40 ff.

196 *Bleckmann* (n 187) 117; 119-120.

197 Chittharanjan Amerasinghe, 'The Law of International Organizations: A Subject which Needs Exploration and Analysis' (2004) 1 *IOLR* 9, 20. *See also* Rebecca Everly, 'Reviewing Governmental Acts of the United Nations in Kosovo' (2007) 8 *German Law Journal* 21-22. With regard to human rights law, *see also Kolb, Porretto and Vité* (n 145) 132ff.

198 *Mégret and Hoffmann* (2003) (n 134) 317; *Murray* (n 191) 518; *Porretto and Vité* (n 125) 46.

199 *Reparation Advisory Opinion* (n 163).

200 *Zwanenburg* (n 16) 234; *Kondoch* (n 7); *Bongiorno* (n 13) 678.

In sum, it appears that IOs, such as the UN, (and, of course, States) are bound by human rights norms of customary nature.

3.1.2. Customary Human Rights Law

That being said, one problem is to pinpoint the human rights norms that are of such nature,[201] the difficulty of which lies in the fact that human rights norms are 'honoured in the breach, not the observance'.[202] Although the UDHR is not legally binding *per se* since it is a UN General Assembly (GA) declaration[203] and its aim was only to set 'a common standard of achievements for all peoples of all nations',[204] the predominant view is that it is, either in whole or in part, of customary nature.[205] There is extensive State practice and *opinio juris* to endorse the position that all rights spelled out in the UDHR[206] are of customary nature. Commentators demonstrate that these rights have been repeated and reinforced[207] in other GA resolutions and have been embraced in various (legally binding) instruments, notably in human rights instruments adopted by regional organisations.[208] They stress the importance of the *opinio juris* element inasmuch as they declare that treaties and GA resolutions reflect the opinion of the international State community regarding human rights. In his separate opinion in the *Namibia* Case, Judge Ammoun declared that the provisions of the UDHR 'can bind States on the basis of custom ... whether because they constituted a codification of customary law ... or because they have acquired the force of custom through a general practice accepted as law ...'.[209]

Accordingly, there are two schools of thought: those who believe 'that the entire corpus of international human rights law or, to be slightly more specific, the substance of the 1948 Universal Declaration of Human Rights, is now to be regarded as

201 *Bongiorno* (n 13) 638-640.

202 Oscar Schachter, *International Law in Theory and Practice* (Martinus Nijhoff, Dordrecht, 1991) 339.

203 *See* Articles 10-14 *UN Charter* (n 140).

204 Cited in Rebecca Wallace, *International Law, Cases and Materials* (3rd ed. Sweet and Maxwell, London, 1997) 65.

205 *See* discussion below.

206 *UDHR* (n 149).

207 As Gunning explains, '[i]t may be difficult for any single resolution or recommendation to create law, but the more often resolutions are reinforced, the greater the likelihood that the resolutions will create the requisite legal expectations and affect other actions of nations. Though the clearest, U.N. General Assembly resolutions are but a single way collective state actions could create custom'. Isabelle R Cunning, 'Modernizing customary international law: The Challenge of Human Rights' (1991) 31 *Va J Intl L* 211, 222-223. *See also* John Humphrey, 'The International Bill of Rights: Scope and Implementation' (1976) 17 *Wm & Mary L Rev* 527.

208 Rhonda Smith, *Textbook on International Human Rights* (3rd ed. Oxford University Press, Oxford, 2007) 37; *Rehman* (n 135) 59.

209 *The Legal Consequences for States of the Continued Presence of South Africa in Namibia*, Advisory Opinion [1971] ICJ Rep 16, Separate Opinion (per Judge Ammoun).

customary law in its entirety;'[210] and those who believe that there is a core of human rights obligations that are of customary nature. In the first category, writers including Humphrey,[211] Sohn,[212] and Nayar[213] have maintained that the UDHR reflects customary law *en bloc*. This is confirmed by national case law, e.g. the *Filartiga*,[214] and *Siderman de Blake*[215] cases. In contrast, Schachter,[216] Meron,[217] Smith,[218] Lillich[219] and Rehman[220] argue that only certain rights have acquired customary status. Among the rights most cited are the prohibition of torture, the prohibition of slavery, summary execution or murder, causing disappearance, prolonged arbitrary detention, genocide,[221] the right to equality before the law and the right to non-discrimination,[222] the prohibition of retroactive penal measures, the principle of *ne bis in idem* and various due process rights.[223]

In contrast, some rights, depending on which court and which jurisdiction adjudicates the matter, might be of customary nature.[224] One of them, of crucial impor-

210 Bruno Simma and Philip Alston, 'The Sources of Human Rights Law: Custom, Jus Cogens, and General Principles' (1988-1989) 12 *Aust YBIL* 82, 84.

211 John Humphrey, 'The Universal Declaration of Human Rights: Its History, Impact and Juridical Character' in Bertrand Ramcharan (ed.), *Human Rights: Thirty Years after the Universal Declaration* (Martinus Nijhoff Publishers, The Hague, 1979) 21, 37.

212 Louis Sohn, 'The Human Rights Law of the Charter' (1977) 12 *Tex Intl L J* 129, 133; Louis Sohn, 'Ideal to Law to Practice: The Universal Declaration Today and Tomorrow' (1999) 11 *Pace Intl L Rev* 71, 76-77.

213 Keladharan Nayar, 'Human Rights: The UN and US Foreign Policy' (1978) 19 *Harv Intl L J* 813, 816-817.

214 Judge Kaufman stated that the prohibition on torture 'has become part of customary international law, as evidenced and defined by the Universal Declaration of Human Rights'. *Filartiga v. Pena-Irala*, 630 F. 2d 876 (2d Cir. 1980), 883.

215 *Siderman de Blake v. Republic of Argentina*, 965 F.2d 699, 719 (9th Cir. 1992).

216 Oscar Schachter, 'International Law in Theory and in Practice: General Course in Public International Law' (1982) 178 *Recueil des Cours de l'Académie de Droit International* 21, 333-342; Oscar Schachter, 'New Custom: Power, *Opinio Juris* and Contrary Practice' in Jerzy Makarczyk (ed.), *Theory of International Law at the Threshold of the 21st Century: Essays in Honour of Krzysztof Skubiszewski* (Kluwer Law International, The Hague, 1996) 531.

217 *Meron* (1989) (n 179).

218 *Smith* (n 208) 36.

219 Richard Lillich, 'Civil Rights' in Theodor Meron (ed.), *Human Rights in International Law: Legal and Policy Issues* (Kluwer Law International, Oxford, 1984) 115, 133; Richard Lillich, 'The Growing Importance of Customary International Human Rights Law' (1995-1996) 35 *Ga J Intl & Comp* L 1.

220 *Rehman* (n 135) 59-60.

221 Andrew Cunningham, 'The European Convention on Human Rights, Customary International Law and the Constitution' (1994) 43 *ICLQ* 537, 544; *Bongiorno* (n 13) 639.

222 *Lillich* (1984) (n 219) 133.

223 *Meron* (1989) (n 179) 96-97, 134.

224 *See e.g.* the right to education, the right to privacy and the right to temporary asylum. *Cunningham* (n 221) 546.

tance in the context of recent peacebuilding missions, is the right to freely dispose of one's property. For instance, in Kosovo, three major problems arose: returning individuals expressed their wish to use their property again, there was confusion regarding occupancy and ownership rights and, often, there were multiple property claims.[225] The existence of a customary right to property in all instances and access to one's property is difficult to ascertain. In particular, on the domestic level, such a right has been denied in US courts. While a State may not expropriate a foreign national's property,[226] it may well do this to the property of its own nationals.[227] This disparity in jurisprudence tends to show that the law is uncertain and this, in turn, suggests that a general right to property may not have yet attained customary status. Thus, it is rather unclear which rules relating to the right to property apply in peacekeeping operations. For example, in the European regional context:

> UNMIK restrictions on property sales in the so-called special zones ... proved highly controversial both for the Kosovo Serbs sellers and the Kosovo Albanian potential buyers alike. The Ombudsperson received multiple complaints from buyers and sellers about the impact on their property rights.[228]

In reaction the Ombudsperson released a report criticising the attitude of UNMIK.[229] Other institutions, such as the HRC,[230] have also expressed their concern that the right to property might have been encroached upon. Yet none of the reports/comments provide any guidance as to which specific element of the right to property was violated.

Other rights that are problematic in certain peacekeeping missions relate to detention. For example, in the context of the ISAF operation in Afghanistan, Canadian forces could detain individuals in pursuance of Theatre Standing Order 312A[231] and 'have the sole discretion to determine whether a detainee "shall be retained in custody, transferred to [the Afghan National Security Forces] or released".'[232] The criteria applied to make such a decision are *prima facie* unclear but the Federal Court of Canada indicated that the rules to be applied in this context are chiefly those of

225 Leopold von Carlowitz, 'Crossing the Boundary from the International to the Domestic Legal Realm: UNMIK Lawmaking and Property Rights in Kosovo' (2004) 10 *Global Governance* 307, 323.

226 *Siderman de Blake* (n 215). *See generally Brownlie* (n 85) 497-527.

227 '[T]he taking by a state of its national's property does not contravene the international law of minimum human rights'. *De Sanchez v. Banco Central de Nicaragua*, 770 F.2d 1385, 1397 (5th Cir. 1985).

228 *Human Rights Watch* (n 71) 14.

229 Ombudsperson Institution in Kosovo, *Special Report No. 5 on Certain Aspects of UNMIK Regulation No. 2001/17 on the Registration of Contracts for the Sale of Real Property in Specific Geographical Areas of Kosovo* (29 October 2001).

230 HRC, 'Concluding Comment, UNMIK' (14 August 2006) UN Doc. CCPR/C/UNK/1, para 18.

231 *Amnesty International Canada* (n 62) para 59.

232 Ibid. para 63.

IHL.[233] In other words, the guarantees offered by human rights law are not available, despite the fact that the right to appeal against one's detention is deemed to be of customary nature.[234] KFOR detained suspects on the basis of military decisions which could not be independently reviewed.[235] Moreover, it is argued that the right to an effective remedy, also considered to be of customary nature,[236] is generally applicable to IOs.[237] Indeed, the ICJ has acknowledged, albeit in a discrete context, that the right to a remedy is binding upon the UN.[238] In spite of that, this right does not appear to be granted to detainees in the hands of peacekeepers. As both rights, the right to a remedy and to appeal against one's detention are deemed to be customary, such detainees should be allowed to challenge their detention in an appropriate forum since these rights are applicable to those involved in peacekeeping operations.

To conclude, certain human rights (those which can be proven to be of customary nature) are applicable to peacekeeping operations.

3.2. Applicability of General Principles of International Law to Peacekeeping Operations

Another source that is apposite in examining the applicability of human rights norms in peacekeeping operations is the general principles of law.[239] Although often viewed as subsidiary to treaty and custom, they should not be easily dispelled, for they provide general legal guidance. While disputes persist as to the exact content of these principles, it is widely conceded that they are part and parcel of international law and thereby binding upon all subjects of international law. As Bongiorno stresses, '[o]nce general principles are identified, they can be strong contenders for international law status'.[240]

Usually, general principles of international law are only relied upon when courts wish to prevent a *non liquet* situation:[241] they are drawn upon to fill in gaps in the law.

233 Ibid. para 162.

234 The customary nature of the prohibition against arbitrary detention was stated in the *Fernandez v. Wilkinson* case (505 F. Supp. 787, 798).

235 *European Commission for Democracy through Law* (n 176) para 51. The Human Rights Committee has also expressed its concern that detention carried out by KFOR troops cannot be reviewed by an independent judicial body, which constitutes a breach of the ICCPR. HRC, '*Concluding Comment, UNMIK*' (n 230) para 17.

236 *See e.g. de Wet* (n 159) 616; Dinah Shelton, *Remedies in International Human Rights Law* (Oxford University Press, Oxford, 1999) 182.

237 Karel Wellens, 'Fragmentation of International Law and Establishing an Accountability Regime for International Organizations: The Role of the Judiciary in Closing the Gap' (2004) 25 *Mich J Intl L* 1159, 1162.

238 *Effects of Awards of Compensation Made by the United Nations Administrative Tribunal*, Advisory Opinion [1954] ICJ Rep 47.

239 *Article 38 ICJ Statute* (n 179).

240 *Bongiorno* (n 13) 639-640.

241 *Boyle and Chinkin* (n 113) 285-286; Hugh Thirlway, 'The Sources of International Law' in Malcolm Evans (ed.), *International Law* (2nd ed. Oxford University Press, Oxford, 2006) 115, 127.

General principles of international law are either derived from natural law or find their origins in national legal systems. Yet, it is also submitted that often judges use the expression 'general principles of international law' to express 'values that international law seeks to promote and protect',[242] thereby placing the promotion of human dignity at the centre of international law.[243]

As the ICJ recognised in the *Corfu Channel* case that 'elementary considerations of humanity' are included in the category of 'general and well-recognised principles',[244] it is clear that peacekeeping troops cannot act in contravention of these basic principles.[245] Moreover, if one maintains that 'general principles of international law form the foundation of the international legal order',[246] then surely certain human rights norms are to be viewed as general principles of international law. This opinion is buttressed by the dissenting opinion of Judge Tanaka in the 1966 *South West Africa* judgment where he declared that '[a]s an interpretation of Article 38, paragraph 1(c), … the concept of human rights and of their protection is included in the general principles mentioned in that Article'.[247]

Although it seems straightforward to declare that human rights as general principles of international law are applicable to peacekeeping operations, the problem as to the exact content of these principles remain. A glaring example of the intricacy of identifying the content of such principles is the meaning of 'elementary considerations of humanity'. Rehman avers that '[m]any principles, particularly those in the criminal justice system (e.g. presumption of innocence and right to fair trial), can be identified as general principles of law'.[248] But what does, for instance, the right to a fair trial as understood as a general principle of law entail? One author, Oswald, posits that in relation to the treatment of detainees by peacekeepers the following general principles of law should be complied with: lawfulness, dignity and humanity, necessity and reasonableness, and accountability.[249] All these principles are derived from various human rights and international humanitarian law treaties and instruments and UN reports.

Another view is to accept that the UDHR contains general principles of law pertaining to human rights. For example, Rodley interprets the ICJ jurisprudence in the *Hostages Case (US v. Iran)*[250] as supporting the view that the UDHR propounds

242 *Legality of the Threat or Use of Nuclear Weapons*, Advisory Opinion [1996] ICJ Rep 226, Dissenting Opinion of Judge Higgins, para 41.

243 *Boyle and Chinkin* (n 113) 289. For Lillich and Meron, general principles are but a necessary passage of human rights into customary law. Richard Lillich, 'The Growing Importance of Customary International Human Rights Law' (1995-1996) 35 *Ga J Intl & Comp L* 1, 16. *Meron* (1989) (n 179) 88. *See also* discussion in Nina Jørgensen, *The Responsibility of States for International Crimes* (Oxford University Press, Oxford, 2005) 129.

244 *Corfu Channel* Case (*United Kingdom v. Albania*), Merits [1949] ICJ Rep 4.

245 *Kondoch* (n 7).

246 *Zwanenburg* (n 16) 235.

247 *South West Africa Cases*, Second Phase [1966] ICJ Rep 4.

248 *Rehman* (n 135) 21.

249 *Oswald* (2008) (n 3) 206-208.

250 'Wrongfully to deprive human beings of their freedom and to subject them to physical

fundamental principles recognised by general international law.[251] More particularly, Haksar depicts the UDHR as the 'conscience of the world - a synthesis, a profession of faith, a common philosophy of human rights - and ipso facto a part of general international law'.[252] In this context, law, understood as rules, principles and justice, is viewed in terms of ideas that might be remote from reality.[253] If such a view is espoused, it may be argued that States and IOs alike are compelled to abide by the provisions set forth in the UDHR since they reflect general principles of international law.[254] Accordingly, peacekeepers must ensure that they act in conformity with the UDHR.

Nonetheless, recourse to the general principles of international law as a source of obligations for peacekeeping missions appears unsuitable due to their vague formulation. Still, unquestionably, they are helpful as general guidelines or 'benchmark[s] against which law and process may be measured'[255] but are of very little avail when it comes to describing the exact content of the rule.

3.3. Applicability of Jus Cogens *Norms to Peacekeeping Operations*

The question as to which rules are unmistakably applicable under any circumstances is answered by reference to *jus cogens*.[256] *Jus cogens* norms embody values which are deemed to prevail over others because they represent a shared hope, demand, and expectation[257] and are viewed as 'the irreducible minimum of public international law'.[258] They are superior rules of international law which assist in solving conflicts

constraint in conditions of hardship is in itself manifestly incompatible with the principles of the Charter of the United Nations, as well as with the fundamental principles enumerated in the Universal Declaration of Human Rights'. *Case Concerning United States Diplomatic and Consular Staff in Tehran* (*US v. Iran*) Merits [1980] ICJ Rep 3, para 91.

251 Nigel Rodley, 'Human Rights and Humanitarian Intervention: The Case Law of the World Court' (1989) 38 *ICLQ* 321, 326.

252 Urmila Haksar, *Minority Protection and the International Bill of Rights* (Allied, Bombay, 1974) 36.

253 Martti Koskenniemi, 'Hierarchy in International Law: A Sketch' (1997) 8 *EJIL* 566, 578.

254 *Zwanenburg* (n 16) 235.

255 *Oswald* (2008) (n 3) 206.

256 Article 53 of the Vienna Convention on the Law of Treaties declares that *jus cogens* norms are norms 'recognized by the international community of states as a whole from which no derogation is permitted'. Vienna Convention on the Law of Treaties (1969) 8 *ILM* 679. The principle of *jus cogens* is also accepted in the 1986 Vienna Convention on the Law of Treaties between States and International Organizations or between International Organizations (1986) 25 *ILM* 543.

257 *Paust* (n 179) 155.

258 *Zwanenburg* (n 16) 236 citing Eric Suy, *Papers and Proceedings of the Lagonissi Conference* 9 (1967). The doctrine of *jus cogens* 'thus incorporates notions of universality and superiority into international law'. Hillary Charlesworth and Christine Chinkin, 'The Gender of Jus Cogens' (1993) 15 *Hum Rts Q* 63, 66.

between different international law norms.[259] Neither the UN nor States may derogate from them[260] because, as the ICJ has stressed, such norms constitute 'intransgressible principles of international customary law'[261] and they rank above UN acts privileged by Article 103 UN Charter.[262] In contrast to customary international law, norms constituting *jus cogens* transcend consent[263] and are thus applicable to all subjects of international law irrespective of their willingness to be bound by them.

While this seems to be straightforward in principle, it is not in practice for, as with customary norms, there is much wrangling as to which norms are of *jus cogens* nature.[264] 'There is still no generally acceptable definition'[265] with regards to the content although legal pundits claim that all *jus cogens* norms must at least be of customary nature[266] and/or find their roots in the UN Charter.[267]

In this vein, there is a need to list those rights that may be of *jus cogens* character. Among the least contentious examples are the prohibition of genocide,[268] the principle of racial non-discrimination, the rules prohibiting trade in slaves, and piracy.[269] Other authors and courts add the prohibition on torture,[270] the right to life, the right

---

259 Ulf Linderfalk, 'The Effect of Jus Cogens Norms: Whoever Opened Pandora's Box, Did You Ever Think about the Consequences?' (2007) 18 *EJIL* 853, 854.

260 *Yassin Abdullah Kadi v. Council of the European Union and Commission of the European Communities*, Case T-315/01 (21 September 2005) para 231. *See also Zwanenburg* (n 16) 236.

261 *The Legality of the Threat or Use of Nuclear Weapons* (n 242) para 79. *See also* Mark Janis, 'The Nature of Jus Cogens' (1988) 3 *Conn J Intl L* 359.

262 *Application of the Convention on the Prevention and Punishment of the Crime of Genocide (Bosnia and Herzegovina v. Serbia and Montenegro)* [1993] ICJ Rep 4, Separate Opinion of Lauterpacht, para 100; Sebastian Recker, 'European Court of Justice Secures Fundamental Rights from UN Security Council Resolutions' (2009) 1 *Göttingen Journal of International Law* 159, 165.

263 *Siderman de Blake* (n 215).

264 Jean-Francois Quéguiner, 'The Principle of Distinction: Beyond an Obligation of Customary International Humanitarian Law' in Howard M Hensel (ed), *The Legitimate Use of Military Force. The Just War Tradition and the Customary Law of Armed Conflict* (Ashgate, Aldershot, 2008) 161, 170.

265 *Linderfalk* (n 259) 854. *See also* Paul Tavernier, 'L'identification des règles fondamentales, Un problème résolu?' in *Tomuschat and Thouvenin* (n 152) 1, 1-2; Anthony Aust, *Modern Treaty Law and Practice* (Cambridge University Press, Cambridge, 2000) 257.

266 *Rehman* (n 135) 23.

267 '[F]rom a substantial point of view, it seems possible to pretend that the Charter constitutes the constitutional "Law of Nations" in the sense that it is the ethical and legal *matrix* for every rule able to be qualified as peremptory'. *Dupuy* (n 147) 11. More particularly, Onuf tends to argue that Chapter I of the UN Charter contains peremptory norms. Nicholas Onuf, 'The Constitution of International Society' (1994) 5 *EJIL* 1, 16-17.

268 The prohibition of genocide is a well-recognised example of a peremptory norm, yet it is unlikely that it will ever find application in the context of peacekeeping operations.

269 *See de Wet* (n 159) 616; *Dupuy* (n 147) 10.

270 *United States v. Matta-Ballesteros*, 71 F.3d 754, 764, n.5 (9th cir. 1995).

to liberty and security of the person, the right to equality, the right to a fair trial, the presumption of innocence and the prohibition of retroactive criminal law.[271] The American Restatement lists genocide, slavery or the slave trade, murder or causing the disappearance of individuals, torture or other cruel, inhuman, or degrading treatment or punishment, prolonged arbitrary detention, systematic racial discrimination, and a consistent pattern of gross violations of internationally recognised human rights[272] while the list generated by the HRC in its General Comment No. 24 On Reservations incorporates even more rights.[273] McDougal goes a step further inasmuch as he posits that the UDHR has become 'established customary international law, having the attributes of *jus cogens* and constituting the heart of a global bill of rights'.[274] Accordingly, it is submitted that, at least, fundamental human rights are encompassed in the *jus cogens* notion.[275]

Other rights, such as the right to property and the right of access to a court, that are of relevance in the context of peacekeeping operations, are not generally viewed as having the status of *jus cogens*.[276] For example, although the right to property is enshrined in Article 17 of the UDHR, it does not figure in the ICCPR or the ICESCR.[277] It is doubtful that it constitutes a *jus cogens* norm, especially since its customary nature is already questioned and it is admitted that *jus cogens* norms are customary norms *per se*. Yet the Court of First Instance of the European Union (CFI) has recognised that the prohibition of *arbitrary* deprivation of property is a norm of *jus cogens*.[278] The CFI has also maintained that the right of access to a court is *jus cogens*, though it is not absolute; limitations to such a right are encompassed in the way it is guaranteed under *jus cogens*.[279] If one accepts the CFI jurisprudence)

---

271 *Rehman* (n 135) 23; 61.

272 Restatement (Third) of the Foreign relations law of the United States, 1987, Section 702(a)-(g).

273 HRC, 'General Comment No. 24 (52)' (4 November 1994) UN Doc. CCPR/C/21/Rev.-1/Add.6, para 8. It must be noted that Clapham believes that the rights identified by the HRC are binding upon the United Nations. *Clapham* (n 183) 124.

274 Myres McDougal, Harold Lasswell and Lung-Chu Chen, *Human Rights and World Public Order* (Yale University Press, New Haven, 1980) 274.

275 As Jørgensen explains, '[i]n theory all basic values of the international legal order give rise to rules of *jus cogens*' and these include many fundamental human rights. *Jørgensen* (n 243) 91.

276 In contrast and with regards to the right to access to courts, *see e.g.* Christian Dominicé, '*Morgan* v. *World Bank* (Ten Years Later)' in Sabine Schlemmer-Schulte and Ko-Yung Tung (eds), *Liber Amicorum Ibrahim F.I. Shihata: International Finance and Development Law* (Kluwer Law International, The Hague, 2001) 155, 166.

277 *ICESCR* (n 132).

278 *Kadi* (n 260) para 242.

279 *Kadi* (n 260) paras 287-288. It must however be noted that this decision was overruled by the European Court of Justice in 2008. The European Court of Human Rights also considers that the right of access to a court is not absolute and may be subject to limitations. Yet, it does not go as far as to say that it is a right of *jus cogens* nature. *See e.g. Al-Adsani v. United Kingdom* (App no 35763/97) ECHR (21 November 2001), para 53.

and applies it to peacekeeping missions, then those involved in such missions cannot arbitrarily deprive an individual of his/her property and must ensure that he/she has access to a court, barring some exceptions.

Overall, in cases where a specific human right is of *jus cogens* nature and its content clear, then incontrovertibly IOs and States must abide by this norm when involved in peacekeeping operations.

4. Applicability of Specific Instruments Relating to Peacekeeping Operations

Besides general public international law norms applicable to both States and IOs, a further source of human rights obligations exists, namely various legal institutional instruments adopted by the UN itself. While the applicability of IHL to peacekeeping operations is acknowledged to a certain extent by the UN[280] there is no equivalent instrument affirming the UN's adherence to human rights standards in peacekeeping operations.[281] Rather, a plethora of internal instruments regulate peacekeeping missions, some of them have beenstandardised over the years while others have a more *ad hoc* character.[282]

4.1. Mandates of Peacekeeping Missions

First and foremost, to enquire whether human rights law is applicable in peacekeeping missions, its mandate, as stipulated in the 'enabling resolution', must be investigated. As Bothe rightly points out, '[t]he mandate of a peace operation is the source of its powers and at the same time the limitation of its powers'.[283] As each mandate is different, attention must be paid to the exact wording used, as there is scope for infinite variations in terms of powers and competences.

The assumption that UN power is 'good' power[284] may be at the root of the problem, for seemingly the UN does not deem it necessary to state expressly that

280 Secretary-General's Bulletin: 'Observance by United Nations Forces of International Humanitarian Law' (6 August 1999) UN Doc. ST/SGB/1999/13. *See* Chapter 3 in the book.

281 *Faite and Labbé Grenier* (n 27) 19.

282 Some authors argue that owing to the variety of peacekeeping missions, universal standards with regards to human rights obligations of UN missions cannot be formulated. *See e.g.* Robert O Weiner and Fionnuala Ni Aolain, 'Beyond the Laws of War: Peacekeeping in Search of a Legal Framework' (1996) 27 *Colum Hum Rts L Rev* 293, 303.

283 Michael Bothe, 'Syndicate Remarks' in Jessica Howard and Bruce Oswald (eds), *The Rule of Law on Peace Operations. A 'Challenges of Peace Operations' Project Conference* (Asia-Pacific Centre for Military Law, 11-13 November 2002) 265.

284 More generally, based on the functionalist theory, it is often assumed that international organisations can do no wrong. Jan Klabbers, 'Kadi Justice at the Security Council?' (2007) 4 *IOLR* 1, 4.

it is bound by human rights law norms[285] and to provide review mechanisms.[286] The mandates conferred by the SC often fail to identify the applicable rules. And when such mandates do provide such guidance, they lack clarity in the sense that they, e.g. 'may declare the right to detain without prescribing any further rules'.[287] In contrast, it is clear from the mandate of UNMIK that it is required to respect human rights.[288]

A further problem to be contemplated is whether the constitutive instruments of peacekeeping missions constitute binding obligations or merely define the internal rules[289] applicable to the organisation. This question cannot be easily solved; the Commentary to Draft Article 3 on the Responsibility of International Organisations reveals that 'the internal law of an international organization cannot be sharply differentiated from international law'.[290] While it is largely accepted that Security Council resolutions belong to the realm of international law, such an assertion cannot be made with regard to other instruments such as those produced by the Secretary-General.[291]

When a mandate (established by the Security Council) deliberately stipulates that a peacekeeping mission is bound by human rights law, then those entrusted with the task of carrying out the mission are bound by human rights law. If, however, reference to human rights law is made in another instrument, it seems less plain that those involved in the peacekeeping mission are bound by human rights norms.

4.2. Administration of Territory: Special Rules?

It is submitted that:

> peace operations in which territory is directly administered by an international organization must be distinguished from those in which an international organization may play a considerable role in advising and supporting local authorities, but has no powers to directly promulgate and/or apply law.[292]

285 Guglielmo Verdirame, 'Compliance with Human Rights in UN Operations' (2002) 2 *HRL Rev* 265, 280-281.

286 *See European Commission for Democracy through Law* (n 176) paras 92-100.

287 *Faite and Labbé Grenier* (n 27) 8.

288 *See* discussion below.

289 As Zwanenburg elucidates, '[t]he internal law of the UN is the law made by the organization or its founders, the subject of which is in the first place the UN itself. However internal law may also have effects outside the UN'. *Zwanenburg* (n 16) 232.

290 ILC, 'Report of the International Law Commission on the Work of its 57th Session' (5 May – 6 June and 7 July – 8 August 2003) UN Doc. A/58/10, Commentary to Draft Article 3, para 9.

291 *Cameron* (n 145) 22.

292 Ibid. 14.

This distinction is linked to the fact that in the former case the UN is able to create and enforce law and thus directly affect the life of individuals whose human rights must be protected.[293]

In this light, one would expect Security Council mandates to specify that international administrations are bound by human rights law. It is thus comforting to see that the Security Council indicated that one of the tasks entrusted to the civil administrations in Kosovo was to protect and promote human rights.[294] As the Ombudsperson in Kosovo correctly noted: 'Resolution 1244 created UNMIK as a surrogate State, with all the ensuing obligations, including affirmative obligations to secure the human rights to everyone within UNMIK jurisdiction'. As a result, Cameron argues that 'the obligation to protect human rights means that it would be a direct contravention of the mandate to violate or fail to respect them in the course of fulfilling other tasks in the mandate'.[295] Yet it is submitted that, in fact, the act would be in violation of the mandate that refers to the protection of human rights rather than human rights law directly as there is reference to the exact source of the obligation to protect human rights law in the mandate.[296] In contrast, UNSC Resolution 1272 that established the UN mission in East Timor does not explicitly subject the UN administration to human rights standards.[297]

Another sore point concerns the endeavours of both UN administrations, in East Timor and Kosovo, to oblige those holding public office to abide by human rights standards. Even though these administrations have issued regulations listing a series of international (and European) instruments binding upon UN personnel,[298] such regulations do not affect the UN *per se* but rather its personnel.[299] With regards to Kosovo, Regulation 1999/24 does not expressly require that instruments emanating from the international administration adhere to human rights standards; neither does the use of the words 'shall observe' seems to lend support to the direct applica-

293 This is also supported by the constitutionalism theory applied to international organisations. As Klabbers explains, '[c]onstitutionalism may help explain why the UN, when administering East Timor or Kosovo, should behave well'. *Klabbers* (2007) (n 120) 6.

294 *UNSC Res. 1244* (10 June 1999).

295 *Cameron* (n 145) 26.

296 For example, the Special Chamber of the Kosovo Supreme Court on Kosovo Trust Agency Related Matters refused to apply a provision of a Regulation issued by the international administration on the basis that it did not comport with human rights standards as stipulated in UNMIK Regulation 1999/24 and not as stipulated in a specific human rights treaty. *See Everly* (n 197) 30.

297 *UNSC Res. 1272* (25 October 1999).

298 Regulation No. 1999/1 On the Authority of the Transitional Administration in East Timor (27 November 1999) UN Doc. UNTAET/REG/1999/1; Regulation No. 1999/1 On the Authority of the Interim Administration in Kosovo (25 July 1999) UN Doc. UNMIK/REG/1; Regulation No. 1999/24 On the Law Applicable in Kosovo (12 December 1999) UN Doc. UNMIK/REG/1999/24, para 1.3.

299 Marcus Brand, 'Institution-building and Human Rights Protection in Kosovo in the Light of UNMIK Legislation' (2001) 70 *Nord J Intl L* 461, 475-476.

bility of human rights law in Kosovo.[300] In contrast, Section 3 of the UNTAET (UN Transitional Administration in East Timor) Regulation No. 1999/1 provides that the Indonesian penal and civil codes remain applicable subject to their compatibility with human rights instruments. As a result 'although UNTAET did not accede to the international human rights treaties or become subject to their monitoring mechanisms, the principles that they contain became part of the law in East Timor'.[301]

Notwithstanding, a further UNMIK regulation appears to be more appropriate, for it obliges the Provisional Institutions of Self-Government (PISG) and their officials 'to promote and fully respect the rule of law, human rights and freedoms, democratic principles and reconciliation' and it indicates the human rights instruments that require compliance.[302] Still, this leaves open the question of the applicability of human rights norms to the activities of the UN administration in Kosovo itself.[303] Moreover, these regulations are interpreted by the international administration[304] and other institutions,[305] rather than by the bodies that are specifically designed to interpret these human rights norms.

It is true that under certain circumstances the UN appears to act like a State. Although the UN is never fully in charge of a certain territory, population and administration/government,[306] it has on numerous occasions, especially in failed States, States coming into being or in entities with a seemingly indefinite status, agreed to fill the vacuum in order to replace a non-existent government.[307] In doing so, the UN is recreating State structures and, thereby, mimicking traditional forms of gov-

300 Ibid. 463-464.

301 *Bongiorno* (n 13) 660.

302 Article 3.3 stipulates that '[t]he provisions on rights and freedoms set forth in these instruments shall be directly applicable in Kosovo as part of this Constitutional Framework'. On a Constitutional Framework for Provisional Self-Government in Kosovo (14 December 2001) UNMIK Regulation 2001/9. This position is stressed in the Comments issued by the HRC. HRC, '*Concluding Comment, UNMIK*' (n 230) para 4.

303 *Marshall and Inglis* (n 70) 102.

304 *See* discussion in *Everly* (n 197) 23.

305 Interestingly the Special Chamber of the Kosovo Supreme Court on Kosovo Trust Agency Related Matters refused to apply a provision of a Regulation issued by the international administration on the basis that it did not comport with human rights standards as stipulated in UNMIK Regulation 1999/24. *See Everly* (n 197) 30.

306 *Mégret and Hoffmann* (2003) (n 134) 325.

307 The UN only 'assumed the role of caretaker of a transition … whereas in Kosovo and East Timor it more closely resembles a midwife to new states'. Michele Griffin and Bruce Jones, 'Building Peace through Transitional Authority: New Directions, Major Challenges' (2000) 7 *Intl Peacekeeping* 82.

ernmental power.[308] In some cases, such as East Timor[309] and Kosovo,[310] the Security Council, by way of a binding resolution under Chapter VII, granted, although not explicitly, some bodies of the UN the powers to 'reign' over a certain territory and population,[311] as a result of which they held legislative, executive and judicial powers.[312] For example, the UNTAET was given 'the overall responsibility for the administration of East Timor', which meant that it would 'exercise all legislative and executive authority, including the administration of justice'.[313] As Mégret and Hoffmann avow, it is 'a rather convoluted way of saying that it was sovereign'.[314]

---

308 In reality, the UN is endowed with all State attributes and is effectively acting as a sovereign power. Jarat Chopra, 'The UN's Kingdom of East Timor' (2000) 42 *Survival* 29; *Griffin and Jones* (n 307) 77. It must however be stressed that all UNSC resolutions pertaining to territories administered by the United Nations underlined the sovereignty of the State, e.g. of the Former Republic of Yugoslavia in the case of Kosovo. *See* for example the preamble of Resolution 1244 (1999) which 'Reaffirm[s] the commitment of all Member States to the sovereignty and territorial integrity of the Federal Republic of Yugoslavia and the other states of the region ...'. *UNSC Res. 1244* (10 June 1999).

309 The United Nations Transitional Administration in East Timor (UNTAET) was given 'the overall responsibility for the administration of East Timor' which meant that it would 'exercise all legislative and executive authority, including the administration of justice'. *UNSC Res. 1272* (25 October 1999) UN Doc. S/RES/1272. UNTAET mandate was conceived following the interpretation and specification of *Resolution 1244* (1999) concerning UNMIK's mandate. *UNSC Res. 1244* (n 294).

310 UNMIK is perceived as the administrator and government of Kosovo. John Williamson, 'Establishing the Rule of Law in Post-War Iraq: Rebuilding the Justice System' (2004) 33 *Ga J Intl & Comp L* 229. See also Report of the Secretary-General, 'United Nations Interim Administration Mission in Kosovo' (12 July 1999) UN Doc. S/1999/779, para 35: 'The Security Council, in its resolution 1244 (1999), has vested in the interim civil administration authority over the territory and people of Kosovo. All legislative and executive powers, including the administration of the judiciary, will, therefore, be vested in UNMIK'.; Ombudsperson Institution in Kosovo, 'Special Report No. 1 on the Compatibility with Recognized International Standards' (26 April 2001) para 23: '... in Kosovo, where the interim civilian administration (United Nations Mission in Kosovo – UNMIK) in fact acts as a surrogate state'. (emphasis added); and *Human Rights Watch* (n 71) 8.

311 Simon Chesterman, 'Virtual Trusteeship' in David Malone (ed), *The UN Security Council. From the Cold War to the 21st Century* (Lynne Rienner, London, 2004) 222.

312 Although the UNSC endowed the Coalition Provisional Authority in Iraq with a mandate quasi equivalent to that attributed to the UNTAET and UNMIK missions, the CPA cannot be considered as a body of the United Nations and cannot, hence, be the subject of the discussion on whether UN administrations act alike governments. *UNSC Res. 1483* (22 May 2003) UN Doc. S/RES/1483, paras 4 and 8.

313 *UNSC Res. 1272* (n 297).

314 *Mégret and Hoffmann* (2003) (n 134) 329. So, Chinkin explains that the UN was endowed in East Timor 'with a broader competence over a territory than ever before bestowed upon an international body'. Christine Chinkin, 'East Timor: A Failure of Decolonisation' (1999) 20 Aus *YBIL* 50.

It is submitted that, even when the mandates of international administrations do not expressly refer to human rights obligations, these institutions are bound by virtue of their State-like status.[315] According to Eagleton, States' obligations and responsibility are based on their capacity to control individuals within their territory.[316] Mégret and Hoffmann emphasise that '[i]t is that capacity for control that simultaneously creates a potential for, and a duty to avoid, human rights abuse'.[317] Along these lines, it is argued that, since the UN is able to control a certain population residing in a certain portion of territory, it acts like a quasi-State and, thus, must comply with relevant rules. As the Kosovo Ombudsperson affirmed, as a surrogate State the international administration had to abide by 'all ensuing obligations, including affirmative obligations to secure human rights to every one within UNMIK jurisdiction'.[318] In other words the UN must adhere to human rights law when administering territories. Such a method can however assuredly only be employed on an *ad hoc* basis after carefully reviewing the factual and legal elements of such operations.

4.3. Codes of Conduct, Rules of Engagement, SOFAs

Other sources of law regarding the applicability of human rights law to peacekeeping operations are the various documents issued to military and civilian police personnel involved in such missions. Most do not mention human rights law or when they do so they are rather elusive. Moreover, these documents do not seem to form a coherent set of rules that could lead to the articulation of general comments on the applicability of human rights law to the UN.

For example, neither the Status of Forces Agreements (SOFA) nor the Participation Agreements include references to human rights law. Even the model agreements drawn up by the UN have paid scant attention to this subject. The model SOFA makes no allusions to human rights law,[319] while the Model Agreement between the UN and member States contributing personnel and equipment to UN peacekeeping operations only refers to IHL instruments.[320]

---

315 *Porretto and Vité* (n 125) 40.

316 Clyde Eagleton, 'International Organization and the Law of Responsibility' (1951) 76 *Recueil des Cours* 386. Recent jurisprudence of the ECtHR suggests that State responsibility may be grounded in States' capacity to exercise control over individuals outside their territory. *Loizidou* (1996) (n 76) and *Ilascu* (n 92).

317 *Mégret and Hoffmann* (2003) (n 134) 323. '[I]nternational institutions have undertaken new and greater operational responsibilities, and with them came the distinct functional capacity to violate fundamental rights'. *Verdirame* (n 285) 267.

318 Ombudsperson Institution in Kosovo, *Special Report No. 2 on Certain Aspects of UNMIK Regulation 24/1999, on the Law Applicable to Kosovo,* para 7. *See also European Commission for Democracy through Law* (n 176) para 91.

319 'Model Status-of-Forces Agreement for Peacekeeping Operations' (9 October 1990) UN Doc. A/45/594.

320 It mentions the Geneva Conventions of 1949 and their Additional Protocols of 1977 and the UNESCO Convention of 1954 on the Protection of Cultural Property. 'Model Agreement between the United Nations and Member States Contributing Personnel

For each operation, peacekeeping personnel are supplied with a document providing the parameters within which they may exercise force. Such operational guidelines are based on international and national law. While they do touch upon IHL, no reference is made to human rights law at all. A second flaw is that it is axiomatic that national contingents apply their own rules of engagement,[321] which frequently results in inconsistencies in application.[322]

The 'Ten Rules - Code of Personal Conduct for Blue Helmets', which is directed towards military personnel, contains some human rights elements.[323] Nevertheless, it must be stressed that this document is not legally binding and is formulated in such a way that it reads rather like the ten Commandments. The three most pertinent sentences are '3. Treat the inhabitants of the host country with respect, courtesy and consideration', '4. Do not indulge in immoral acts of sexual, physical or psychological abuse or exploitation of the local population or UN staff, especially women and children', and '5. Respect and regard the human rights of all'. While the first two directives concentrate on human dignity and can to a certain extent be viewed as rather explicit, the latter is more wide-ranging inasmuch as it alludes to human rights more generally. Unfortunately, this directive does not define the term 'human rights' by reference to any legal instruments, which thereby provides States with a certain margin of appreciation in interpreting these terms.

The Code of Conduct for Law Enforcement Officials,[324] in contrast, addresses human rights more fully. Article 2 explicitly spells out that '[i]n the performance of their duty, law enforcement officials shall respect and protect human dignity and maintain and uphold the human rights of all persons'. While the text itself does not cite specific human rights instruments, the commentary does, listing *inter alia* the UDHR and the ICCPR and insisting that national commentaries to the provision should also include regional instruments. Torture and inhuman treatment are unambiguously prohibited under Article 5, which refers to the Declaration against Torture.[325] In the specific circumstance of detention, Article 6 stipulates that law enforcement officials are responsible for ensuring the protection of the health of the detainees. No reference is made to the right to challenge one's detention, a bone of contention in past and current peacekeeping operations.

---

and Equipment to United Nations' (23 May 1991) UN Doc. A/46/185 and Corr.1, para 28.

321 The only exception appears to be the International Security Assistance Force in Afghanistan. 'Overview of Protection Issues in the Context of Multinational Peace Operations' in *Faite and Labbé Grenier* (n 27) 8.

322 *Faite and Labbé Grenier* (n 27) 8.

323 'Ten Rules - Code of Personal Conduct for Blue Helmets' available at: <www.un.org/Depts/dpko/dpko/Conduct/ten_in.pdf> (accessed 28 August 2009).

324 Code of Conduct for Law Enforcement Officials, *UNGA Res. 34/169* (17 December 1979) UN Doc. A/RES/34/169.

325 Declaration on the Protection of All Persons from Being Subjected to Torture and Other Cruel, Inhuman or Degrading Treatment or Punishment, *UNGA Res. 30/3452* (9 December 1975) UN Doc. A/RES/30/3452. This is due to the fact that the CAT was adopted after the issuance of the Code of Conduct for Law Enforcement Officials.

The document 'We are United Nations Peacekeepers', which is directed towards a broader category of peacekeepers, including both civilian and military components, follows much of the Code of Conduct in terms of respect for human dignity.[326] However, in contrast, human rights *per se* are not mentioned in the operative but rather in the preambular paragraph. The second preambular paragraph reads '[w]e will comply with … the applicable portions of the Universal Declaration of Human Rights as the fundamental basis of our standards'.

Overall, as far as specific documents produced by the UN are concerned, the legal situation appears unacceptable. Whereas some do not mention human rights law at all, those which do, do so incompletely since they do not provide any definition of the term 'human rights'. This is a serious cause of concern because these are the instruments that are used on a daily basis by those involved in peacekeeping missions. It might be argued that the lack of a definition of human rights is not problematic as, in contrast to listing a few rights, it caters for a broad interpretation of the term. Unfortunately such an interpretation is often left to States that are usually inclined to opt for a more restrictive interpretation. Thus, this issue needs to be addressed by the UN.

4.4. Internal Customary Law

More generally, in view of the fact that the UN and other IOs involved in peacekeeping missions have declared on several occasions that they are bound by human rights law for specific missions, it is argued that 'the more secure legal peg upon which to hang the argument that IOs are bound by international human rights law is that such obligations are in fact customary law for the organisation itself'.[327] For example, the Brahimi report emphasised '[t]he essential importance of the United Nations system adhering to and promoting international human rights instruments and standards … in all aspects of its peace and security activities'[328] and Kofi Annan reminded in his report *In Larger Freedom* that 'United Nations peacekeepers and peacebuilders have the solemn responsibility to respect the law themselves, and especially to respect the rights of the people whom it is their mission to help'.[329] Further, legal pundits claim that, read in conjunction with Articles 1 and 55 of the UN Charter, the customary internal law of IOs obliges peacekeepers to abide by human rights standards.[330] Furthermore, the UN expects its personnel to abide by

---

326 'We will always: … Treat the inhabitants of the host country with respect, courtesy and consideration'. 'We will never: … Commit any act that could result in physical, sexual or psychological harm or suffering of the local population, especially women and children'. We Are United Nations Peacekeepers, available at: <www.un.org/Depts/dpko/dpko/Conduct/un_in.pdf> (accessed 27 August 2009).

327 *Cameron* (n 145) 40.

328 'Report of the Panel on United Nations Peace Operations' (21 August 2000) UN Doc. A/55/305, S/2000/809, para 6(e).

329 Kofi Annan, 'In Larger Freedom: Towards Development, Security and Human Rights for all' (21 March 2005) UN Doc. A/59/2005, para 113.

330 *Cameron* (n 145) 40.

human rights standards. Several UN training manuals[331] and courses offered by this institution to its personnel incorporate human rights elements.[332] This indicates that the internal law of the UN contains human rights norms.

Yet, owing to limited practice regarding the protection of all human rights,[333] it cannot be firmly stated that a customary rule obliging the UN to abide by human rights law has developed. As a matter of fact, although 'general commitments [to international human rights standards] have become the norm' in practice such discourse is 'associated with high moral standards and motivations' rather than concrete acts.[334]

5. Conclusion

While there appears to be a wealth of sources obliging both States and IOs involved in peacekeeping missions to abide by human rights standards, there is a concomitant plethora of interconnected legal problems. While the problem of the extra-territoriality of human rights treaties is only pertinent with regard to States, other issues concern both States and IOs.

A series of general problems must be highlighted. First, whilst States are clearly bound by human rights law in peacekeeping operations, this seems less true for IOs. Hence, White's constructive suggestion that the UN recognise formally, in a single instrument, the application of human rights law to its activities should be adopted.[335] This would clear up any doubts as to the applicability of human rights norms to the UN and its peacekeeping missions.

Second, '[u]nder international law, it appears that peace forces have concrete obligations'.[336] Unfortunately, '[i]n legal frameworks and in practice, their obligations are extremely ambiguous, vague, and/or supplanted by national obligations'.[337] The lack of definition and/or the vagueness of certain human rights norms endow both States and IOs with a wide margin of interpretation. In the absence of any monitoring mechanisms, both subjects of international law are free to interpret such rights as it suits them. Therefore, it is submitted that a special mechanism is needed to review the activities of States and IOs in peacekeeping missions.

Third, the lack of clearly identified sources of international law binding peacekeeping missions to human rights law works to the detriment of legal certainty

331 *See e.g. United Nations Civilian Police Handbook* (Turin, International Training Centre of the ILO, 1995); UN, *Military Observers Handbook*, 1995 available at: <www.ejercito.mil.uy/instit/imae/Archivos/GR-SGTM1v2006XEOPE/Reference%20Library/072-un_military_observers_handbook.pdf> (accessed 18 September 2009).

332 *Clapham* (n 183) 127.

333 *See generally Marshall and Inglis* (n 70) 95.

334 *Brand* (n 299) 465. Nevertheless, it must be conceded that the UN, at least, acknowledges some human rights violations by its troops.

335 Nigel White, 'Towards a Strategy for Human Rights Protection in Post-Conflict Situations' in *White and Klaasen* (n 7) 463.

336 *Zwanenburg* (n 16) 240.

337 *Zwanenburg* (n 16) 240.

and against individuals whose rights have been violated. Indeed, the local population may not even find a forum that can readily address the human rights violations they have suffered at the hands of peacekeepers, since it is impossible to point to the sources of such human rights obligations. Failing to identify a legal forum, the use or creation of general or *ad hoc* monitoring mechanisms thus appears as the best solution to fill the gap, at least for preventative purposes.

A fourth and related issue is that victims of human rights violations perpetrated by peacekeeping personnel are subject to different rules and procedures, depending on whether the violations are attributable to States or IOs. This is, to say the least, regrettable, for 'it is axiomatic that human rights are inherent and inalienable entitlements that appertain to the individual; by definition, they cannot be contingent upon the 'banner' under which power is vested and authority exercised'.[338]

The current state of the law is rather unsatisfactory. States and IOs should plainly acknowledge that they are generally bound by, or that they accept, human rights norms in peacekeeping missions. At the moment, the plethora of legal sources applicable to States and IOs make it difficult to keep an overview of their human rights obligations. Therefore, it is recommended that States and IOs involved in peacekeeping missions adopt a legal instrument that clarifies their human rights duties.

338 *Verdirame* (n 285).

Chapter 6

Rules of Engagement

Ben Klappe

Whether or not an obligation to protect civilians is explicit in the mandate of such a force, the United Nations and other actors must be prepared to respond to the expectation of protection created by their very presence.[1]

1. Introduction

The phrase above originates from a report analysing United Nations (UN) actions surrounding the 1994 genocide in Rwanda and clearly illustrates the difficulties civilian and military leaders have had in the past to fathom mandates and to comprehend Rules of Engagement (RoE). If 'reluctance to use force' was the name of the game during peace operations in the early 1990's, today's focus is on the side-effects of the apparent non-reluctance to use force - civilian casualties - jeopardising peace operations as a result of losing hearts and minds.

After-action reports of peace operations have often hinted at obfuscated mandates or unclear RoE. But failures involving the use of lethal force, or the lack thereof, might also be the result of a lack of willingness to deploy sufficient troops. Failures may also stem from the inclination of political leaders to interpret the mandate too restrictively, and occasionally too widely, and the oftentimes unfounded dormant fear of commanders of criminal prosecution in case a decision has to be made when a situation of hostile intent occurs. The latter is connected to generic difficulties when troops are increasingly engaged in stability operations or peace enforcement: opponents hiding amongst the civilian population with great risks of civilian casualties when using deadly force. This chapter will assess the term 'Rules of Engagement' (RoE) and analyse why decisions to use force have caused difficulties in the past and why RoE are still perceived as a burden, causing considerable inconvenience for commanders and soldiers during military operations nowadays. Subsequently the chapter will explore what possible remedies may entail and examine why only a very few cases involving the use of (excessive) force may lead to prosecution.

1 'Conclusions of the Independent Inquiry into actions of the United Nations during the 1994 genocide in Rwanda addressed to the Secretary-General' (16 December 1999) UN Doc. S/1999/1257.

M. Odello and R. Piotrowicz (eds.), International Military Missions and International Law.
2011 Koninklijke Brill NV. Printed in The Netherlands. ISBN 978 9004 17437 5. pp. 145–160.

2. Rules of Engagement – Authority, Prohibitions and Limitations

Rules of Engagement are directives to operational commanders which delineate the parameters within which force may be used. Rules are based on a mandate - be it international (UN Security Council, regional organisation) or national (Government) - authorising a multinational force or national force to deploy and execute tasks in order to achieve military objectives. Such a mandate will be translated at the highest military level into an initial concept of military operations. It will leave necessary space for planners at subordinate headquarters, adjusting plans to situations as they occur. Despite the necessary room for interpretation, clarity is needed when it comes to the authority to use force. Not only will this clarity protect individuals against excessive use of force, it also protects peacekeepers from prosecution when force is used within the parameters of the RoE. RoE in military parlance may appear in various forms, linked to various levels: strategic, operational and tactical, the latter usually supplemented with a so-called pocket card or soldiers' card with, in clear soldiers' language, a repetition of the basic rules on how and when to use force.

A phrase that is nowadays almost a standard in Security Council resolutions is the authorisation 'to use force, up to and including deadly force, to protect civilians under imminent threat of physical violence…'.[2] It should be clearly understood at all levels that this is at the heart of the *raison d'être* of peacekeeping: if peacekeepers are unable, unwilling or not authorised, then what is their role in the first place? Attention should be paid to the precise wording. It raises questions whether there is a difference in the execution of the mission when the wording reads: 'to protect', 'to ensure protection'[3] or 'to contribute to the protection'.[4] The answer should be in the mission implementation plan, the operational plans and orders for military and police components.

Although RoE traditionally are developed for military personnel, police forces are also using RoE or similar directives, such as Directives for the Use of Firearms (DUF). Specific RoE are often developed for maritime operations and interception and engagement of aircraft. As private contractors are increasingly participating in peace operations, rules on the use of force will exist for such personnel. In peacekeeping operations, small groups of soldiers rather than large formations of military units are deployed to execute tasks. Often junior leaders will have to take decisions on the use of force. No commander or superior when monitoring the situation from headquarters or a command post with live-camera images can substitute for the common sense of the leader on the spot. Only they are able to make a final analysis

2 UNAMID, Darfur, *UNSC Res. 1769* (31 July 2007) and MONUC, Democratic Republic of Congo, *UNSC Res. 1565* (1 October 2004).

3 MONUC, Democratic Republic of Congo, *UNSC Res. 1565* (1 October 2004): to ensure the protection of civilians, including humanitarian personnel, under imminent threat of physical violence.

4 UNAMID, Darfur, *UNSC Res. 1769* (31 July 2007): to contribute to the protection of civilian populations under imminent threat of physical violence and prevent attacks against civilians, within its capability and areas of deployment, without prejudice to the responsibility of the Government of the Sudan.

and assessment and decide how best to defuse or control the situation on the ground. It is therefore crucial that rules should be clear and simple, understandable for junior leaders and soldiers.

RoE impose political, operational and legal limitations upon commanders at all levels. They are the primary means by which international organisations or national governments provide guidance to the armed forces on the use of force during military operations. RoE may impose political limitations to ensure that relevant international or national policy will be followed. The UN, for example, prohibits the use of mines and incendiary weapons, but may authorise and limit the use of riot control means. International law and treaties may not be applicable to the specific situation (during peace operations the Geneva Conventions and Additional Protocols do not apply *de-jure*) or States may not have signed up to certain treaties, while it is in the interest of the operation to abide by certain rules. In an attempt to address the issue and for the purpose of setting out fundamental principles and rules of international humanitarian law that apply to forces conducting operations under UN command and control, the UN Secretary-General (SG) has issued a Bulletin.[5] Section 1 of the Bulletin states that the fundamental principles and rules of IHL set out in the Bulletin are applicable to UN forces when in situations of armed conflict they are actively engaged therein as combatants, to the extent and for the duration of their engagement. They are accordingly applicable in enforcement actions, or in peacekeeping operations when the use of force is permitted in self-defence.[6] Shortly after its promulgation, the Bulletin triggered questions in the military and legal community on the threshold for the 'situation of armed conflict'. A practical solution for the applicability of the Bulletin may be found by declaring the fundamental principles specified in the Bulletin to be applicable at all times. To adhere to such fundamental principles as humane treatment of the wounded, women, children and detainees should be a matter of standard policy, regardless of the situation at hand.

5 Secretary-General's Bulletin: 'Observance by United Nations forces of international humanitarian law' (6 August 1999) UN Doc. ST/SGB/1999/13.

6 The Bulletin does not affect the protected status of members of peacekeeping operations under the 1994 UN Safety Convention or their status as non-combatants, as long as they are entitled to the protection given to civilians under the international law of armed conflict.

RoE may limit the use of force when the target is close to civilian populations.[7] Although under international law this would be a regular precaution,[8] RoE may add extra precautionary measures, not required under treaty law.[9]

RoE may contain operational considerations of importance to the commander and may limit the use of force in such a way that it will be used in a manner consistent with the overall military objective. This may include the prohibition to destroy critical infrastructure, communication facilities and other potential military targets, whilst allowing the disabling or disruption of such objects. Limitations may also regulate command involvement in battle by vesting authority in a commander to authorise pre-planned strikes, use of certain weapon systems or aircraft.[10]

The legal authority for the use of force derives from international or national sources (Security Council Resolutions, decisions by national governments). Rules are also based on customary international law (IHL and HRL) and national laws (both sending States and host States). In the absence of a Status of Force Agreement or other form of agreement, host State law may impact upon a soldier's use of force.

As a basic rule, all individuals, including soldiers, enjoy the right to defend themselves against attacks. The right of self-defence has developed over centuries under both international law (self-defence between States) and national law. Self-defence under national criminal law would generally exculpate someone from criminal charges when he acts necessarily to defend himself or someone else against an imminent assault. National law may vary considerably. When it comes to multinational operations, relevant differences under national laws might lead to so-called national caveats, limiting national contingents in their conduct of operations. In practice during coalition operations dozens of caveats may exist. Caveats may restrict contingents to conduct operations in certain geographical areas based on security considerations or for reasons related to logistic sustainability, with a view to cumbersome infrastructure and availability of (air) assets. Other caveats are related to the use of force. Application of certain RoE may violate national (criminal) law. Rather than fighting the problem, commanders should categorise caveats, dividing

7 API, Article 51 (Protection of the civilian population) [...] prohibits indiscriminate attacks e.g. an attack which may be expected to cause incidental loss of civilian life, injury to civilians, damage to civilian objects, or combination thereof, which would be excessive in relation to the concrete and direct military advantage anticipated.

8 API, Article 57 (Precautions in attack) [..] those who plan or decide upon an attack shall take all feasible precautions in the choice of means and methods of attack with a view to avoiding, and in any event to minimizing, incidental loss or civilian life, injury to civilians and damage to civilian objects; and refrain from deciding to launch any attack which may be expected to cause incidental loss of civilian life, injury to civilians, damage to civilian objects, or a combination thereof, which would be excessive in relation to the concrete and direct military advantage anticipated.

9 Such measures could be the visual identification of a selected target or the obligation to deploy forward observers before using long-range artillery.

10 In NATO-led operations a matrix is often used to indicate specific authorisation levels or commanders to release weapons or weapon systems. Use of heavy weapons may have a high risk of escalation and senior commanders, with their additional staff capacity, are in a better position to oversee all consequences of employing those weapons.

them into those that may realistically cause problems, those that are inconvenient or caveats irrelevant for the conduct of operations. The commander and his staff will subsequently develop plans while taking into consideration national limitations. When some contingents are not authorised under national law to use deadly force to protect infrastructure, that situation may change when such infrastructure is used by internally displaced persons who come under attack by rebel forces. Then the authority to use force to protect civilians under imminent threat of physical violence will prevail.

In RoE, the terms 'hostile act' and 'hostile intent' play a prominent role. A hostile act during UN peacekeeping operations may be defined as: 'An attack or other use of force, intended to cause death, bodily harm or destruction'.[11] At first sight this may seem quite clear, but how will the individual soldier make his decisions when an action is likely to demonstrate hostile intent? Hostile intent may be defined as: 'The threat of imminent use of force, which is demonstrated through an action which appears to be preparatory to a hostile act'.[12] The soldier fortunately may find some support in the remainder of the definition, namely: 'only a reasonable belief in the hostile intent is required, before the use of force is authorised'. Whether or not hostile intent is being demonstrated must be judged by the on-scene commander, on the basis of one or a combination of factors, including: the capability and preparedness of the threat, the available evidence which indicates an intention to attack and the historical precedent within the mission's area of responsibility.[13]

An analysis by Canadian forces[14] following the use of deadly force in Somalia in 1994 revealed that the RoE authorised forces to use 'deadly force' in responding to a 'hostile act' or when confronting 'hostile intent'. There appeared to be no distinction between a hostile act and a hostile intent, and many soldiers accepted that this was the case. A senior officer sought to make it clearer by advising the soldiers that 'hostile intent' existed if someone held a weapon 'parallel to the ground'. Another officer viewed the attempted definition as unworkable, since his squadron operated in an area where many Somalis carried weapons. In a related vein, the RoE were deficient in failing to address adequately the question of the level of threat and the need for a graduated response depending on the severity of the threat encountered. The RoE left the impression that the response to unarmed harassment could be exactly the same as that envisaged for an armed threat (i.e. deadly force). Other RoE interpretations authorised the use of up to deadly force against thieves.[15] Soldiers were uncertain as to whether they were required to obey this new interpretation of the RoE, or whether they could resist it as an unlawful order. Far from clearing up confusion about the RoE, the interpretation given increased it significantly. Understood literally, it authorised lethal force against all thieves; nonetheless, some soldiers under-

11 UN Department of Peacekeeping Operations, *Guidelines for the Development of Rules of Engagement for UN Peacekeeping Operations* (March 2002).

12 Ibid.

13 Ibid.

14 Report of the Somalia Commission of Inquiry, available at: <www.forces.gc.ca/somalia/vol2/v2c22e.htm>.

15 Ibid.

stood that deadly force would be employed only when stolen materiel was 'critical equipment', although nothing made clear what materiel counted as critical equipment. Another source of confusion was the target toward which soldiers were to aim once they had decided to fire on an intruder. The commanding officer instructed soldiers to shoot 'between the skirt and the flip-flops', that is, at the legs. Some thought that the instruction could represent a positive step: it placed a shot to kill another step away.[16] However, even the commander was uncertain about the effect of the instruction, since he acknowledged that soldiers are trained from the outset to shoot at the centre of visible mass. It is equally probable that it had the opposite effect, making the conditions for resorting to force easier.[17]

3. Senior Leaders and Use of Force Decisions.

3.1 Rwanda 1994

A particular lesson can be learned from the UN Assistance Mission in Rwanda (UNAMIR) in 1993.[18] The Security Council decided that UNAMIR should contribute to the security of Kigali, i.e. within a weapons-secure area established by the parties in and around the city. Although it had been proposed by the Secretary-General that UNAMIR assist in the recovery of arms, the resolution was silent on the issue.[19]

Approximately 800,000 people were killed during the 1994 genocide in Rwanda. The systematic slaughter of men, women and children, which took place over the course of around 100 days, will be remembered as one of the most abhorrent events of the twentieth century. Rwandans killed Rwandans, brutally decimating the Tutsi population of the country, but also targeting moderate Hutus. The failure by the UN to prevent and, subsequently, to stop the genocide was a failure by the UN system as a whole. The fundamental failure was the lack of resources and political commitment devoted to developments in Rwanda and to the UN presence there. There was a persistent lack of political will by member States to act, or to act with enough assertiveness.[20] Although UNAMIR suffered from a chronic lack of resources and political priority, it must also be said that serious mistakes were made with those resources which were at the disposal of the UN.[21]

On 23 November 1993, the Force Commander sent UN Headquarters a draft set of RoE for UNAMIR. The draft included an article specifically allowing the mission to use force in response to crimes against humanity and other abuses ("There may also be ethnically or politically motivated criminal acts committed during this man-

16 Ibid.

17 Ibid.

18 *UNSC Res. 872* (5 October 1993).

19 Letter dated 15 December 1999 from the members of the Independent Inquiry into actions of the United Nations during the 1994 genocide in Rwanda addressed to the Secretary-General (16 December 1999) S/1999/1257.

20 Ibid.

21 Ibid.

date which will morally and legally require UNAMIR to use all available means to halt them. Examples are executions, attacks on displaced persons or refugees").[22] UN Headquarters never responded to the Force Commander's request for approval. On 11 January 1994, the Force Commander sent a cable to UN Headquarters which has come to figure prominently in the discussions about how much the UN knew about the risk of genocide. The telegram stated that the Force Commander had been put in contact with a top level trainer in the Interahamwe militia, and contained several key pieces of information. The first related to a strategy to provoke the killing of Belgian soldiers and the Belgian battalion's withdrawal. The informant had been in charge of demonstrations a few days earlier, with the aim of targeting opposition deputies and Belgian soldiers. The Interahamwe hoped to provoke the Rwandese Patriotic Front battalion into firing at the demonstrators. The deputies were to be assassinated. Belgian troops were to be provoked. If the Belgian soldiers used force, a number of them were to be killed; this was to force the withdrawal of the Belgian contingent. Secondly the informant said that the Interahamwe had trained 1700 men in the camps of the Rwandan Government Forces, scattered in groups of 40 throughout Kigali. He had been ordered to register all Tutsi in Kigali, and suspected this was with the aim of securing their extermination. He said his personnel were able to kill up to 1000 Tutsi in 20 minutes. Thirdly the informant had told of a major weapons cache with at least 135 weapons (G3 and AK 47 assault rifles). He was prepared to show UNAMIR the location if his family was given protection. Having described the information received from the informant, the Force Commander went on to inform UN headquarters that it was UNAMIR's intention to take action within the next 36 hours.[23]

The first response from UN Headquarters to UNAMIR was that there was cause for concern but that there were certain inconsistencies. It ended: 'No reconnaissance or other action, including response to request for protection, should be taken by UNAMIR until clear guidance is received from Headquarters'.[24] UNAMIR responded by pointing to the 24 to 48 hours before the informant was to distribute the arms, requesting further guidance on how to handle the situation, including the request for the protection of the informant. The final paragraph stated that the Force Commander was prepared to pursue the operation in accordance with military doctrine with reconnaissance, rehearsal and implementation. UN Headquarters replied that they could not agree to the operation stated in the final paragraph, as in their view this clearly went beyond the mandate entrusted to UNAMIR under Resolution 872 (1993). Subsequently UNAMIR was instructed to arrange a meeting with the President to inform him about the subversive activities that constituted a clear threat to the peace process.[25]

The Force Commander continued to press for permission to take a more active role in deterrent operations against weapon caches in the Kigali Weapons Secure

22 Ibid.

23 Ibid.

24 Ibid.

25 Ibid.

Area (KWSA). UN Headquarters insisted that UNAMIR could only support the efforts of the gendarmerie. The Force Commander referred to a previous recommendation that deterrent actions supported by the gendarmerie and army be initiated, pointing out that neither of these Rwandan institutions had the resources to conduct cordon and search operations themselves. UN Headquarters emphasised that public security was the responsibility of the authorities and must remain so, referring to Resolution 792 authorising UNAMIR only to contribute to the security of Kigali, i.e., within a weapons-secure area established by the parties.

Whether the decision to raid the weapon cache was within the mandate of the mission or not is of key importance. The Force Commander maintained that it was; UN Headquarters firmly believed that the raid was not in the mandate. The key is the interpretation of the phrase 'weapons secure area established by the parties' in the mandate. It should be recalled in this context that the Security Council had deliberately weakened the role of UNAMIR in relation to the KWSA, as compared with the role foreseen by the Arusha Agreement.[26] The instruction cables from the Secretariat show concern about the possibility that the information might be a trap, and a concern for the safety of the mission: "the overriding consideration is the need to avoid entering into a course of action that might lead to the use of force and the unanticipated repercussions". Given the context, the Inquiry did not see reason "to criticize the decisions taken by the Secretariat on the mandate issue; however the issue should have been raised with the Security Council as a fundamental weakness in the mandate of the mission, which the Council should consider rectifying because of the dire risks involved".[27] The Independent Inquiry concluded that whether or not an obligation to protect civilians was explicit in the mandate of such a force, the UN and other actors must be prepared to respond to the expectation of protection created by their very presence.[28]

A final remark should be made whether or not the decision to search for a possible weapon cache, in essence a tactical operation, should have been discussed at all between Force Commander and superiors at UN Headquarters, the strategic level or, as suggested by the Independent Inquiry, with the Security Council at the political level. During time-sensitive operations it is widely known that referring decisions up in the chain of command risks losing momentum. This effect may be reinforced by the inability to make a correct assessment of the urgency when superior headquarters are operating at great distance or in different time-zones. Had the Force Commander at the time decided that it was within his command responsibility to authorise the search, there would not have been reasonable ground for questioning the commander for ordering the search, regardless of the outcome of the raid.

26 Africa - Miscellaneous, Declaration adopted by the Regional Summit on the Occasion of the Signing of the Peace Agreement between the Government of the Republic of Rwanda and the Rwandese Patriotic Front (4 August 1993) available at: <www.unhcr.org/refworld/docid/3ae6b4ffe.html> (accessed 24 February 2010).

27 Ibid.

28 Ibid.

3.2 Democratic Republic of Congo (DRC) 2004

A clear and tragic example of a too-narrow interpretation of the mandate and RoE involving the Mission of the UN in the Democratic Republic of Congo (MONUC)[29] occurred at the end of May 2004 in Bukavu, DRC. Laurent Nkunda, a renegade dissident ex-RCD-Goma,[30] refusing to adhere to a ceasefire agreement, marched from North Kivu with ex-ANC soldiers to join Mutebutsi[31] north of Bukavu, a city of 600,000 inhabitants. He was reinforced along the route and his force grew to about 2,000 men. MONUC's deputy-force commander was on-scene and planning to disarm Mutebutsi's units, as well as using attack helicopters to channel Nkunda's troops along Lake Kivu so as to prevent the seizure of Bukavu.[32] The tactics were to warn Nkunda verbally, if needed followed by warning shots, and finally, if Nkunda still did not turn back, to attack his advance units. HQ MONUC Kinshasa then decided that in the given situation deadly force was prohibited. Nkunda passed Bukavu airport and headed for Bukavu on 1 June 2004. MONUC troops blocked the road and delayed the attack for 18 hours. On 2 June 2004 Nkunda's troops reached Bukavu and spread out in the city. Private houses and shops were looted and citizens robbed. Summary executions and widespread rape occurred; hundreds of lives were lost and many citizens were injured.[33] UN Headquarters had expected MONUC and the Kivu Brigade to use force and did not share the views of HQ MONUC Kinshasa about taking a neutral posture in Bukavu. The Bukavu crisis influenced the peace process seriously, delaying it politically and militarily for more than five months. When Nkunda arrived in Bukavu, demonstrations started in all major cities in the DRC. The UN was blamed for not stopping Mutebutsi and Nkunda. MONUC HQ, pressed by severe attacks on UN establishments in Kinshasa, prepared for evacuation, which definitely brought a halt to the peace process.[34] UN property was destroyed. The main cause of the failure to protect the populations is considered the misinterpretation of the mandate by HQ MONUC Kinshasa during the crisis and the consequent restrictions (not justified by existing RoE) put on the proposed military course of action to protect the civilians of Bukavu.[35]

It is important here to consider how imminent is the threat and who will determine the imminence, the available means to respond to a situation and prioritisa-

29 *UNSC Res. 1565* (n 3).

30 Rassemblement Congolais pour la Démocratie-Goma.

31 A former regional commander of the Army of the Federal Republic of Congo (FARDC) since 2007 detained in Rwanda.

32 Brigadier General Jan Isberg, Former Deputy Force Commander and Brigade Commander, 'Experiences from UN Military Peace, Enforcement Operations in the DRC April 2003 – January 2005' (United Nations Mission in the Democratic Republic of Congo (MONUC)) available at: <www.dtic.mil/cgi-bin/GetTRDoc?AD=ADA472816&Location=U2&doc=GetTRDoc.pdf>.

33 UNSC, Third Special Report of the Secretary-General on MONUC (16 August 2004) S/2004/650.

34 Ibid.

35 *Jan Isberg* (n 32).

tion in case of conflicting responsibilities. How imminent is 'imminent'? Should it be instant and overwhelming, or do we need to wait for a smoking gun? The answer will have to be given by commanders on the ground as the situation develops, in line with the overall mission strategy and the mandate, detailed in operation plans and in line with the RoE. If intelligence reveals plans and credible evidence that armed elements are preparing an attack on civilians in villages nearby, the commander may conclude that the threat is imminent: within hours killing may start. No time should be lost and the armed elements should be engaged, if necessary by using deadly force. Radio stations broadcasting inciting language and ordering violence should be stopped as well. This may eventually include the use of force, which must be proportionate and necessary. When information reveals the location of weapon caches, commanders are supposed to act forthwith, not wait until the weapons are distributed and used against the population.

Although the present approach may deviate from peace operations of a decade ago, the mandates and rules have not changed that much, although it should be noted that the language in resolutions today is more explicit.[36] The authority to act is contained in the resolution and the permission to use force is in the RoE. What is new is the awareness at both political and military levels, based on dramatic experiences and failures in the past, that peacekeepers cannot stand idly by when civilians are threatened. Although in the particular situation of the Bukavu crisis the commander on the ground was overruled by the political leadership of the mission, another scenario would have been a commander pushing for robust action and eventually taking action as originally planned. It should be said here that to date no commander has ever been disciplined or prosecuted for having used force to protect civilians under imminent threat of physical violence, while quite a few have suffered trauma for not taking action and subsequently having to observe the slaughter of civilians.

3.3 Afghanistan 2009

Another, more recent, example involves the discussion amongst senior leaders after the issuance of guidelines extending the definition of military targets. A NATO senior commander has issued 'guidance' providing troops with the authority to attack directly drug producers and facilities throughout Afghanistan.[37] The guidelines state 'deadly force is to be used even in those cases where there is no proof that suspects are actively engaged in the armed resistance against the Afghanistan government or against Western troops' and it is 'no longer necessary to produce intelligence or other evidence that each particular drug trafficker or narcotics facility in Afghanistan meets the criteria of being a military objective'.[38] The senior commander rationalises his directive by writing that the alliance has decided that drug traffickers and narcotics facilities are inextricably linked to the opposing military forces, and thus may be attacked. Two subordinate commanders have criticised and ignored the guide-

36 *UNSC Res. 1565 and 1769* (n 3 and n 4).

37 S. Koelbl, 'NATO High Commander Issues Illegitimate Order to Kill' (2009) *Spiegel Online International*.

38 Ibid.

lines, declaring the order 'to be illegitimate, violating both International Security Assistance Force[39] (ISAF) rules of engagement and international law'.[40] Commander ISAF considers that the new created category in the RoE for dealing with opposing forces would 'seriously undermine the commitment ISAF has made to the Afghan people and the international community to restrain our use of force and avoid civilian casualties to the greatest degree predictable'.[41] The example once more underlines the need for greater clarity. In absence of a widely accepted and detailed implementation plan, based on the mandate, commanders may fill in the void by issuing controversial guidelines, causing difficulties for both subordinates and superiors.

4. Use of Force and Prosecution of Excessive Use of Force

In a soldier's war journal,[42] a lieutenant based in Iraq illustrates that fear of investigations and prosecutions, followed by media scrutiny, is part of the day-to-day use of force dilemma for soldiers and junior leaders. He wrote: 'Light 'em up. A quick burst or two of 50-caliber rounds should suffice. I've never tasted bloodlust before, not the lethal brew anyhow, but it seeped into my soul this night. I didn't come here to kill, and never felt the impulse or desire to truly end a man's life. But here it was, arriving as quickly as the crawling terrorists had. Kill or be killed. Never has this war been so clear, so pure, so obvious, so clean. And yet ... The platoon leader in me knew we couldn't shoot yet, and tugged at my brain like a giant anchor holding in place a battleship on full throttle. Escalation of force, rules of engagement... They haven't technically dug anything yet, thus, haven't begun emplacing anything'.[43]

The narrator-lieutenant has just established outer cordon security positions with his platoon and is alarmed by his sergeant: two shady figures are crawling low onto the road, down from the canal. The lieutenant orders his sergeant to keep watching and asks if he observes any heat signatures. He then orders a team to dismount to arrest the individuals and to beam the targets with a bright naked-eye laser to let them know they are watching. Next, he orders them to open fire and engage the targets if they run. The lieutenant reports to the command post: 'we have a possible IED (Improvised Explosive Device) emplacement happening at our location. We're employing RoE, and will engage with fire if they run and detainment is no longer a viable option'.[44] The captain responds unexpectedly and immediately: 'Negative, you will not engage! Try to detain the individuals and do not open fire until the individuals directly engage you'. Next the two individuals start running and disappear in the dark, leaving a state of art pressure plate IED designed specifically for attacks

39 International Security Assistance Force has a peace-enforcement mandate under Chapter VII of the UN Charter. Nine *UNSC Resolutions – 1386, 1413, 1444, 1510, 1563, 1623, 1707, 1776* and *1833* – relate to ISAF.

40 API, Article 51 (n 7).

41 Ibid.

42 Milblog Kaboom, Lt.G. (April 2008) available at: <http://kaboomwarjournalarchive.blogspot.com> (accessed May 2008).

43 Ibid.

44 Ibid.

on armoured vehicles. One of the individuals, a teenager, is detained 48 hours later by another unit during an attempt to emplace another IED. The lieutenant then reflects things are different now: 'Everyone's so scared to make a mistake, convinced they'll end up on the cover of Time. The IED wouldn't have hit the vehicle of the guy who tweaks the rules of engagement, or the guy who would have been appointed the investigating officer if we had shot. The IED would have cut through me, or my men, or some of my comrades, in an instantaneous fireball of death'.[45] He concludes with: 'I will not hesitate again, even for just a few seconds, nor will I call up an update until after the fact. There's too much at stake now for me to not employ those lessons learned. The next time, we might not be able to find the damn thing until after it explodes and we're separating scrap metal from human remains'.

The event is exemplary for conditions soldiers have to cope with and the split second character of decisions to be made by them. The sensitivity and restraint is based on the mounting awareness worldwide of civilian casualties. The changing character of military operations – patrolling streets in built-up areas and in crowded slums instead of patrolling in deserted buffer zones between States – inevitably will lead to an increased risk of civilian casualties once soldiers use force as a last resort. Civilian casualties as a result of soldiers' actions may jeopardise the operation and may lead to demonstrations and revenge or have other far reaching political consequences. A few examples may reveal some particularities in case of a decision to prosecute.

4.1 Iraq 2003

In 2003 a shooting incident took place between the two Iraqi towns of Al Khidr and As Samawah, in which a Dutch soldier fired two warning shots in the direction of a group of men allegedly looting containers with military supplies. As a result an Iraqi man died. The soldier stood trial for having fired warnings shots while the criteria as laid out in the *Aide-Mémoire* (Soldier's card) and the Instructions/RoE for firing warning shots were not met.[46]

The prosecutor appealed the trial chamber's decision to acquit and subsequently the appeal chamber decided that the soldier, while firing warning shots, acted in line with the specific rules, taking into consideration 'commander's intent' regarding force property and the requirements of force protection with a view to the imminent breach of the security cordon.[47] The appeal chamber gave further consideration to the specific situation at the scene, in particular that earlier warning shots in the air did not result in the expected outcome, namely the dispersal of the crowd threatening the soldiers. Under those circumstances and according to the prevailing views at the

45 Ibid.

46 LJN: AR4029, Rechtbank Arnhem, 05/097011-03, available at: <http://zoeken.rechtspraak.ro.minjus/default.aspx>.

47 LJN: AT4988, Gerechtshof Arnhem, 21-006275-04, available at: <http://zoeken.rechtspraak.ro.minjus/default.aspx>.

time, firing a shot in the ground (allegedly hitting the Iraqi man) was neither grossly negligent nor considerably careless.[48]

4.2 Iraq 2005

Another case leading to criminal procedures involving the use of force is the so-called Haditha incident on 19 November 2005 in Iraq.[49] A roadside bomb exploded beneath a vehicle belonging to a US Marine convoy, killing one member of the squad and injuring two others. Nineteen civilians were subsequently shot and killed by the squad, commanded by a staff sergeant, as it searched houses for those responsible for the bombing and subsequent small arms fire. Five men who emerged from a car that drove up immediately after the bombing were also shot. Eight Marines were originally charged with wrongdoing: four enlisted men were charged with murder while the battalion commander and three other officers faced charges related to failing to order a full-scale probe into the Haditha incident.[50] Charges against seven of the eight were dismissed or withdrawn. The staff sergeant who led the squad that killed the Iraqis and shot the men who emerged from the car was first charged with multiple counts of murder. After an investigative hearing in 2007, those charges were reduced to nine counts of voluntary manslaughter.[51] In early 2010, the trial was still ongoing.

The case has evolved into a far more complex examination of the Marine Corps' RoE and the general conduct of wartime operations in hostile residential areas. Another complication seems to be the misinterpretation of rules. Rules may not be explained properly by superiors. Such may be the case after a change of theatre of operations. Soldiers who have operated in a situation where civilians were evacuated, limiting the risk of civilian casualties, may have been given latitude when using deadly force.

Maintaining discipline and the handling of disciplinary and criminal cases by commanders or national prosecutors varies widely. A commander may have an interest not to report criminal conduct as it may discredit the commander and his unit. If reported, there is still the question whether a prompt and thorough professional investigation is possible, preferably by national criminal investigators, into relevant facts and circumstances. Operational circumstances, the ongoing skirmishes in the area, logistical limitations to transport forensic experts to the scene, the availability of independent witnesses, and interpreters all may have serious impact on the reliability of the investigation. Subsequently, prosecutors will review investigations that have been completed and have considerable liberty to decide whether to forward the case to an independent court. If the case is forwarded, judges will review if the evidence produced is sufficient to prove beyond reasonable doubt that a crime has been committed.

---

48 Ibid.

49 Available at: <www.nctimes.com/articles/2008/06/17/military/zeca5018258ba2e208825746b005ae619.txt>.

50 Ibid.

51 Ibid.

Military justice systems in States vary widely. Traditionally, most countries have a strict division separating military justice through a court-martial system convened for the individual military case. That is the situation in most Asian, middle-East and African countries, the USA, Canada, the UK (court-martial convening authority, prosecutors and court-members separated from the military chain of command) and Ireland (independent director of prosecution and military judges serving until retirement). In these countries the general opinion is that military society is unique (and sometimes parallel to civilian society) in the sense that soldiers are given extraordinary tasks and supposed to take exceptional risks, including being exposed to life-threatening situations to accomplish the mission. Therefore, those who are familiar with the organisation and have clear understanding of the pressure and stress soldiers are exposed to, are considered best capable of prosecuting, defending and judging military criminal offences.

5. Conclusion

Failure to adhere to the RoE in wartime and peacetime is not a new phenomenon. What is new is the circumstances on the battlefield, as well as the availability of mass communications technology reporting on alleged mistakes when applying deadly force, involving the death of civilians. Such reports may instantly influence the international community and international support for military operations. Violating RoE and causing civilian casualties will lay the foundation for losing hearts and minds and losing the battle. Civilian leaders and military commanders are ultimately responsible for formation, training, execution of tasks and the behaviour of their troops. Adequate training of troops is an ongoing process and a useful tool to prevent violation of norms by individual soldiers. It is a responsibility of leaders at all levels. Misinterpretation of rules by soldiers and excessive force may also result from the fact that troops are not trained adequately or appropriately selected for specific tasks. Proper troop-to-task analysis and extensive training on the use of force are important first steps to prevent excessive force.

Simultaneously, reluctance to resort to the use of force may cause casualties as well. Examples include Rwanda in 1994, Srebrenica in 1995 and the less known Bukavu crisis in 2004, as discussed previously. It is therefore of extreme importance that RoE are developed thoroughly and carefully, within an operational, legal and political framework. It is equally important that political leaders of multinational missions (e.g. Special Representatives of the Secretary-General) and national political leaders understand the complexities on the ground once military operations have started and soldiers have set foot on foreign/host state territory. Political leaders should have a thorough knowledge of the essential principles and definitions of the RoE. This would assist them in understanding their overall leadership roles, leaving the operational and tactical day-to-day decisions to military commanders and the commander on-scene.

Despite large-scale deployments of troops in UN peacekeeping operations (from 2005-2009 annual turnover of roughly 200,000 UN peacekeepers)[52] and

52 For a detailed overview *see* <www.un.org/en/peacekeeping/contributors>.

deployments of coalitions of the willing (Iraq[53] and Afghanistan[54] 200,000 soldiers annually), comparatively limited numbers of commanders and soldiers have been prosecuted and convicted of inappropriate or criminal behaviour, particular for having used excessive force. Concluded from special reports concerning criminal behaviour[55] and regular reports in the media related to misconduct by soldiers, cases that lead to criminal conviction are limited. There seems no ground to believe that large numbers of cases are not reported as international media and human rights organisations follow military operations closely.

A variety of reasons explain the small percentage of soldiers who have been prosecuted and convicted of criminal behaviour during military operations.

From a positive point of view, the increased attention given to conduct and behaviour during recruit training/initial training and during pre-deployment training have borne fruit. Continued training during deployment is a priority of many commanders. Specific training packages on IHL, IHRL, conduct and discipline and RoE have been developed over the years and are used widely by armed forces. In addition, armed forces have set minimum training standards before units or individuals are to be deployed. The effect is strengthened by the increased awareness of political leaders, commanders and soldiers that conduct and behaviour is a force-multiplier and a precondition for winning hearts and minds on a rapidly changing battlefield where soldiers interact on a daily basis with civilians. The behaviour of soldiers is therefore also directly linked to force protection and safety of the unit and is a prerequisite for bringing the mission to a successful conclusion.

Moreover, the arrests, the subsequent trials and convictions of senior political leaders and military commanders since the establishment of International Criminal Tribunals for the Former Yugoslavia and Rwanda, the Special Court for Sierra Leone and the International Criminal Court have contributed to the consciousness at all levels that soldiers and civilians alike have to abide by the rules and will serve as a warning and deterrence to commanders and soldiers.

Finally, when force is used, after-action reports usually excel in clarity while leaving room for many questions.[56] These questions may never be answered properly, as remoteness of the area and dire circumstances will prevent the timely collection of evidence and the hearing of independent witnesses. When, days later, allegations of civilian casualties are reported during the same period and place, it will be extremely difficult for criminal investigators and prosecutors to obtain evidence that will prove

53 For a detailed overview *see* <www.brookings.edu/iraqindex>.

54 For a detailed overview *see* <www.isaf.nato.int/en/troop-contributing-nations/index.php>.

55 Schlesinger, *Final Report of the Independent Panel to Review US DoD Detention Operations* (2004) available at: <www.defense.gov/news/AUG2004/d20040824finalreport.pdf>; *Aitkin Report, An Investigation into Cases of Deliberate Abuse and Unlawful Killing in Iraq in 2003 and 2004*, MOD UK (25 January 2008) available at: <*www.mod.uk/NR/rdonlyres/7AC894D3.../aitken_rep.pdf.*>.

56 Soldiers' language is short and situations may be described as: 'At 14.00h platoon received fire. Responded with approximately 700 rounds of 7.62 mm in self-defence. Approximately 12 attackers killed'.

beyond reasonable doubt that under the prevailing circumstances at the time, soldiers have used excessive force.

Chapter 7

Crisis Response Operations in Maritime Environments

*Ulf Häußler**

1. Introduction

Contemporary crisis, whether inter-State or intra-State, is usually perceived as a primarily land-based phenomenon. Protracted armed violence without solid ground beneath the feet of those fighting is an exceptional phenomenon; long-term air campaigns are the choice of the small number of States possessing the necessary resources, and long-term world-wide sea campaigns have not occurred since the end of World War II.[1] The maritime environment is different from the land environment, both factually and from a legal perspective, and so is the use of the oceans for the purposes of military operations compared to ground operations.[2] Accordingly, oceans have played a different role for military purposes, including as theatres of contemporary military operations, than they hitherto did. Maritime environments have nevertheless faced developments capable of threatening, or aggravating threats to, international peace and security. The UN Security Council has imposed maritime embargoes on e.g.

* The views expressed herein are my own; they do not necessarily correspond with the official position of NATO or the Headquarters, Supreme Allied Commander Transformation.

1 In particular, control of vast maritime areas is no longer a primary military objective since global oceanic warfare seems no longer to be the preferred choice of States in conflict. *See* D.P. O'Connell, *The International Law of the Sea* (Clarendon Press, Oxford, 1984) 1094sqq.

2 The essence of armed conflict has not changed significantly over time; requiring control of territory continues to be the means of choice of those taking up arms, except in the small number of cases where a desired political end-State can be reached without it. The only case at hand seems to be Operation Allied Force (1999) which helped convincing the Government of the Federal Republic of Yugoslavia (Serbia and Montenegro) and the Government of Serbia that they would better withdraw their forces from Kosovo.

M. Odello and R. Piotrowicz (eds.), International Military Missions and International Law.
2011 Koninklijke Brill NV. Printed in The Netherlands. ISBN 978 9004 17437 5. pp. 161–210.

Southern Rhodesia after its Unilateral Declaration of Independence[3] and on the parties to the conflict in the former Yugoslavia[4] for exactly that reason.

Recently, the number and visibility of threats linked to maritime environments has increased and their nature has become more complex. International Organisations (IOs) and States – mainly in coalitions yet in certain cases also individually – have responded with various operations. The aims pursued have been: to maintain international security on the high seas, to deny the use of the high seas to those attempting to sustain conduct threatening international peace and security on land, to ensure freedom of navigation including for the purposes of humanitarian access from sea, and combinations thereof. Moreover, the international community has recently moved towards containing threats posed by conduct occurring in certain States' territorial waters[5]. From the perspective of international law, the actions taken

3 The embargo, established by para 8 of *UNSC Res. 217* (12 November 1965) was enforced by the UK at sea by way of trying to divert shipments of oil which might have reached Southern Rhodesia through a pipeline installed at the Mozambique port of Beira. These measures came within the ambit of 'appropriate measures which would prove effective in eliminating the authority of the usurpers and bringing the minority régime in Southern Rhodesia to an immediate end', as contemplated by para 5 of *UNSC Res. 217* (above). When the *Joanna V*, an oil tanker owned by a Panamanian company, flying the Greek flag and chartered to a South African company, did not obey the order of diversion given by the frigate Plymouth, the UK obtained *UNSC Res. 221* (9 April 1966), which characterised the situation resulting from the possibility that significant oil supplies might reach Southern Rhodesia a threat to the peace (para 1) and, *inter alia*, called upon the UK government 'to prevent, by the use of force if necessary, the arrival at Beira of vessels reasonably believed to be carrying oil destined for Southern Rhodesia' (para 5). Although the Security Council did not mention Chapter VII of the UN Charter expressly, the determination that a breach to the peace existed assimilates the authorisation of the use of force to the use of force based upon this chapter. *UNSC Res. 221* (above) was used to justify the interception of another vessel, the *Manuela*. *Cf.* H. Strydom, 'South Africa' in V. Gowlland-Debbas (ed), *National Implementation of United Nations Sanctions* (Martinus Nijhoff Publishers, Netherlands, 2004), 403, 406.

4 The general and complete embargo on all deliveries of weapons and military equipment was enacted by virtue of para 6 of *UNSC Res. 713* (25 September 1991). It applied to all States that came into existence after the Socialist Federal Republic of Yugoslavia's dismemberment (para 6 of *UNSC Res. 727* (8 January 1992) read together with para 33 of UN document S/23363). To support the embargo, NATO launched Operation Maritime Monitor (16 July to 22 November 1992), which was followed by Operation Maritime Guard in an area in International waters off the Montenegro coast, approved by the North Atlantic Council on 20 November 1992 in support of *UNSC Res. 787* (16 November 1992) – the first of the quoted resolutions included decisions based on Chapter VII of the UN Charter – and co-ordinated with the WEU Operation Sharp Fence which patrolled the Otranto Straits in international waters. On 15 June 1993, NATO and the WEU launched the combined Operation Sharp Guard which prevented all unauthorized shipping from entering the territorial waters of the Federal Republic of Yugoslavia (Serbia and Montenegro) and all arms from entering the former Yugoslavia in accordance with UN sanctions. *See* <www.nato.int/IFOR/general/shrp-grd.htm> for further details (accessed 1 March 2009).

5 The phrase 'territorial waters' is used to cover both internal waters and territorial sea (Article 8 and Article 2(1)) of the UN Convention on the Law of the Sea 1982, respec-

entail collective self-defence,[6] and pre-emptive[7] or preventive[8] measures. While not all of these operations are crisis response operations proper, they represent part of the broader spectrum of naval operations, which (theoretically) ranges from law enforcement at sea to geographically unlimited warfare during international armed conflict. Focusing on the maritime aspect of the United Nations Interim Force in Lebanon (UNIFIL) and the operations at the Horn of Africa, this chapter will analyse how maritime crisis response operations implement, enforce and develop the existing legal framework, in particular the interplay of the UN Charter and the UN Convention on the Law of the Sea (UNCLOS).

2. Defining Maritime Crisis Response Operations

Maritime environments have lots to offer for those posing threats. The freedom of navigation facilitates sea transport of all sorts of weaponry, up to and including weapons of mass destruction (WMD); or parts thereof or centrifuges; pirates can acquire their own peculiar kind of revenue; and terrorists can reach their targets on land while approaching from sea (as in Bombay, 2008) or target sea-going vessels from coastal bases (as in the USS Cole incident, 1999). These examples indicate that the sea is, in its own particular way, exposed to the whole range of contemporary challenges and threats to international peace and security known on land. With this in mind, it is appropriate to integrate international military operations at sea in the legal and policy frameworks of international military operations in general and, to that end, to adapt the terminology developed mainly for land operations tackling contemporary challenges and threats to their equivalent at sea. However, using this terminology is indeed a matter of adaptation in light of the characteristics of maritime environments and the specifics of the law of the sea. This section outlines the full spectrum of maritime military operations and defines maritime crisis response operations as one element thereof.

2.1 Maritime Operations and the Strategic Importance of the Oceans

From 1945 to the early 1980s alone, some one hundred-odd naval operations were conducted involving about fifty navies.[9] Examples include the Falklands War of 1982, the proclamation of maritime war zones by both belligerents during the Iran-Iraq

---

tively (hereinafter referred to as UNCLOS).

6 Examples include the maritime aspect of Operation Enduring Freedom, Operation Active Endeavour, and the maritime aspect of UNIFIL.

7 Examples include NATO Operation Ocean Shield (successor to Allied Provider and Allied Protector), and EU Operation Atalanta – Counter-Piracy and Assistance to WFP at the Horn of Africa.

8 The key example is the Proliferation Security Initiative (PSI). For NATO support to the PSI see para 6 of NATO's Comprehensive, Strategic-Level Policy for Preventing the Proliferation of Weapons of Mass Destruction (WMD) and Defending against Chemical, Biological, Radiological and Nuclear (CBRN) Threats dated 01 September 2009, online at http://www.nato.int/cps/en/natolive/official_texts_57218.htm.

9 *Cf. O'Connell* (n 1) 1095.

War (1980-1988),[10] the maritime component of Operation Desert Storm (1991), maritime support of UN embargos (Southern Rhodesia, former Yugoslavia), NATO's Operation Active Endeavour in the Mediterranean and the maritime detachment of Operation Enduring Freedom at the Horn of Africa (both responding to the attack on the US on 11 September 2001), Tamil Tigers maritime warfare, and the maritime component of Operation Iraqi Freedom (since 2003).

The strategic importance of the oceans, including for the purpose of projecting power at strategic distance, is reinforced by the contemporary practice of military operations at sea. At the low intensity end of the spectrum, maritime embargoes and maritime interdiction operations continue to be a prime choice where the aim is to contain, or de-escalate, a threat, crisis or conflict. Conversely, at the high intensity end, sea-based platforms offer multiple options to support land operations. Warships can provide strategic mobility where airlift capabilities are lacking, or insufficient, or where their use would expose the forces airlifted to unacceptable threats. On a more general scale, international waters are attractive in lieu of land bases with a view to decreasing both the dependence on access being granted by foreign governments[11] and the degree of exposure to asymmetric threats.[12] In support of actual land operations, apart from making naval artillery capabilities available to forces involved in ground combat, warships are capable of launching fighter aircraft, tactical rotary-wing capabilities (helicopters), and both manned and unmanned aerial and/or underwater reconnaissance and/or combat vehicles. However unlikely geographically unlimited warfare on the high seas may have become, States and the international community have a major range of maritime security interests, both 'soft' and 'hard' in nature, they may want to protect. The strategic importance of the oceans for that purpose is highlighted, from the international community's perspective, by the preamble of UNCLOS which stresses 'the significance of this Convention as an important contribution to the maintenance of peace, justice and progress for all peoples of the world'.[13]

'Soft' maritime security interests relate to the use of the sea for the flow of goods, as a resource of food supplies, energy, and raw materials, and as a source of revenue through e.g. leisure and tourist purposes: activities on which most States are heavily dependent.[14] Some States even produce goods on the high seas in order to prevent them from becoming subject to country-specific import quotas.[15] Interference

---

10 *See* Wolf Heintschel von Heinegg, 'The United Convention on the Law of the Sea and Maritime Security Operations', 48 *German Yearbook of International Law* (*GYIL*) 151, 162sq for further details.

11 *Cf.* the observation that: '... freedom of navigation is of paramount importance for the rapid deployment of armed forces to almost every region of the world' Ibid. 151, 154).

12 This aspect is addressed by the 'Sea Basing' concept developed under the umbrella of 'Sea Power 21' by the US Navy. For a legal assessment of this concept and further references *see* Ibid. 151, 167sqq.

13 UNCLOS Preamble, first paragraph. The seventh paragraph of UNCLOS contains similar language.

14 *Heintschel von Heinegg* (n 10) 151/154.

15 To give but one example, *see* the discussion of off-shore production of cotton products in P. Rivoli, *The Travels of a T-Shirt in the Global Economy* (John Wiley & Sons, Hoboken NJ, 2005).

with any of these economic activities can have significant adverse effects on national interests and/or shared interests of the international community; it can become a threat to national or international security if it – using the language devised by the High-level Panel on Threats, Challenges and Change[16] – 'leads to large-scale death or lessening of life chances and undermines States as the basic unit of the international system'. As rightly observed by the High-level Panel, '[e]conomic and social threats, including poverty, infectious diseases and environmental degradation' are among the range of 'threats without boundaries' the international community needs to be concerned about. Disruption of sea lines – that is, the freedom of peaceful navigation – can cause, contribute to or exacerbate such threats, including by seriously jeopardising or denying humanitarian access. Moreover, the protection of a State's nationals – consumers (tourists) and merchants alike – and their property involves national security interests, as well. These 'soft' security interests are particularly at stake if other States fail to afford the minimum standards of protection owed in accordance with the general principles of international law relating to the treatment of foreigners.[17] These minimum standards apply off shore no less than they do on land (and in the air); supplementing *inter alia* the obligation that any State must effectively exercise its jurisdiction and control over ships flying its flag,[18] they require that States provide reasonable protection, in maritime environments, against harm inflicted by the State's own nationals or from aboard a ship flying its flag or sailing within its territorial waters and adjacent contiguous zone. Maritime crisis response operations may protect any of these 'soft' security interests.

As to 'hard' security interests below the threshold of international hostilities at sea, the proliferation of small arms as well as WMD are as much a matter of concern as attempts made by certain States to curb the freedom of peaceful navigation of warships.[19] Certain cases of proliferative sea transport of weaponry may run counter to existing prohibitions embodied in globally applicable UN regimes and embargoes,[20] touching hence on security interests of the international community also, while many such cases of sea transport will stay within the scope of the freedom of navigation.[21] However, freedom of navigation cannot prevent such unpleasant sur-

16 The following quotations are taken from 'A more secure world: our shared responsibility', UN document A/59/565 at 12 (synopsis) and 17, respectively.

17 Security of foreign investments, the subject-matter of many international agreements as well as the ICJ's *Barcelona Traction* Case [1970] ICJ Rep. 3 and many cases in the US-Iran Claims Tribunal, is the key economic example in this category. Physical security of a State's own nationals abroad is equally important, as highlighted by cases of, and/or announcements of the preparedness to conduct, non-combatant evacuation operations or hostage release operations.

18 *See* Article 94 of UNCLOS.

19 Such attempts take the shape of claims to excessive baselines or security zones, or the imposition of unjustified limitations on navigational rights. *See Heintschel von Heinegg* (n 10) 151, 161.

20 *Cf.* para 2(a) of *UNSC Res. 1373* (28 September 2001); paras 1, 2, 3(c)/(d) of *UNSC Res. 1540* (28 April 2004).

21 If sea transport is protected by the freedom of navigation, warships must release any vessels they may have inspected. *Cf.* the discussion of the *So San* incident by *Heintschel*

prises as the capture of the *Sirius Star*[22] and *MV Faina*[23] by Somali pirates. These incidents brought unexpected security concerns to broader awareness. Returning, finally, to the freedom of peaceful navigation of warships, it seems worthwhile to recall that warships are means of projection of maritime power not only for the purposes of legitimate use of force but also, as acknowledged by UNCLOS, for the exercise of flag State jurisdiction over commercial vessels at sea;[24] theirs is, moreover, the belligerent aspect of combating piracy (to which this chapter will return when analysing naval operations at the Horn of Africa).

Like their counterparts on land, contemporary crisis response operations in maritime environments represent segments of the entire spectrum of military operations, including the threat or use of force. Even if robust capabilities are not put to actual use their deterrent effect may be key to creating a permissive environment.[25] For the purpose of legal analysis, the existing factual diversity must be aligned with the relevant legal framework(s). Law disconnected from practical realities is an empty shell; still, relying on practice too much might amount to making the law subordinate to mere power politics. Yet what legal framework should be considered in the first place? There are three primary sources, namely the UN Charter, the law of naval warfare,[26] and UNCLOS. Moreover, troop contributing States' national laws governing military operations in maritime environments might also have a role to play, and so might any affected coastal State's law. Another issue is the impact of international human rights law. The range of potentially applicable sources indicates that the effort of identifying the legal framework of contemporary crisis response operations in maritime environments faces the same challenges as does the effort of examining the legal principles and rules governing land-based crisis response operations. The challenges comprise, but are not limited to, the impact of the UN Charter on the classical war-and-peace divide in light of the post-Cold War Chapter VII practice, a lack of clarity concerning the accountability of IOs entrusted with exercising (quasi-supra-

---

von Heinegg (n 10) 151, 175sqq.

22 On the hijacking of the Sirius Star, a supertanker commissioned in March 2008 and owned by the Saudi oil company Aramco, *see* <http://en.wikipedia.org/wiki/MV_Sirius_Star> (accessed 29 May 2009).

23 On the MV Faina, a Belize-flagged Ukrainian vessel carrying a cargo of arms and ammunition, which was captured on 25 September 2008 and only released, after a ransom of US$3.2 million had been paid, on 5 February 2009, *see* paras 145-146 of the report of the Monitoring Group dated 20 November 2008 (UN document S/2008/769).

24 Since it addresses only cases where a warship encounters a foreign ship, Article 110 of UNCLOS has left States' sovereign power to task warships with exercising flag State jurisdiction at sea untouched.

25 A permissive environment is characterised by a level of consent to, and/or compliance with, e.g. a cease-fire, armistice, or peace settlement, including such terms and conditions as may have been imposed by a Chapter VII UNSC Res. which, on comparison with a non-permissive environment, is less uncertain and the resulting threat of disruption is reduced.

26 The examples given in the first paragraph of the introduction indicate that in warfare on the high seas, the principles and rules of IHL pertaining to air and land warfare may also play an important role. Related questions are, however, beyond the scope of this chapter.

national) transitional authority over governmental institutions and/or individuals by virtue of the relevant mandates, and with operational control of the troops conducting them; the standards governing, and bodies competent for ensuring, the protection of the rights of the human person; and the proper delineation of responsibilities and tasks of military and civilian agencies involved in, or supporting, the operation. What then does it mean that the UN Security Council has added a maritime component to UNIFIL and authorised operations to suppress piracy and armed robbery at sea in the Gulf of Aden and the territorial waters of Somalia? This chapter will argue that – apart from confirming the huge value, both strategic and tactical, of maritime environments and the military capabilities put to use therein for the maintenance and/or restoration of international peace and security – the UN Security Council has made the same choice as it did with respect to crisis response operations on land, namely, a choice in favour of a legal framework that overcomes the classical war-and-peace divide in international law and facilitates, from the perspective of international law, the effective and efficient neutralisation of such threats to international peace and security as are genuine to maritime environments.

2.2 Crisis Management and (Maritime) Crisis Response Operations

It seems easy to argue that certain customarily accepted military uses of the sea should not be regarded as crisis response operations, namely nuclear tests (to the extent still permitted), naval exercises, maritime weapons tests and marine scientific research for military purposes.[27] However, that still leaves a broader range of naval operations than a single legal definition could capture. The definitional challenge lies within the fact that neither 'crisis management' nor 'crisis response operations' have traditionally been legal categories. However, unlike many policy creations which come and go they have stayed prominent on the policy agenda,[28] the notion of 'crisis management' is well established in Article 43 of the Treaty on European Union (TEU)[29]; it is also used in a related UN-EU Joint Declaration.[30] Although not

27 For these examples *see Heintschel von Heinegg* (n 10) 151, 152.

28 To give but one example, NATO's Comprehensive Political Guidance (endorsed by NATO Heads of State and Government at the Riga Summit on 29 November 2006 – <www.nato.int/docu/basictxt/b061129e.htm> (accessed 20 March 2008) keeps both 'crisis management' and 'crisis response operations', phrases already used in the Strategic Concepts 1991/1999, on the alliance's policy agenda (paras 3, 4, 6, 7(e) 11).

29 The consolidated version of the Treaty on European Union is available as EU document 6655/1/08 REV1 (dated 30 April 2008). The previous Article 17(2) TEU; (*cf.* (2002) *Official Journal of the European Union*, No. C 325) had codified the Petersberg Tasks adopted by the Western European Union (WEU) in Part II para 4 of its Petersberg Declaration of 9 June 1992 (<www.weu.int/documents/920619peten.pdf> (accessed 1 March 2009).

30 *Cf.* the Joint Declaration on UN-EU Co-operation in Crisis Management of 24 September 2003, available at: <http://ochaonline.un.org/Coordination/FieldCoordinationMechanisms/TheFribourgProcess/EuropeanCoordinationProcess/tabid/1393/language/fr-FR/Default.aspx> (accessed 1 March 2009). Note, however, that neither of the two most important recent UN policy documents, the reports *A more secure world* (n 16) and 'In larger freedom: towards development, security and human

codified, the notion of 'crisis response operations' is not disconnected from any legal framework, either: NATO repeatedly speaks of 'non-Article 5 crisis response operations', indicating thus that such operations do not amount to collective defence as contemplated by the said article of the North Atlantic Treaty[31] yet still come within the ambit of this treaty (although probably without an expressly written legal basis).[32]

Being comparably young creations still, the notions of 'crisis management' and 'crisis response operations' are not defined as legal terms of art. An initial legal definition of these phrases is nevertheless fully warranted in light of their close links to important international treaties. While the notion of 'crisis management' is actual treaty language, the notion of 'crisis response operations' supplements treaty language; both phrases should hence be defined in accordance with their ordinary meaning as contextualised in the Treaty on European Union and as complementing, in light of relevant policy decisions, the North Atlantic Treaty, respectively. Moreover, since both NATO and the EU engage in 'crisis management' and conduct 'crisis response operations' in accordance with UN mandates or in support of the principles of the UN,[33] the legal framework created by the UN Charter, in particular Chapter VII, must be borne in mind for the purpose of defining these phrases even though they are not Charter language.

---

rights for all' (UN document A/59/2005) uses the terms 'crisis management' and 'crisis response'.

31 NATO's Comprehensive Political Guidance distinguishes expressly between 'operations for collective defence and crisis response' (at para 11). This is congruent with NATO's Strategic Concept 1991 which introduced the differentiation between 'crisis management and defence' (at para 52); *see* text accompanying note 18 for the relationship between the phrases 'crisis management' and 'crisis response operations'.

32 Whilst not ignoring opposite views (e.g. the political remnant of the 'German Democratic Republic', under its then existing name 'Partei des Demokratischen Sozialismus', unsuccessfully challenged NATO's power to launch 'non-Article 5' operations; *see* the judgment of Germany's Federal Constitutional Court (22 November 2001) – case no. 2 BvE 6/99 – BVerfGE 104, 151 – English summary available at: <www.bundesverfassungsgericht.de/entscheidungen/es20011122_2bve000699en.html>), NATO's consolidated practice complements its constituent treaty. From a legal perspective, one line of argument would derive the non-Article 5 powers *a maiore ad minus* from Article 5 of the North Atlantic Treaty; another would characterise them as implied powers, and yet another one would rely on the North Atlantic Treaty's repeated references to the UN Charter and the purposes of the UN which encapsulate both UN-mandated operations and operations supporting the said purposes without a UN mandate. Indeed, para 10 of NATO's Strategic Concept 1999 (<www.nato.int/docu/pr/1999/p99-065e.htm> (accessed 1 March 2009)) contains a reference to Article 7 of the North Atlantic Treaty, which stipulates that:

> This Treaty does not affect, and shall not be interpreted as affecting in any way the rights and obligations under the Charter of the Parties which are members of the United Nations, or the primary responsibility of the Security Council for the maintenance of international peace and security.

A more detailed discussion of this issue is beyond the scope of this chapter.

33 *See* the reference to the UN Charter, in para 10 of NATO's Strategic Concept 1999 (Ibid.) as well as Article 21 TEU (which adapts the former Article 11(1) TEU) (n 29).

In the absence of definitions in legal instruments or jurisprudence, a legal definition can best be derived from relevant practice of States and IOs. Looking first at the nexus between 'crisis management' and 'crisis response operations', it appears from NATO's Comprehensive Political guidance that 'crisis response operations' are a subset of 'crisis management'.[34] The language of Article 43 TEU permits a similar approach. It specifies various 'tasks ... in crisis management.' It also expressly mentions that they may be performed using 'civilian and military means'. It follows that Article 43 TEU confirms the existence of civilian crisis management tasks. Moroever, there are two primary sources of actual definitions: policy level practice (contained in official documents) and operational practice (represented by actual conduct in theatre and by the documents containing related direction and guidance). As far as can be established, the only releasable definition of 'crisis management' is contained in the *NATO Glossary of Terms and Definitions*.[35] NATO has defined crisis management so as to comprise 'the coordinated actions taken to defuse crises, prevent their escalation into an armed conflict and contain hostilities if they should result'.[36] This definition is supplemented by the language used in the NATO Handbook 2006[37] which, in its capacity as a public relations tool rather than an official document, illustrates the object and purpose of crisis management as defined. *Sub specie* '[v]arying forms of crises and crisis response', the chapter on crisis management contains the observation that:

> Crisis management can involve both military and non-military measures to respond to a crisis situation threatening national or international security. A crisis may be essentially political in nature, or military, or humanitarian, and may be caused by political disputes or armed conflict, technological incidents or natural disasters. Crisis management consists of the different means of dealing with these varying forms of crises.[38]

---

34 At para 6, the Comprehensive Political Guidance highlights NATO's readiness:

> 'To contribute to effective conflict prevention and *to engage actively in crisis management, including through non-Article 5 crisis response operations*, as set out in the Strategic Concept'

(emphasis by the author).

35 The NATO Glossary (Allied Administrative Publication No. 6 – AAP-6 (2010)) is available at: <www.nato.int/docu/stanag/aap006/aap6.htm> (accessed 09 July 2010). The US has developed its own definition for primarily domestic purposes. *Cf.* the *Department of Defense Dictionary of Military and Associated Terms* (DoD Dictionary (Joint Publication 1-02 – JP 1-02 as amended through April 2010)), available at: <www.dtic.mil/doctrine/ new_pubs/jp1_02.pdf> (accessed 09 July 2010) as well as Joint Publication 3-28 which deals with Civil Support, available at: <www.fas.org/irp/doddir/dod/jp3-28.pdf> (accessed 1 March 2009).

36 *AAP-6* (2010) (Ibid.) at 2-C-19 (definition adopted 2 May 1995).

37 The NATO Handbook 2006 is available through the NATO E-Bookshop at: <http://193.219.98.16/index.php?inc=languages&idpub=62&orderby=language&taal=ENG>.

38 Ibid. 44. Note, however, that it seems that in the passages following the quote the terminology gets somewhat blurry as – unlike in the quote – the phrases 'crisis management operations' and 'crisis response operations' are used as though they had a synonymous meaning.

This NATO description has much in common with the analysis of relevant EU treaty law. The NATO Handbook 2006 goes on to distinguish 'two broad categories of crisis management operations ..., namely operations calling for collective defence, and other crisis response operations in which collective defence is not involved'.[39] In light of this differentiation, '[o]ther crisis response operations include all military operations that the Alliance may decide to conduct in a non-Article 5 situation'.[40] This differentiation creates a fairly broad non-Article 5 category.[41] From a policy perspective, the category of 'crisis situation threatening national or international security' yet short of international armed conflict (the latter being captured by Article 5 of the North Atlantic Treaty) conforms with the equally broad approach taken by then UN Secretary-General Annan, who canvassed the idea that the whole range of threats identified by the High-level Panel[42] is capable of triggering intervention

39 Ibid.

40 Ibid. 45.

41 The narrative of examples given for the non-Article 5 category (Ibid.) begins with peace support operations supporting the peace process in a conflict area, to continue that 'however, they include a range of other possibilities including conflict prevention, peacekeeping and peace enforcement measures, peace-making, peace-building, preventive deployment and humanitarian operations'. By way of contrast, the *NATO Glossary* (n 35) captures 'conflict prevention, peacemaking, peace enforcement, peacekeeping, peacebuilding and/or humanitarian operations' under the heading of peace support operation (2-P-3; definition adopted 14 October 2002). One might wonder to what extent the phrases 'crisis response operation' and 'peace support operation' overlap or if there is a difference between them at all.

The *NATO Handbook* (n 37) narrative mentions further examples such as support for Polish troops contributed to the Multinational Force in Iraq (MNF-I), the NATO Training Mission for Iraq (NTM-I), Operation Pakistan Earthquake Relief (2005) and assistance to Ukraine with respect to devastating floods – which, again, would all come within the ambit of peace support operation as per the NATO Glossary. In this context, the reference to NATO's supporting role for Polish troops contributed to the Multinational Force in Iraq (MNF-I) might create a wrong impression. In that case, NATO did by no means support the participation of one of its members in an armed conflict beyond the ambit of the North Atlantic Treaty under the guise of crisis response; rather it supported this member's support for the legitimate Government of Iraq in accordance with *UNSC Res. 1511* (16 October 2003) and 1546 (8 June 2004).

Even more blurry is the definition, by the NATO Glossary, of crisis response shipping which covers '[a]ll shipping employed in support of allied military operations, including ships taken up from trade, chartered shipping and, when appropriate, national prepositioned ships' (AAP-6 (2010) at 2-C-19; definition adopted 3 August 1998); that is, it integrates, *sub specie* 'allied military operations', shipping related to collective defence in the 'crisis response' category.

42 The Report *A more secure world: our shared responsibility* (n 16) identifies the following challenges:

- 'Economic and social threats, including poverty, infectious diseases and environmental degradation',
- 'Inter-State conflict',
- 'Internal conflict, including civil war, genocide and other large-scale atrocities',
- 'Nuclear, radiological, chemical and biological weapons',
- 'Terrorism', and

by the UN Security Council should national authorities be unable or unwilling to protect their citizens.[43] From a legal perspective, however, it encapsulates not only situations to which a military response involving the use of force would be lawful and legitimate but also situations to which, in light of the relevant practice, only responses excluding the use of force (except in self-defence) would be permissible; in particular, if they stand on their own, essentially economic and social threats to international security and threats thereto posed by transnational organised crime do not, under current international law, justify the use of force.[44] On that basis, the differentiation between 'military and non-military measures' responding to a crisis captures 'military measures' (this phrase being synonymous to 'military crisis response operations') and two sub-categories of 'non-military measures', namely 'non-military crisis response operations' including those conducted by armed forces exercising non-military tasks (reflecting the absence of purely civilian capabilities within NATO) and the entire repertoire of crisis diplomacy as e.g. referred to in Article 33 of the UN Charter.

For the purposes of this chapter, crisis management covers military crisis response operations, non-military crisis response operations, and non-military measures addressing a crisis. The notion of 'crisis response operations' covers all operations implementing a (preferably comprehensive) crisis management strategy which aims at resolving a crisis. Crisis response operations in maritime environments are those conducted mainly by naval and amphibious forces, and primarily off-shore, that is, regardless of whether in the territorial waters or the contiguous zones of one or more States, or on the high seas including the exclusive economic zones of one or more States, or in archipelagic waters.

Crisis response operations are military in nature if it is their purpose, by way of performing military tasks with military means and measures, to prevent the escalation of a given situation into an armed conflict, or to contain actual or imminent hostilities, including all kinds of the use of force by actors possessing paramilitary and/or military capabilities.[45] Non-military crisis response operations are those abstaining from the use of military means and measures, and the performance of military tasks; apart from the purposes of preventing the escalation of a given situation into an armed conflict and containing actual or imminent hostilities by diplomatic means, they also serve the purpose of keeping crises at a level of escalation not involving the imminence of an outbreak of large-scale violence or hostilities. To differentiate between military crisis response operations and non-military crisis response operations, the rule of thumb is that armed forces receive mandates to perform military

---

· 'Transnational organized crime'.

At paras 17-23, and 12 – executive summary, and 25 – synopsis of part two.

43 *See In larger freedom* (n 30) para 135.

44 It would be hard to demonstrate that the post-Cold War policy level practice constitutes a legal policy consensus concerning military responses involving the use of force in response to these kinds of threats. *See* U. Häußler, 'Enforcing the Rule of Law: Military Contributions to Comprehensive Security' (2008) 8 *NZAFLR* 47, 55-58.

45 The criterion referring to paramilitary/military capabilities is derived from the practice of international peace missions. *Cf.* U. Häußler, *Ensuring and Enforcing Human Security* (Wolf Legal Publishers, Nijmegen, 2007) 91 and 97sqq.

crisis response operations. Since, however, armed forces may (exceptionally) have to perform non-military tasks and use corresponding means and measures, confirmation of this presumption might be required in cases of doubt, relying on the following criteria:

- the level of the threat tackled by the operation as identified in the mandate and other relevant documents;[46]
- the purpose of the operation as per its mandate;
- the responsibilities and tasks defined by the mandate of the operation; and
- the authority conferred on the operation (or, more precisely, its lead organisation[47]) to perform its responsibilities and tasks.

With respect to these criteria, the presumption that an operation mandated to armed forces is a military crisis response operation is usually confirmed:

- if the threat addressed by the operation arises from the existence, or imminent or actual use, of paramilitary or military capabilities;
- if the operation shall contribute to the establishment of conditions within which a local government can increasingly exercise effective, efficient, and accountable control over territory and population;
- if the operation shall suppress on-going hostilities, or the re-emergence thereof contrary to a cease-fire or peace settlement; or
- if the operation shall exercise transitional authority on the basis of Chapter VII of the UN Charter[48] or support the exercise of a state's inherent right of self-defence.

As a rule, the coincidental existence of threats of a lower level, the inclusion of purposes other than suppressing paramilitary or military violence, and of e.g. humanitarian responsibilities and tasks, do not alter the military nature of a crisis response operation.

The presumption that armed forces receive mandates to perform military crisis response operations is based on the general empirical insight that the operations of armed forces, while serving political ends, are of a military nature. There is no reason why this empirical insight should not be valid in the field of crisis management. Exceptions from the presumption in question are usually rooted in express legal provision. The UNCLOS provisions concerning the exercise of flag State jurisdiction and/or otherwise conducting law enforcement at sea are an apt example. These provisions define non-military tasks serving a non-military purpose, as reflected in the object and purpose of the part of UNCLOS to which they belong – that is, exercise of jurisdiction at sea. The mandates of crisis response operations in maritime environments may likewise contain provision justifying the characterisation of the operation as non-military

46 The mandate may not address such aspects of a threat as available in classified information only. Such information will, however, usually be accessible by those approving, planning, and executing the operation; it will, accordingly, influence their decisions.

47 For the role of the lead organisation *see Häußler* (n 45) 62sqq.

48 Note, however, that as demonstrated by the relevant mandates, non-military crisis response operations such as UNMIK and hybrid crisis response operations with a distinct non-military component such as UNTAET may also possess transitional authority based on Chapter VII of the UN Charter.

in nature; they must hence, like any other mandate, be analysed in light of the mentioned presumption, taking the criteria specified above duly into account.

2.3 The Legal Framework of Crisis Response Operations in Maritime Environments

Being an umbrella term for operations mandated by the UN or supporting the principles of the UN as laid down in its Charter, the notion of crisis response operations is linked closer to the UN Charter than to legal differentiations between separate areas at sea and/or the legal nature of given situations according to classical categories of international law. The UN Charter, Chapter VII in particular, has overcome the classical war-and-peace divide for the purpose of maintaining and restoring international peace and security.[49] Since the end of the Cold War the consolidated practice of international peace missions has continuously supplemented the framework of the UN Charter with a growing body of customary international law.[50] As indicated in the course of discussing the criteria to distinguish military crisis response operations from their non-military counterpart, recent UN-mandated crisis response operations on land have mainly served the purpose of suppressing, or preventing the re-emergence of, armed conflict or hostilities, based on the principle of impartiality;[51] or they have been (or are being) conducted in support of legitimate governments involved in an armed conflict or hostilities with insurgents and/or IOs assisting these governments under a civilian mandate.[52] At sea, the primary focus of the recent UN-mandated crisis response operations – the maritime component of UNIFIL, the EU Operation Atalanta, and NATO's operations at the Horn of Africa – is maritime support of legitimate governments and IOs. NATO's Operation Active Endeavour[53] and the maritime component of the US-led multina-

49 *See* U. Häußler, 'General Principles of International Humanitarian and Human Rights Law: A Tool to Overcome the War-and-Peace Divide in International Law' in C.M. Bailliet (ed), *Security: A Multidisciplinary Normative Approach* (Martinus Nijhoff, Leiden, Boston, 2009) 49sqq.

50 *For examples see* the discussion in *Häußler* (n 45) 106sq and 138sq.

51 Examples are the UN-mandated NATO- and, respectively, EU-led peace forces deployed to Bosnia and Herzegovina following the Dayton Agreement (IFOR/SFOR/NHQ Sarajevo and EUFOR ALTHEA), to Kosovo following the ceasefire agreed upon trough the Military-Technical Agreement Between the International Security Force ('KFOR') and the Governments of Federal Republic of Yugoslavia and the Republic of Serbia of 9 June 1999 (KFOR) and the UN peace force in the Democratic Republic of the Congo (MONUC).

52 Examples are the UN-mandated International Security Assistance Force in Afghanistan (ISAF) and Multinational Force in Iraq (MNF-I) after the end of the occupation by the Iraqi Freedom coalition (*see* para 9 of *UNSC Res. 1546* (n 41)); for the initial authorization of MNF-I *see* para 13 of *UNSC Res. 1511* (n 41). The mandates of ISAF and MNF-I (have) provide(d) for support to UNAMA, the United Nations Assistance Mission in Afghanistan, and UNAMI, the United Nations Assistance Mission in Iraq, respectively. MONUC is likewise mandated to support the government of the Democratic Republic of the Congo.

53 *Cf.* <www.afsouth.nato.int/JFCN_Operations/ActiveEndeavour/Endeavour.htm> (acces-

tional Operation Enduring Freedom support the US's inherent right to self-defence in accordance with Article 51 of the UN Charter.[54]

Unlike Operations Active Endeavour and Enduring Freedom, the maritime component of UNIFIL, the EU Operation Atalanta, and NATO's Operation Ocean Shield (which followed Allied Provider and Allied Protector) have detailed UN mandates. This section will analyse the mentioned mandates and key aspects of their implementation in light of the criteria for assessing the military nature of crisis response operations.

2.4 UNIFIL

UNIFIL, originally established by UN Security Council Resolutions 425 and 426 (1978), had its maritime component added after the adoption of UN Security Council Resolution 1701 (2006).[55] Although initially drafted with a focus on ground operations,[56] the new UNIFIL mandate proved to be sufficiently flexible to cover naval operations, too. Upon a request made by the Lebanese Prime Minister,[57] the UNIFIL Maritime Task Force was established and became operational on 15 October 2006.[58] No doubts were raised at this stage about the utilisation of Resolution 1701 (2006) for the UNIFIL Maritime Task Force; the fact that the mandate was extended repeatedly with full knowledge of the members of the Security Council of this Task Force and its operations,[59] confirms that it covers the Task Force and its operations *ab initio*.

---

sed 1 March 2009).

54 The exercise of this right was endorsed by *UNSC Res. 1368* (12 September 2001) and *1373* (n 20). – This chapter will not discuss the question of whether Article 51 of the UN Charter can still be relied upon with respect to Operations Active Endeavour and Enduring Freedom. Suffice it to say that the UN Security Council has never questioned the validity of *UNSC Res. 1368* (above) and that States seem to treat it as still being good law, as well: for instance, Germany has repeatedly extended its national mandate for contributing forces to these operations with parliament approving the cabinet decision to continue the deployment 'in support of the combined response to terrorist attacks on the US on the basis of Article 51 of the UN Charter and Article 5 of the North Atlantic Treaty as well as *UNSC Res. 1368* and *1373*'. *See e.g.* the title of the cabinet decision submitted to parliament as print 16/10720, available at: <http://dip21.bundestag.de/dip21/btd/16/107/1610720.pdf> (accessed 1 March 2009; my translation).

55 The mandate was subsequently extended by *UNSC Res. 1773* (21 August 2007), *1832* (27 August 2008) and *1884* (27 August 2009).

56 Like the discussions in the Security Council meeting where the mandate was first adopted (*see* the meeting record (11 August 2006) UN document S/PV.5511) the resolution does not make any express reference to the Maritime Task Force.

57 *Cf.* para 36 of the United Nations Secretary-General's Report (12 September 2006) UN document S/2006/730.

58 *See* United Nations Secretary-General's Report (1 December 2006) UN document S/2006/933, 2, and the related UNIFIL press release at <www.un.org/Depts/dpko/missions/unifil/pr065.pdf>.

59 In the preamble of *UNSC Res. 1773* (n 55) the Security Council:

Reaffirm[s] UNIFIL's authority to take all necessary action in areas of deployment of

2.4.1 Threat Assessment

Resolution 1701 (2006) responded to the brief period of hostilities following the abduction of Israel Defence Force soldiers by Hezbollah whereupon, as determined by the UN Security Council, the situation in Lebanon constituted a threat to international peace and security; it seems beyond debate that the elements of this threat are not either solely economic and social in nature or posed by transnational crime only and that they hence justify a response involving the use of force.

2.4.2 Purpose

UNSCR 1701 (2006) complements *UNSCR 425* (1978) in requiring UNIFIL to support the Government of Lebanon in its effort to exercise its authority throughout the territory of Lebanon.[60] As will be discussed shortly, this effort is severely hampered by armed groups present in southern Lebanon. Countering them justifies a military response.

2.4.3 Responsibilities and Tasks

While UNIFIL has been fulfilling land-based responsibilities and tasks concerning movements of ground forces since its establishment, *UNSCR 1701* (2006) has added further responsibilities and tasks to its mandate, namely to:

- assist the Lebanese armed forces in taking steps towards the establishment between the Blue Line and the Litani river of an area free of any armed personnel, assets and weapons other than those of the Government of Lebanon and of UNIFIL deployed in this area (para 11(e) read together with para 8), and
- assist the Government of Lebanon, at its request, in securing its borders and other entry points to prevent the entry into Lebanon without its consent of arms or related materiel (para 11(f) read together with para 14).

These responsibilities and tasks imply a military response.

2.4.4 Authority

UNIFIL's authority is based on the consent of the Government of Lebanon, as illustrated by the UN Security Council's observation that it acted 'in support of a request

---

> its forces and as it deems within its capabilities, to ensure that its area of operations is not utilized for hostile activities of any kind and to resist attempts by forceful means to prevent it from discharging its mandate.

In the meeting where this resolution was adopted, Indonesia made express reference of 'its intended contribution of additional assets to UNIFIL's Maritime Task Force' (meeting record (24 August 2007) UN document S/PV.5733, 4); it would seem counter-intuitive, therefore, to assert that the quoted language was not meant to apply to the Maritime Task Force.

60 As per para 3 of *UNSC Res. 425* (19 March 1978) the key purpose of the deployment of UNIFIL was 'assisting the Government of Lebanon in ensuring the return of its effective authority in the area'. *UNSC Res. 1701* (11 August 2006) endorsed a request for additional support.

from the Government of Lebanon to deploy an international force to assist it to exercise its authority throughout the territory'. By way of that consent, Lebanon has conferred authority on the UN which the Security Council has granted to UNIFIL in its capacity as a subsidiary organ of the United Nations established in accordance with Article 7(2) of the UN Charter.

The scope of UNIFIL's authority derives from the determination that it may:

> take all necessary action in areas of deployment of its forces and as it deems within its capabilities, to ensure that its area of operations is not utilized for hostile activities of any kind, to resist attempts by forceful means to prevent it from discharging its duties under the mandate of the Security Council ...[61]

This language is slightly different from authorisations of the use of force under Chapter VII of the UN Charter ('all necessary means' / 'all necessary measures') and has, accordingly, given raise to doubts concerning the degree of force so authorised.[62] Considering, however, that the phrase 'all necessary action' had been used to legitimise the use of force on previous occasions[63] and that the term 'action' encapsulates

61 Para 12 of *UNSC Res. 1701* (Ibid.).

62 German commentators have suggested that in light of its content the resolution cannot be considered to fit in either of the frameworks created by Chapters VI and VII of the UN Charter. *See* M. Asseburg,'Der Bundeswehreinsatz im Libanon: Die Maritime Task Force im Rahmen von »UNIFIL plus«' in St. Mair (ed), *Auslandseinsätze der Bundeswehr* (Stiftung Wissenschaft und Politik, Berlin, 2007) 101. (available at: <www.swp-berlin.org/common/get_document.php?asset_id=4355>). This, however, is a erroneous conclusion from the correct assessment that UNIFIL has 'a robust yet not an offensive mandate' reached by D. Weingärtner 'Das UNIFIL-Mandat der Bundeswehr – politische und rechtliche Aspekte' (2007) *Journal of International Law of Peace and Armed Conflict* 116-119, on which M. Asseburg relies.

63 Examples at hand comprise Annex 1A to the Dayton Agreement (Article I(2)(b): '... to authorise the IFOR to take such *actions* as required, *including the use of necessary force* ...'; Article IV(2)(b): '...*military action* by the IFOR, *including the use of necessary force* ...' – the same language is used in Article IV(2)(c)(4) & (6), IV(4), IV(6), VI(6), VI(9)(a), and VI(9)(b)(2)) available at: <www.nato.int/Ifor/gfa/gfa-home.htm> (accessed 26 May 2009) and Article I(2) of the Military Technical Agreement between the International Security Force ('KFOR') and the Governments of the Federal Republic of Yugoslavia and the Republic of Serbia available at: <www.nato.int/kosovo/docu/a990609a.htm> (accessed 19 March 2009) provides that:

> The State Governmental authorities of the Federal Republic of Yugoslavia and the Republic of Serbia understand and agree that the international security force ('KFOR') will deploy following the adoption of the UNSC Res. referred to in paragraph 1 and operate without hindrance within Kosovo and with the authority to take *all necessary action* to establish and maintain a secure environment for all citizens of Kosovo and otherwise carry out its mission.

(all emphases by the author). – Note, however, that only some members of the UN Security Council were aware of the MTA-Kosovo when *UNSC Res. 1244* (10 June 1999) whose para 7 authorised the establishment of KFOR 'with all necessary means to fulfil its responsibilities', was adopted.

'the use of armed force' e.g. within NATO,[64] this phrase is equally capable of expressing an authorisation of the use of the full spectrum of force as the usual language. In the absence of indications to the contrary, the phrase 'all necessary action' confers authority to use military force on UNIFIL.

Nothing to the contrary can be derived from the fact that unlike many other military crisis response operations, UNIFIL does not have a mandate expressly based on Chapter VII of the UN Charter. The practice of the Security Council indicates that a UN mandate adopted with the consent of that State does not need a legal basis in Chapter VII of the UN Charter.[65]

2.4.5 UNIFIL Practice: Support to the Government of Lebanon – UNCLOS – Self-Defence

The Area of Maritime Operations (AMO) assigned to the UNIFIL Maritime Task Force covers some 110 x 43 nautical miles,[66] including all of Lebanon's territorial waters and significant portions of the high seas.[67] The novelty – and in particular here it is true that, as observed by then UN Secretary-General Kofi A. Annan, '[a] large maritime element presents a new challenge for a peacekeeping operation'[68] – is that with respect to the UNIFIL Maritime Task Force, one single mandate covers two areas of a legally different nature and in which different measures of authority may be exercised under the usually applicable legal framework embodied in UNCLOS. The key question is whether it makes a difference, legally, whether the UNIFIL Maritime Task Force exercises its authority in Lebanon's territorial waters only, or also in those adjacent parts of the high seas which form part of the AMO.

So far, the practice of the UNIFIL Maritime Task Force has avoided tackling the challenge because it focused the exercise of actual authority under its mandate on Lebanon's territorial waters.[69] For that purpose, the Task Force has made arrange-

64 *See Article 5 of the North Atlantic Treaty* (n 32).

65 As far as maritime environments are concerned, the authorisation of the use of force, by the UK, to enforce at sea the embargo against Southern Rhodesia is the key example. *UNSC Res. 1701* (n 60) adapts the South Rhodesia precedent to the exigencies of UNIFIL. In both cases, the relevant resolutions contain the determination that either a threat to the peace or a threat to international peace and security exists (or existed), yet in neither of them did the UN Security Council state that it acted on the basis of Chapter VII of the UN Charter. From my perspective, nothing to the contrary can be derived from the mandate of Operation Desert Storm (*UNSC Res. 678* (29 November 1990)) where the UN Security Council made use of its Chapter VII powers in support of the Government-in-exile of Kuwait.

66 *Cf.* the information on UNIFIL given at <www.einsatz.bundeswehr.de> (accessed 1 March 2009).

67 *Weingärtner* (n 62) 116, 118: up to 50 nautical miles off the Lebanese coast.

68 Para 36 of the *United Nations Secretary-General Report* (n 57).

69 None of the relevant reports submitted by the United Nations Secretary-General to the UN Security Council specifies any exercise of authority in the high seas part of the AMO. That might be without prejudice to the tracking of vessels, though: *cf. Weingärtner* (n 62) 116, 118. The author also discusses, by way of hypothesis, what questions concerning exercise of authority might cause concerns, namely transfer of detain-

ments with the Lebanese Navy concerning access to Lebanese territorial waters, the conduct of boarding and inspections, communications and reporting procedures.[70] These arrangements differentiate between four sub-zones of the part of the AMO covering Lebanon's territorial waters, namely the portions of the Lebanese territorial waters north and south of UNIFIL's Area of Operations on land (i.e. the Litani River), and within these portions those between the coast-line and six nautical miles and those between six and twelve nautical miles off shore. In these sub-zones, the UNIFIL Maritime Task Force collaborates closely with the Lebanese Navy and performs such tasks as checking and confirming the identity of vessels, and diverting suspicious vessels to Lebanese ports for inspection by Lebanese naval and customs officials upon arrival.[71] In light of this practice, limited both *ratione loci* and *ratione materiae*, the scope of UNIFIL's authority has not been a matter of practical challenge:[72] the vessels whose identity the Maritime Task Force has checked and confirmed, have complied with orders diverting them to Lebanese ports.[73]

UNIFIL's dormant maritime authority in the portion of the high seas integrated in its AMO was never waived by this restrictive practice. The 'request from the Government of Lebanon to deploy an international force to assist it to exercise its authority throughout the territory' facilitates the assessment of UNIFIL's authority within the AMO both inside Lebanon's territorial waters and beyond. As far as the territorial waters are concerned, the supplementing arrangements between the UNIFIL Maritime Task Force and Lebanon define the nature of the assistance needed by the Government of Lebanon; for the purposes of interpreting Resolution 1701 (2006) it can be understood as confining the range of 'necessary action' to measures aimed at supporting the Lebanese Navy and Customs. Beyond Lebanon's ter-

ees, were they be taken by UNIFIL, to Lebanon whose criminal law still permits capital punishment (Ibid. 119).

70 Para 16 of the United Nations Secretary-General Report (14 March 2007) UN document S/2007/147. In accordance with these arrangements, Lebanese naval liaison officers are on board the ship commanding maritime interdiction operations (*see* text accompanying n 96 for the definition) as well as at UNIFIL headquarters: *see* para 30 of the United Nations Secretary-General Report (28 February 2008) UN document S/2008/135.

71 *See* Para 16 of the United Nations Secretary-General Report (Ibid.); para 26 of the United Nations Secretary-General Report (28 June 2007) UN document S/2007/392.

72 The exercise of authority in accordance with the mandate under *UNSC Res. 1701* (n 60) must be distinguished from certain sporadic incidents with the Israeli Defence Force (IDF). Most of these incidents were resolved in a more or less diplomatic manner. *See, for instance*, para 26 of the United Nations Secretary-General Report (27 June 2008) UN document S/2008/425, concerning the hailing, by the IDF on 22 May 2008, of a passenger vessel coming from Larnaca, Cyprus, and heading to Naqura that was being utilized for UNIFIL troop rotation.

73 The United Nations Secretary-General Report (18 November 2008) UN document S/2008/715 mentions that since October 2006, the Maritime Task Force has hailed and queried more than 19,700 ships in the area of maritime operations. All 185 vessels that were identified as suspicious since October 2006 were subsequently inspected and cleared the Lebanese Navy and Customs (at para 27). The earlier reports, all of them quoted above, contain no information to the contrary.

ritorial waters, the request's language, as reproduced in Resolution 1701 (2006), does not in and of itself contain a limitation of UNIFIL's authority *ratione loci*; it merely reinforces that UNIFIL operations outside Lebanon's territory (i.e. including its territorial waters) shall serve the purpose of the overall mandate. However, can Lebanon's consent be a legal basis for any operations of the UNIFIL Maritime Task Force on the high seas? It can: because while Lebanese territorial sovereignty ends at the outer limits of its territorial waters, some of its sovereign rights extend beyond. Indeed, nothing indicates that the Government of Lebanon is precluded from requesting, or did not intend to request, assistance in exercising such sovereign rights as it may have on the high seas, for the purpose of being able to fully exercise its territorial authority within Lebanon's borders regardless of whether at land or at sea. Now that the UN Security Council has given full effect to the request of the Government of Lebanon, UNIFIL may indeed support the exercise of such Lebanese sovereign rights as applicable *ratione loci* in that part of the AMO beyond Lebanon's territorial waters. To explore the details of UNIFIL's authority in that respect, the analysis will now turn to the sovereign rights which Lebanon may exercise on the high seas.

The most obvious (confirmatory) source of Lebanese sovereign rights applicable on the high seas is UNCLOS. Since the request made by the Government of Lebanon as endorsed by the UN Security Council has conferred Lebanese sovereign rights on the UN, Resolution 1701 (2006) empowers UNIFIL vessels, regardless of which State contributed them, to exercise the same rights as Lebanese warships; their authority to do so is demonstrated by flying the UN flag. In particular, UNIFIL vessels may exercise jurisdiction on behalf of Lebanon as envisaged by Article 110(1) of UNCLOS. Second, Lebanese commercial vessels are not 'foreign ships' if encountered in the course of an operation conducted by the UNIFIL Maritime Task Force. As a result, they are not protected by Article 110 of UNCLOS. However, UNIFIL's conferred powers extend beyond the categories of suspicion justifying the boarding, by a warship, of a foreign ship encountered on the high seas. The phrase 'reasonable ground for suspecting' activities pertaining to those categories indicates that the said provision is concerned with law enforcement at sea – more precisely, its jurisdictional aspects. By contrast, the responsibilities and tasks assigned to UNIFIL including its Maritime Task Force are not limited to law enforcement. In particular, UNIFIL's authority, on the high seas, to establish an area free of any opposing armed personnel, assets and weapons – a 'de-militiarised' zone (cf. para 11(e) read together with para 8 of Resolution 1701 (2006)) – and to secure Lebanon's borders to prevent the unauthorised entry of arms or related materiel (cf. paras 11(f) and 14 of Resolution 1701 (2006)),[74] is not addressed by Article 110(1) of UNCLOS. Accordingly, these responsibilities can only flow from a source other than this provision, and in fact external to UNCLOS – and so does the authorisation of the use of force for the purposes of enforcing their implementation (cf. para 12 of Resolution 1701 (2006)).

Where the threshold of armed attack is crossed, a State may rely on its inherent right of self-defence in accordance with Article 51 of the UN Charter to justify the use of military force action against opposing armed personnel, assets and weaponry on its territory. It may rely on the same right with respect to supplies destined

74 For a similar assessment *cf. Weingärtner* (n 62) 116, 118.

to such opposing armed personnel and reaching its territory from the high seas. As will be demonstrated shortly, that is what the Government of Lebanon did when it conferred the right to take action beyond the scope of UNCLOS on the United Nations.

Before the present analysis can focus on the substantive criteria for the exercise of the right of self-defence, it must briefly deal with the questions of whether the law of the sea does in any way affect the applicability of this right. This question had already been discussed with respect to the predecessor norm of Article 110 of UNCLOS; it must be answered in the negative since '[t]here can be little doubt that in the normative hierarchy Article 51 is antecedent to Article 22, which gives no directions as to the case of self-defence'.[75] The applicability of the right of self-defence on the high seas is not only a matter of normative hierarchy though. Armed attacks may first occur at sea, e.g. initiated by or embodied in seaborne acts of aggression. Indeed, the whole range of acts of aggression captured by the UN Definition of Aggression[76] can be committed on the high seas or in a manner involving the use of the high seas. In the present context, '[t]he sending by or on behalf of a State of armed bands, groups, irregulars or mercenaries, which carry out acts of armed force against another State of such gravity as to amount to the acts listed above, or its substantial involvement therein' (Article 3(g)) is particularly relevant. Now that an armed attack can occur at or from sea there is no reason why self-defence on the high seas should not be covered by Article 51 of the UN Charter. Just like, accordingly, nothing prevents Lebanon from requesting UN support in the exercise of its inherent right of self-defence at sea as a means of collective self-defence, there is nothing in the UN Charter that prevents the UN Security Council from providing support to Lebanon's national self-defence through UNIFIL under its authority and responsibility, defined by Article 51 of the UN Charter, 'to take at any time such action as it deems necessary in order to maintain or restore international peace and security'.

As to the substantial criteria for the exercise of Lebanon's inherent right of self-defence with UNIFIL support, the question is whether there does indeed exist a threat to Lebanon's national security which at the same time jeopardises the exercise, by the Government of Lebanon, of its authority throughout the territory and meets the threshold that 'an armed attack' occurs, or has occurred and is on-going. While the request made by the Government of Lebanon did not use language which openly identified that Lebanon was continuously under attack at the time the request was made, including by way of provision of supplies from the high seas, a brief analysis of the circumstances as depicted in relevant UN documents provides sufficient clarity to that extent. The threat to international peace and security which triggered Lebanon's inherent right of self-defence was twofold, namely it consisted (and still consists) of the presence of opposing armed groups in southern Lebanon which prevented (and still prevents) the Government of Lebanon from exercising the full scale of its sovereign rights in the area, and the infliction of hostilities, by the said armed groups, on Israel which provoked and may again provoke legitimate countermeas-

75 *O'Connell* (n 1) 804; the quote goes to Article 22 of the Geneva Convention on the Law of the Sea 1958.

76 *UNGA Resolution 3314* (XXIX) (14 December 1974).

ures to the ultimate detriment of Lebanon and its government in the capacity as the repository of Lebanon's sovereignty.

The request referred to by the UN Security Council reiterates a concern shared by Lebanon and the international community for extended periods of time. In particular, following Israel's withdrawal from southern Lebanon (through which Israel had fulfilled its obligations under Resolutions 425 and 426 (1978))[77] the UN Security Council has repeatedly noted the lack of the full exercise of Lebanon's sovereign rights by its government.[78] The source of the lack of full exercise of Lebanon's sovereign rights by its government was aptly identified when the UN Security Council dealt with the fact that apart from non-Israeli foreign forces;[79] Lebanese and non-Lebanese militias – which still awaited disbanding and disarmament – remained present in Lebanon in September 2004.[80] That is, the situation in Lebanon had not improved in this respect since 22 May 2000, on which day a Report submitted by the UN Secretary-General had noted that:

> Lebanese and other armed groups in Lebanon and Member States having influence over them, must provide their cooperation and support to UNIFIL to implement resolution 425 (1978). Only with the support of all parties concerned will it be possible for peace and security to be restored in southern Lebanon.[81]

77 *See* the Statement by the President of the Security Council (18 June 2000) UN document S/PRST/2000/21, which endorsed the United Nations Secretary-General's conclusion (contained in the report of 16 June 2000, UN document S/2000/590, at paras 15-18) that as of 16 June 2000 Israel had withdrawn its forces from Lebanon in accordance with resolution 425 (1978). The UN Security Council has subsequently recalled that it has endorsed the quoted conclusion reached by the United Nations Secretary-General, in the preamble of *UNSC Res. 1310* (27 July 2000), *1337* (31 January 2001), *1365* (31 July 2001), *1391* (28 November 2002), *1428* (30 July 2002), *1461* (30 January 2003), *1496* (31 July 2003), *1525* (30 January 2004), *1553* (29 July 2004), *1559* (2 September 2004), *1583* (28 January 2005) and *1655* (31 January 2006).

78 Initially it did so by way of expressing that the Government of Lebanon shall ensure the return of its effective authority and presence in the south, including with a significant deployment of the Lebanese Armed Forces as soon as possible. *See* para 6 of *UNSC Res. 1310* (Ibid.), para 5 of *UNSC Res. 1337* (Ibid.), para 5 of *UNSC Res. 1365* (Ibid.), para 5 of *UNSC Res. 1391* (Ibid.). Note that in the United Nations Secretary-General Report (22 May 2000) UN document S/2000/460, para 28, the United Nations Secretary-General had recommended that '[t]he Lebanese Armed Forces should ensure that all national territory falls under the effective authority of the Government' following Israel's withdrawal, dealing with this question separately from Lebanon's pledge to re-establish local civilian administration and to assume local law enforcement functions. Later, the UN Security Council commended that steps in that direction had been taken (*see* para 5 of *UNSC Res. 1428* (Ibid.), para 5 of *UNSC Res. 1461* (Ibid.)), then welcomed these steps (*see* para 4 of *UNSC Res. 1496* (Ibid.)) yet still encouraged the Government of Lebanon to continue its effort (*see* para 4 of *UNSC Res. 1525* (n 77), para 4 of *UNSC Res. 1553* (n 77)).

79 *See* para 2 of *UNSC Res. 1559* (n 77).

80 Para 3 of *UNSC Res. 1559* (n 77) '*call[ed] for* the disbanding and disarmament of all Lebanese and non-Lebanese militias'; *see also* para 2 of *UNSC Res. 1680* (17 May 2006).

81 *United Nations Secretary-General Report* (22 May 2000) (n 78) para 43.

This careful language succeeds in keeping the reader aware that the continued presence of any opposing armed group is irreconcilable with the return of the Government of Lebanon's effective authority over southern Lebanon (cf. para 3 of UNSCR 425 (1978)). The continued presence of foreign, and foreign-influenced, armed groups (militias) constitutes a violation of Article 2(4) of the UN Charter[82] amounting to an act of aggression on Lebanon.[83] Article 3(g) of the UN Definition of Aggression – in that respect reflecting customary international law[84] – includes 'the sending by or on behalf of a State of armed bands, groups, irregulars or mercenaries, which carry out acts of armed force against another State'; it also specifies that this kind of activities, if attributable to a State, as well as a State's 'substantial involvement therein', can be 'of such gravity as to amount to' an actual armed attack conducted by regular forces of that State. According to the ICJ, the relevant criterion is the gravity of the activity; thus, an act of aggression is committed by way of 'sending by a State of armed bands to the territory of another State, if such an operation, because of its scale and effects, would have been classified as an armed attack rather than as a mere frontier incident had it been carried out by regular armed forces'. In that context, 'assistance to rebels in the form of the provision of weapons or logistical or other support' – including from the high seas – likewise constitutes an armed attack.[85]

The presence of foreign-influenced opposing armed groups in southern Lebanon meets this criterion which in essence assimilates using a proxy to conduct of a State's own armed forces. In the case of southern Lebanon, the foreign-influenced opposing armed groups have functioned as a proxy for an occupation of Lebanon by the States having influence over them;[86] hence the inability of the Government of Lebanon

82 Article 2(4) of the UN Charter has established the customary and peremptory principle of international law that States shall refrain in their international relations from the threat or use of force against the territorial integrity or political independence of any State, or in any other manner inconsistent with the purposes of the United Nations. The UN General Assembly has explained, in the Friendly Relations Declaration (*UNGA Resolution 2625* (XXV) (24 October 1970) Annex), that according to this principle, *inter alia*:

> Every State has the duty to refrain from organizing or encouraging the organization of irregular forces or armed bands including mercenaries, for incursion into the territory of another State.
>
> Every State has the duty to refrain from organizing, instigating, assisting or participating in acts of civil strife or terrorist acts in another State or acquiescing in organized activities within its territory directed towards the commission of such acts, when the acts referred to in the present paragraph involve a threat or use of force.

83 Note that according to the ICJ the threshold of aggression under Article 3(g) of the UN Definition of Aggression is slightly higher than threshold of the prohibition of the use of force in international relations established by Article 2(4) of the UN Charter which also encapsulates less grave forms of the use of force. *See* the judgment of the International Court of Justice of 27 June 1986 – *Case concerning Military and Paramilitary Activities in and against Nicaragua* (*Nicaragua v. United States of America*) [1986] ICJ Rep. 14, para 191.

84 As per the judgment of the ICJ in *Nicaragua v. United States of America* (Ibid.) para 195.

85 Ibid. Note that the ICJ considered such activities to run counter the principle of non-intervention, as well (at paras 202sqq).

86 Like the UN Security Council, I have no intention to identify these States.

to re-establish its authority by way of a significant deployment of its armed forces. As a result, it was appropriate that the UN Secretary-General identified, albeit in diplomatically cautious language, this presence as threatening international peace and security. As the resolutions concerning the situation in the Middle East and focusing on Lebanon under this agenda item never ceased to contain the implication that the presence of opposing armed groups in southern Lebanon prevented the Government of Lebanon from re-establishing full authority,[87] this aggression amounting to an armed attack against Lebanon has never ceased to exist, either.

The armed attack against Lebanon had, moreover, an unpleasant side effect, namely – in the, initially again diplomatically careful, language of the UN Security Council – cases of use of force from the territory of Lebanon;[88] that is, against Israel.[89] This side effect constitutes in itself a violation of international law. Article 3(f) of the UN Definition of Aggression requires the Government of Lebanon to prevent the use of Lebanon's territory for the purposes of an aggression against another State, reflecting the laws of neutrality which prohibit that such use be permitted with respect to any armed conflict to which a State is not a party. It may have been with this requirement in mind that the UN Security Council called upon 'the Government of Lebanon … to exert control and monopoly over the use of force on its entire territory and to prevent attacks from Lebanon across the Blue Line'.[90] Later on, it named Hezbollah as responsible for initiating hostilities on 21 November 2005 and mentioned the firing of rockets from Lebanon into Israel on 27 December 2005, for the first time identifying Israel as the victim of hostilities committed from Lebanon.[91] As a result, the proxy occupation of southern Lebanon by foreign-influenced opposing armed groups effectively deprived Lebanon of the ability to fulfil its obligation to prevent an aggression from being perpetrated from its territory, rendering this aggression attributable to the armed groups in question, maybe even the States having influence over them. Moreover, as the activities of armed groups not authorised in the 'de-militiarised' area ultimately triggered Israel's campaign, they had a direct adverse effect on Lebanon's territory and nationals and hence separately triggered Lebanon's inherent right of self-defence against the said armed groups and their sponsors. It should be noted in this context that Lebanon cannot predict what future aggressive activities perpetrated by opposing armed groups might trigger further countermeasures by Israel; Lebanon can, accordingly – using the famous *Caroline* formula – rely on the 'necessity of self-defence, instant, overwhelming, leaving no choice of means, and no moment for deliberation' to pre-empt any further activities by, or supportive of, these armed groups – including provision of supplies from the high seas. In light of recent developments of the principles and rules of international law concerning the inherent right of self-defence the above

87 *See UNSC Res. 1583* (n 77) para 4.

88 This fact emerges in para 4 of *UNSC Res. 1583* (n 77) which calls upon the Government of Lebanon to *inter alia* 'exert control over the *use of force* on its territory and *from it*' (my emphasis).

89 *See also UNSC Res. 1614* (29 July 2005) para 4.

90 *UNSC Res. 1614* (Ibid.) para 6. In the preamble of same resolution, the UN Security Council had also referred to fighting which had occurred in May 2005 as to 'hostilities'.

91 *See* the preamble of *UNSC Res. 1655* (n 77).

conclusions would even retain their validity if – unlike suggested here – the aggressive activities perpetrated by opposing armed groups were not attributable, or for the time being could not be attributed, to any other State.[92] Noting finally that the UN Security Council expressly referred to seaborne activities to the detriment of Lebanon in the relevant context,[93] Lebanon may, as a matter of principle, exercise its inherent right of self-defence in the maritime space – and, in light of the continued presence of opposing armed groups after the 2006 campaign,[94] receive UN support for that purpose, as well.

As to the activities against which the right of self-defence may be exercised, this is a matter of the *jus in bello* rather than the *jus ad bellum*. In particular, shipments of arms or related materiel destined for any armed group obligated to disarm and disband in accordance with pertinent UN Security Council demands constitute a direct participation, by virtue of providing supplies of paramilitary or military capabilities, in the hostilities committed against Lebanon by these groups through the proxy occupation as well as the provocation of Israeli countermeasures against aggressive activities perpetrated from Lebanese territory. From the perspective of UNIFIL, fulfilment of the obligation 'to ensure that its area of operations is not utilized for hostile activities of any kind'[95] is tantamount to support to Lebanon for that aspect of self-defence.

In the absence of any express limit in the request made by the Government of Lebanon or in UNSCR 1701 (2006), the range of self-defence measures available to UNIFIL comprises, subject to the exigencies of each case, the full spectrum of force. Accordingly, UNIFIL may *inter alia* conduct maritime interdiction operations – which the NATO Glossary defines as '[a]n operation conducted to enforce prohibition on the maritime movement of specified persons or material within a defined geographic area'.[96] Maritime interdiction operations comprise visit, boarding, search, and seizure (frequently referred to as 'VBSS') operations which are appropriate belligerent measures – i.e. beyond mere exercise of (law enforcement) jurisdiction under UNCLOS – for purposes of national self-defence in accordance with Article 51 of the UN Charter.[97] VBSS operations on the high seas in support of Lebanon's national self-defence would have to respect the generally accepted limits of self-defence, namely immediacy, necessity, and proportionality;[98] *ratione loci* the clear definition of the Area of Maritime Operations – which excludes geographically unlimited warfare for self-defence purposes – meets the proportionality[99]

92 *Cf. Heintschel von Heinegg* (n 10) 151, 170.

93 *See UNSC Res. 1655* (n 77) para 4.

94 *See UNSC Res. 1701* (n 60) para 8.

95 Ibid. para 12.

96 *AAP-6* (2010) (n 35) at 2-M-3 (definition adopted 1 January 2006). The NATO Glossary defines the notion of maritime operation as follows: 'An action performed by forces on, under, or over the sea to gain or exploit control of the sea or to deny its use to the enemy' (definition adopted 1 March 1973).

97 *Heintschel von Heinegg* (n 10) 151, 170.

98 Ibid.

99 Ibid.

requirement. It should finally be noted that beyond the mandate under Resolution 1701 (2006), the warships contributed to the UNIFIL Maritime Task Force have the individual right to self-defence if 'illegally subject to force on the high seas'[100] as well as in Lebanon's territorial waters.

2.4.6 Conclusion on UNIFIL

The maritime component of UNIFIL is (*inter alia*) mandated to support the Government of Lebanon in the exercise of Lebanon's inherent right of self-defence. Supporting a legitimate government's effort to re-establish its full sovereignty and to suppress the infliction of hostilities, it is a military crisis response operation. As its legitimacy is rooted in Lebanon's sovereignty and Article 51 of the UN Charter, UNCLOS cannot be relied upon to derive any substantial limits on UNIFIL's maritime authority within the Area of Maritime Operations. Outside that area, of course, the warships contributed to UNIFIL's Maritime Task Force are subject to the same legal framework under UNCLOS as any other warship.

3. Horn of Africa

The Gulf of Aden is both a very important sea route and a trouble spot. Incidents such as the attack on the USS Cole on 12 October 2000, the discovery of Scud parts during the interception of the So San in December 2002 by a Spanish navy vessel[101] and other cases of trafficking in arms, as well as the capture of vessels carrying armaments, oil· or humanitarian supplies, and of various private vessels, by *inter alia* Somali Pirates operating in the Gulf of Aden and all along the coastline of Somalia around the Horn of Africa, illustrate the broad range of challenges in that area. Part of these challenges is rooted in the lack of effective control being exercised by the governments of certain coastal States, the most notorious example being Somalia which has long been regarded as a failed State and did not have a central government in many years since 1991.[102]

Following the termination of UNOSOM II, the situation in Somalia was not a prominent agenda item in the UN Security Council until 2001. By then, this situation had not changed significantly. Hostilities had never ceased; neither had the flow of weapons into Somalia in violation of the UN arms embargo imposed in 1991; in

100 This right is distinct from State self-defence: *O'Connell* (n 1) 804.

101 *Cf. Heintschel von Heinegg* (n 10) 151, 175sqq; at the reference, *v. Heinegg* also explains the link between the So San incident and the Proliferation Security Initiative (PSI).

102 Reference is made, by way of example, to the resolutions in which the UN Security Council noted that it was 'having regard to the exceptional circumstances, including in particular [the] absence of a government in Somalia', in the last preambular paragraph of *UNSC Res. 897* (4 February 1994). *See also* the last preambular paragraph, respectively, of *UNSC Res. 923* (31 May 1994) and 954 (4 November 1994). Currently, the UN Security Council recognises the Transitional Federal Government (TFG) as Somalia's legitimate government (*see for instance*, the reference in the fourth preambular paragraph of *UNSC Res. 1851* (16 December 2008)), its limited ability to exercise effective control in Somalia notwithstanding.

sum, international peace and security in the region had continuously been in jeopardy for almost two decades.[103]

Presumably with the UNOSOM writing on the wall in mind, the UN Security Council has taken a cautious approach towards authorising new crisis response oper-

103 Since November 1991, heavy fighting occurred between competing factions in Mogadishu, Somalia, involving two protagonists (the Interim President Ali Mahdi Mohamed and General Mohamed Farah Aidid of the United Somali Congress) and heavily armed elements, some of which operated independently of the named protagonists (*see* United Nations Secretary-General, 'Report on the Situation in Somalia' (11 March 1992) UN document S/23693 at paras 3, 4, and 11). This report was delivered pursuant to para 10 of *UNSC Res. 733* (23 January 1992), the first resolution adopted by the UN Security Council with respect to the situation in Somalia. Although this resolution did not contain an express determination that the situation in Somalia poses a threat to international peace and security in the region, it '[s]trongly urge[d] all parties to the conflict to cease hostilities and agree to a cease-fire' (para 4) and imposed 'a general and complete embargo on all deliveries of weapons and military equipment to Somalia' for which Chapter VII of the UN Charter was quoted as a legal basis (para 5). A cease-fire was agreed upon on 3 March 1992 yet not maintained (*cf.* para 9 of *UNSC Res. 767* (24 July 1992); para 11 of *UNSC Res. 775* (28 August 1992)). In the sixth preambular paragraph of *UNSC Res. 751* (24 April 1992), the UN Security Council noted that it was 'concerned that the situation in Somalia constitutes a threat to international peace and security' (*see* also the seventh paragraph of *UNSC Res. 767* (above) and the sixth preambular paragraph of *UNSC Res. 775* (above)). Moreover, the UN Security Council recognised 'that the provision of humanitarian assistance in Somalia is an important element in the effort of the council to restore international peace and security in the area' (ninth paragraph of *UNSC Res. 767* (above) which it later reaffirmed (eighth preambular paragraph of *UNSC Res. 775* (above)). Eventually, the UN Security Council determined formally, in the third preambular paragraph of *UNSC Res. 794* (3 December 1992):

> that the magnitude of the human tragedy caused by the conflict in Somalia, further exacerbated by the obstacles being created to the distribution of humanitarian assistance, constitutes a threat to international peace and security.

Later resolutions upheld the determination that the situation in Somalia threatens peace and security in the region (*see* the last preambular paragraph of *UNSC Res. 814* (26 March 1993); the thirteenth preambular paragraph of *UNSC Res. 837* (6 June 1993); the last preambular paragraph of *UNSC Res. 897* (Ibid.); the last preambular paragraph of *UNSC Res. 923* (n 102); and the last preambular paragraph of *UNSC Res. 954* (n 102). The second preambular paragraph of *UNSC Res. 1356* (19 June 2001) – the first resolution since *UNSC Res. 954* (Ibid.) – contains the expression of the UN Security Council's 'desire to *see* peace and security return to Somalia', indicating that the situation had not substantially changed since UNOSOM II had left the country. The seventh preambular paragraph of *UNSC Res. 1474* (8 April 2003) contains once again the determination that the situation in Somalia constitutes a threat to international peace and security in the region. Since then, all relevant resolutions contain a similar determination (*UNSC Res. 1519* (16 December 2003); *1558* (17 August 2004); *1587* (15 March 2005); *1630* (14 October 2005); *1676* (10 May 2006); *1724* (29 November 2006); *1725* (6 December 2006); *1744* (21 February 2007); *1766* (23 July 2007); *1772* (20 August 2007); *1801* (20 February 2008); *1811* (29 April 2008); *1814* (15 May 2008); *1816* (2 June 2008); *1831* (19 August 2008); *1838* (7 October 2008); *1844* (20 November 2008); *1846* (2 December 2008); *1851* (n 102); *1853* (19 December 2008); and *1897* (30 November 2009)).

ations mandated to address the situation in Somalia; for a couple of years its preferred choice was a series of monitoring operations (which might be characterised as civilian crisis response operations). The first military post-UNOSOM crisis response operation was launched by the African Union with UN support and endorsement in 2007 (AMISOM),[104] to be followed by further – and, unlike in the case of UNIFIL, separate – crisis response operation mandates adopted in 2008. The mandate which attracted the most publicity responded to an endemic increase in piracy and armed robbery at sea – which had long been a matter of concern[105] in light of their multiple adverse effects, including as an increasingly significant source of warlord revenue and supplies.[106] The current Horn of Africa maritime mandate, contained in UN Security Council Resolutions 1851 (2008) and 1897 (2009), merges multiple authorisations contained in a variety of resolutions in separation. These resolutions focus on ensuring humanitarian access (in particular the delivery of humanitarian aid including

104 African Union Mission in Somalia, *UNSC Res. 1844* (Ibid.), *1859* (22 December 2008) and *1863* (16 January 2009).

105 The evolution of piracy in Somalia is discussed in the report (5 April 2006) of the Monitoring Group tasked with surveying the arms embargo imposed by *UNSC Res. 733* (n 103). According to the report, initially separate activities, namely those of armed sea robbers posing as law enforcement officers in order to board ships in the late 1980s and those of self-described coast guard(s) taking care of fisheries enforcement of the early 1990s were the basis of 'the much more sophisticated and lucrative money-making activity of today' (*see* UN document S/2006/229, Annex, at paras 77-81).

106 Although the UN Security Council only expressed that it is '*[c]oncerned about* the increasing incidents of piracy and armed robbery against ships in waters off the coast of Somalia, and its impact on security in Somalia' in the ninth preambular paragraph of *UNSC Res. 1676* (n 103), it had long before been aware of the matter. As far as possible to establish, the United Nations Secretary-General reported to the UN Security Council on piracy for the first time on 19 December 2000, noting that '[e]xtended parts of coastal areas ... continue to be dominated by pirates ...' (UN document S/2000/1211, at para 34). Later on, he reported that '[p]iracy and forcible detention of sailors on trawlers fishing illegally in Somali territorial waters has continued' (UN document S/2001/963, at para 53). The Panel of Experts appointed by the United Nations Secretary-General upon the UN Security Council's request and tasked with investigating in violations of the arms embargo (para 3 of *UNSC Res. 1425* (2002)) observed that '[t]he Horn of Africa has become a haven for pirate activity' yet believed that mainly 'unrelated actions' occurred – 'the 'defence' of the Somali coast against illegal fishing notwithstanding' (report dated 24 February 2003 – UN document S/2003/233, Annex, at para 163). It also noted that '[l]egitimate naval forces operating around the Horn of Africa have not taken action despite international agreements on piracy interdiction' (Ibid. para 164; *see* the case study at paras 165-168). In its follow up report, the Panel of Experts pointed at the fact that the sale of fisheries licenses around Puntland had become 'indistinguishable in most respects from common piracy' (report dated 27 October 2003 – UN document S/2003/1035, Annex, at para 147). Later reports received by the UN Security Council address the link between piracy and warlord activities; they will be discussed separately. The Monitoring Group which took over from the Panel of Experts in accordance with para 2 of *UNSC Res. 1519* (2003) reported on 22 July 2004 that, during a meeting with the International Maritime Organization, there was agreement on the need of urgent action to promote 'maritime and port security, including with regard to piracy and armed robbery on ships' (UN document S/2004/604, Annex, at para 109).

food),[107] enforcement of the arms embargo concerning Somalia,[108] and, to these ends, the fight against and/or suppression of piracy and armed robbery at sea.[109]

Both the focus of the Horn of Africa maritime mandate on activities beyond the *prima facie* perception of hostilities and its strict separation from AMISOM ground operations in Somalia might create the impression that the UN Security Council may have intended to address essentially economic and social threats and/or threats posed by transnational crime to international peace and security. Accordingly, the nature of the crisis response operations authorised by the maritime mandate warrants closer analysis.

3.1 Threat Assessment

The UN Security Council has adopted all resolutions contributing to the AMISOM and Horn of Africa maritime mandates under the agenda item 'The Situation in Somalia'. The resolutions contributing to the maritime mandate might, accordingly, address the threat as part of the overall situation in Somalia rather than as pertaining to the maritime environment only. The present analysis must hence first ask whether in the UN Security Council's assessment there is a maritime threat standing on its own or an overall threat composed of land-based and maritime factors. After demonstrating that the UN Security Council has addressed the situation in Somalia in a holistic manner, it will turn to the nature of the comprehensive threat posed thereby. Finally, considering that the threat at hand is rooted in paramilitary/military and civilian factors, it will then focus on the nature of piracy and armed robbery at sea, taking into account both relevant legal definitions, and pirates' and armed robbers' activities.

3.1.1 The Nexus between the Land and Maritime Threat Factors

By mandating AMISOM and the Horn of Africa naval operations under the same agenda item, the UN Security Council has created the presumption that these mandates address different aspects of the same situation, that is, different factors threatening international peace and security in the region. This presumption might, however, be rebutted in light of the language used in the mandates. The phrase 'maritime security' and essentially similar terminology – which occurs in a couple of resolutions[110] – might indicate that the UN Security Council intended to deal with a distinct category of threat to international security which may be considered disconnected from the land-based threat. However, the use of this language does not create a distinction between separable and indeed separate land-based and maritime threats at the Horn of Africa. Suffice it to say that the UN Security Council has not defined the notion

---

107 Para 18 of *UNSC Res. 1772* (n 103), para 11 of *UNSC Res. 1814* (n 103).

108 Paras 6/7 of *UNSC Res. 1814* (Ibid.); *cf.* para 13 of *UNSC Res. 1772* (Ibid.).

109 Para 18 of *UNSC Res. 1772* (Ibid.), para 7 of *UNSC Res. 1816* (Ibid.), paras 2-4 of *UNSC Res. 1838* (n 103), paras 9/10 of *UNSC Res. 1846* (n 103); *see also UNSC Res. 1811* (n 103).

110 Para 5 of *UNSC Res. 1816* (n 103) and para 5 of *UNSC Res. 1846* (n 103); *see* also para 2 of *UNSC Res. 1838* (n 103): 'security of maritime activities'; para 4 of *UNSC Res. 1851* (n 102): 'long-term security of international navigation off the coast of Somalia'.

of 'maritime security' in a manner indicating that it wanted to use this language as new a legal or policy term of art; other documents are similarly silent.[111]

Moreover, the cross-references between different resolutions demonstrate that the UN Security Council considers piracy and armed robbery at sea, and the factors threatening international peace and security on land to be interdependent. On the one hand, it determined:

> that the incidents of piracy and armed robbery against vessels in the territorial waters of Somalia and the high seas off the coast of Somalia exacerbate the situation in Somalia which continues to constitute a threat to international peace and security in the region.[112]

On the other hand, it has recognised 'that the ongoing instability in Somalia contributes to the problem of piracy and armed robbery at sea off the coast of Somalia'.[113]

Threats to international peace and security are frequently rooted in multiple factors, and oftentimes in factors which in isolation would not amount to such threat. It is then the cumulative effect of such factors which justifies the UN Security Council in determining that a given situation constitutes a threat to international peace and security. To have such cumulative effect, the factors in question – in the present context the land and maritime factors – must be interdependent, e.g. in light of a substantial factual exists between them or because they reciprocally influence one another. The UN Security Council has specifically tackled a mutually reinforcing link between arms embargo violations and piracy when noting with concern the Monitoring Group's findings:

---

111 Note that, as observed by the United Nations Secretary-General in his 2008 report on Oceans and the law of the sea (UN document A/63/63), there is no universally accepted definition of the phrase 'maritime security'. The report outlines the following lowest common denominator (at para 39):

> At its narrowest conception, maritime security involves protection from direct threats to the territorial integrity of a State, such as an armed attack from a military vessel. Most definitions also usually include security from crimes at sea, such as piracy, armed robbery against ships, and terrorist acts.

The UN Security Council has not remedied this definitional challenge. To the contrary, by way of attaching an attribute *ratione loci* – the geographical reference to the international waters off the coast of Somalia – to the notion of 'maritime security' the UN Security Council has, for the time being, denied it a meaning beyond the given context. That also means that in attaching the said attribute the UN Security Council has refrained from introducing 'maritime security' as a new and distinctive subcategory of the notion of 'international security' as captured by the UN Charter. It follows that it has not relied on the phrase 'maritime security' as a legal basis for authorising the use of force in the maritime mandate. Moreover, the attribute *ratione loci* confirms rather than discards the existence of a link between the maritime aspect of the threat and its land-based counterpart.

112 *UNSC Res. 1816* (n 103), last preambular paragraph; *see also UNSC Res. 1838* (n 103), last preambular paragraph; *UNSC Res. 1846* (n 103), last preambular paragraph; *UNSC Res. 1851* (n 102), last preambular paragraph.

113 *UNSC Res. 1872* (26 May 2009), fifteenth preambular paragraph.

> that escalating ransom payments are fuelling the growth of piracy in waters off the coast of Somalia, and that the lack of enforcement of the arms embargo ... has permitted ready access to the arms and ammunition used by the pirates and driven in part the phenomenal growth in piracy.[114]

Likewise, in determining that piracy and armed robbery at sea 'exacerbate the situation in Somalia' the UN Security Council has referred to an effect which presupposes a substantial factual link between these factors and the land-based threat (the latter being primarily represented by the hostilities inflicted by warlords and militias opposing the Transitional Federal Government – TFG). In recognising that the instability on land 'contributes to the problem [at sea]' it has made this point crystal clear. Moreover, the Horn of Africa maritime mandate echoes earlier practice: the resolutions addressing the denial of humanitarian access, including from sea,[115] in the 1990s likewise hold the situation in Somalia to be exacerbated thereby.[116] The use of both verbs – 'to exacerbate' and 'to contribute' – reflects that denial of humanitarian access, and piracy and armed robbery at sea, respectively, are factors which do not only occur *in* Somalia[117]. This is obvious as far as piracy is concerned because piracy can, by definition, only occur on the high seas – that is, *outside* Somalia. The disruption of humanitarian access can likewise occur *outside* Somalia because humanitarian assistance is being provided *inter alia* from sea – that is, from *outside* Somalia. Accordingly, by using the verbs 'to exacerbate' and 'to contribute' the UN Security Council has included cases in its threat assessment where threatening factors occurred *outside* Somalia and nevertheless adversely affected – namely exacerbated – or were influenced by, the situation *in* Somalia.[118]

---

114 Para 9 of *UNSC Res. 1851* (n 102).

115 *See* the observation by the representative of the People's Republic of China in the 3145th meeting of the UN Security Council that 'ships carrying relief supplies cannot reach ports in safety, and the goods that have arrived at ports cannot be delivered safely' (UN document S/PV.3145, at 16). *See also* the remarks by the UK representative (n 33), and the United Nations Secretary-General's letter (24 November 1992) UN document S/24859.

116 In the third preambular paragraph of *UNSC Res. 794* (n 103), the UN Security Council determined:

> that the magnitude of the human tragedy caused by the conflict in Somalia, further exacerbated by the obstacles being created to the distribution of humanitarian assistance, constitutes a threat to international peace and security.

117 Note that the relevant meeting record does not contain an explanation why the term 'exacerbate' was used in *resolution 794* (n 103). The President of the Security Council, speaking in his capacity as the representative of India, used this language, too, yet without further explanation (UN document S/PV.3145, at 49). The United Nations Secretary-General's letter (29 November 1992) UN document S/24868, to which he referred does not use this language.

118 It may be added in this context that in addressing the threat to international peace and security posed by the situation in Somalia, the UN Security Council has repeatedly taken note of, or expressed value judgments concerning, incidents which represent the substantial factual link between the land-based and maritime factors contributing thereto. It has done so in resolutions adopted both prior to resolutions *1816/1838/1846* (all n 103) and thereafter.

The substantial factual link between the factors at issue surfaces in various elements of

UN Security Council practice, with two specific perspectives on the interdependence between maritime and land-based aspects of the overall threat. The first perspective – of which the UN Security Council is cognisant since it received a related report in 2005 and which it later addressed implicitly in a resolution – captures the supportive role of piratical activities for the generation of revenue by warlords.

The first discussion of the link between piracy and arms embargo violations is contained in the 'Analysis of the trends and patterns of arms embargo violations' submitted by the Monitoring Group in its report (14 February 2005) UN document S/2005/153, Annex. The narrative on 'Transport' *sub specie* 'Finance', a subsection of the examination of the 'Role of finance, transport and customs' specifies that '[t]he Somali coastline has one of the highest rates of sea piracy in the world' (at para 71). As requested by the UN Security Council (para 3(i) of *UNSC Res. 1587* (n 103), on 22 August 2005 the Monitoring Group submitted a further report in which it specified that '[t]he main motive behind acts of piracy in Somali waters appears to be an attempt by local administrations or individual warlords and militias to obtain large sums of money through ransom demands' (UN document S/2005/625, Annex, at para 100). Para 3(i) of *UNSC Res. 1630* (n 103) requested yet another report which was submitted on 5 April 2006; it observes that 'monies obtained through ransom are used to purchase arms' (UN document S/2006/229, Annex, at para 89). The UN Security Council has taken note of that report in *UNSC Res. 1676* (n 103) – which made express mention of piracy for the first time, and, as it focused on arms embargo violations, alluded at the factual link between the two.

The second perspective – addressed in statements of the President of the UN Security Council in 2005 and 2006 and likewise addressed in a resolution subsequently – focuses on the disruption of humanitarian access as well as of peaceful navigation by pirates (and armed robbers at sea). For the Presidential Statements *see* UN document SPRST/2005/54 (9 November 2005):

> The Security Council expresses serious concern over the increasing incidents of piracy off the coast of Somalia. The Council condemns recent hijackings of vessels in the area, particularly of ships carrying humanitarian supplies to Somalia.

See, moreover, UN document S/PRST/2006/11 (15 March 2006) and para 18 of *UNSC Res. 1772* (n 103).

The UN Security Council addressed the substantial factual link between the factors contributing to the threat posed by the situation in Somalia. Concerning disruptions of peaceful navigation and humanitarian access, the eighth preambular paragraph of *UNSC Res. 1816* (n 103) deplored:

> incidents of attacks upon and hijacking of vessels in the territorial waters and on the high seas off the coast of Somalia including attacks upon and hijackings of vessels operated by the World Food Program and numerous commercial vessels and the serious adverse impact of these attacks on the prompt, safe and effective delivery of food aid and other humanitarian assistance to the people of Somalia, and the grave dangers they pose to vessels, crews, passengers, and cargo …

The matter of embargo violations (*inter alia* by warlords) being facilitated with piratical revenue was again addressed in the terms of reference of the re-established Monitoring Group. As per para 3 of *UNSC Res. 1853* (n 103), the Monitoring Group is tasked, *inter alia*, with investigating 'all activities, including in the financial, *maritime* and other sectors, which generate revenues used to commit arms embargo violations' (subpara (c)) and 'any means of transport, routes, *seaports*, airports and other facilities used in connection with arms embargo violations' (emphases by the author). The same tasks had already been defined in para 3(b)/(c) of *UNSC Res. 1676* (n 103) which, as discussed *supra*, was

As a result, the UN Security Council's threat assessment tackles the situation in Somalia, including its territorial waters, and the high seas off its coast, in a holistic manner.

3.1.2 The Nature of the Threat

As indicated earlier, the UN Security Council has never closed the agenda item 'The Situation in Somalia'. Conversely, its practice indicates that, the pause in UN or UN-mandated action between 1994 and 2001 and factual developments notwithstanding, this situation has retained essentially the same legal nature over the years. In the final resolution on UNOSOM the UN Security Council had expressly called the situation in Somalia a conflict.[119] In its first post-UNOSOM resolution it expressed its desire to see peace and security return to Somalia,[120] indicating thus that the situation had not changed substantially ever since. Moreover, the UN Security Council adopted resolutions 1356 (2001), 1407 (2002) and 1425 (2002) under Chapter VII of the UN Charter, once again indicating that its assessment, made in the 1990s,[121] that the situation in Somalia threatens international peace and security, had not changed. When again determining expressly that the situation in Somalia constitutes a threat to international peace and security in the region, the UN Security Council noted with regret the continuous violations of the arms embargo imposed in 1992, including since the signing of the 'Declaration on Cessation of Hostilities and the Structure and Principles of the Somalia National Reconciliation Process' (Eldoret Declaration) in October 2002.[122] This language does not only reinforce the continued and unchanged nature of the threat. The reference to the Eldoret Declaration also indicates that hostilities had not ceased in spite of this declaration (as well as subsequent similar instruments). It follows that the UN Security Council did not alter its assessment of the paramilitary/military nature of the overall threat, either.[123]

---

the first resolution to expressly address the link between piracy and embargo violations.

119 Para 1 of *UNSC Res. 954* (n 102).

120 *See* the second preambular paragraph of *UNSC Res. 1356* (n 103).

121 This assessment had tackled the military nature of the threat by way of reference to rearmaments and troop build-ups by Somali factions, and by 'continued incidents of fighting and banditry', including 'violence and armed attacks against persons engaged in humanitarian and peace-keeping efforts'. *See* the sixth and seventh preambular paragraphs of *UNSC Res. 897* (n 102).

122 Second preambular paragraph of *UNSC Res. 1474* (n 103).

123 The UN Security Council has repeatedly referred to the situation in Somalia as to a conflict and called upon the parties to avoid any indiscriminate attacks on populated areas. *See* paras 19 and 21 of *UNSC Res. 1772* (n 103); paras 13 and 15 of *UNSC Res. 1801* (n 103); 17 and 18 of *UNSC Res. 1814* (n 103); and the third preambular paragraph of *UNSC Res. 1853* (n 103). *Cf.* also the sixth preambular paragraph of *UNSC Res. 1744* (n 103); and the ninth preambular paragraph of *UNSC Res. 1831* (n 103) (indicating future 'post-conflict' efforts of the United Nations).

3.1.3 The Nature of the Threatening Activities

Like any other multi-factor threat, the paramilitary/military threat posed by the situation in Somalia can be exacerbated both by paramilitary/military factors and civilian factors.[124] However, like in any other case to date, the UN Security Council has not expressly determined[125] the nature of the factors captured by the maritime mandate. Hence the need to analyse whether it intended to include these factors in the authorisation of military crisis response operations or wanted to address them specifically with the authorisation of law enforcement support[126] to its pre-existing effort to counter the threat to international peace and security posed by the situation in Somalia.

Concerning piracy and armed robbery at sea, the UN Security Council has repeatedly reaffirmed

> ... that international law, as reflected in the United Nations Convention on the Law of the Sea of 10 December 1982 (UNCLOS), sets out the legal framework applicable to combating piracy and armed robbery at sea, as well as other ocean activities.[127]

This language, specifically the word 'reflected', confirms that the principles and rules of the law of the sea derive from UNCLOS and, beyond the scope of this codification (and specifically for the States and IOs not parties thereto), from relevant co-existing customary international law.[128] Accordingly, the legal nature of piracy and armed robbery at sea must be examined with the whole of the law of the sea in mind.

---

124 To give but two examples of military factors exacerbating a given situation, if mortar or artillery becomes available this factor will exacerbate any threat heretofore posed by infantry units without fires support, and if a shortage of food occurs in territory under belligerent occupation the need to support civilians suffering from hunger will reduce the occupying forces' capabilities available for e.g. containing the militant activities of any resistance movements that might exist.

125 The UN Security Council has called on States 'to assist the TFG in its effort to strengthen its operational capacity to bring to justice those who are using Somali territory to plan, facilitate or undertake *criminal acts of piracy and armed robbery at sea*' (para 7 of *UNSC Res. 1851* (n 102); emphasis by the author). The characterisation 'criminal acts' seems to be nothing more than a reference to pertinent Somali criminal law.

126 *Note that* G. Breda & J.P. Pierini have not even considered the possibility that counter-piracy could be anything else than a matter of law enforcement when discussing the impact of the Medvedyev judgment on a broader range of maritime operations. 'Legal Issues Surrounding Maritime Counterdrug Operations and the Related Question of Detention as Highlighted in the Medvedyev and Others v. France decision of the European Court of Human Rights' (2008) 48 *The Military Law and the Law of War Review* 167-198, specifically at 191 ('recent maritime law enforcement operations such as those to combat piracy'). A couple of German Ministry of Defence lawyers have also considered the Horn of Africa mandate to be an authorization of law enforcement only when the matter was discussed in the national military legal community.

127 Fourth preambular paragraph of *UNSC Res. 1851* (n 102); *see also UNSC Res. 1838* (n 103), third preambular paragraph; *UNSC Res. 1846* (n 103), fourth preambular paragraph.

128 According to the eighth preambular paragraph of UNCLOS 'matters not regulated by

Although Article 101 of UNCLOS, a *verbatim* reproduction of Article 15 of the 1958 Convention on the High Seas, defines the notion of piracy it leaves its legal nature undetermined. Composed of three categories of elements, it tackles a variety of acts, specifies what purpose they must be committed for, and identifies possible victims thereof. The UNCLOS definition has not gone beyond customary international law,[129] and even in its limited scope it has attracted criticism for being 'both tautologous and imprecise', that is, for its 'elliptical nature'.[130] This lack of precision alone prevents the UNCLOS definition from determining that the legal nature of piracy is a crime because it fails to meet the increased legal certainty requirement imperative for provisions pertaining to criminal law. Moreover, the context of Article 101 of UNCLOS, represented by the sequence of provisions to which this article belongs, is preoccupied with questions of jurisdiction. It namely enables States to extend their domestic criminal jurisdiction over piracy should they actually penalise it.[131] This jurisdictional approach is limited to lifting exclusive flag State jurisdiction (Article 92(1) of UNCLOS)[132] for the purpose of suppressing piracy.

---

this Convention continue to be governed by the rules and principles of general international law'. On the co-existence of UNCLOS and customary international law *cf.* M.R. Nordquist, *UNCLOS Commentary* (Vol. I, 1985) 464sq.

Note that not all members of NATO are parties of UNCLOS. NATO, the African Union and the EU are not parties either although they would all qualify as party in accordance with Article 305(1)(f) of UNCLOS (The European Community is a party to UNCLOS but EU naval operations at the Horn of Africa are not conducted within the framework of the European Community.) *See* <www.un.org/Depts/los/reference_files/status2008.pdf> (accessed 30 July 2009).

129 *Cf.* the assessment by *O'Connell* (n 1) who considers the definition 'not innovatory' if analysed 'in light of the precedents of customary law', 769.

130 *O'Connell* (n 1) 769sq.

131 It may be noted in this context that there seems to be a lack of criminal law tackling piracy specifically. Para 15 of *UNSC Res. 1846* (n 103) expressly urges States parties to the Convention for the Suppression of Unlawful Acts Against the Safety of Maritime Navigation (SUA Convention) to fully implement their obligations thereunder and to support judicial capacity-building for the successful prosecution of persons suspected of piracy and armed robbery at sea off the coast of Somalia.

132 Inasmuch as Article 100 of UNCLOS assigns the repression of piracy on the high seas to the co-operation of all States this rule pertains to international co-operation in matters of justice even though it does not require States to either extradite or prosecute pirates they capture (*aut dedere aut iudicare*). Articles 108 and 109 again illustrate that Section I of Part VII of UNCLOS is preoccupied with jurisdictional matters. Jurisdictional provisions are not usually meant to impact matters of substantive law. Various passages in S.N. Nandan & Sh. Rosenne *UNCLOS Commentary* (Vol. III, 1995) confirm this analysis. At Art. 105.1 the learned authors note that 'Article 105 provides an exception from the general rule set out in Article 92, that a ship is subject to the exclusive jurisdiction of its flag on the high seas'. Likewise, at Art. 105.10(a) they observe that 'Article 105 gives expression to the universal jurisdiction which any State can exercise against any pirate or pirate ship or aircraft'. *See also* Art. 100, Ibid. The need to include such jurisdictional provision in UNCLOS derives inter alia from the determination, by virtue of Articles 104 and 110(1)(a)/(d) of UNCLOS, that piracy does not automatically render a ship stateless – except if the law of the original flag State so provides in accordance with Article 91(1) of UNCLOS.

Accordingly, it does not entail a determination whether piracy is a crime *jure gentium*; it merely takes into account that piracy may be a crime under States' domestic criminal law. The Horn of Africa maritime mandate has not altered international law in this respect. It nevertheless contains two innovations, namely it has assimilated armed robbery at sea – i.e. for instance in Somalia's territorial waters – to piracy and it has authorised naval operations in Somalia's territorial waters, including hot pursuit of pirates entering them from the high seas ('reverse hot pursuit'). However, as repeatedly affirmed by UN Security Council, these innovations:

> apply only with respect to the situation in Somalia and shall not affect the rights or obligations or responsibilities of Member States under international law, including any rights or obligations under UNCLOS, with respect to any other situation, and ... shall not be considered as establishing customary international law, including any rights or obligations under UNCLOS, with respect to any other situation.[133]

It follows that, like UNCLOS, they concern jurisdiction only, and that the sovereignty of coastal States over their territorial waters is unfettered. Like the focus on jurisdictional questions, the limited scope of the Horn of Africa maritime mandate – reflected by its focus on the situation in Somalia at the exclusion of the high seas in general – indicates that the UN Security Council did not intend to determine the legal nature of piracy.[134] UN practice otherwise contains no such determination, either, yet it indicates that piracy need not necessarily be characterised as criminality.[135] It follows that the Horn of Africa maritime mandate does not address the legal nature of piracy and armed robbery at sea.

Customary international law has attached a dual nature to piracy. Being still[136] considered *hostes humani generis*, pirates may be targeted with military force; once

133 Para 10 of *UNSC Res. 1851* (n 102). *See* also para 11 of *UNSC Res. 1846* (n 103), para 8 of *UNSC Res. 1838* (n 103), and para 9 of *UNSC Res. 1816* (n 103). Note also that several members of the UN Security Council have stressed in relevant meetings that no new customary international law shall be established. *See* the meeting record (UN document S/PV.6050) concerning *UNSC Res. 1851* (n 102).

Without that express statement, the emergence of new customary international law would indeed have been quite probable. The Horn of Africa maritime mandate does not only limit Somalia's exclusive coastal State jurisdiction over armed robbers at sea and such pirates as have reached its territorial waters (*cf.* Article 100 of UNCLOS), it also lifts the limits on certain action by warships in foreign States' territorial waters which otherwise are confined to innocent passage (*cf.* particularly Articles 19 and 20 of UNCLOS)

134 The official record (UN document S/PV.6050) indicates that its members may have different views concerning that question.

135 See, for instance, *UNGA Res. 63/111* whose preamble differentiates between 'transnational organized crime committed at sea' and 'threats to maritime safety and security', capturing 'piracy, armed robbery at sea, smuggling and terrorist acts against shipping, offshore installations and other maritime interests' in the second category.

136 The characterization of pirates as *hostes humani generis* – enemies of all mankind – has never lost its validity because the definition of the notion of 'piracy' by Article 101 of UNCLOS 'corresponds' to it, *Nandan and Rosenne* (n 132) Art. 101.8(a).

captured, they may be tried as criminals. According to still good jurisprudence, 'a pirate is deemed *hostis humani generis* because he commits hostilities upon the subjects and property of any or all nations'.[137] Accordingly, 'with professed pirates there is no state of peace. They are the enemies of every country and at all times, and therefore are universally subject to the extreme rights of war'.[138] Nothing in the Horn of Africa maritime mandate indicates that the UN Security Council intended overturn this jurisprudence and to deny States and IOs the option to make pirates (and armed robbers at sea) 'subject to the extreme rights of war'. Rather, it seems to have considered this option one possible sovereign choice with which it might even sympathise when it repeatedly called upon States 'to take part actively in the fight against piracy and armed robbery at sea off the coast of Somalia'[139]. This language – 'take part actively', 'fight' – resembles the terminology for the use of military force in an armed conflict rather than for law enforcement purposes. In comparable language, the UN Security Council authorised the use of force against land bases of pirates and armed robbers at sea subject to the limits deriving from 'applicable international humanitarian and human rights law',[140] likewise indicating thus that it considered combat force an option. Other sources of international law do not affect this assessment. In particular, the use of force against pirate vessels does not qualify as an act of aggression (and hence a fortiori not as a use of force prohibited in accordance with Article 2(4) of the UN Charter). Although pirate ships do not automatically lose their nationality in accordance with Article 104 of UNCLOS, using force against them does not represent '[a]n attack by the armed forces of a State on the ... marine ... fleet[] of another State'.[141]

Finally, the UN Security Council has specifically addressed disruptions of humanitarian access and arms embargo violations by persons designated by the 751 Sanctions Committee as non-compliant actors[142] (hereinafter referred to as 'other non-compliant activities') because they involve the use of force and/or the provision of supplies to armed groups and may for that reason alone – i.e. notwithstanding

---

137 J. Storey in *Harmony* v. *US* (The Brig Malek Adhul) [1844] 2 How 210, 232; this quote is taken from *O'Connell* (n 1) 968.

138 Lord Stowell in *Le Louis* [1817] 2 Dods 210/244; this quote is taken from C.J. Colombos, *The International Law of the Sea* (Longmans, London, 1951) para 368.

139 Para 2 of *UNSC Res. 1838* (n 103), para 9 of *UNSC Res. 1846* (n 103), para 2 of *UNSC Res. 1851* (n 102).

140 *See* para 6 of *UNSC Res. 1851* (n 102) by which the UN Security Council authorises that:

> States and regional organizations cooperating in the fight against piracy and armed robbery at sea off the coast of Somalia ... may undertake all necessary measures that are appropriate in Somalia, for the purpose of suppressing acts of piracy and armed robbery at sea, ... provided, however, that any measures undertaken pursuant to the authority of this paragraph shall be undertaken consistent with applicable international humanitarian and human rights law.

Note that operations on the land territory of Somalia under this provision are contingent on advance notification by the TFG to the United Nations Secretary-General and a request of the TFG.

141 *See* para 3(d) of the UN definition of aggression (*UNGA Resolution 3314* (n 76)).

142 *Cf.* paras 7 & 8(b)/(c) of *UNSC Res. 1844* (n 103), reinforced by para 2 of *UNSC Res. 1853* (n 103).

the membership of the individuals concerned in any such group – amount to direct participation in the hostilities in Somalia. These threatening factors are of a para-military/military nature.

3.1.4 Conclusion on the Threat Assessment

The UN Security Council has upheld its assessment, made in the 1990s, according to which the situation in Somalia constitutes an essentially paramilitary/military threat to international peace and security. It has, however, not determined the nature of piracy and armed robbery at sea which exacerbate this situation. In this respect, it has shown restraint, merely building upon the dual nature of piracy under customary international law, and indicating the sources of limits of action to suppress them, both of a military nature and law enforcement. As a result, the UN Security Council's threat assessment justifies the authorisation of both military crisis response operations and law enforcement support to the overall effort to restore international peace and security in the region.

3.2 Purpose

As a whole, the mandates of AMISOM and the Monitoring Group as well as the Horn of Africa maritime mandate serve the overall purpose of curing Somalia from the calamitous effects of failing statehood. To achieve sustainable success, this cure must enable the situation in Somalia to be so transformed that only legitimate and accountable public authority be exercised in Somalia, and that it be effectively exercised throughout the territory of Somalia. The exercise of transitional authority based on Chapter VII of the UN Charter, co-operation with the TFG, and mitigation of the adverse effects caused by the absence of effective government on the lives and livelihoods of the Somali people shall cumulatively contribute to this process. Within these co-ordinates, the purpose of the maritime mandate is to restore effective control of Somalia's territorial waters. This purpose captures security of navigation off the Somali coast (including fulfilment of Somalia's related legal obligations on the high seas such as combating piracy), improvement of food security for the recipients of humanitarian aid, and security from paramilitary and military violence for everyone throughout Somalia (including through the prevention of arms embargo violations). Countering the threats addressed in this context justifies a military response.

3.3 Responsibilities and Task

Initially addressed in separation, the responsibilities and tasks assigned to Horn of Africa naval operations by the maritime mandate were soon amalgamated in practice.[143] The Horn of Africa maritime mandate followed suit; the consolidated man-

143 This amalgamation might also reflect the practice of NATO 'to counter piracy off the Somalia coast, including by escorting vessels of the WFP' and the EU decision 'to launch … a naval operation to protect WFP maritime convoys …, and to repress acts of piracy and armed robbery at sea off the coast of Somalia'. *See* para 6 of *UNSC Res. 1846* (n 103).

date will hence be the subject-matter of analysis. Given, however, its still composite nature, the maritime mandate does not contain a single and conclusive list of the responsibilities and tasks assigned to the operations conducted thereunder. The following responsibilities form its common ground:

- facilitating humanitarian access (in particular the delivery of humanitarian aid including food); and
- contributing to the enforcement of the arms embargo concerning Somalia by way of preventing that any revenues be raised from which embargo violators might benefit, and that material supplies be provided to embargo violators.

To fulfil these responsibilities, the maritime mandate assigns two key tasks to the naval operations at the Horn of Africa. Each of these tasks – namely the fight against piracy and armed robbery at sea,[144] and the protection of individual commercial vessels[145] – supports both of the above responsibilities. These tasks overlap with the task to prevent activities which directly or indirectly support spoilers of the peace process, designated arms embargo violators, and persons obstructing humanitarian access.[146] Depending on their links and behaviour, pirates and armed robbers at sea may come in any of those categories.

In and of themselves, these responsibilities and tasks do not necessarily imply, but neither do they preclude a military response.

144 Para 2 of *UNSC Res. 1838* (n 103), para 9 of *UNSC Res. 1846* (n 103), para 2 of *UNSC Res. 1851* (n 102). Para 3 of *UNSC Res. 1816* (n 103) used less determined language, urging States 'to render assistance to vessels threatened by or under attack by pirates or armed robbers'.

The UN Security Council had first encouraged that action be taken against pirates in a Presidential Statement (15 March 2006) UN document S/PRST/2006/11), taking note of the resolution passed by the Assembly of the International Maritime Organization concerning Piracy and Armed Robbery against Ships in Waters off the Coast of Somalia (Resolution A.979(24) (6 February 2006); *cf.* also the reference in the *Monitoring Group's report* (5 April 2006) (n 105) at para 143:

> encouraging Member States whose naval vessels and military aircraft operate in international waters and airspace adjacent to the coast of Somalia to be vigilant to any incident of piracy therein and to take appropriate action to protect merchant shipping, in particular the transportation of humanitarian aid, against any such act, in line with relevant international law.

It used identical language in para 18 of *UNSC Res. 1772* (n 103) and again in para 12 of *UNSC Res. 1801* (n 103) – both of which it adopted under Chapter VII of the UN Charter. The latter resolution also welcomed French and Danish support to World Food Programme naval convoys, as did para 11 of *UNSC Res. 1814* (n 103).

145 The UN Security Council initially phrased this task, acting on the basis of Chapter VII of the UN Charter, by calling for 'action to protect shipping involved with the transportation and delivery of humanitarian aid to Somalia and United Nations-authorized activities'. (para 11 of *UNSC Res. 1814* (n 103)). Later, it urged States and regional organizations 'to continue to take action to protect the World Food Programme maritime convoys' (para 5 of *UNSC Res. 1838* (n 103)). *Cf.* also para 4 of *UNSC Res. 1851* (n 102).

146 Paras 7 & 8(b)/(c) of *UNSC Res. 1844* (n 103), reinforced by para 2 of *UNSC Res. 1853* (n 103).

3.4 Authority

By mid-2009, all mandates concerning the situation in Somalia – for AMISOM,[147] the Monitoring Group,[148] and the Horn of Africa naval operations[149] – are based on Chapter VII of the UN Charter. Within that legal framework, the UN Security Council frequently authorises operations substituting the exercise of transitional authority for the exercise of parts of the public authority by the government(s) responsible for the theatre of operations – that is, in the present context, the TFG. Such exercise of transitional authority may take different forms, including supporting and/or empowering the TFG as well as protecting and defending humanitarian operations (specifically those conducted by the UN) and the exercise by individuals and legal persons of their rights.

The choice of Chapter VII reflects the assessment concerning the TFG's capacity to exercise legitimate and accountable authority on behalf of the State of Somalia. As the relevant resolutions reveal, the UN Security Council does not consider the TFG capable of extending its authority throughout its country[150]; the mandate as it currently stands is, accordingly, not concerned with supporting the exercise of such authority.[151] A lack of capacity was specifically taken into account with respect to Somalia's maritime environment.[152] In light of this assessment, the Horn of Africa maritime mandate focuses on protecting and defending humanitarian operations and the exercise by individuals and legal persons of their rights. It brings together

147 *UNSC Res. 1872* (n 113).

148 *UNSC Res. 1853* (n 103).

149 *UNSC Res. 1851* (n 102) and *1846* (n 103).

150 In the sixth preambular paragraph of *UNSC Res. 1814* (n 103), the UN Security Council has welcomed 'the commitment of all Somali parties that have agreed to engage in dialogue with each other with a view to establishing peace and security in Somalia'. This assessment implies by necessity that the TFG cannot establish peace and security in Somalia of its own because it lacks the capacity to do so.

151 *UNSC Res. 1818* (13 June 2008) and subsequent resolutions do not deal with any State's sovereign rights; if commissioned by the United Nations or an organisation which is part of the UN family, 'the transportation and delivery of humanitarian aid to Somalia and United Nations-authorized activities' (para 11 of *UNSC Res. 1818* (above)) is not within the ambit of such rights.

152 In the seventh preambular paragraph of *UNSC Res. 1814* (n 103), the UN Security Council has welcomed the United Nations Secretary-General's assessment 'that the political situation in Somalia currently provides a renewed opportunity for the international community to give practical support to domestic initiatives'. The notion of giving support to 'domestic initiatives' rather than the TFG implies that neither empowering nor supporting the TFG would suffice to achieve the desired effect. Later resolutions do even refer expressly to:

> the lack of capacity of the Transitional Federal Government (TFG) to interdict pirates or patrol and secure either the international sea lanes off the coast of Somalia or Somalia's territorial waters.

UNSC Res. 1816 (n 103), seventh preambular paragraph; *see also UNSC Res. 1846* (n 103) fifth preambular paragraph as well as para 5; *UNSC Res. 1851* (n 102) fifth preambular paragraph.

three elements, namely the UN Security Council's call upon 'States and regional organisations that have the capacity to do so, to take part actively in the fight against piracy and armed robbery at sea off the coast of Somalia'[153] – which includes taking 'the necessary means, in conformity with international law, as reflected in the Convention, for the repression of acts of piracy';[154] the authorisation, for 'States and regional organisations cooperating with the TFG', to enter into Somalia's territorial waters and use, therein, 'all necessary means to repress acts of piracy and armed robbery at sea';[155] and the decision authorising operations on land to suppress pirates and armed robbers at sea with 'all necessary measures'.[156] All relevant resolutions establish mechanisms to keep the TFG fully involved; doing so is currently the key method to both empower it and support it in growing legitimacy.[157]

The UN Security Council has also recommended certain measures 'in particular', namely 'deploying naval vessels and military aircraft', and 'seizure and disposition of boats, vessels, arms and other related equipment used in the commission of piracy and armed robbery at sea off the coast of Somalia'.[158] The use of the phrase 'in particular' indicates that these measures do not from an exhaustive catalogue of the authority available in the fight against piracy and armed robbery at sea; these measures as such are capable of serving both law enforcement and combat purposes.

As a result, the UN Security Council expects that States, including through 'appropriate international agencies' (Article 48(2) of the UN Charter), and regional organisations exercise the existing authority to 'repress', i.e. combat (under customary international law) and/or 'suppress' (as per UNCLOS), piracy on the high seas; that it assimilates armed robbery at sea to piracy and extends, co-operation with the TFG provided, the authority to take action against activities of both kinds in Somalia's territorial waters; and also makes, a TFG request provided, equivalent authority available for land operations – for which the applicability of international humanitarian law is expressly assumed. In sum, the authority thus conferred on the Horn of Africa naval operations includes a military response.

153 Para 2 of *UNSC Res. 1851* (n 102) para 9 of *UNSC Res. 1846* (n 103), para 2 of *UNSC Res. 1838* (n 103). Less determined language ('be vigilant') was used in para 2 of *UNSC Res. 1816* (n 103).

154 Para 3 of *UNSC Res. 1838* (n103). Less determined language ('render assistance') was used in para 3 of *UNSC Res. 1816* (n 103).

155 As far as this aspect of authority is concerned, para 10 of *UNSC Res. 1846* (n 103) expressly requires that it be exercised 'in a manner consistent with such action permitted on the high seas with respect to piracy under relevant international law'. This authorisation repeats para 7 of *UNSC Res. 1816* (n 103).

156 As far as this aspect of authority is concerned, para 6 of *UNSC Res. 1853* (n 103) expressly requires that it be exercised 'consistent with applicable international humanitarian and human rights law'.

157 Introduced by para 7 *UNSC Res. 1816* (n 103), entry into Somalia's territorial waters for the purpose of repressing acts of piracy and armed robbery at sea is subject to an advance notification requirement. The same applies to the exercise of the authority to conduct land operations for the purpose of suppressing acts of piracy and armed robbery at sea, pursuant to a TFG request, in accordance with para 6 of *UNSC Res. 1853* (n 103).

158 Para 2 of *UNSC Res. 1851* (n 102), para 9 of *UNSC Res. 1846* (n 103).

3.5 Horn of Africa Practice

Since the adoption of the Horn of Africa maritime mandate, *inter alia*, NATO and the EU[159] as well as Canada, Denmark, France, India, the Netherlands, the Russian Federation, Spain, the UK, and the US[160] have launched initiatives to counter piracy off the coast of Somalia. Moreover, one private security contractor has made an offer – though did not receive any response – to support such initiatives.[161]

The range of naval operations conducted at the Horn of Africa covers the deployment of Vessel Protection Detachments (VPDs) on merchant ships and forming of maritime convoys under the protection of naval vessels as well as countering piracy and armed robbery at sea. As far as possible to establish, the authority to conduct land operations against pirates and armed robbers at sea has not yet been used.

Apart from reported cases of use of force,[162] naval operations countering piracy and armed robbery at sea may involve the diversion[163] or hailing, stopping and boarding of suspected pirate ships, detention of suspected pirates, and seizure of weapons/ammunition they might have in their possession as well as the ships they use. Such operations may be conducted both in a deliberate offensive manner and in preparation of self-defence and/or extended self-defence of vulnerable commercial vessels as well as pre-emptive action in case of a demonstration of hostile intent or preventive action responding to a hostile act. Follow-up on these operations may also involve criminal prosecution of detained pirate suspects, either by the judiciary of the detaining State or following transfer to States in the region[164]. However, this example must not be confused with hostage and/or vessel release operations like the one conducted by US forces in whose course deadly force was also used.[165]

---

159 NATO operations under the Horn of Africa maritime mandate comprise Ocean Shield (successor to Allied Provider and Allied Protector); the European Union is conducting Operation Atalanta in accordance with Council Joint Action 2008/851/CFSP (10 November 2008) *Official Journal of the European Union* No. L 301/33.

160 For the list of States and IOs *see* para 6 of *UNSC Res. 1846* (n 103).

161 *See* the press release entitled 'Backwater Worldwide's Maritime Operations ready to assist Shipping Industry' dated 16 October 2008 (<http://blackwatermediacenter.com/images/pdf/10-16-08%20Maritime-Release.pdf> (accessed 29 July 2009)).

162 For instance, on 19 November 2008, the Indian vessel *INS Tabar* fired on a pirate mother vessel which, following the explosion of ammunition stored thereon, sunk. The Indian Navy claimed that the warship had fired in self-defence, responding to a threat by and fire from the pirates whom it had stopped in order to search the vessel. *See* <www.cbc.ca/world/story/2008/11/19/pirate-somali.html> and <www.nytimes.com/2008/11/19/world/asia/19iht-20pirate.17953692.html> (both accessed 24 July 2009).

163 Note that it might be challenging to identify a suitable port for diversion in the maritime environment at the Horn of Africa.

164 On co-operation in the exercise of jurisdiction *see* para 11 of *UNSC Res. 1816* (n 103) and para 3 of *UNSC Res.* 1851 (n 102), respectively. The EU used to have a cooperation agreement with Kenya which was later denounced by the latter, and has a similar agreement with the Seychelles. These agreements breathe the spirit of law enforcement through their detailed human rights regimes.

165 On 12 April 2009, US Navy snipers shot three pirates holding an American cargo-ship captain hostage and threatening him with an AK-47. *See* <www.cnn.com/2009/

VPD and convoy operations also involve diversion as well as hailing, stopping and boarding. Moreover, detention and seizure may be authorised, as well. While deliberate offensive operations are an option under a Chapter VII mandate, it is more likely that VPD/convoy operations will focus on responding to activities which, as a minimum, involve demonstrations of hostile intent. To date, VPD/convoy practice has rarely involved the use of lethal force against non-compliant actors.[166] In sum, to date the Horn of Africa naval operations do not exhaust the authority available under the rules of customary international law co-existing with UNCLOS, UNCLOS itself, or stemming from the maritime mandate. In particular, counter-piracy practice focuses on military support to maritime law enforcement rather than the fight against pirates and armed robbers at sea.

The focus on law enforcement reflects a policy choice made by the States and IOs implementing the mandate rather than a legal requirement. As demonstrated, relevant international law has not limited the range of options available. In applying international law to the situation at the Horn of Africa, the only legal reason for denying States and IOs the authority to combat pirates and armed robbers at sea, leaving them with law enforcement as the sole option, could hence have been an overarching proportionality concern. However, combating pirates and armed robbers at sea is neither *per se* unproportional nor is it unproportional in light of the peculiarities of the situation at the Horn of Africa. In particular, the interests of the international community whose protection the Horn of Africa naval operations shall bring about have sufficient weight to outbalance the private interests affected by a military response; they are, moreover, not irreconcilably in conflict with the sovereign interests of Somalia for as long as their implementation does not jeopardise the realisation of the desired end-State, viz. curing Somalia from the calamitous effects of failing statehood.

3.6 International Community Interests

The international community interests adversely affected by piracy and armed robbery at sea as well as other non-compliant activities are essentially freedom of navigation at sea, the UN's capacity to perform its functions, and non-proliferation of illicit small arms and light weapons in the region. Apart from arms embargo violations, the threatening activities, namely denial of humanitarian access and disruption of sea lines, affect international security from an economic or social angle; being caused by *inter alia* piracy and armed robbery at sea at the Horn of Africa, they coin-

WORLD/africa/04/12/somalia.pirates/> (accessed 24 July 2009). The Department of Defense Dictionary of Military and Associated Terms (as amended through 17 March 2009) – JP 1.02 – defines the related US doctrinal term 'hostage rescue' as: '[a] personnel recovery method used to recover isolated personnel who are specifically designated as hostages'. As the relevant military doctrine, JP 3-50 'Personnel Recovery' indicates, these operations are perceived to be a national responsibility (passim). Accordingly, it is unlikely that the US considered the Horn of Africa maritime mandate to have any bearing on this operation.

166 That might also be related to the fact that to facilitate these operations, SOFA-like agreements with the flag States of the vessels so protected might be required.

cidentally have part of their roots in transnational crime.[167] Customary international law concerning the fight against piracy notwithstanding, threatening factors of that nature would not in and of themselves justify an authorisation of the use of force under Chapter VII of the UN Charter if they stood in isolation. The authorisation of the use of all necessary means/measures in spite of the foregoing indicates that the UN Security Council considers measures exclusive of the use of force inadequate. This is a sound judgment. Like a catalyst, the TFG's lack of capacity to influence the situation in Somalia in conjunction with the mutually reinforcing link between piracy / armed robbery at sea and arms embargo violations, enable the adverse effects at issue to transcend the economic/social and criminal domains. Additionally, as humanitarian access is denied to the World Food Programme[168], the UN's capacity to effectively and efficiently exercise its functions is also adversely affected. Putting the UN's capacity to contribute to food security in jeopardy amounts to challenging its credibility as a provider of international peace and security – at any event in the region. The gravity of the denial of humanitarian access, demonstrated by the continuing humanitarian catastrophe, also transcends the economic/social domain[169]. Moreover, piracy as an activity of *hostes humani generis* is the paradigmatic case of paramilitary/military violence inflicted on all States individually as well as the international community of States as a whole, and as represented by the United Nations. As far as piracy is concerned, the UN Security Council could have authorised the use of force no matter whether it has a substantial factual link with other factors contributing to a complex composite threat like that posed by the situation in Somalia.

3.7 Limits of Authority and Proportionality Concerns

As discussed, the Horn of Africa maritime mandate confirms customary international law concerning the use of force and UNCLOS concerning jurisdictional ques-

---

167 More precisely, representing part of its dual nature, piracy may *inter alia* be considered transnational crime; the Horn of Africa maritime mandate has assimilated armed robbery, a domestic crime by nature, to transnational crime.

168 The WFP is a programme which was jointly established by the UN and the Food and Agriculture Organization of the United Nations (FAO), a Specialized Agency within the meaning of Article 57 of the UN Charter, for the purposes of food aid support to development, emergency and protracted relief food, and promoting world food security. *See* Articles I and II(1) of the WFP General Regulations – <http://one.wfp.org/aboutwfp/how_run/GeneralRegulations_E.pdf> and Article XII(1) of the FAO Constitution – <www.fao.org/docrep/010/k1713e/k1713e01.htm#1> (both accessed 24 July 2009).

169 A similar conclusion could probably be based on the notion of 'UN self-defence' which could be developed by way of analogy to the right of self-defence for situations like the one at hand where – through interests which it considers indispensable for the purpose of maintaining or restoring international peace and security – the raison d'être of the UN is at stake. There can be no doubt that the UN has the legal capacity it needs to defend its interests (*cf.* the ICJ's Advisory Opinion, *Reparations for the Injury Suffered in the Service of the United Nations* (Bernadotte) (Advisory Opinion) [1949] ICJ Rep. 174, 178sq). There should be no doubt either that it may exercise the said capacity by way of authorising the use of force under Chapter VII of its Charter.

tions of international co-operation in maritime law enforcement, both on the high seas, against pirates and their vessels, which it extends to armed robbers at sea and Somalia's territorial waters. It also authorises the use of force against vessels and/or persons on board them who, even if neither pirates nor armed robbers at sea, disrupt humanitarian access or violently deprive others of the freedom of navigation, as well as against designated arms embargo violators. This authority does not come without limits. Operations on the high seas, regardless of whether military in nature or law enforcement, do not occur in a legal vacuum. Moreover, when extending the legal rules for fighting and prosecuting pirates to armed robbers at sea and Somalia's territorial waters, the UN Security Council has also extended thereto the limits placed on such action on the high seas under relevant international law.[170] (The authority to conduct land operations for the purpose of suppressing acts of piracy and armed robbery at sea is beyond the scope of this analysis.)

The formula that the limits of authority shall derive from 'relevant international law' does not relieve those applying and implementing the Horn of Africa maritime mandate from the need to determine what international law is actually relevant. The same variety of legal sources from which authority derives is also relevant in determining the limits of authority. For the purpose of analysis, the following will be differentiated: deliberate offensive operations against pirates, armed robbers at sea, and other non-compliant actors; certain aspects of the legal framework concerning persons belonging to any of these categories in a law enforcement framework; and follow-up operations, in particular transfer of detainees as well as other forms of support to criminal prosecution.

Deliberate offensive operations against pirates target them as *hostes humani generis* – that is, in a belligerent manner. Being assimilated to pirates by the Horn of Africa maritime mandate, armed robbers at sea may be targeted in the same manner. Other non-compliant actors, viz. those disrupting humanitarian access or freedom of navigation outside a piratical context, are also belligerently targetable because the use of force against them is authorised under Chapter VII of the UN Charter. Part of belligerent targeting is that the vessels controlled by persons belonging to any of these categories may be treated as though they were enemy warships. That being so, fighting pirates and armed robbers at sea (as opposed to 'suppressing' them), and the use of force against other non-compliant actors, is legally equivalent to a non-international armed conflict. In that context, the authority to belligerently target entails lethal neutralisation of individuals and sinking of the vessels in their control. Targeting is subject to the same criteria as apply otherwise in non-international armed conflict; as common Article 3 of GCs I-IV[171] does not specifically address tar-

170 The Horn of Africa maritime mandate consistently requires that both entry into Somalia's territorial waters for the purpose of repression of piracy and armed robbery at sea as well as the use of all necessary means to achieve this end must be conducted 'in a manner consistent with such action permitted on the high seas with respect to piracy under relevant international law'. Para 9 of *UNSC Res. 1846* (n 103), para 7(a) of *UNSC Res. 1816* (n 103).

171 AP II is applicable to non-international armed conflicts 'which take place on the territory of a High Contracting Party between its armed forces and ... other armed groups ...', that is, not extraterritorially.

geting, they primarily stem from customary international humanitarian law as far as States are concerned and from general principles of international humanitarian law as far as IOs are concerned. If international human rights treaty law is considered applicable it may require prudent planning and execution of individual operations should they possibly involve adverse effects on the lives of those not specifically targeted.[172]

By contrast, neither pirates nor armed robbers at sea nor other non-compliant actors may claim combatant immunity for their activities. Lacking a link to a legitimate belligerent, they do not enjoy status under international humanitarian law. Being the quintessential outlaws at sea, pirates historically did not even enjoy any protections at all. By contrast, contemporary international law does not leave them and persons belonging to the other categories without protection; they can namely rely on common Article 3 of GCs I-IV, including in case of capture. Moreover, they may also rely on such protections as the shipwrecked benefit from in non-international armed conflict. According to the ICRC's Customary International Humanitarian Law Study, after an engagement the shipwrecked must be searched for, collected and evacuated without delay; they must receive the medical treatment and attention required by their condition to the fullest extent possible and without delay; and they must be protected against ill-treatment and pillage of their personal property.[173]

Deliberate offensive operations may also aim to neutralise the targeted individuals and their vessels non-lethally. For that purpose, diversion, VBSS, and capture are covered by the authority both under customary international law or Chapter VII of the UN Charter. If they target pirates, armed robbers at sea, or other on-compliant actors, diversion, VBSS, and capture are not legally equivalent to belligerent prize measures of the same nature which may be taken against merchant vessels and/or their cargoes;[174] the latter are directed against civilians not taking a direct part in hostilities[175] and/or civilian objects not effectively contributive thereto.[176] However, VBSS, diversion and capture are also measures available in the exercise of law enforcement jurisdiction at sea in accordance with Article 110 of UNCLOS. In

172 *See* the judgments by the European Court of Human Rights in *Isayeva v. Russia* (24 February 2005) Application No. 57950/00 – at paras 179sqq and *Isayeva et al. v. Russia* – Applications No. 57947/00, 57948/00, and 57949/00 – at paras 174sqq.

173 *See* J. M. Henckaerts & L. Doswald-Beck (eds), *Customary International Humanitarian Law Vol I: Rules* (Cambridge University Press, Cambridge, 2005) Rules 109-111. It might be a matter of debate whether practice in non-international armed conflicts involving hostilities at sea would indeed support the customary nature of the essence of Articles 7 and 8 of GP II as implied by these rules. Attempting to analyse this would, however, exceed the scope of this chapter.

174 *Heintschel von Heinegg* (n 10) 151, 156; *cf.* 'San Remo Manual on International Law Applicable to Armed Conflicts at Sea' (12 June 1994) paras 112-158.

175 Note that the ICRC's Interpretive Guidance (2009) does not address the belligerent activities of pirates.

176 Note that according to the ICRC, the definition of targetable objects is concerned, the 'effective contribution' and 'definite military advantage' standards apply in non-international armed conflict, as well. *Henckaerts and Doswald-Beck* (n 173) Rule 8 and commentary thereon, 30sq.

that case, the notion of 'relevant international law' may refer to international human rights law – to the extent it is considered extraterritorially applicable to the conduct of States and/or capable of having binding force upon the conduct of IOs not parties to human rights treaties.[177]

Both military and law enforcement operations against pirates, armed robbers at sea, and other non-compliant actors require appropriate preparation. As far as military operations are concerned, regardless of whether they aim at achieving a lethal or non-lethal effect, prudent planning must give effect to the principle of distinction and the prohibition of unnecessary suffering and should involve a targeting process for that purpose; it must also give effect to the principle of humane treatment. As far as targeting is concerned, target selection will be the most challenging part – how does one identify a pirate, armed robber at sea, or otherwise non-compliant actor? To meet the challenge with respect to pre-planned operations against individuals, a three-step analysis has become state-of-the-art, comprising the positive identification of the targeted individual(s), an assessment of his/her pattern of life which facilitates precautions concerning collateral damage and effects, and proof of evidence – information and intelligence – in order to justify targetability.

At the Horn of Africa, the key indicators to assess whether the crew of a vessel are indeed pirates or armed robbers at sea comprise the presence of weapons, in particular weapons of war such as e.g. AK-47s and RPGs; ladders and similar equipment; a lack of fishing equipment, less provisions of food and water than would be required for a fishing tour; and the fact that the number of persons on board a vessel exceeds the usual size of a fishing crew. Intelligence, e.g. that pirates or armed robbers at sea are operating in a given area, may support such assessment.

On a separate note, as far as designated non-compliant actors are concerned, it may be assumed that any information available to the 751 Sanctions Committee will also be available for targeted operations against them. Their ignorance or resistance towards a diversion order or the order to receive a boarding party may also be considered indicative of piracy, armed robbery at sea, or other non-compliance. In the framework of belligerent VBSS, such ignorance or resistance may be considered as sufficient to engage. By contrast, in law enforcement as contemplated by Article 110 of UNCLOS, engagement might be disproportionate in these cases.

Law enforcement at sea requires prudent preparation of operations, as well. In particular, the criterion of suspicion of piracy under Article 110 of UNCLOS has certain commonalities with the steps 'positive identification' and 'proof of evidence'. This article establishes a rule of doubt, a presumption of entitlement to freedom of navigation on the part of an intercepted vessel (*in dubio pro libertate*). It applies when a warship encounters 'a foreign ship', that is, a ship that prima facie – by virtue of flying a certain flag[178] – enjoys the protection of another than the warship's flag State. As this rule of doubt pertains to a freedom granted under international law,

177 This chapter will not engage in the discussion concerning (i) the extraterritorial applicability of human rights treaty law and (ii) the binding force of both international humanitarian law treaties and international human rights treaty law on IOs (including the intergovernmental pillar of the EU). For my position regarding these questions *see* *Häußler* (n 49) 49sqq.

178 Article 110(2) of UNCLOS: 'its flag'.

the notion of 'foreign' must also be derived from international law. Echoing the International Court of Justice's *Nottebohm* judgment,[179] Article 91(1) of UNCLOS requires expressly that '[t]here must exist a genuine link between the State and the ship'. The genuine link is missing, and the presumption under Article 110 of UNCLOS rebutted accordingly, if pirates (and, at the Horn of Africa, armed robbers at sea) are caught in the act or after having been pursued, or (albeit that might happen in movies only rather than in reality) fly the pirate flag. Moreover, if not caught in the piratical act, a vessel may be nevertheless be considered (that is, there is reasonable ground for suspecting that it is) piratical if is does not fly a flag or does not give satisfactory information concerning its origin and destination.[180] As UNCLOS is silent on the substantial criteria for determining when a reasonable ground for suspecting piracy exists, this will differ in various States and ultimately reflect the requirements of law enforcement concerning police investigations and evidence gathering in criminal cases. Moreover, planning of law enforcement operations must also ensure that:

> during each deployment of warships (and military aircraft), due regard has to be paid to the legitimate interests of other States and to the safety of international navigation and aviation.[181]

In self-defence and extended self-defence, the use of force is not limited by international law. National (criminal) law may determine what use of force is permitted in such situations from a legal perspective.

While operations against pirates, armed robbers at sea, and other non-compliant actors can be conducted both in a belligerent manner and under the auspices of law enforcement, follow-up operations against pirates and armed robbers at sea always pertain to the realm of law enforcement. By contrast, follow-up operations concerning other non-compliant actors may also involve operational detention for as long as their contribution to the threat to international peace and security in the region is expected to prevail. Operational detention may specifically be an option where persons are detained following a demonstration of hostile intent or the commission of a hostile act which does not qualify as criminal activity.

Once captured, pirates and armed robbers at sea may be brought to trial in the court determined by the flag State of the capturing vessel or a State to which they have been transferred. The UN Security Council encourages criminal prosecution; it has invited States and IOs to embark law enforcement officials and make their citizens and vessels available for forensic investigation.[182]

179 Judgment of the International Court of Justice, *Liechtenstein v. Guatemala* [1955] ICJ Rep. 4. – To justify the exercise of protection in the realm of international law, nationality under domestic law 'must correspond with the factual situation', i.e. be effective; it must be the expression of 'factual ties' (at 22) – of a 'genuine connection' (at 23) – between the national and his or her State.

180 *Cf. Heintschel von Heinegg* (n 10) 151, 171 with respect to statelessness.

181 *Heintschel von Heinegg* (n 10) 151, 170 (including further references).

182 *See* paras 3 and 12 of *UNSC Res. 1851* (n 102).

Article 105 of UNCLOS has not limited the sovereign right of States to determine whether they charge them in a military court – historically an Admiralty Court – or an ordinary criminal court, because it does not attach any qualifying attribute to the notion of 'court'. No matter what the nature of the court, the minimum standards governing criminal trials in accordance with pertinent (general principles of) international humanitarian and human rights law apply. The choice of jurisdiction must not be made with a view to depriving the suspects – or to-be-accused – of that protection. An apt example of a transfer agreement was concluded between the EU and Kenya.[183] This agreement addressed the transfer of detainees and their belongings as well as possible evidence and specified the terms and conditions under which military personnel involved in detention and seizure may be called as witnesses.

3.8 Conclusion on the Horn of Africa

When in 1992 the UN Security Council authorised the use of force by a military crisis response operation to deal with the situation in Somalia for the first time, it did so to ensure a secure environment for humanitarian access.[184] This legacy resonates in the contemporary Horn of Africa maritime mandate which addresses not only the disruption of humanitarian access but also disruptions of the freedom of navigation, piracy and armed robbery at sea, as well as arms embargo violations occurring in the maritime environment. The maritime mandate is tailored to the situation in the maritime environment off the coast of Somalia and forms part of the overall effort to restore international peace and security in the region through curing Somalia from the calamitous effects of failing statehood. To that end, it confirms counter-piracy authority stemming from customary international law co-existing with UNCLOS as well as UNCLOS itself, both of which it extends *ratione materiae* (to armed robbers at sea) and *ratione loci* (to Somalia's territorial waters). It also authorises the use of force against other non-compliant actors, thus defending the interest of the international community represented by UN efforts to contribute to food security in

183 Exchange of Letters (EOL) with Kenya on the conditions and modalities for the transfer of persons suspected of having committed acts of piracy and detained by the European Union-led Naval Force (EUNAVFOR), and seized property in the possession of EUNAVFOR, from EUNAVFOR to Kenya and for their treatment after such transfer (OJ 2009 L 79/49). This EOL is no longer in force.

184 *UNSC Res. 794* (n 103) authorised the use of force by a multinational force, namely 'all necessary means to establish as soon as possible a secure environment for humanitarian relief operations in Somalia' (para 10). The multinational force – the Unified Task Force (UNITAF) – had been offered by the US and recommended, as one of five options, by the United Nations Secretary-General, as an 'enforcement operation'; the United Nations Secretary-General had *inter alia* suggested that its mandate 'could also stipulate that the operation would be conducted with full respect for the applicable rules of humanitarian law' (Letter dated 29 November 1992 from the United Nations Secretary-General addressed to the President of the Security Council – UN document S/24868 – at 4sq). The language used in both the letter and the subsequently adopted resolution indicates without ambiguity that the multinational force was considered a military crisis response operation entrusted with authority to use force with military means and measures.

Somalia, unimpeded freedom of navigation on the high seas, and non-proliferation of illicit small arms and light weapons. The mandate authorises, accordingly, military crisis response operations which need to be augmented by law enforcement capabilities for follow-up purposes; at the same time, it does not preclude that maritime law enforcement only is conducted.

4. Conclusion

Crisis response operations in maritime environments face specific legal and practical challenges which derive namely from the concurrent, if competing, exercise of sovereign rights pertaining to multiple jurisdictions in the same geographical area and from the fact that international law of the sea relies on enforcement by States both through their armed forces and their criminal jurisdictions. Apart from that, they have many challenges in common with their land-based counterparts. The exact relationship between the specific ingredients of the legal framework – international humanitarian law, international human rights law, and the law of IOs – is not settled any better than with respect to crisis response operations on land. UN mandates authorising the use of all necessary means, measures, or action require States and IOs implementing them to make a policy choice concerning the necessity of exhausting the UN mandate by using military force for military purposes, and determining to what extent they limit themselves to focusing on military support to law enforcement. Fully cognisant of the need to limit the transitional authority conferred upon crisis response operations by a UN mandate and/or consent of the government responsible for the theatre of operations, in order to balance the exercise of such transitional authority with the sovereignty of the State(s) and the rights of the human person enjoyed by the individuals affected, those making the relevant policy decisions should duly take into account the lesson repeatedly learned in the 1990s that under-implementation may go hand-in-hand with failure.

The mandates specifically reviewed combine elements of the legitimisation of the use of force and the specification of the conditions under which legitimate force may lawfully be used. Both mandates also enhance the law enforcement options available at sea; they do not, however, make them the legally preferred choice. The UNIFIL mandate illustrates how the UN may contribute to collective self-defence including at sea; the Horn of Africa maritime mandate shows that multiple interests of the international community – freedom of navigation at sea, the UN's capacity to perform its functions, and non-proliferation of illicit small arms and light weapons – as well as the goal of curing Somalia from the calamitous effects of failing statehood may be amalgamated into a uniform effort. Doing this may require, as the Horn of Africa maritime mandate indicates, that the UN Security Council adjusts the legal framework to the exigencies of the theatre of operations. In the given maritime context, it has confirmed that it considers its resolutions hierarchically superior to UNCLOS,[185] reaffirming the superior rank of the UN Charter and the obligations

185 For an earlier example *see* the non-proliferation regime concerning weapons of mass destruction (WMD) established by *UNSC Res. 1540* (n 20) and the related analysis by *Heintschel von Heinegg* (n 10) 151, 181.

stemming from its Chapter VII in particular vis-à-vis any other international treaty to which the members of the UN are party.

Chapter 8

Criminal Responsibility of International Military Missions and Personnel

Paolina Massidda

1. Introduction

There can be little doubt that members of international military missions have been involved in the commission of serious criminal acts. Media and human rights organisations in particular have documented the involvement of members of International Military Missions (IMM) in criminal acts and abuses in operations ranging from those in Bosnia-Herzegovina and Kosovo in the early 1990s to Cambodia and Timor-Leste in the early and late 1990s, to West Africa in 2002 and the Democratic Republic of the Congo in 2004.

A report of Amnesty International issued in 2000 said that forces belonging to the Economic Community of West African States Military Observer Group (ECOMOG) also committed human rights violations. In particular, during the rebels' incursion into Freetown, a large numbers of captured or suspected rebels were extra-judicially executed by ECOMOG. Children, including an eight-year-old boy caught in possession of a gun, were among the victims. Ill-treatment, including beating, whippings and public humiliation, was common at ECOMOG checkpoints. At least ten Sierra Leonean staff of humanitarian organisations and the International Committee of the Red Cross (ICRC) were detained by ECOMOG forces in January 1999; most were beaten.[1]

Human Rights Watch, in its Report issued in 2002, reported several cases of sexual violence by members of the United Nations Mission in Sierra Leone (UNAMISIL), including the rape of a twelve-year-old girl in Bo by a soldier of the Guinean contingent and the rape of a woman by two Ukrainian soldiers near Kenema.[2]

Members of IMM are bound by the provisions of International Humanitarian Law (IHL) and are subject to domestic jurisdiction in respect of crimes commit-

---

1 *See* Amnesty International, Report on Sierra Leone (2000) AI Index available at: </www.unhcr.org/refworld/publisher,AMNESTY,SLE,3ae6aa127,0.html>. *See also* J. L. Poole, 'Conflict Justice in Sierra Leone' in *Conflict Mapping in Sierra Leone, Violations of IHL from 1991 to 2002* (Smiths, Gambette & Longley (eds), (No Peace Without Justice) 2004).

2 Human Rights Watch, 'We'll Kill You if You Cry: Sexual Violence in the Sierra Leone Conflict' (2002) available at: <www.hrw.org/reports/2003/sierraleone/sierleon0103.pdf>.

M. Odello and R. Piotrowicz (eds.), International Military Missions and International Law.
2011 Koninklijke Brill NV. Printed in The Netherlands. ISBN 978 9004 17437 5. pp. 211–243.

ted during their operations. Under the model status-of-forces agreement (SOFA),[3] military members of peacekeeping operations are subject to the criminal authority of the troop-contributing country concerned. Because military members of national contingents are not subject to the criminal jurisdiction of the host State, the model SOFA, which has been repeatedly endorsed by the United Nations Security Council, specifically envisaged that the United Nations Secretary-General would obtain formal assurances from the troop-contributing country concerned that it would exercise jurisdiction with respect to crimes that might be committed by its forces in the mission area.

This chapter examines briefly the legal basis for criminal responsibility of members of IMM and evaluates how national jurisdictions have complied with their obligation to investigate and prosecute crimes committed by their citizens when deployed to operations abroad. The chapter also evaluates the few cases conducted by international tribunals and courts in respect of events which could be qualified as crimes occurring during missions and, finally, considers briefly the role of the International Criminal Court when the national jurisdiction is unable and/or unwilling to genuinely investigate and prosecute crimes falling under its jurisdiction committed by members of IMM.

2. Legal Basis for Criminal Responsibility of International Military Missions and Personnel

Although there was originally some doubt about the applicability of international humanitarian law to members of IMM, it is now generally accepted that humanitarian law binds such forces.[4]

Members of IMM, including peacekeeping and/or peace-enforcement operations, are subject to the same substantive and procedural rules of criminal law as ordinary defendants and international criminal responsibility is a viable and practical concept with respect to such personnel. The question arises whether international criminal law indeed applies without restrictions to individuals acting under the supervision of an international organisation or a group of States. Criminal prosecution of members of IMM is subject to a significant degree of controversy on a number of points. This controversy relating to the scope of the potential prosecution

3 Report of the Secretary-General 'Model Status-of-Forces agreement for Peace-Keeping Operations' (1990) UN Doc. A/45/594. *See also*, 'Model Agreement Between the United Nations and the Member States Contributing Personnel and Equipment to United Nations Peace-Keeping Operations' (1991) UN Doc. A/46/185.

4 *See* P. Benvenuti, 'The Implementation of International Humanitarian Law in the Framework of United Nations Peace-keeping Operations', in *European Commission, Law in Humanitarian Crisis*, Vol. 1 (Office for Official Publications of the European Communities, Luxembourg, 1995) 83. *See also*, Van Hegelson, 'The Law of Armed Conflicts and the United Nations Peace-Keeping and Peace-Enforcing Operations' (1993) 6 *Hague Yeabook of International Law*, 95; L.C. Green, 'Humanitarian Law and the Man in the Field' (1976) 14 *Can. Y. B. Int-l Law*, 96; D. Shraga UN Peacekeeping Operations: Applicability of International Humanitarian Law and Responsibility for Operations-Related Damages' (2000) 94 *AJIL*, 406.

of members of IMM has evolved around the question as to whether jurisdiction is national or international.

In United Nations operations, agreements are usually concluded between the UN and troop-contributing States (the so called Participation Agreements), and between the UN and the host State (the so called SOFA). These agreements exempt the members of the force, to a certain extent, from the criminal jurisdiction of the host State: they are 'immune from legal process'.[5] The reason for this arrangement, in the words of the Secretary-General, is that: 'it is essential to the preservation of the independent exercise of the functions of the force'.[6] These specific arrangements are supported by the provisions of the Convention on the Privileges and Immunities of the United Nations,[7] which confer immunity from legal process on UN officials.

In the absence of host State jurisdiction, however, it is not the UN that exercises jurisdiction. The UN does not have a court martial structure or other integrated penal system to deal with crimes committed by peacekeepers. Instead, agreements between the contributing States and the UN provide that the troop-contributing States exercise criminal jurisdiction over the troops they contribute. Thus, it is left to the State of nationality of a peacekeeper to prosecute crimes. National (military) criminal law is used to prosecute peacekeepers, and there is in principle no international jurisdiction. In certain cases States will have asserted universal jurisdiction over serious crimes committed by non-nationals. This is certainly not the case for all States and all the core crimes. For example, the Dutch War Crimes Act of 1952[8] establishes universal jurisdiction over war crimes, including breaches of common Article 3 of the Geneva Conventions of 1949, but not over crimes against humanity.

That the exercise of criminal jurisdiction is left to the troop-contributing States is illustrated by practice. Members of IMM have been subjected to criminal prosecution by national tribunals for crimes allegedly committed during military or peace operations. This arrangement has not remained immune from criticism. Indeed, to some authors it appears inconsequent that troop-contributing States have criminal jurisdiction over forces for which the United Nations is responsible. Also, different States may have different views on which, if any, crimes allegedly committed by their troops they want to investigate and/or prosecute.[9]

Just as there is no general framework regulating criminal jurisdiction with regard to UN operations, nor is there any for non-UN operations. For each operation, an *ad hoc* arrangement is agreed upon. Since there are many different types of

5 *See e.g.* ONUC SOFA, reproduced in R. Higgins, *UN Peacekeeping 1946–1967 — Documents and Commentary*, III Africa (1980) 199–206, para. 9 and *Model Status-of-Forces Agreement for Peacekeeping Operations* (n 3) para. 46.

6 *See* 'Summary Study on the experience derived from the establishment of UNEF I' (9 October 1958) UN Doc. A/3943 para. 136.

7 Convention on the Privileges and Immunities of the United Nations, UNGA Res. 22 A (I) (13 February 1946) (Privileges and Immunities of the United Nations).

8 Official Title: Wet oorlogsstrafrecht (Wartime Offences Act 1952).

9 *See* M. Zwanenburg, 'Compromise or Commitment: Human Rights and International Humanitarian Law Obligations for UN Peace Forces' (1998) 11 *Leiden Journal of International Law*, 229.

military operations, many different types of arrangements are consequently possible. A common characteristic of such agreements, however, is the concern of troop-contributing States for their sovereignty. This implies a strong presumption against any other criminal jurisdiction than that of the troop-contributing State. Examples of this principle are found in the arrangements with regard to IFOR and SFOR in Bosnia-Herzegovina, laid down in Annex IA to the Dayton Agreement[10] and Appendix B thereto. Article 7 of that Appendix B provides that: 'NATO military personnel shall under all circumstances and at all times be subject to the exclusive jurisdiction of their respective national elements'.[11] Another example is the Multinational Forces and Observers (MFO). Article 11(a) of the Protocol regarding the MFO states that:

> Military members of the MFO shall be subject to the exclusive jurisdiction of their respective national states in respect of any criminal offences which may be committed by them in the Receiving State. Any such person who is charged with the commission of a crime will be brought to trial by the respective Participating State, in accordance with its laws.[12]

Furthermore, over two decades, international military missions have begun to develop ways to bridge the gap between general application of IHL and practice through the setting of specific general principles and rules. The Rules of Engagement (RoE) can be defined as prescriptive guidelines meant to govern the application of military force promulgated by governmental or international institutional bodies.[13] The purpose of the RoE is to constrain the use of unlawful and unreasonable force during military operations, irrespective of their nature.

Juridical and operational aspects of the RoE are inextricably linked with certain aspects of international criminal law liability. In particular, the question of whether

10 General Framework Agreement for Peace in Bosnia and Herzegovina (21 November 1995, signed in Paris on December 14, 1995). Full agreement found at: <www.ohr.int/dpa/default.asp?content_id=379>.

11 Ibid. (See Annex IA, Appendix B, Article 7 (1996) 35 *ILM* 75).

12 *See* 'Appendix to the Annex to the Protocol between the Arab Republic of Egypt and the State of Israel', 3 August 1981, reproduced in R. C. R. Siekmann (ed), *Basic Documents on United Nations and Related Peace-keeping Forces* (1991) 292–305.

13 *See* T. Westunsing, 'Taking Terrorism and ROE seriously' (2003) 1 *J. Mil. Ethics*, 4. The US military defines RoE as 'directive issued by a competent military commander which delineate the circumstances and limitations under which United States forces will initiate and/or continue combat engagement with other forces encountered'. *See also* the Department of Defense Joint Publication 1-02 (1998) DOD Dictionary of Military and Associated Terms, Washington DC, Joint Chief of Staff. The definition of Rules of Engagement in the Standing United Nations Rules of Engagement for Peace-Enforcement Operations reads: 'Rules of Engagement provide general guidelines of self-defense and specific guidance governing the use of force consistent with mission accomplishment'. The Rules of Engagement Catalogue of NATO states: 'Rules of Engagement are the authorization for or limits on the use of force during military operations'.

RoE may function as sources for international criminal responsibility insofar as they involve general principles of law is not without practical relevance.

An example can be found in the criminal prosecution of a Dutch officer of the Royal Netherlands Marines Corps, a member of the Quick Reaction Force of the Dutch Battalion, engaged in the Stabilization Force Iraq (SFI) during the operation 'Telic', the US-led coalition that on 20 March 2003 started to overthrow the Iraqi regime. On 1 January 2004, a Dutch Sergeant-Major was charged with murder and involuntary manslaughter. Allegedly, he shot an Iraqi civilian during a salvage operation of a relief supply container following a looting by numerous Iraqi individuals. The Sergeant-Major fired two warning shots in the vicinity of the crowd, one in the air and one to the ground. The charges, based upon violation of the Dutch Penal Code, were indirectly substantiated with the assertion that the RoE were infringed, particularly the provision concerning the use of 'non-deadly force'. This example seems to imply that criminal courts could derive international criminal law liabilities from the RoE presupposing that these provisions are norms of international criminal law and that their application is in compliance with the principle of legality.[14]

The relevance of the RoE for the determination of criminal responsibility is further demonstrated by the criminal case against the Belgian Colonel Marchal with respect to the killings of ten Belgian peacekeepers in Rwanda. On 7 April 1994, ten Belgian soldiers who were brought into action as part of the United Nations peacekeeping force in Rwanda (UNAMIR) were killed during a massacre in Kigali while escorting Prime Minister Agathe Uwiliniyimana. In 1996, the Prosecutor-General in Brussels brought charges under Belgian criminal law against Colonel Marchal, at the time of the event operational commander of the Belgian peacekeeping contingent, for negligence for the death of the ten Belgian soldiers, due to the fact that he allegedly refrained from taking precautionary measures. In particular, the prosecution argued that Marchal could have reasonably known that Rwandan paramilitary activists (the so called Interhamwe) were planning to kill Belgian soldiers in order to force a withdrawal from the mandate so that the internal tribal war could continue. In its judgement of 4 July 1996,[15] the military court in Brussels acquitted Marchal, considering that he had strictly complied with the UN mandate and with the RoE. Indeed, the order given to Marchal in his capacity as commander of the Kigali sector, on 7 April 1994 by General Dallaire – at the time Commander of the UNAMIR - to organise an escort for the Rwandan Prime Minister, was legitimate in accordance with the mandate of the force and the RoE, which served to safeguard prominent Rwandan politicians, including the Rwandan Prime Minister. Therefore, the court concluded that Marchal was neither juridically nor factually in a position to doubt the legitimacy and/or the political basis of the UN mandate.[16]

---

14 *See* (2004) *YIHL* 545-546.

15 Judgement and case summarised in (1998) 1 *YIHL* 413.

16 For a description of the case, *see* G.J. Knoops, *Defenses in Contemporary Criminal Law* (Transnational Publishers, New York, 2001) 143-156, 181, 182. *See also*, R. Dallaire, *Shake Hands with the Devil: The Failure of Humanity in Rwanda* (Carrol & Graf Publishers, New York, 2003).

It is therefore established in practice that members of IMM are subject to national jurisdiction for crimes committed during operations.

3. Practice of National Jurisdictions in Investigating and Prosecuting Members of International Military Missions, Including Peacekeeping and/or Peace-enforcement Operations

Cases have occurred in which peacekeepers and members of military operations were subject to investigations and tried by national courts for crimes allegedly committed during operations. In the course of several international, as well as internal, armed conflicts in the past which led to courts martial, examples emerge that realistically could occur within the context of military, peacekeeping or peace enforcement operations.

The following examples, taken from 1901-1902 US court martial cases which resulted in trials against several military superiors charged with various violations of the laws of war committed in the course of the US counter-insurgency operation in the Philippines in 1901, demonstrate the practical importance of international criminal law liability for members of international military forces. Indeed, principles of law established in such cases, may still be relevant and applied by analogy to cases involving members of IMM.

In May 1902 US Major Glenn was charged with the crime of torture (forcing the victim to drink large quantities of water) perpetrated for the purpose of obtaining information or confessions. The defendant justified his behaviour by arguing that he acted on the ground of military necessity.[17] The potential relevance of this example for members of international military forces is in the fact that they are sometimes ordered to assist in locating and apprehending individuals, for instance in order to surrender them to international tribunals. An example is the involvement of Stabilisation Force in Bosnia and Herzegovina (SFOR) troops assisting in the arrest of suspects indicted by the International Criminal Tribunal for the Former Yugoslavia (ICTY) and the interrogation of persons who could contribute to such arrest.[18]

In the case of US First Lieutenant Preston Brown, the defendant was charged with the crime of murder for shooting and killing an escaping prisoner of war, a Philippino who refused to answer Brown's questions about the death of a US soldier. In July 1901, a US court martial reached a guilty verdict of manslaughter and condemned Brown to five years of hard labour and recommendation for dismissal from army services.[19] The relevance of this example derives from the potential paral-

---

17 G. Mettraux, 'US Courts-Martial and the Armed Conflict in the Philippines (1899-1902): Their Contribution to National Case Law on War Crimes' (2003) 1 *Journal of International Criminal Justice*, 135-150.

18 The RoE of the SFOR provided that troops can arrest any individual against whom an indictment has been issued by the International Criminal Tribunal for Former Yugoslavia (ICTY) for crimes under its jurisdiction.

19 *Knoops* (n 16) 146-147.

lel with the crimes committed by troops engaged in the military mission in Iraq in 2003, which will be discussed *infra*.

At the time of these cases, the international criminal law system was not developed in the way it exists now. It is therefore interesting to discuss how similar cases have been solved in practice under contemporary international criminal law.

Practice has shown that criminal responsibility of IMM can be relevant essentially in three areas: treatment of civilians and/or persons imprisoned or otherwise detained, superior responsibility and joint criminal enterprise.

3.1 Treatment of Civilians and/or Persons Imprisoned or Otherwise Detained

The issue of the treatment of civilians and/or of prisoners/detainees is so far the one which has lead to the majority of cases investigated and prosecuted.

The practice shows on one side a reluctance on the part of national jurisdiction to investigate and prosecute crimes committed by members of IMM, and, on the other side, the inadequacy of national legislation insofar as conducts which could fall under the category of international crimes are not included as such in the relevant national legislation and/or are included as different crimes, of less gravity.

The matter of the applicability of humanitarian law to IMM in the framework of treatment of civilians or persons imprisoned was considered in various cases. One of the first cases arose from incidents that occurred during the Canadian participation in the UNITAF mission during March 1993. These events led to a military board of inquiry, several courts martial and appeals and led to the establishment of a Commission of Enquiry into the Deployment of Canadian Forces to Somalia. The leading case in the matter is *R v. Brocklebank*. The accused was arrested for aiding and abetting the torture of a Somali teenager who entered the Canadian Forces compound and was tortured and beaten to death while in custody.[20] The court took the view that as there was no declared war or armed conflict in Somalia, and as the Canadian forces deployed as part of the UNITAF mission were performing peacekeeping duties, they were not engaged in an armed conflict. As a consequence, the court ruled that Private Brocklebank had no legal obligation to ensure the safety of the prisoner because neither the Geneva Conventions nor the Additional Protocols applied in the circumstances.

This analysis seems flawed in a number of respects. First, the court qualified the mission of the Canadian forces as a 'peacekeeping mission', despite the fact that UNITAF had been authorised by the Security Council under Chapter VII of the UN Charter in circumstances that indicated that the previous mission (UNOSOM I) was being replaced by a peace enforcement operation comprising a coalition of States and condemning all violations of IHL committed in Somalia,[21] recognising therefore that the conflict in Somalia was of sufficient degree and intensity to trigger the application of IHL. Surprisingly, the court found that there was no evidence of an armed conflict, despite the fact that it does not seem to have heard any

20 Court Martial Appeal Court of Canada (1996) 134 DLR (4th) 377.

21 *See UNSC Res. 794* (3 December 1992).

evidence related to this aspect of the case, namely on the level of killings amongst the armed factions and the casualties amongst other members of the mission.[22] Furthermore, the court failed to consider properly the relevance of Articles 4 and 29 of the Fourth Geneva Convention, which provide the definition of persons protected by the Convention as well as the obligations in respect of the treatment of such persons when in the hands of a party to the conflict.[23] Indeed, it could be argued that Canadian Forces may have been a party to the conflict or occupying part of Somalia within the meaning of the Fourth Geneva Convention. If so, this would create a group of 'protected persons' in the sense of the said provisions, a category that the court failed to recognise.

It is worth noting that a Belgian military court also came to the conclusion that the Geneva Conventions and the Additional Protocols were not applicable to the armed conflict in Somalia. In June 1997, a Brussels military court acquitted Kurt Coelus and Claude Baert, two Belgian ex-paratroopers, of the war crime of threatening and committing assault and battery on Somali children at a checkpoint. They had been identified from a photograph in the Belgian daily 'Het Laatste Nieuws,' which appeared to show them swinging a boy over a camp fire. The military court held that the Belgian Act of 16 June 1993 relative to the punishment of grave breaches of the Geneva Conventions of 12 August 1949 and their two Additional Protocols was not applicable since the situation in Somalia in 1993 could not be defined as an international armed conflict because the United Nations troops were conducting a peace-keeping mission and could not be considered as a party to the conflict or an occupying power. The court further held that the events in Somalia in 1993 could not be regarded as a non-international armed conflict within the meaning of Article 3 common to the four Geneva Conventions, since the hostilities did not take place

---

22 *See* J.M. Simpson, *Law Applicable to Canadian Forces in Somalia 1992/93: A Study Prepared for the Commission of Inquiry into the Deployment of Canadian Forces to Somalia* (Ottawa, 1996) 30-33 (also known as the Simpson Study).

23 Article 4 of the Fourth Geneva Convention reads as follows: 'Persons protected by the Convention are those who, at a given moment and in any manner whatsoever, find themselves, in case of a conflict or occupation, in the hands of a Party to the conflict or Occupying Power of which they are not nationals. Nationals of a State which is not bound by the Convention are not protected by it. Nationals of a neutral State who find themselves in the territory of a belligerent State, and nationals of a co-belligerent State, shall not be regarded as protected persons while the State of which they are nationals has normal diplomatic representation in the State in whose hands they are. The provisions of Part II are, however, wider in application, as defined in Article 13. Persons protected by the Geneva Convention for the Amelioration of the Condition of the Wounded and Sick in Armed Forces in the Field of 12 August 1949, or by the Geneva Convention for the Amelioration of the Condition of Wounded, Sick and Shipwrecked Members of Armed Forces at Sea of 12 August 1949, or by the Geneva Convention relative to the Treatment of Prisoners of War of 12 August 1949, shall not be considered as protected persons within the meaning of the present Convention'. Article 29 reads as follows: 'The Party to the conflict in whose hands protected persons may be, is responsible for the treatment accorded to them by its agents, irrespective of any individual responsibility which may be incurred'.

between organised armed forces, but between irregular factions behaving in an anarchical manner without an established chain of command.[24]

The decision of the military court was heavily criticised and raised serious concerns about the lack of accountability for peacekeepers on the basis of legal technicalities. As a result, a separate case involving Sgt. Dirk Nassel concluded in May 1998 with a guilty verdict for several offences based on violations of human rights involving serious mistreatment of Somali youths. Sgt. Nassel forcibly fed a Somali child with pork and salted water until he vomited; tied a Somali child to a military vehicle and ordered the vehicle to move off; and procured and offered a Somali girl as a 'present' at a birthday party for a paratrooper under his command. The Somali girl was subsequently subjected to sexual abuse. The military court found the Belgian sergeant posted with the UNOSOM II troops guilty of assault and battery, threats and racial discrimination with regard to a Somali child, as well as incitement to immorality and indecent assault in a military camp. As indicated above, it is significant to note that the charges brought against Nassel were not in relation to violations of IHL but of human rights law. This choice in charges ensured that the military court did not repeat its judgment resulting in the acquittal of Coelus and Baert.[25]

An Italian Commission of Inquiry into events in Somalia also had difficulties grappling with the issue of the applicability of IHL, and it failed to make any legal evaluation of the facts, especially from the perspective of humanitarian law. The Italian cases also show the inadequacy of national legislation not only in investigating and prosecuting cases of international crimes, but also in implementing in the national legislation the core crimes codified under international criminal law.

After the publication in the Italian weekly magazine 'Panorama' of photographs concerning presumed maltreatment of and violence towards Somali civilians by Italian soldiers, both the military and ordinary judicial authorities commenced investigations. Indeed, under the Italian law a specific legal regime for operations of this kind does not exist. Under Article 9 of the Military Penal Code (MPC) applicable in time of war, provisions of the MPC are extended to Italian military contingents abroad. However, the MPC has not been deemed applicable to this specific case by virtue of the law decree authorising the mission, which provided, in derogation from the above-mentioned Article 9, that the Italian contingent in Somalia be subject to the MPC applicable in time of peace. This latter contains also provisions which deal with crimes committed by military persons against civilian and military enemies. However, the specific crimes of torture and maltreatment against civilians are not provided for in the MPC applicable in time of peace. Moreover, according

24 C.M. 17 déc. 1997, *Coelus en Baert* (1998) II, 3, D, *J.T.* 289. *See* M. Cogen, 'Correspondents' Report : Belgium' (1998) 1 *YIHL* 145 in which the following citation for the case is provided: Judgment of the Belgian Military Court regarding violations of IHL committed in Somalia and Rwanda, Nr 54 AR (1997) 20 November 1997, published in *Journal des tribunaux* (24 April 1998) 286-89. *See also* A. Weyembergh, 'La notion de conflit armé, le droit international humanitaire et les forces des N.U. en Somalie (à propos de l'arrêt de la Cour militaire du 17 déc. 1997)', (1999) *RDPC* 177-201.

25 *See* O. Dubois, 'Implementation of International Humanitarian Law: Biannual Update of National Legislation and Jurisprudence – January to June 1998' (1998) 325 *IRRC*, 732.

to the Italian law, military offences are normally judged by the military jurisdiction on the basis of military laws. The MPC applicable in time of peace, however, does not deal with common offences; thus, a military person responsible for an offence not foreseen by military regulation must be judged by the ordinary jurisdiction. In this legal context, both the military and ordinary judicial authorities can commence investigations for different offences, each on the basis of its own competence.

On 16 June 1997, the Italian government established a Fact-Finding Commission for a preliminary verification that the events actually took place. The Commission was mandated with ascertaining whether the illegal events reported had occured and verifying any malfunction in the management of the mission which could have undermined its humanitarian aims. Its mandate was confined to a non-judicial assessment. On 8 August 1997, the Commission presented its 'Conclusive Report on the Events which Occurred in Somalia', asserting the 'absolutely individual' nature of the episodes of maltreatment reported. It also stressed that those episodes had the character of 'exceptional gravity'.[26]

The Commission examined eight episodes of alleged violations of human rights, recognising them as founded. The Commission excluded responsibility for events concerning Somali prisoners 'hooded and bound' during patrols, in that such treatment is allowed by military law for transfer of individuals whose freedom must be restricted. The first episode, in which the Commission verified that the allegation was *prima facie* founded, took place on 9 April 1993 in the Johar camp and concerned the interrogation of a Somali citizen where a telephone wire was used to cause electric shocks. The Commission concluded that the offence had taken place but could not attribute responsibility. The other two cases took place during the course of the UNOSOM II operation. The first concerned the rape of a Somali female citizen perpetrated around 14-15 June 1993 at the Mogadishu port. On this occasion, the victim reported that she was forced into a container by a junior officer and there raped by a group of soldiers. The Commission found that the incident occurred but did not draw any conclusions on the question of criminal responsibility. The last episode took place between 17 and 19 November 1993 at a checkpoint controlled by the Italian contingent and concerned an allegation of rape with a rifle flare of a Somali woman. For the other episodes, the unreliability of the witnesses, the contradictions in depositions and the lack of objective evidence of the events reported were decisive elements in concluding that the facts were unfounded.

At the end of the investigation, the Commission reached the conclusion that the responsibilities ascertained were limited to the lower levels of the military hierarchy, including non-commissioned officers and subordinate officers who were responsible for illicit tolerance or omission of control, contributing to causing the events. In the Commission's view, the patronising attitude of subordinate officers apparently determined their failure to report the events to superior officers, whose responsibility in the events, either direct or indirect, was thus excluded.[27]

---

26 *See* N. Lupi, 'Report by the Enquiry Commission on the Behavior of Italian Peacekeeping Troops in Somalia' (1998) 1 *YIHL* 375.

27 Ibid. 378.

A number of trials were initiated before the ordinary Italian judge for offences actually committed by military persons in a war context. However, the Italian criminal code does not criminalise specific conducts as described below in the context of an armed conflict. As a result, nobody was ever convicted of war crimes.

The cases described above show the dilemma of national courts in applying rules of IHL to their forces when engaged abroad in military missions despite the fact that the applicability of such rules is now universally recognised. In any case, even assuming that the Geneva Conventions and the Additional Protocols did not apply, some of the relevant international instruments contain a principle, the so called Martens clause, which holds that in cases not explicitly covered by treaty law, civilians and combatants remain under the protection of the principles of humanity. The clause imposes at all times the minimal but overriding obligation to act in accordance with the laws of humanity and the dictates of public conscience.[28]

In recent years, the UK-US led military intervention in Iraq in March 2003 has shown that the treatment of detainees is an area of prime importance and concern in relation to the obligation of military personnel to ensure that the treatment and interrogation of such persons, captured under the authority of the intervening power, is in compliance with norms of both IHL and international criminal law.

The report of the International Committee of the Red Cross (ICRC), on the 'Treatment by the Coalition Forces of Prisoners of War and Other Persons Protected by the Geneva Conventions in Iraq During Arrest, Internment and Interrogation', issued in February 2004, raised essential issues of international criminal liability for military personnel.[29] The main violations allegedly committed by the coalition forces during arrest, internment and interrogation which are analyzed in the ICRC Report, covering the period between March and November 2003, include:

(1) Brutality against protected persons upon capture and initial custody, sometimes causing death or serious injury;
(2) Absence of notification of arrest of persons deprived of their liberty to their families, causing distress amongst persons deprived of their liberty and their families;
(3) Physical or psychological coercion during interrogation to secure information;
(4) Prolonged solitary confinement in cells devoid of daylight; and
(5) Excessive and disproportionate use of force against persons deprived of their liberty resulting in death or injury during their period of internment.

28 *See* T. Meron, 'The Martens Clause, Principles of Humanity, and Dictates of Public Conscience' (2000) 94 *AJIL* 78-89. *See also*, A. Cassese, 'The Martens Clause: Half a Loaf or Simply Pie in the Sky?' (2000) 11 *EJIL* 187-286.

29 *See*, 'The Damning Red Cross Report of February 2004', in *EIR Executive Intelligence Review*, vol. 31, Nr. 20 (21 May 2004) available at: <www.larouchepub.com/eirtoc/2004/eirtoc_3120.html>. The Report is available at the following address: <www.derechos.org/nizkor/us/doc/icrc-prisoner-report-feb-2004.pdf> (thereafter referred to as The ICRC Report).

The Report also points out other 'serious problems of conduct by the coalition forces affecting persons deprived of their liberty', namely:

(1) Seizure and confiscation of private belongings of persons deprived of their liberty;
(2) Exposure of persons deprived of their liberty to dangerous tasks;
(3) Holding persons deprived of their liberty in dangerous places where they are not protected from shelling.

According to the Report, ill-treatment during capture was frequent, indicating a 'consistent pattern with respect to times and places of brutal behaviour during arrest'. Whereas ill-treatment during interrogation 'was not systematic except with regard to persons arrested in connection with suspected security offences or deemed to have an 'intelligence' value', the ICRC noted that in these cases (interrogation relating to suspected security offences) persons deprived of their liberty under the supervision of the Military Intelligence were at high risk of being subjected to a variety of harsh treatments ranging from insults, threats and humiliations to both physical and psychological coercion, which in some cases was tantamount to torture, in order to force cooperation with their interrogators.[30]

The nature of criminal liability in this area is demonstrated by the Report mentioning that the military authorities should ensure that 'battle group units arresting individual and staff in charge of internment facilities receive adequate training enabling them to operate in a proper manner and fulfil their responsibilities without resort to ill-treatment or using excessive force'.[31]

Following publication of the Report, and pressure by the media and civil society, at the end of January 2004, the commander-in-chief of the multinational troops in Iraq, General Ricardo Sanchez, instructed General Antonio Taguba to set up an inquiry into the affair. The findings of his investigation were handed over to the authorities in charge on 4 April 2004. The Taguba Report concludes that American soldiers carried out acts of humiliation which severely violated international law. It states that numerous 'sadistic abuses' were inflicted upon detainees of Abu Ghraib between October and December 2003. The guards had set up their own rules, which were condoned more or less explicitly by their superiors. The Report mentioned numerous examples of maltreatment towards detainees, such as physical and sexual abuse, torture, intimidation by using military dogs and the threat of rape and killing.[32]

The Report specifically named seven suspects, against whom several charges were brought by the US military justice for mistreatment of detainees.[33]

30 *ICRC Report* (n 29) 3 and 4.

31 Ibid. para. 63.

32 *See* The Report on the Treatment of Abu Ghraib Prisoners in Iraq, available at: <www.npr.org/iraq/2004/prison_abuse_report.pdf>.

33 All cases related to the abuses in the Abu Ghraib prison are reported on the website of the Swiss organisation TRIAL (Track Impunity Always) at the following address: <www.trial-ch.org/en/trial-watch/profil/db/facts/jeremy-c._sivits_554.html>.

On 14 May 2004, a US court martial convicted the reservist Jeremy Sivits for his participation in the mistreatment of Iraqi detainees[34]. He was sentenced to one year's imprisonment, discharged from duty for dereliction of duty and demoted to the rank of private for his role in the Iraqi prisoner abuse events on 8 November 2003. The sentence was a result of a plea agreement which was accepted by a special court martial to all three criminal charges against him:

(1) Conspiracy to maltreat subordinates or detainees;
(2) Dereliction of duty for wilfully failing to protect detainees from abuse, cruelty and maltreatment; and
(3) Maltreatment of detainees (including taking pictures of naked Iraqi prisoners being humiliated).

Interestingly, the fact that Sivits was a reservist did not prevent the court martial from holding him criminally liable as, according to the judge, the defendant was well aware that the treatment of the prisoners violated the Geneva Conventions of 1949.

An element of this plea agreement was to ensure Sivits' ability to testify against other military servicemen charged with mistreatment of Iraqi detainees at the Abu Ghraib prison. Following the Sivits trial, a total of seven US soldiers (reservists with the 372nd Military Police Company) have been indicted for abuse of Iraqi prisoners at the Abu Ghraib prison.[35]

34 Details on the Sivits case and charges can be found at <www.cdi.org/news/law/sivits-court-martial.cfm>.

35 The cases, held between 2004 and 2005, concerned: Armin Cruz, tried by a special tribunal which applies an expedited procedure and which cannot issue sentences that exceed one year of imprisonment, was found guilty of conspiring to mistreat prisoners and sentenced to eight months' imprisonment. Javal Davis pleaded guilty and was sentenced to six months imprisonment for dereliction of duty, forgery of official documents and violence against detainees. Lynndie England pleaded guilty to conspiring to maltreat detainees and maltreatment of detainees. However, the presiding judge of the military court rejected the plea of guilty on account of Charles Graner's testimony. According to Graner, England was not aware of her guilt at the time of her crimes. On 26 September 2005, Lynndie England was sentenced to 3 years' imprisonment on counts of conspiracy to maltreat detainees, maltreatment of detainees and indecent acts. Charles Graner was tried before a court martial made up of officers and reservists from the USA army. In his defence, Charles Graner affirmed that he was executing orders from his superiors, who had demanded that he demonstrate toughness against the Iraqi prisoners, in order to break down their resistance before interrogation. The court martial did not accept the argument of obeying orders from superiors. He was found guilty of all of the charges levelled against him: conspiracy to mistreat prisoners, neglect of duty, cruel and inhumane treatment, assault and battery and indecent acts and sentenced to 10 years' imprisonment. Ivan L. Frederick II was charged with the following offences: conspiracy to mistreat detainees; dereliction of duty to protect detainees from maltreatment; violence against detainees; indecent acts (watching detainees perform sexual acts). The trial was held before a regular military tribunal. He claimed he had acted on orders from his battalion commander. He pleaded guilty and was sentenced to eight years' imprisonment. Sabrina Harman was indicted for conspir-

In the United Kingdom, allegations of mistreatment of civilians and persons detained in Iraq have also been investigated.[36] In February 2005, a military tribunal convicted three British soldiers of having abused prisoners in May 2003.[37] The abuse came to light when a film of photographs was handed to a photo-development shop by a soldier. These photographs depicted Iraqis being forced to simulate oral and anal sex, as well as a man being tied up in a net and suspended from a forklift truck.[38]

The case of the 15-year old Ahmed Jabber Karheem, who died after having been arrested with three other suspected looters on 8 May 2003, caused the indictment for manslaughter of four soldiers, accused of taking the suspects to the banks of a canal in a British Warrior vehicle where they forced them to enter the water at gunpoint. The prosecution case was that the activities of the four accused fell significantly and unlawfully outside what could be described as 'minimum necessary force'. However, the court martial determined that the practice of 'wetting' constituted minimum force in the circumstances.

---

acy to maltreat detainees, dereliction of duty to protect detainees from abuse, and cruelty against detainees. A military tribunal found her guilty on six of the total of seven counts and sentenced her to six months imprisonment. Roman Krol pleaded guilty on the charges of maltreatment of prisoners and conspiracy to maltreat prisoners. He was sentenced by a military tribunal to ten months in prison.

36 From the invasion of Iraq in March 2003 to January 2008, over 120,000 members of the UK Armed Forces have served in the region. As of January 2008, 229 allegations of criminal activity were investigated, 20 of which were dealt with, either by court martial trial or by summary dealing within the chain of command. The range of incidents investigated included investigations into shooting incidents, traffic accidents, fraud and other crimes. All cases concerned allegations of unlawful conduct outside the scope of normal military operations. They all relate to the period of occupation: the first case concerned events in May 2003 and the last in May 2004. *See* The Aitken Report: An Investigation into Cases of Deliberate Abuse and Unlawful Killing in Iraq in 2003 and 2004 (25 January 2008) available at: <www.mod.uk/NR/rdonlyres/7AC894D3-1430-4AD1-911F-8210C3342CC5/0/aitken_rep.pdf>. *See also*, 'Memorandum to the UK Ministry of Defence on the Aitken Report: An Investigation into cases of deliberate abuse and unlawful killing in Iraq 2003 and 2004' Redress (31 January 2008) available at: <www.redress.org/publications/Memo%20on%20Aitken%20Report%2031%20Jan%2008.pdf>.

37 All three accused were dismissed from the army and sent to military prison by a court martial panel. Corporal Daniel Kenyon was convicted of aiding and abetting abuse by failing to report it to more senior officers and sentenced to 18 months' imprisonment. Lance-Corporal Mark Cooley was found guilty of abuse for an incident in which he suspended an Iraqi man from the prongs of a forklift truck and sentenced to 2 years' imprisonment. Fusilier Gary Bartlam, pleaded guilty to aiding and abetting Cooley and to taking 'trophy' photographs and was sentenced to 18 months' youth custody for disgraceful conduct of a cruel and indecent kind. Lance Corporal Darren Larkin admitted assaulting an Iraqi prisoner and was sentenced to 140 days' imprisonment.

38 For a comprehensive account of the different cases, *see* R. Kerr, *The Military on Trial: The British Army in Iraq* (Wolf Legal Publishers, Nijmegen, The Netherlands, 2008).

Another case involved a soldier named Williams who was charged with the murder of Hassan Said on 3 August 2003 in Ad Dayr in southern Iraq. He had been part of a patrol that stopped six Iraqis moving a cart containing ammunition. Three of the men were detained, but Said ran away and was cornered by two soldiers and shot; he died the next day. The commanding officer concluded that this was not a case of unlawful killing and that the soldier had acted in accordance with the RoE, ruling out a court martial. However, the Army Prosecuting Authority disagreed and passed the case to the Attorney-General who, in turn, referred it to the Crown Prosecution Service. Following investigation, Williams was charged with murder in September 2004 and the case was committed to trial. This is one of only a handful of cases in which members of the British armed forces have been charged with murder whilst on active duty. At issue was whether, in opening fire, Williams had used reasonable and proportionate force. The test in law was the soldier's 'actual perception of danger'. Williams had consistently declared that, in a moment of crisis, he believed that his colleague's life, and that of his own, was at risk. In these circumstances, the context in which the incident took place was crucial, including the soldiers' perception of danger. In February 2005, the trial judge concluded that: 'the troops worked in dreadful physical conditions, never knowing when, in a moment, an apparently benign situation would turn into a lethal attack'.[39]

The most controversial of the UK cases has been that of Payne and others, concerning the death of Baha Da'oud Salim Mousa, aged 28, who died in Basra on 15 September 2003 after being subjected to numerous assaults over 36 hours when he was in the custody of British soldiers[40] and whose family also brought a case before the European Court of Human Rights (ECtHR) against the Secretary of State for Defence for the same alleged incident (see *infra*).

---

39 Ibid. 28.

40 Mousa, together with six others, was arrested on the morning of Sunday 14 September 2003 following a raid on the Haitham Hotel in Basra where he worked as a receptionist. Found inside the hotel were rifles, ammunition, grenades, a sniper scope, timings believed to be indicative of bomb making devices, forged identity documents and a large quantity of Iraqi money, all of which appeared to confirm intelligence that the hotel, together with others in the city, was being used as a base for insurgents and extremists. Accordingly, employees at the hotel were taken to a temporary detention facility at the Lancashire Regiment Main Headquarters while it was determined whether or not they should be interned on the basis that they posed a threat to coalition forces. It was alleged that they were subjected to ill-treatment at the hotel, prior to being arrested and taken to the temporary detention facility, but the majority of the beatings took place at that facility. It was alleged that much of the abuse was to keep them in stress positions as part of the conditioning procedure for detainees. The detainees were made to stand with their backs against the wall, their knees bent so that their thighs were parallel to the ground and their arms outstretched in front of them, again parallel to the ground. The precise cause of Mousa's death is unknown, but pathologists agreed that it was either postural asphyxia or the net result of his multiple injuries. At the *post mortem*, it was reported that his body had 93 visible external injuries, strangulation marks, broken ribs and a broken nose. Another of the Iraqi civilians had such serious injuries to his kidneys that he suffered renal failure, and others had identifiable injuries consistent with being assaulted, being punched or being kicked.

A total of nine charges were brought against seven soldiers: Corporal Payne, who had immediate control of the soldiers guarding the detainees, was charged with the civil offence of unlawful killing (manslaughter) contrary to Section 70 of the Army Act 1955, war crimes contrary to Section 51(1) of the International Criminal Court Act 2001 (inhumane treatment) and perverting the course of justice for having told members of his regiment to tell anyone in authority investigating the death of Baha Mousa, to say that he had died because he banged his own head accidentally, an account which he knew to be untrue. Lance-Corporal Wayne Crowcroft and Kingsman Darren Fallon were jointly charged with war crimes contrary to Section 51(1) of the International Criminal Court Act 2001 (inhumane treatment). Whilst guarding the detainees during the course of Sunday 14 September 2003, it was alleged that they subjected them to continuous beatings. A Sergeant was charged with a civil offence of assault occasioning actual bodily harm contrary to Section 47 of the Offences Against the Person Act 1861 and, alternately, battery contrary to Section 39 of the Criminal Justice Act 1988. It was alleged that he had kicked the feet from under one of the Iraqi detainees, causing him to collapse to the ground and, once he was on the ground, had proceeded to kick and punch him, directing blows to his body and to his head. Staff Sergeant Davies, Major Michael Peebles and Colonel Jorge Mendonca were charged separately with negligently performing a duty contrary to Section 29(a) of the Army Act 1955. They were alleged to have failed in their duty to take such steps as were reasonable in all circumstances to ensure that military personnel under their effective control did not ill-treat Iraqi civilians being detained for tactical questioning. Major Peebles and Staff Sergeant Davies had effective control of the soldiers guarding the detainees and Colonel Mendonca had overall responsibility as commanding officer. It was alleged that they failed to provide adequate instructions or guidelines on the handling of detainees to those with immediate responsibility, that the handling of detainees within the Lancaster Regiment amounted at the very least to bad practice, and that there was no adequate monitoring system. Moreover, given that the abuse took place almost continuously over 36 hours and there was no effort made to cover it up, it was alleged that it must have been heard by numerous soldiers and officers within the camp, including those three, and that they failed in their duty to investigate the situation.

Corporal Payne pleaded guilty to one count of inhumane treatment, and became the first British soldier convicted of a war crime under the International Criminal Court Act.[41] He was jailed for one year and dismissed from the army.

3.2 Superior Responsibility[42]

As some of the cases above show, obedience to orders of superiors is still used as a defence to invoke exemption from liability in criminal proceedings involving soldiers,

---

41 N. Rasiah, 'The Court-martial of Corporal Payne and Others and the Future Landscape of International Criminal Justice' (2009) 7(1) *Journal of International Criminal Justice* 177-199.

42 In this section the terms 'superior responsibility' and 'command responsibility' are used interchangeably.

despite the fact that such excuse is constantly ruled out in trial under contemporary international criminal law. Furthermore, the principle of superior responsibility appears to be a relevant mechanism through which superiors engaged in military missions and/or peacekeeping operations can be held criminally liable for crimes committed by their subordinates during such missions or operations.

Command responsibility is by now well established in customary international law and three elements are necessary to establish liability based on this doctrine:

(1) The existence of a *de jure* or *de facto* superior–subordinate relationship of effective control;
(2) The superior knew or had reason to know that the criminal act was about to be or had been committed;
(3) The superior failed to take the necessary steps to prevent or punish the offences.[43]

Application of the command responsibility doctrine is relatively straightforward when a superior actually 'knew' his subordinates had committed or were about to commit crimes. In at least some of its permutations, superior responsibility resembles complicity liability, and while some domestic legal systems require that an accomplice act (or omit to act, where the law imposes a duty to act) with the purpose (and not merely knowledge) of aiding the principal, not all legal systems do.[44] With proof of knowledge the international standard thus does not deviate so substantially from widespread principles of criminal law as to give rise to concern. Things begin to become more complicated when one leaves the realm of actual knowledge and moves into the realm of 'had reason to know', 'should have known' and various other formulations that have been given to command responsibility doctrine over the years. This is the contested terrain of conscious and unconscious negligence, recklessness, *dolus eventualis* and other gradations of risky behaviour, and it is in this area that national (as well as international) courts have run into trouble in attempting to articulate a clear, coherent standard of liability.

Under the doctrine of command responsibility, liability can be imposed on a commander for violations of the law of war committed by his forces, if the commander failed in his duty to prevent, suppress or punish such crimes. The doctrine has gained the status of customary international law and has been codified in a number of international treaties and statutes.[45] However, the doctrine remains for the majority of the cases unapplied in domestic prosecutions of international crimes.

43 On the development of the doctrine of superior responsibility, *see* J.S. Martinez, 'Understanding Mens Rea in Command Responsibility from Yamashita to Blaškić and Beyond' (2007) 5(3) *Journal of International Criminal Justice*, 638-664.

44 *See* ICTY, *The Prosecutor v. Krstić* [2004] (IT-98-33-A) Appeals Chamber, Judgement, 19 April 2004, at para. 141 (discussing French, German, Swiss, English, Canadian, Australian and US law on the *mens rea* required for aiding and abetting).

45 *Martinez* (n 43). *Also see*, B. Womack, 'The Development and Recent Applications of the Doctrine of Command Responsibility: With Particular Reference to the Mens Rea Requirement' (2003) *International Crime and Punishment, Selected Issues*, 101 - 117.

An example is the case of Lieutenant-Colonel Jordan, who was indicted by the US military on 27 April 2006. He was the highest ranking officer in the Abu Ghraib torture scandal and the only officer accused of prisoner abuse. The charges related to several violations under the US Uniform Code of Military Justice (UCMJ): dereliction of duty to supervise soldiers under his control, which led to the abuse of prisoners; maltreatment of prisoners, using military working dogs in interrogations without permission and making false official statements. His defence argued that although he was nominally in charge of the interrogation centre, Jordan did not have direct control over the interrogations. Jordan was cleared of mistreatment charges, but convicted of disobeying orders not to discuss the inquiry. Finally he received an administrative reprimand, which leaves no written judicial record of the case. The case shows once again the inadequacy of national legislation to deal with international crimes. Indeed, under the US UCMJ there is no adequate mechanism to hold commanders and supervisors criminally accountable for the law of war violations committed by forces under their command. If a commander ordered, directed, participated in or otherwise facilitated the detainee abuse at Abu Ghraib, there are adequate provisions under the UCMJ to affix criminal liability. The fact is, however, that there is simply not sufficient evidence to show that commanders and senior officers engaged in this kind of criminal conduct, because there is no evidence of shared intent between the commander and the subordinate(s).

The principle of superior responsibility also applies to cases in which the superior should have taken measures to investigate the behaviour of his/her subordinates in order to prevent them from continuing to commit or committing crimes.

At the time the Iraqi conflict broke out, Jeffrey Chessani was Lieutenant-Colonel in the Marines, in command of Kilo Company based in an agricultural region situated on the Euphrates, some 250 km to the north-west of Baghdad. In this zone, the American and Iraqi forces had fought unsuccessfully against foreign and local insurgents during a large part of the war. On the morning of 19 November 2005, a bomb exploded as a convoy of marines was passing not far from the village of Haditha. The men from this unit allegedly reacted by raking a taxi with machine gun fire, killing its five occupants, aged between 18 and 25 years. According to reports the soldiers then entered the village of Haditha. They are then said to have broken into several houses and killed in cold blood anyone they came across. Twenty four civilians in all were reportedly murdered. Afterwards, several villagers went to the military base seeking justice. It is alleged that being eager to cover up the facts, the marines offered up to US$2500 to certain families affected in exchange for their silence.[46]

Despite the accusations from Iraqi witnesses, no enquiry was opened until January 2006. In April 2006, soldiers of the Kilo Company were relieved of their duties and repatriated to California. Chessani was relieved of his command, together with two of his company commanders. Moreover, Chessani was accused before a military jury of violation of a lawful order and dereliction of duty in violation of Article 92 of the UCMJ for incorrectly reporting the facts to his superior and for not opening an investigation, when it appeared more than likely that a violation of

46 *See* <www.trial-ch.org/en/trial-watch/profil/db/facts/jeffrey_chessani_724.html>.

the laws of war had taken place. The defendant admitted that he had never given the order to open an investigation. He maintained that the civilian deaths were the result of a legitimate fight between his Company and the insurgents. The action for which he was being admonished was therefore, in his opinion, collateral damage for which no investigation was officially required. According to the Defence, substantial evidence existed to show that the marines could legitimately, however wrongly, believe that they were the target of armed attacks by men without uniform and using human shields for protection. On 17 June 2008, a military judge dropped charges against Chessani after finding that a decision to press charges may have been unduly influenced by a Haditha investigator.

Initially, four marines had been charged with participating in the killings and four officers for not having opened up an investigation into this serious blunder. At the time of writing, two of these soldiers and two of the officers have had charges dropped after a ruling that there are insufficient grounds for prosecution. Two other marines await the decision on whether or not to have them brought before a court martial. In the same affair, an American General and two other officers received a reprimand but were not subjected to judicial proceedings. Marine Lieutenant Max Frank, who arrived at the scene after the incident, received immunity from prosecution in return for his testimony. Since the opening of investigations, several charges have been dropped. At the time of writing, no single person has been charged with murder. Chessani remains the highest ranking officer to appear before a court martial for an act or a decision taken during combat.[47]

In the UK case discussed above of Payne and others, Colonel Mendonca was charged with negligently performing a duty by failing to take such steps as were reasonable in all the circumstances to ensure that Iraqi civilians being held at the temporary holding centre under his command were not ill-treated. It was not suggested that he condoned the abuse, but that, as a commanding officer, he either failed to impose a sufficiently robust culture of intolerance towards such abuses or failed to have a sufficiently firm grip on his soldiers. The particulars of the charges can be summarised as follows: knowing that detainees were subjected to a conditioning process involving maintaining a stress position and deprivation of sleep whilst hooded and cuffed, Colonel Mendonca (i) failed to ensure that such a conditioning process was not causing the detainees undue and unacceptable suffering amounting to ill-treatment; (ii) failed to make any or any adequate enquiries during their detention to ensure that they were not ill-treated; (iii) failed to enquire how this process was to be achieved without causing ill-treatment to the detainees; (iv) failed to make any enquiry on the length of time this conditioning process was being imposed on the detainees or to be imposed; (v) failed to make any or any adequate enquiry during his visit to the detention facility about the instructions the guards had been given in relation to the handling of the detainees; (vi) failed to introduce proper procedures to prevent ill-treatment of detainees when there was a risk that soldiers under his command might ill-treat the detainees when the Brigade Commander had issued a warning that soldiers under his command had been acting over-robustly in rela-

47 Ibid.

tion to Iraqi civilians; and (vii) failed to take adequate steps to ensure that any soldier under his command found ill-treating a detainee would properly be dealt with.[48]

The Judge Advocate found that the charge against Mendonca concerned events after 13 September 2003, when the delegation of responsibility for the processing and treatment of detainees to the Battle Group Internment Review Officers (Major Royce and Major Peebles) or the procedure and operation of the processing of detainees were already adopted by the Lancaster Regiment on the basis of instructions issued by the Brigade Headquarters. Indeed, the Lancaster Regiment Internment Procedure was drawn up by Major Royce, who had been appointed on 9 July 2003. The procedure was adopted to maintain the shock of capture so that detainees would be more responsive to questioning and involved the hooding of detainees and the use of stress positions in order to continue the unease of the detainees, so as to make the tactical questioning an easier process. According to Major Royce, the procedure was cleared with Brigade Intelligence and Brigade Legal and discussed fully with Colonel Mendonca as Commanding Officer, including specific questions relating to the use of hooding and stress positions. Major Royce handed over his role to Major Peebles before leaving Iraq on 24/25 August 2003. The Judge found that no witness has given any evidence to the effect that Colonel Mendonca did anything he should not have done or that Colonel Mendonca failed to do something he should have done in relation to the charge against him. Furthermore, nothing untoward was brought to Colonel Mendonca's attention in a system that worked well in the period up to 14/15 September 2003. The ill-treatment on 14 and 15 September 2003 was a 'one-off' occurrence which Colonel Mendonca had no reason to believe was taking place until he was informed of the death of Baha Mousa. It is plain that Colonel Mendonca did not know and had no reason to suppose that the detainees were being ill-treated nor is there any suggestion to the contrary.[49]

These criminal prosecutions show that the concept of criminal liability, under norms of international criminal law, has become pivotal for military forces and this development may increase the responsibilities of members of IMM under international criminal law.

In the ICRC Report of February 2004 it is observed that 'widespread abuse of power and ill-treatment by the Iraqi police which is under the responsibility of the occupying powers'[50] is documented.

These observations are not without practical consequences for members of IMM because they may indeed be held liable for parallel chains of command, even when delegation of command occurs. This relevance is reaffirmed by the Court Martial Appeal Court of Canada in the 1996 case of Major AG Seward, a peacekeeping operational commander, charged with and convicted of, *inter alia*, neglect in performing his military duty during the peace operation in Somalia in 1993. In particular, the charges stated that Major Seward, by issuing an instruction to his subordinates that prisoners could be abused, failed to properly exercise command over

48 *See* Rasiah (n 41).

49 Ibid.

50 *Damning Red Cross Report* (n 29) 4.

his subordinates. The result of this failure was that some of the peacekeepers under his command had beaten up and killed a Somali civilian. The Court Martial Appeal Court of Canada held Major Seward criminally accountable for this failure.[51]

The call of the ICRC in its report of February 2004 'to ensure that battle group units arresting individuals and staff in charge of internment facilities receive adequate training enabling them to operate in a proper manner and fulfil their responsibilities without resorting to ill-treatment or using excessive force',[52] seems also particularly relevant to members of IMM. It seems hardly imaginable that the defences of mistake of fact and/or law and that of superior orders can play a role with respect to these forms of criminal behaviour, even when one bears in mind that the majority of members of the armed forces are not legally trained or educated in the law of war, including rights of others and the duties that they owe to others.

The overriding notion which may govern superior responsibility of international military operations is that of operational command and control.

Regarding UN-led international peacekeeping operations, superior responsibility seems indeed profoundly shaped by this notion. This proposition is supported by two sources:

(1) The 1991 Secretary-General's Report concerning command and control over United Nations peacekeeping operations, where it is said that 'in general United Nations Command is not full command and is closer in meaning to the generally recognised military concept of 'operational command". This command enhances full authority to issue operational directives within the limits of the mandate;
(2) The 1995 Report of the Special Committee on Peacekeeping Operations, stressing that 'the authority of the United Nations Force Commander is based on the concept of operational control'.[53]

The structure, like most operational command structures, is based on the normative belief that although peacekeeping operational commanders are not to depart from UN policies or orders given by the peacekeeping authorities, they bear personal legal responsibility in terms of superior responsibility. Peacekeeping operations are conducted under the operational command of a Force Commander who is monitored by either a group of participating States or the UN, responsible for the mission. It should be noted that the exact level of operational command attributed to the Force Commander is, in principle, specified in the participating State agreement and/or document named 'Transfer of Authority' (ToA), which transfers command from the national level to the UN. In principle, the operational premises outlined in such documents cannot alter the idea and elements of superior responsibility.

---

51 *Major A.G. Seward v. Her Majesty the Queen, Canadian Court Martial Appeal Court* [1996] (Crim.)(Ont.)(CMAC) available at: <http://csc.lexum.umontreal.ca/en/bulletin/1996/96-11-08.bul/96-11-08.bul.html>.

52 *See Meron* (n 28) 24.

53 *See* G. Knoops, *The Prosecution and Defense of Peacekeepers Under International Criminal Law* (Transnational Publishers, New York, 2004).

According to some authors, three different models of command structure can be identified in international military missions:[54]

(1) Operations under UN command and control, in which a force is composed of national contingents placed under UN command and control pursuant to agreements between the participating States and the UN. This model was used in the context of UNIFIL (United Nations Interim Force in Lebanon), UNFICVP (United Nations Force in Cyprus), UNIKCOM (United Nations Iraq/Kuwait Observer Mission), and UNIIMOC (United Nations Iran/Iraq Military Observer Group);

(2) Operations conducted under national command and control but authorized by the UN Security Council. This was the model adopted in the Gulf conflict, where Security Council Resolution No. 678 (1991) authorised 'States co-operating with the Government of Kuwait' to 'use all necessary means' to achieve the objectives set out in the resolution;

(3) Operations in which a force under UN command has operated alongside other forces under national command and control. In Somalia, UNOSOM and UNOSOM II operated under UN command but alongside separate forces which remained under national command. In Bosnia and Herzegovina, UNPROFOR was a UN force but the NATO air force units which conducted air strikes in support of UNPROFOR did not come under UN command and control, even though they operated under authorisation from the Security Council and even though the UN requested assistance. The ISAF troops in Afghanistan operate under command of NATO.

IMM are likely to have a division of command in that a commander exercises operational and not administrative control. The question arises whether the absence of administrative control precludes superior responsibility of a commander who has operational control and command. Legal literature does not exclude criminal responsibility of the latter commander. A pre-condition for this assumption seems to be that the particular commander should at least have some level of control at the administrative level; otherwise the principle of personal guilt would be infringed.

Another argument which supports this observation indicates that delegation of command is not perceived as a circumstance that may diminish command responsibility. This notion may be deduced from the Yamashita case, tried by a US military commission. In that case, two particularities arose: the existence of undisciplined soldiers and the delegation of command to three generals. Contrary to the orders of General Yamashita, who still had overall command, the units of the two other generals did not refrain from fighting and became implicated in mass killings. Despite the apparent reasonableness of delegation of command, General Yamashita was held criminally responsible, although he had not been able to maintain proper communication with the two other units.[55]

---

54 C. Greenwood, 'International Humanitarian Law and UN Military Operations' (1998) *YIHL* 12-13.

55 A.F. Reel, *The Case Against General Yamashita* (Chicago University Press, Chicago,

The question remains whether the applicability of superior responsibility, even in the event of delegation of command, allows exceptions, a question of relevance to military missions. As far as members of such missions are concerned, the argument of delegation of powers as a potential defence to superior responsibility seems only warranted when the delegation fulfilled the criteria that it was: (1) partial, (2) precise, (3) specific, that (4) the delegates were functionally in a position to be able to fulfil the functions delegated to them and (5) the commander in question took sufficient care in selecting, supervising and controlling his staff.

These observations lead to the conclusion that criminal liability of commanders is as such not attenuated by the existence of a command structure. In conclusion, the multinational features of military contingents engaged in international crisis operations do not create a distinct regime of superior responsibility. Rather, they leave intact the responsibility of every operational commander for their unit. In addition, within the legal parameters of superior responsibility, these features may give raise to criminal responsibility of the particular overall force commander for all units operating within such contingents, even for members from other (participating) States.

3.3. The Applicability of the Theory of 'Joint Criminal Enterprise'

The theory of 'joint criminal enterprise' has been developed by the *ad hoc* international tribunals for the former Yugoslavia (ICTY) and for Rwanda (ICTR) in the context of international crimes. The theory establishes the criminal liability of several persons involved in the same event for aiding and abetting (or encouraging) the main perpetrator. In a joint criminal enterprise it is required that the participants must intend the criminal object of such enterprise and must participate in some way in the accomplishment of that objective.[56] The principle of accomplice liability or the common purpose doctrine holds members of a group responsible for each other's criminal acts. So, if three people commit a bank robbery and one fatally shoots a person in the process, for example, the law considers all guilty of murder.

Members of IMMs may fall within the ambit of the extended form of joint criminal enterprise in the event of implication in a potentially systematic violation of the laws of war and therefore such theory seems applicable *mutatis mutandis*.

During the UNITAF mission in Somalia in 1993, which was a peace enforcement operation under Chapter VII of the UN Charter and conducted under US command, several Canadian soldiers were charged with torturing to death a 16 year-

1949). *See also*, Volume IV *Law Reports of Trials of War Criminals* (1947) 35 United Nations War Crimes Commission.

56 *See* the research paper by J. Martinez and A. Marston Danner, 'Joint Criminal Enterprise, Command Responsibility, and the Development of International Criminal Law' (2004) Vanderbilt Public Law Research Paper No. 04-09; Stanford Public Law Working Paper No. 87. For an analysis of the ICTY practice, *see* N. Piacente, 'Importance of the Joint Criminal Enterprise Doctrine for the ICTY Prosecutorial Policy' (2004) *Journal of International Criminal Justice* 2(2) 446-454. *See also*, G. Boas & W. Schabas, *International Criminal Law Developments in the Case Law of the ICTY* (Brill, Leiden, 2003).

old unarmed Somali civilian. The boy, Shidane Arone, was apprehended during the night of 16 March 1993 after his attempt to enter the camp of Belet Huen. During his incarceration, Shidane Arone was mistreated by Canadian Chief Corporal Matchee. While in custody, the Somali civilian underwent torture and was beaten to death mainly at Matchee's hands. Although another soldier, Private Brocklebank, did not actually participate in the acts of torture, he knew about them whilst performing his guard duty. Due to his failure to intervene and report this mistreatment to Matchee's superior, Brocklebank was indicted for violation of Section 269(1) of the Canadian Criminal Code, based upon the offence of aiding and abetting in the commission of the crime of torture.[57]

The prosecution asserted that Private Brocklebank, who was aware of the alleged acts of torture, neither attempted to terminate this behaviour nor to report it to his superiors. Ultimately Brocklebank was acquitted as it was not proven beyond reasonable doubt that he aided or abetted with the intention of supporting Corporal Matchee in the commission of the crime of torture.[58] Notably, the court martial did not address the charge of negligent performance of military duty or dereliction of military duty due to the failure to apply the Geneva Conventions, especially the provisions relating to the protection of civilians.

However, the Brocklebank case raises the question whether soldier A can be held criminally liable on the basis of joint criminal enterprise for actions of soldier B that go beyond the initial (implicit) common intention or common criminal design, for instance, when the original purpose was only to detain certain individuals, but one of the soldier tortures or mutilates one of these persons contrary to the original plan.

The following examples show that indeed the theory of joint criminal enterprise can be applied to members of IMM. Between December 1992 and June 1993, Canadian Forces were deployed in Somalia as part of the United Nations Operation in Somalia (UNOSOM I) and as part of the Unified Task Force in Somalia (UNITAF). During 1993 and 1994 reports reached Canada which indicated that the Airbone Regiment was responsible for at least four Somali deaths and it appeared that the circumstances were such as to be incompatible with the RoE, both of the UN and the Canadian Defence Department. It has always been understood that personnel on a UN peacekeeping mission may only use deadly force in defence of their own persons or of their vital supplies. In one case it was reported that three unarmed young Somali civilians intercepted while trying to infiltrate a Canadian base had been fatally shot in the back whilst fleeing. It appeared that the troops were acting in compliance with a superior order permitting the use of firearms against infiltrators failing to stop when summoned, so long as the fire was directed between the waist and the ground. When the commanding officer was court martialled, in accordance with Canadian law, he contended in his defence that the RoE were mere

57 *See Her Majesty the Queen v. Private D. J. Brocklebank*, Court Martial Appeal Court of Canada, [2 April 1996] 134 DLR (4th) 377. *See also*, K. Boustany, 'Brocklebank: A Questionable Decision of the Court Martial Appeal Court of Canada' (1998) *YIHL* 371-374.

58 Ibid.

guidelines subject to discretionary amendment if that were considered necessary in the circumstances of the case, and maintained that his instruction with regard to the use of fire was not an order but equally a guideline. He was finally acquitted.[59]

Neither he nor the court seem to have considered how ordinary soldiers were to decide when an apparent instruction issued by the commander amounted to an order and when it was to be construed as a guideline. Moreover, it might be suggested that the court might have reached a somewhat different decision had they had their attention drawn to the decision of the Canadian War Crimes Court, which had tried Kurt Meyer and rendered so significant a guideline on the issue of command responsibility. Indeed, in the case of Meyer, the judges found that 'There is no evidence that anyone heard any particular words uttered by the accused which would constitute an order, but it is not essential that such evidence be adduced. The giving of the order may be proved circumstantially; that is to say, you may consider the facts you find to be proved bearing upon the question whether the alleged order was given, and if you find that the only reasonable inference is that an order that the prisoners be killed was given by the accused at the time and place alleged, and that the prisoners were killed as a result of that order, you may properly find the accused guilty'.[60]

Another case was more distressing. A young Somali had been caught whilst attempting to infiltrate the Canadian compound. He was unarmed. His arms and legs were bound by his captors, again members of the Airborne Regiment, prior to removal to an underground bunker. There, he was subjected to ill-treatment and torture that culminated in his death. A number of members of the Canadian force were tried in connection with this killing, although the prime offender will never be brought to trial since he is alleged to have attempted to hang himself and was not cut down until after sufficient damage was done to his brain as to make it unlikely that he would ever be fit enough to understand any proceedings instituted against him.[61] One of his colleagues was charged with participation in the murder and torture. He agreed that he had participated in the beating and ill-treatment, that he knew that matters had got out of hand but said that *'l'ésprit de corps'* prevented him reporting the facts to higher authority. Moreover, the defendant claimed that there was an order authorising 'abuse' of such prisoners in order to serve as an example. The accused was found guilty of manslaughter and sentenced to five years' imprisonment. Others involved in the same incident were given virtually nominal sentences and, in the case of the officer who had issued the order, a mere reprimand.[62]

59 Ibid.

60 *See* Law-Reports of Trials of War Criminals, The United Nations War Crimes Commission, Volume IV, London, HMSO, [1948] Case No. 22, The Abbaye Ardenne Case Trial of S.S. Brigadefuhrer Kurt Meyer, Canadian Military Court, Aurich, Germany (10/28 December 1945) available at: <www.ess.uwe.ac.uk/WCC/meyer.htm>.

61 *See* 'Dishonoured legacy: the lessons of the Somalia Affair: Report of the Commission of Inquiry into the Deployment of Canadian Forces to Somalia: executive summary' (1997) Ottawa.

62 *See* the Report of the Somalia Commission of Inquiry, the Courts Martial, available at: <www.forces.gc.ca/somalia/vol1/v1c14e.htm>.

In the case of Evans and others, concerning an incident involving British troops in the village of Al Ferkah, Maysan Province, Iraq, in May 2003, it was alleged that British soldiers stopped a vehicle to carry out a routine search and then brutally assaulted a number of unarmed Iraqis using helmets, rifle butts, fists and feet, causing fatal injuries leading to the death of 18-year old Nadhem Abdullah. It was alleged that the deceased and the driver of the vehicle were dragged out and made to lie down, upon which they were attacked, rendering both unconscious. Two women who tried to intervene (one of whom was pregnant) were also said to have been harmed and a dog was shot dead. The soldiers were accused of 'gratuitous violence meted out to unarmed civilians in unjustified and wholly unprovoked attacks'. Seven soldiers of the 3rd Battalion, Parachute Regiment were charged with murder and violent disorder on the basis of 'joint enterprise' in that they had either inflicted blows or had later protected those who carried out the assaults.

Although the evidence showed that the patrol was in Al Ferkah on the day in question (radio messages from the patrol confirmed they had followed a car from a checkpoint to the village of Al Ferkah, but no incident was reported to the commanding officer, Captain Andrew Blackmore), and Nadham Abdullah died as the result of an assault carried out by the patrol (forensic evidence taken at the scene included boot marks on one of the victims matching those worn by several of the members of the patrol and blood on one of the accused's rifle butt which matched the DNA profile of Mr Abdullah's family), the prosecution could not prove which of the soldiers had carried out the assault or that there was a joint enterprise. Stopping and searching vehicles was a regular occurrence in light of the fact that groups of locals and insurgents regularly used pick-up trucks, such as the one involved in this incident, for smuggling arms, drugs and large quantities of money and the stopping and searching of vehicles was an inherently dangerous activity, because of the risk of attack by gunmen. Therefore, it was legitimate to manhandle civilians who did not immediately comply and to use 'reasonable force' to enable a search to be carried out. What was at issue therefore was not the fact of having used force against Iraqi civilians, but whether such use of force was reasonable and proportionate or 'gratuitous and unprovoked'.[63]

These cases show that the following three modes of criminal liability have practical relevance in the context of international military operations:

(1) Direct participation in the event;
(2) Indirect participation by means of aiding and abetting the persons involved in the event ;
(3) Potential involvement of senior authorities in the events through the judicial concept of superior responsibility and/or joint criminal enterprise.

63 *See Kerr* (n 38) 26.

4. Practice of International Jurisdictions in Investigating and Prosecuting Members of International Military Missions, including Peacekeeping and/or Peace-enforcement Operations

The criminal responsibility of members of IMM has also been discussed before international tribunals and courts. The Prosecutor of the ICTY conducted investigations of war crimes allegedly committed by Dutch peacekeepers engaged in UNPROFOR, although no peacekeeper was ultimately indicted.[64]

The ICTY Prosecutor also initiated a preliminary criminal investigation against NATO following its air strike campaign in Yugoslavia in 1999 (the so-called Operation Allied Force). This investigation related to charges of violation of IHL. The Final Report of the Commission of Inquiry which was established to advise the ICTY Prosecutor with respect to these charges concluded that there was no sufficient basis to pursue a criminal investigation against NATO.[65]

NATO conducted a bombing campaign against Yugoslavia from 24 March to 9 June 1999. During and since that period, the ICTY Prosecutor received numerous requests that she investigate allegations that senior political and military figures from NATO countries committed serious violations of IHL during the campaign, and that she prepare indictments pursuant to Article 18(1) and (4) of the Statute of the Tribunal.[66] Criticism of the NATO bombing campaign has included allegations of varying weight: a) that, as the resort to force was illegal, all NATO actions were illegal, and b) that the NATO forces deliberately attacked civilian infrastructure targets (and that such attacks were unlawful), deliberately or recklessly attacked the civilian population, and deliberately or recklessly caused excessive civilian casualties in disregard of the rule of proportionality by trying to fight a 'zero casualty' war for their own side. Allegations concerning the 'zero casualty' war involved suggestions that, for example, NATO aircraft operated at heights which enabled them to avoid attack by Yugoslav defences and, consequently, made it impossible for them to properly distinguish between military or civilian objects on the ground. Certain allegations went so far as to accuse NATO of crimes against humanity and genocide.[67]

---

64 Dutch Parliamentary History (1999 – 2000) 26 122 No. 17, at 35.

65 *See* 'Final Report to the ICTY Prosecutor by the Committee Established to Review the NATO Bombing Campaign against the Federal Republic of Yugoslavia', available at: <www.un.org/icty/pressreal/nato061300.htm.>. *See also*, P. Benvenuti, 'The ICTY's Prosecutor and the Review of the NATO Bombing Campaign against the Federal Republic of Yugoslavia' (2001) 12(3) *EJIL* 503 -530.

66 Article 18 of the ICTY Statute provides that: 'The Prosecutor shall initiate investigations *ex officio* or on the basis of information obtained from any source, particularly from Governments, United Nations organs, intergovernmental and non-governmental organizations. The Prosecutor shall assess the information received or obtained and decide whether there is sufficient basis to proceed'.

67 *See* 'Civilian Deaths in the NATO Air Campaign' HRW Report, available at: <www.hrw.org/legacy/reports/2000/nato/>.

On 14 May 1999 the ICTY Prosecutor established a Committee to assess the allegations and material accompanying them, and advise the Prosecutor whether or not there was sufficient basis to proceed with an investigation into some or all of the allegations or into other incidents related to the NATO bombing. In the course of its work, the Committee did not address the issue of the fundamental legality of the use of force by NATO members against the former Yugoslavia as, if such activity were unlawful, it could constitute a crime against peace and the ICTY has no jurisdiction over this offence. In the course of its review,[68] the Committee applied to NATO activities the same criteria that the Office of the Prosecutor had applied to the activities of other actors in the territory of the former Yugoslavia. The Committee paid particular attention to the following questions:

(1) Are the prohibitions alleged sufficiently well-established as violations of international humanitarian law to form the basis of a prosecution, and does the application of the law to the particular facts reasonably suggest that a violation of these prohibitions may have occurred? and
(2) Upon the reasoned evaluation of the information by the committee, is the information credible and does it tend to show that crimes within the juris-

---

68 The key incidents and target categories were:

a. the attack on a civilian passenger train at the Grdelica Gorge – 12/4/99 – 10 or more civilians killed, 15 or more injured,
b. the attack on the Djakovica Convoy – 14/4/99 – 70-75 civilians killed, 100 or more injured,
c. the attack on Surdulica, - 27/4/99 – 11 civilians killed, 100 or more injured,
d. the attack on Cuprija – 8/4/99 – 1 civilian killed, 5 injured,
e. the attack on the Cigota Medical Institute – 8/4/99 – 3 civilians killed,
f. the attack on Hotels Baciste and Putnik – 13/4/99 – 1 civilian killed,
g. the attacks on the Pancevo Petrochemical Complex and Fertilizer Company – 15/4/99 and 18/4/99 – no reported civilian casualties,
h. the attack on the Nis Tobbaco Factory – 18/4/99 – no reported civilian casualties,
i. the attack on the Djakovica Refugee Camp – 21/4/99 – 5 civilians killed, 16-19 injured,
j. the attack on a bus at Lu`ane – 1/5/99 - 39 civilians killed,
k. the attack on a bus at Pec – 3/5/99 – 17 civilians killed, 44 injured,
l. the attack at Korisa village – 13/5/99 – 48-87 civilians killed,
m. the attack on the Belgrade TV and Radio Station – 23/4/99 – 16 civilians killed,
n. the attack on the Chinese Embassy in Belgrade – 7/5/99 – 3 civilians killed, 15 injured,
o. attack on Nis City Centre and Hospital – 7/5/99 – 13 civilians killed, 60 injured,
p. attack on Istok Prison – 21/5/99 – at least 19 civilians killed,
q. attack on Belgrade Hospital – 20/5/99 – 3 civilians killed, several injured,
r. attack on Surdulica Sanatorium – 30/5/99 – 23 killed, many injured,
s. attack on journalists convoy Prizren-Brezovica Road – 31/5/99 – 1 civilian killed, 3 injured,
t. attack on Belgrade Heating Plant – 4/4/99, - 1 killed,
u. attacks on trade and industry targets.

diction of the Tribunal may have been committed by individuals during the NATO bombing campaign?

The Committee conducted its review relying essentially upon public documents, including statements made by NATO and NATO member States at press conferences and public documents produced by the former Yugoslavia. The Committee did not speak to those involved in directing or carrying out the bombing campaign. NATO admitted that mistakes did occur during the bombing campaign; errors of judgment may also have occurred.

On the basis of the information reviewed, the Committee was of the opinion that neither an in-depth investigation related to the bombing campaign as a whole nor investigations related to specific incidents were justified. In all cases, either the law was not sufficiently clear or investigations were unlikely to result in the acquisition of sufficient evidence to substantiate charges against high level or lower level suspects for particularly heinous offences. The Committee recommended therefore that no investigation be commenced by the ICTY Prosecutor in relation to the NATO bombing campaign or incidents occurring during the campaign.[69]

More interesting are the recent precedents before the ECtHR relating to alleged responsibility of the British troops engaged in Iraq. The firm Public Interest Lawyers has represented the families of victims in four high profile cases brought against the UK Ministry of Defence under the European Convention on Human Rights (ECHR). Two of these concern British victims. The other two involve allegations of abuse and unlawful killing of Iraqi civilians by British forces.

One is the case of *R (Al-Skeini and others) v. Secretary of State for Defence*.[70] In 2004, relatives of six Iraqis killed by British forces brought a claim under the ECHR, seeking judicial review of the Secretary of State's alleged failure and/or refusal to conduct independent inquires into their deaths, to accept liability for those deaths and to pay satisfaction. All six deaths occurred in the period from the end of major combat operations on 1 May 2003 to the transfer of sovereignty to the Interim Government Coalition, on 28 June 2004, i.e. the period of occupation. Five of the six cases involved shooting incidents in which Iraqi civilians were killed or fatally injured and died later.[71]

69 *See* 'Final Report to the Prosecutor by the Committee Established to Review the NATO Bombing Campaign Against the Federal Republic of Yugoslavia' (2000) available at: <www.icty.org/sid/10052>. *See also*, P. Benvenuti, 'The ICTY Prosecutor and the Review of the NATO Bombing Campaign against the Federal Republic of Yugoslavia' (2001) 12(3) *EJIL*, 503-530.

70 *See* Judgements – *Al-Skeini and others (Respondents) v. Secretary of State for Defence (Appellant); Al-Skeini and others (Appellants) v. Secretary of State for Defence (Respondent) (consolidated Appeals)*. [2007] UKHL 26. Available at: <www.publications.parliament.uk/pa/ld200607/ldjudgmt/jd070613/skeini-1.htm>.
See also the website of the Public Interest Lawyers at: <www.publicinterestlawyers.co.uk/cases/cases.php?id=34> *which includes links to the relevant decisions and judgements in the case.*

71 In particular, Hazim Jum'aa Gatteh Al-Skeini was shot dead in the street with another

In all but two of the cases, the Secretary of State accepted that the victims were killed by British troops. In the third case, the Secretary of State accepted that the victim was killed during an exchange of fire between British troops and Iraqi gunmen but said that the provenance of the bullet that killed the victim has not been established. In the sixth case, of Baha Mousa, it was accepted that the victim died whilst in the custody of British troops.

In all but two of these cases, the commanding officer determined that the soldiers involved had acted in line with the RoE and no investigation was launched. In one case, the Special Investigations Branch launched an investigation, and in another case, the Commanding Officer referred the situation for investigation to the Special Investigation Branch, which eventually gave rise to a court martial of seven soldiers of the Queen's Lancashire Regiment, including the Commanding Officer Colonel Jorge Mendonca (see under 2. above).

On 14 December 2004, the ECtHR ruled on two preliminary issues, namely:

(1) Whether the ECHR and 1998 Human Rights Act were applicable; and
(2) Whether the Secretary of State had violated his procedural duty to investigate.

The court ruled that the British government had to launch an inquiry into the death of one of the persons concerned, but the other cases were dismissed. It was found that whilst the ECHR and 1998 Human Rights Act applied to detention cases, it did

man in the Al Majidiyah area of Basra just before midnight on 4 August 2003 on his way to a funeral ceremony. Waleed Fayayi Muzban was shot on the night of 24 August 2003 at a checkpoint in the Al Maqaal area of Basra. In the ECtHR case, it is alleged that the soldier involved in the incident said he was on patrol carrying out a perimeter check and became suspicious of a minibus being driven towards the patrol. He ordered it to stop, which it did, but the driver started shouting to people behind the curtains in the van. The driver then pushed the soldier away and made a grab for his weapon before he drove away, swerving in the direction of other members of the patrol. The soldier fired at the vehicle's tyres and it came to a halt upon which the driver appeared to be reaching for a weapon, so the soldier fired into the vehicle. Muhammad Abdul Ridha Salim was shot dead shortly after midnight on 6 November 2003 during a house search being carried out by a British patrol in Basra. The soldiers concerned said that it was in self-defence since the deceased and another man rushed at them with weapons. Hannan Mahibas Sadde Shmailawi was shot on 10 November 2003 at the Institute of Education in Basra where her husband worked as a night porter, and where they lived. According to her husband, there was a sudden burst of gunfire into the building. According to the army, she was shot during a fire fight. Raid Hadi Sabir Al Mousawi was shot in the Al Hayyaniyah area of Basra at about midnight on 26 August 2003. The soldiers on patrol heard gunshots which they suspected were coming from an alley-way in which a man was holding an AK rifle and shouting to people in a courtyard out of sight. One soldier illuminated the alley-way and shouted warnings, but was fired upon by the man. A single shot was fired in response, which inflicted a fatal injury. The last case, concerning Baha Mousa, was the most controversial and was very different in nature. Whilst the first five cases concerned the deaths of Iraqi civilians as a result of soldiers opening fire in combat situations, the Mousa case concerned the alleged mistreatment of Iraqi civilians in British custody. *See Kerr* (n 38) 31.

not apply to the other cases of unlawful killing. This finding was upheld in the judgment on appeal before the UK jurisdiction dated 21 December 2005.[72]

The importance of the ECtHR judgment lies in the fact that ultimately, on 13 June 2007, a ruling by the Law Lords confirmed that the Human Rights Act applies to civilians arrested and detained by British forces in Iraq.[73]

Another case, *R (Khuder Al-Sweady and Hussain Fadhi Abbas) v. The Secretary of State for Defence* concerned allegations of mutilation and torture of Iraqi civilians in southern Iraq in May 2004. In 2004 an investigation was launched into claims that a number of Iraqis had been tortured and mutilated following a firefight involving British troops on the road from Al-Amara to Basra, near Majar-al-Kabir, on 14 May 2004. These allegations were contained in the official death certificates for seven of the 21 bodies handed over to hospital authorities by British troops written by Dr Adel Salid Majid, the director of the hospital in Majar al Kabir, on 15 May 2004, the day after the battle. Another doctor, who had examined one of the seven bodies, disputed the allegation. Following the investigation involving interviewing over 200 witnesses, the Royal Military Police found no evidence of criminal conduct.[74]

In October 2007, lawyers acting for the families of the victims brought the case to the High Court, arguing that the Ministry of Defence was obliged to launch an independent inquiry into the alleged incident.[75] They claimed that the evidence, including a video taken by relatives of the dead Iraqis showing bodies being removed from body-bags, showed evidence of gouged-out eyes, serious injuries to genitals, asphyxiation and hanging. At the time of writing, the case is pending.

In the context of criminal responsibility of IMM, the establishment of the ICC may have a significant impact on the future willingness and ability of States to investigate and prosecute their nationals participating in IMM. Once a State has ratified the Statute, then all nationals of that State will be subject to its provisions. Under the Statute, the principle of complementarity governs the relationship between the ICC and national jurisdictions. This principle intends to reconcile the State's duty to exercise criminal jurisdiction over international crimes with the establishment of a

---

72 The judgement is available at: <www.publicinterestlawyers.co.uk/uploaded_documents/al_skeini-court_of_appeal_judgment_211205%20.doc>.

73 *See* Y. Hu, Champion, J. Taylor and Others '*Al-Skeini and Others v. The Secretary of State for Defence* [2007] UKHL 26', Research Paper: Humanitarian Law Perspectives 2009, Topic 9, available at: <www.redcross.org.au/ihl/media/9883391_1_HLP_2009_-_Al_Skeini.pdf>.

See also, Al Skeini and Others v. United Kingdom, Application n. 55721-07, Written Comments by the Bar Human Rights Committee, the European Human rights Advocacy Centre, Human Rights Watch, Interights, the International Federation for Human Rights, Liberty, the Law Society of England and Wales pursuant to Article 36 § 2 of the European Convention on Human Rights and Rule 44 § 2 of the Rules of the European Court of Human Rights, available at: <www.interights.org/documentbank/index.htm?id=542>.

74 Available at: <www.lawreports.co.uk/WLRD/2009/QBD/R(Al-Sweady)_v_SSD_No2.html>.

75 Article 18 ICTY Statute (n 66). The information appears on the website of Public Interest Lawyers.

permanent court having jurisdiction over the same crimes. The fundamental objective is 'to put an end to impunity' for crimes of concern to the international community as a whole and 'thus to contribute' to their prevention.[76]

In substance, the system set out in the Statute is that of 'successive' jurisdiction, first of national authorities and then of the ICC, which implies primacy recognised to the exercise of domestic jurisdictions. However, when the court is satisfied that the relevant State is unwilling or unable genuinely to carry out national proceedings, it is entitled to act on the basis of its jurisdictional powers. As the Experts Paper for the Office of the Prosecutor underlines, ICC proceedings will then 'provide independent and impartial justice, demonstrate the determination of the international community to repress international crimes, and the real prospect of ICC action, thus encouraging prosecution by states in the future'.[77]

Therefore, the Rome Statute envisages a realistic and equitable mechanism to reconcile States' prerogatives in prosecuting international crimes with the need to have in place a permanent court with jurisdiction over the same crimes. The complementarity regime results in a division of labour between national courts and the ICC, which is aimed at achieving the fundamental objective of preventing and punishing the core crimes under international humanitarian law. The purpose of the Court is not to 'compete' with States for jurisdiction, but to ensure that the most serious international crimes do not go unpunished.[78]

---

76 5th Preambular paragraph of the Statute.

77 *See* Expert Paper on Complementarity, available at: <www.icc-cpi.int/iccdocs/doc/doc654724.PDF.>.

78 According to Article 17, a case is inadmissible before the Court if:

(a) The case is being investigated or prosecuted by a State which has jurisdiction over it, unless the State is unwilling or unable genuinely to carry out the investigation or prosecution;

(b) The case has been investigated by a State which has jurisdiction over it and the State has decided not to prosecute the person concerned, unless the decision resulted from the unwillingness or inability of the State genuinely to prosecute;

Article 17(2) specifies further criteria for determining unwillingness in a particular case:

(a) The proceedings were or are being undertaken or the national decision was made for the purpose of shielding the person concerned from criminal responsibility for crimes within the jurisdiction of the Court referred to in Article 5;

(b) There has been an unjustified delay in the proceedings which in the circumstances is inconsistent with an intent to bring a person to justice;

(c) The proceedings were not or are not being conducted independently or impartially, and they were or are being conducted in a manner which, in the circumstances, is inconsistent with an intent to bring the person concerned to justice.

Article 17(3) lays down as further criteria for determining inability in a particular case:

whether, due to a total or substantial collapse or unavailability of its national judicial system, the State is unable to obtain the accused or the necessary evidence and testimony or otherwise unable to carry out its proceedings.

States remain under the duty to exercise their criminal jurisdiction over individuals responsible for these crimes. No alibi for inaction is thus granted anymore to national judicial systems.

On the one hand, and beyond considerations of principle, it is evident that the ICC will not be able to bring to justice each and every perpetrator of all international crimes falling within its competence *ratione materiae*. Even if the ICC had primacy over domestic jurisdictions, practical reasons would impose inevitable choices, and complementarity makes it possible for national courts to operate as a sort of 'first line of defence' against impunity. It is only when national action is lacking or does not meet certain basic requirements of genuineness and fairness that the court is meant to come into play. In these cases, the ICC is called to dispense justice as an exemplary reminder of the international community that no impunity will be tolerated for egregious crimes of the kind covered by the Statute.

On the other hand, the primacy of national courts does not mean that the ICC should play a residual and basically minor role in dealing with international crimes. This concept was rejected from the beginning of the ICC process, as inconsistent with the idea of a meaningful institution to fight and end impunity. And the logic and provisions of the Statute point in the same direction. Deference to national action is indeed the principle which governs the system, but the existence of a genuine willingness and ability to investigate and prosecute at domestic level is the essential condition for its application: while the competence to determine, at the various stages of the proceedings, whether this condition is met, remains with the ICC. In other words, the court is supposed to operate as an active monitor of national jurisdictions, ready to supplement certain key deficiencies and failures, in order to achieve the objective of bringing to justice those responsible for the most heinous crimes.

It is in this framework that the possibility of investigating and prosecuting crimes committed by members of IMMs before the ICC has to be evaluated.

It is clear that the Statute does entail changes with regard to criminal jurisdiction over members of IMM. It creates a novel international jurisdiction, next to the existing national jurisdiction, which goes beyond accepted regimes of universal jurisdiction. In this regard, the Statute is only one manifestation of a wider trend toward the acceptance of international criminal jurisdiction for certain serious crimes. Taken together, Articles 17 to 19 of the Statute are the result of a very strict concept of complementarity and all these provisions tilt heavily towards the primacy of national jurisdiction.

Chapter 9

The Responsibility of International Organisations for Military Missions

Nicholas Tsagourias*

1. Introduction

International Organisations (IOs) are very active in organising and in deploying military missions. The United Nations (UN) is the organisation with primary responsibility in peace and security[1] but a plethora of other organisations exist which can deploy forces independently from, in conjunction with or under the authority of the UN.[2] The multiplication as well as diversification of such missions has increased the risk of human rights or humanitarian law violations being committed.[3] Such violations will engage the responsibility of the sending IO if they constitute breaches of its obligations and are attributed to that particular IO.[4]

This chapter will not deal with the obligations of IOs but will rest on the assumption that IOs have both customary International Humanitarian Law (IHL) and Human Rights Law (HRL) obligations, and a customary law obligation to 'respect and ensure respect' of such obligations.[5] Instead, this chapter will focus on

* I am grateful to Aurel Sari and Yael Ronen for comments on a draft of this chapter. The usual disclaimer applies.

1 Chapter VII of UN Charter (24 October 1945) 1 UNTS XVI.

2 Ibid. Chapter VIII.

3 For example, *see* the Report of the UN Secretary-General, 'A Comprehensive Strategy to Eliminate Future Sexual Exploitation and Abuse in United Nations Peacekeeping Operations' (24 March 2005) UN Doc. A/59/10.

4 Article 4 of Draft Articles on the Responsibility of International Organisations, A/64/10 (2009) (hereinafter referred to as DARIO). Also Article 1 and 2 of Articles on State Responsibility (12 December 2001) UN Doc. A/RES/56/83 (hereinafter referred to as ASR).

5 *See* Common Article 1 GCI-IV. *Case Concerning Military and Para.military Activities in and against Nicaragua,* [1986] ICJ Rep. 14 para. 220 (hereinafter referred to as *Nicaragua Case)*; *Legality of Threat or Use of Nuclear Weapons, Advisory Opinion* [1996] ICJ Rep. paras. 79-97; *Legal Consequences of the Construction of a Wall in the Occupied Palestinian Territories, Advisory Opinion* [2004] ICJ Rep. 200, paras. 106, 107-181; *Case Concerning Armed Activities on the Territory of the Congo (Democratic Republic of Congo* v. *Uganda)* [2005] ICJ Rep paras. 215-217 (hereinafter referred to as *Congo* v. *Uganda*). 'Basic Principles and Guidelines on the Right to a Remedy and Reparation for Victims of Gross Violations of International Human Rights and Serious Violations of International Humanitarian

M. Odello and R. Piotrowicz (eds.), International Military Missions and International Law.
2011 Koninklijke Brill NV. Printed in The Netherlands. ISBN *978 9004 17437 5. pp. 245-265.*

the conditions under which wrongful conduct can be attributed to an IO for international responsibility purposes and, in this regard, it will also examine issues of multiple attribution and responsibility in view of the multinational character of military missions. The final section will deal with consent, self-defence and necessity as circumstances precluding wrongfulness.

2. Attribution of Conduct

It is a well-established principle in the law of international responsibility that a State or an IO is responsible for the acts of its organs or agents.[6] Regarding UN peacekeeping forces, they are subsidiary organs of the UN if they have been established by the General Assembly or the Security Council and have been placed under the UN chain of command,[7] comprising the United Nations Secretary-General (UNSG) who exercises executive and administrative authority over the force through his Special Representative, and the Force Commander, who exercises operational authority.

The UN confirmed this in its submissions to the International Law Commission (ILC), according to which 'a United Nations peacekeeping force established by the Security Council or the General Assembly is a subsidiary organ of the United Nations'[8] and in the same vein it submitted to the European Court of Human Rights (ECtHR) that 'UNMIK was a subsidiary organ of the UN..., it was headed by a Special Representative of the Secretary-General and reported directly to the UN Security Council via the Secretary-General'.[9]

Law', A/RES/60/147 (21 March 2006). L. Condorelli and L. Boisson De Chazournes, 'Common Article 1 of the Geneva Convention Revisited: Protecting Collective Interests' (2000) 82 *IRRC* 67. For human rights obligations *see Velásquez Rodríguez* v. *Honduras* (Judgment of 19 July 1988) Inter-Am.Ct.H.R (Ser. C) No. 4 (1988) paras. 166-172.

6 Article 5 DARIO (n 4) and Article 4 ASR (n 4).

7 *UN Charter* (n 1) Article 22 and 29. *Certain Expenses of the United Nations (Article 17, Para.graph 2, of the Charter)* (Advisory Opinion) [1962] ICJ Rep.151, at 165. With regard to UNEF I *see UNGA Res. 1000* (ES-I) (5 November 1956) and *UNGA Res. 1001* (ES-I) (7 November 1956) as well as the Report of the Secretary-General, 'Summary Study of the Experience derived from the establishment and operation of the force' (9 October 1958) UN Doc. A/3943, para. 127. With regard to ONUC *see* the *Regulations for the United Nations Force in the Congo of 15 July 1963* which state: '[t]he United Nations Operation in the Congo (ONUC) is the subsidiary organ of the United Nations established by authority of the Security Council resolution [143] of 14 July 1960 and of which the United Nations Force in the Congo is an integral part' (ST/SGB/ONUC/1 (mimeographed) chap. I, para. 5, b). Also Article 6 of *UNSC Res. 1244* (10 June 1999) establishing UNMIK; Article 5 of *UNSC Res. 1279* (30 November 1999) establishing MONUC; Articles 1-4 of *UNSC Res. 1542* (30 April 2004) establishing MINUSTAH.

8 Statement by the United Nations Legal Counsel, Mr. Hans Corell in A/CN.4/541 (2004) 18, para. 36.

9 Application no. 71412/01 by Agim Behrami and Bekir Behrami against France and Application no 78166/01 by Ruzhidi Saramati against France, Germany and Norway, European Court of Human Rights, Grand Chamber Decision as to the Admissibility (4 May 2007) 45 EHRR SE10, para. 118 (hereinafter referred to as *Behrami/Saramati).*

The same holds true for certain European Union (EU) missions[10] to the extent that they have been established by the Council of the European Union and the chain of command, as described for example in EUJUST THEMIS, the EU Rule of Law operation in Georgia is the following: '1. EUJUST THEMIS, ... shall have a unified chain of command, as a crisis management operation. 2. The EUSR [EU Special Representative] shall report to the Council through the SG/HR [Secretary-General/High Representative]. 3. The PSC [Political and Security Committee] shall provide the political control and strategic direction. 4. The Head of Mission shall lead EUJUST THEMIS and assume its day-to-day management. 5. The Head of Mission shall report to the SG/HR through the EUSR. 6. The SG/HR shall give guidance to the Head of Mission through the EUSR'.[11]

In those cases where the force is a subsidiary organ of an IO, any wrongful act is, in principle, 'imputable to the Organization, and if committed in violation of an international obligation entails the international responsibility of the Organization and liability for compensation'.[12]

That having been said, one needs to make a distinction between civilian and military missions, as well as between the civilian and military components of mixed operations. Civilian missions such as, for example, the EU rule of law or police missions,[13] and civilian personnel in mixed operations, may consist of staff belonging to an IO or staff seconded to an IO. In both cases their acts will be attributed to the receiving IO because the former are its organs whereas the latter are its agents.[14] The status of military personnel is however different. States place their own troops at the disposal of an IO to whom they transfer operational command[15] or opera-

10 N. Tsagourias, 'EU Peacekeeping Operations: Legal and Theoretical Issues' in M. Trybus and N. White (eds), *European Security Law* (Oxford University Press, Oxford, 2006) 102. Also F. Naert, 'Accountability for Violations of Human Rights Law by EU Forces' and M. Zwanenburg, 'Towards a More Mature ESDP: Responsibility for Violations of International Humanitarian Law by EU Crisis Management Operations' in S. Blockmans (ed), *The European Union and Crisis Management: Policy and Legal Aspects* (TMC Asser Press, The Hague, 2008) at 375 and 395, respectively.

11 Article 1 and Article 8 of Council Joint Action 2004/523/CFSP (2004) OJ L 228/2. *Also see* Article 7 of Council Joint Action 2004/847/CFSP (2004) OJ L 367/30 with regard to EUPOL Kinshasa and Article 1 and 5 of Council Joint Action 2008/736/CFSP (2008) OJ L 248/26 with regard to EUMM Georgia (2008).

12 A/CN.4/541 (n 8) para. 36; Letter of United Nations Secretariat in A/CN.4/545 (2004) 17.

13 For example EUJUST LEX, the European Union Integrated Rule of Law Mission for Iraq, Council Joint Action 2005/190/CFSP (2005) OJ L 62/37 or the civilian monitoring mission EUMM Georgia (2008) Council Joint Action 2008/736/CFSP (2008) OJ L 248/26.

14 'Report of the International Law Commission' GAOR 59th Sess (2004) Supp No 10, UN Doc. A/59/10 Supp, 110, para. 1: 'In this case, the [seconded] organ's conduct would clearly be attributable only to the receiving organisation'. Also see A/64/10 (2009) (n 4) 62. For the EU *see* Council Decision 2003/479/EC OJ 2003 L 160/72.

15 Operational command is 'the authority granted to a commander to assign missions or tasks to subordinate commanders to deploy units, reassign forces, and to retain or delegate operational and tactical control; it is the highest level of operational author-

tional control,[16] but retain full command over their forces. As the *Capstone Doctrine* for UN peacekeeping operations states, '[i]n the case of military personnel provided by Member States, these personnel are placed under the operational control of the United Nations Force Commander or head of military component, but not under United Nations command'.[17] The same holds true for EU operations. For example, Troop Contributing Nations (TCN) transfer operational and tactical command and/or control to the EU military commander, whereas they retain full command over their forces.[18] Furthermore, TCNs retain criminal and disciplinary jurisdiction over assigned troops.[19]

---

ity which can be given to an appointed commander who is acting outside of his own national chain of command, and is seldom authorized by Member States'. *Glossary of UN Peacekeeping Terms* (1998) <www.un.org/Depts/dpko/glossary>. *See also NATO Glossary of Terms and Definitions*, modified version 02, AAP-6 at 2-O-2 and Joint Chiefs of Staff, Joint Publication 3-16, Joint Doctrine for Multinational Operations (5 April 2000) II-3 –II-4 at <www.dtic/,il/doctrine/jel/new_pubs/jp3_16.pdf>.

16 Operational control is 'the authority granted to a commander to direct forces assigned so that the commander may accomplish specific missions or tasks which are usually limited by function, time or location by troop-contributing countries in the Security Council Resolution/mandate, to deploy units and retain or assign tactical control of those units; it is a more restrictive level of authority than operational command: a commander cannot change the mission of those forces (sic) or deploy them outside the area of responsibility previously agreed to by the troop-contributing country without the prior consent of this country; further he cannot separa.te contingents by assigning tasks to components of the units concerned'. *Glossary of UN Peacekeeping Terms* (1998) <www.un.org/Depts/dpko/glossary>. *See also NATO Glossary of Terms and Definitions* (n 15) 2-O-2.

17 *United Nations Peacekeeping Operations: Principles and Guidelines* (2008) 68. Also Presidential Decision Directive 25 (PDD-25) (9 May 1994) lit V: 'The President retains and will never relinquish command authority over U.S. forces. On a case-by-case basis, the President will consider placing appropriate U.S. forces under the operational control of a competent UN commander for specific UN operations authorised by the Security Council'. (1994) ILM 33.

18 Council Joint Action 2008/736/CFSP (2008) OJ L 248/26 (EUMM Georgia), Article 5 (4): 'All seconded staff shall remain under the full command of the national authorities of the seconding State or EU institution concerned. National authorities shall transfer Operational Control (OPCON) of their personnel, teams and units to the Civilian Operation commander'. *Also see* Article 10 of Agreement between the European Union and the Republic of Turkey establishing a framework for the participation of the Republic of Turkey in the European Union crisis management operations (2006). OJ L 189/17 and Council Decision 2006/482/CFSP of 10 April 2006 concerning the conclusion of the Agreement between the European Union and the Republic of Turkey establishing a framework for the participation of the Republic of Turkey in the European Union crisis management operations (2006) OJ L 189/16.

19 Articles 9 and 15 'Model Agreement between the United Nations and Member States Contributing Personnel and Equipment to the United Nations Peacekeeping Operations' (23 May 1991) UN Doc. A 46/185; 'Model Status-of-Forces Agreement for Peacekeeping Operations (9 October 1990) UN Doc. A/45/594, Articles 47-48; Draft Model Agreement on the Status of the European Union-led forces between the European Union and a Host State', Article 8. *See also* Agreement between the Member States of the European Union

In this case, and in order to determine to whom the conduct of military personnel should be attributed, what needs to be established is who exercises command and control over the force and whether such command and control is effective. Command is a military term that provides a *prima facie* indication as to who exercises authority over the force. Although command and control may coincide, this is not always the case as it became apparent during the UN operation in Somalia (UNOSOM II). As the UNSG opined, 'the Force Commander of UNOSOM II was not in effective control of several national contingents which, in varying degrees, persisted in seeking orders from their home countries …'.[20]

Thus, a wrongful act committed during a military mission will be attributed to an IO and engage its responsibility only if command is accompanied by effective control. Effective control as the determining test in such cases has been adopted in Article 6 of the ILC's DARIO[21] and has been affirmed by international jurisprudence.[22] The UNSG also confirmed recently that 'the international responsibility of the United Nations will be limited in the extent of its effective operational control'.[23]

This means that the UN cannot be held responsible for the acts of authorised or recommended forces. In both instances, the military forces do not operate under the UN chain of command but under the command structures that have been agreed by participating States or organisations. As the UNSG has said, 'in authorised Chapter VII operations … the conduct of the operation is imputable to the State or States conducting the operation' and this view has been repeated in the UN submissions to the ILC.[24] For example, the multinational force that furnished assistance to Korea acting upon a UN recommendation[25] was placed under 'unified command under the United States'.[26] As a result, wrongful conduct was attributed to the US or to indi-

---

concerning the status of military and civilian staff seconded to the institutions of the European Union, of the headquarters and forces which may be made available to the European Union in the context of the prepara.tion and execution of the tasks referred to in Article 17(2) of the Treaty on European Union (TEU), including exercises, and of the military and civilian staff of the Member States put at the disposal of the European Union to act in this context (EU SOFA) (2003) OJ C321/6, Article 17.

20 UN Doc. A/59/10 (n 14) 7.

21 A/64/10 (2009) (n 4). Also see A/CN.4/541 (n 8) paras. 29-50; A/CN.4/545 (n 12) 17-19; UN Doc. A/60/10 (12 May 2005) 104. Its suitability for military operations has also been commented by certain states. See A/CN.4/610 (27 March 2009), para. 25.

22 *Nicaragua Case* (n 5) para. 115; *Application of the Convention on the Prevention and Punishment of the Crime of Genocide (Bosnia and Herzegovina v. Serbia and Montenegro)* [2007] ICJ Rep. paras. 389-400.

23 S/2008/354, para. 16.

24 'Report on Administrative and Budgetary Aspects of the Financing of the United Nations Peacekeeping Operations' UN Doc. A/51/389 para. 17-18; A/CN.4/541 (n 8) para. 32; A/CN.4/545 (n 12) 17-18.

25 *UNSC Res. 83* (27 June 1950); *UNSC Res. 84* (7 July 1950); and *UNGA Res. 498* (V) (18 December 1981).

26 S/1501 (1950) and S/1511 (1950). Statement by the President, 8 July 1950 in United States Policy in the Korean Crisis (Department of State Publication 3922, 1950) 67.

vidual States depending on the degree of control they exercised over the specific operation.[27] With regard to the 1991 Allied action against Iraq, the force was authorised by the United Nations Security Council (hereinafter known as the UNSC)[28] but operational command and control over Western forces was exercised by the US and by Saudi Arabia over Islamic forces.[29]

That said, it has been claimed that the decisive criterion for attributing conduct in authorised operations is: who exercises overall authority and control over the force.[30] The overall control criterion has also been employed by the ICTY in the *Tadic* case. According to the Appeals Chamber, responsibility for the conduct of armed forces, militias or para.military forces is borne by the entity that exercises overall control over such forces manifested in organising, coordinating and planning military actions irrespective of whether specific instructions were issued.[31] Were the overall control criterion to apply to UN authorised operations, it would mean that the conduct of authorised forces would be attributed to the UN engaging its responsibility. This line of reasoning was followed in the *Saramati* case where the ECtHR opined that the impugned act, Mr Saramati's unlawful detention by KFOR forces, was attributable to the UN; KFOR being the North Atlantic Treaty Organisation's (NATO's) operation in Kosovo that was authorised by the UNSC.[32] According to the Grand Chamber, the impugned acts are attributed to the UN because the SC 'retained ultimate authority and control' even if 'effective command of the relevant operational matters was retained by NATO'. [33]

Although the ECtHR spoke of ultimate control instead of overall control, the difference is only a matter of linguistics because the court's reasoning bears a lot of

27 Third Report on State Responsibility by Mr. Roberto Ago, Special Rapporteur A/CN.4/246 YILC (1971) vol II, part 1, 272, para. 211; A.V. Freeman, 'Responsibility of States for the Unlawful Acts of their Armed Forces' 88 RC (1955 II), 263 at 355-358; F. Seyersted, *United Nations Forces in the Law of Peace and War* (A.W. Sijhoff, Leiden, 1966), 110-112 and 120-126. Contra D. Bowett, *United Nations Forces* (Stevens & Sons, London, 1964) 45-47.

28 *UNSC Res. 678* (29 November 1990).

29 Final Report to Congress: *Conduct of the Persian War* (1992) 546 and 556.

30 D. Sarooshi, *The United Nations and the Development of Collective Security* (Oxford University Press, Oxford, 1999) 163-166.

31 *Prosecutor* v. *Dusko Tadic*, Case No. IT-94-1-A, Judgment of Appeal Chamber (15 July 1999) paras. 118-141.

32 *UNSC Res. 1244* (n 7).

33 *Behrami/Saramati* (n 9) paras. 140-141. The same line of reasoning was followed by the British Government in *R (on the application of Al-Jedda) (FC)* v. *Secretary of State for Defence* [2007] UKHL 58. It claimed that the Multinational Force in Iraq was authorised by *UNSC Res. 1511* (16 October 2004) and for that reason its actions were attributable to the UN. The majority of the Law Lords rejected this argument for whom the US and UK forces were not under the effective command and control of the UN (*see* per Lord Bingham paras. 23-24). For a critique of both cases *see* A. Sari, 'Jurisdiction and International Responsibility in Peace Support Operations: The Behrami and Saramati Cases', (2008) 8 *Human Rights Law Review*, 151ff and A. Sari, 'The Al-Jedda Case before the House of Lords', (2009) 13 *Journal of International Peacekeeping*, 181ff.

resemblance to that behind the 'overall control' criterion.[34] The ECtHR applied the overall/ultimate control criterion by relying heavily on the UNSC's power to designate the mandate of the operation and to oversee the operation through reports.[35] However, as the ILC repeatedly said, attribution is a factual exercise of establishing a link between the specific misdeed and its author. Overall/ultimate control on the other hand is neither factual, nor detailed and specific. Even if the UNSC or the UNGA delineate the objectives of the operation, often the terms of the operation are open-ended and States enjoy a wide margin of appreciation. In Kosovo, for example, the authorisation to establish a safe environment for all people[36] or to promote substantial autonomy and self government[37] is very broad; likewise the authorisation to restore peace and security in the region following Iraq's invasion of Kuwait.[38] As for the reports, these are not always detailed and, above all, they are compiled by those whom the UN supposedly tries to control. The Gulf War in 1991 is a case in point, where the Allies submitted reports but in real terms the UN was kept at bay after giving its authorisation.[39] Moreover, even if the UNSC asserts its authority by either terminating the operation or amending its mandate, this can only happen *ex post facto* and not contemporaneously with the act, which is what control is about. For these reasons it is submitted that the overall/ultimate control criterion is not suitable for attribution purposes.

Had the ECtHR applied the effective control test in the joint *Behrami* and *Saramati* cases, its findings would have been partially different. The first case concerned death and injuries caused by the explosion of cluster units in Kosovo. The ECtHR attributed these acts to the UN by treating UNMIK as a UN subsidiary organ.[40] Indeed, UNMIK was the civilian operation in Kosovo, which was established by the UN and was placed under the authority of the UNSG's Special Representative.[41] UNMIK also had *de facto* full control over de-mining, which was carried out by UNMIK Mine Action Coordination Centre (MACC) with the help and participation of KFOR.[42] Thus, its acts or omissions were correctly attributed to the UN not only because UNMIK was a subsidiary organ of the UN but also because the UN exercised effective control over the impugned act.[43] The applicants

34 For example in *Beric and others v. Bosnia-Hergegovina* (App. No. 36257/04). Decision as to the Admissibility (16 October 2007) para. 27 the Court was speaking of effective overall control by referring to its Behrami and Saramati cases.

35 *Behrami/Saramati* (n 9) paras. 132-139.

36 *UNSC Res. 1244* (n 7) Article 4 and Annex 2.

37 Ibid. Article 11.

38 *UNSC Res. 678* (n 28) Article 2.

39 T. Gazzini, *The Changing Rules on the Use of Force in International Law* (Manchester University Press, Manchester, 2006) at 47. With regards to Korea again the UN had no input. *See Seyersted* (n 27) 41.

40 *Behrami/Saramati* (n 9) para. 142-143.

41 *UNSC Res. 1244* (n 7) Article 6.

42 *Behrami/Saramati* (n 9) paras. 52-60; 125-127.

43 *Behrami/Saramati* (Ibid.) para. 143.

claimed that the responsible party was France because it was her troops that failed to de-mine the area. However, in view of UNMIK's command and control structures, France could have been held responsible only if in the particular instance it had acted independently of UNMIK, something that was not proven.[44] The *Saramati* case on the other hand concerned unlawful detention by KFOR personnel. KFOR was not a subsidiary organ of the UN; it was established by NATO and was placed under its command, which was separate from that of UNMIK.[45] The Court could have examined in the first place KFOR's legal status and, had it satisfied itself that KFOR was a subsidiary organ of NATO, perhaps attributed its conduct to NATO. Indeed, KFOR has been established by the North Atlantic Council (NAC), and the European Commission for Democracy through Law (the Venice Commission) has treated KFOR as NATO's subsidiary organ.[46] Furthermore, the Council of Europe made arrangements with NATO to facilitate its visits to detention facilities administered by KFOR.[47] That said, NATO has never claimed that forces operating under its umbrella are its subsidiary organs. The Court did not examine this issue at all but attributed the impugned act to the UN because, for the Court, it exercised ultimate control over KFOR. However, the critical question was who exercised effective control over the force that committed the impugned act. Although Saramati was detained on the orders of Norwegian and French Multinational Brigade (MNB) commanders, they acted on NATO orders[48] and in the name of NATO.[49] In fact the ECtHR admitted that NATO exercised effective control over KFOR and also admitted that there was no 'suggestion or evidence of any actual TCN's orders concerning, or interference in, the present operational (detention) matter'.[50] Thus, Saramati's detention should not have been attributed to the UN. Whether it should have been attributed to NATO or/and its member States is an issue that will be discussed below, as it depends on whether NATO has legal personality.

44 *Behrami/Saramati* (Ibid.) paras. 125-126. Similar reasoning was followed by the Hague District Court in Case 265615/HA ZA 06-1671 *[H.N]* v. *The State of the Netherlands* (Judgment of 10 September 2008).

45 *UNSC Res. 1244* (n 7) para. 6; *Behrami/Saramati* (n 9) para. 118: 'KFOR was established as an equal presence (with UNMIK) but with a separa.te mandate and control structure: it was a NATO led operation authorised by the UN Security Council under unified command and control. There was no formal or hierarchical relationship between the two presences nor was the military in any way accountable to the civil presence'.

46 'Avis sur les droits de l'homme: Etablissement eventual de mechanisms de controle' Avis No 280/2004 (11 October 2004) CDL-AD (2004) 033.

47 Agreement between the United Nations Interim Administration Mission in Kosovo and the Council of Europe on technical arrangements related to the European Convention for the Prevention of Torture and Inhuman or Degrading Treatment or Punishment (23 August 2004) <www.cpt.coe.int/documents/srb/2004-08-23-eng.htm>. Such visits finally took place after an exchange of letters in 2006 between the Secretaries of the Council of Europe (CoE) and NATO.

48 Directive 42.

49 *Nissan v. Attorney-General* [1967] ALL E.R. 200 at 220.

50 *Behrami/Saramati* (n 9) paras. 138-140.

Having said that, even if the UN cannot be held responsible for authorised operations because it does not micromanage authorised forces, it exercises some form of political oversight, which can give rise to political accountability. As the UN acknowledged in its submissions to the ILC, 'a measure of accountability was nonetheless introduced in the relationship between the Security Council and Member States conducting an operation under Security Council authorisation, in the form of periodic reports' which provide an important 'oversight tool'[51] but 'the Council itself or the United Nations as a whole cannot be held responsible for an unlawful act by the State conducting the operation, for the ultimate test of responsibility remains 'effective command and control'.[52]

3. Multiple Attribution and Responsibility

Effective control, as the determining criterion for attributing conduct, tries to discover the direct perpetrator of a wrongful act and, consequently, more often than not, leads to single attributions. However, in view of the multinational character of military missions, one needs to consider whether there are circumstances under which multiple attribution and responsibility can arise. Apparently, the same conduct can be attributed simultaneously to two or more entities only if effective command and control over the force that committed the act is exercised jointly and is indivisible, or when different actors co-perpetrate the same act. If the entities that exercise command and control can be distinguished, or the act of each perpetrator can be distinguished, then each entity is responsible for the conduct over which it exercised effective command and control, or for the act that it committed.[53] As the UNSG put it:

> In joint operations, international responsibility for the conduct of the troops lies where operational command and control is vested according to the arrangements establishing the modalities of cooperation between the State or States providing the troops and the United Nations. In the absence of formal arrangements between the United Nations and the State or States providing troops, responsibility would

51 A/CN.4/556 (12 April 2005) 46.

52 CN.4/545 (25 June 2004) 46.

53 For example *see Saddam Hussein v. Albania and others* (App no 23276/04), Decision as to the Admissibility (14 March 2006) where the European Court of Human Rights said: 'The Court considers these jurisdiction arguments to be based on submissions which are not substantiated. While the applicant referred to certain UN documents, press releases and academic publications, these referred, without more, to coalition partners acting together. The applicant did not address each respondent State's role and responsibilities or the division of labour/power between them and the US. He did not refer to the fact or extent of the military responsibility of each Division for the zones assigned to them. He did not detail the relevant command structures between the US and non-US forces except to refer to the overall Commander of coalition forces who was at all relevant times a US General. Finally, and importantly, he did not indicate which respondent State (other than the US) had any (and, if so, what) influence or involvement in his impugned arrest, detention and handover'.

> be determined in each and every case according to the degree of effective control exercised by either party in the conduct of the operation. The principle that in coordinated operations liability for combat-related damage in violation of international humanitarian law is vested in the entity in effective command and control of the operation or the specific action reflects a well-established principle of international responsibility.[54]

This principle was reiterated in the UN Secretariat's submissions to the ILC, according to which 'in joint operations, namely those conducted by a United Nations peacekeeping operation and an operation conducted under national or regional command and control, international responsibility lies where effective command and control is vested and practically exercised'.[55]

It follows from the above that joint responsibility can arise in the case of UNAMID, the joint UN/AU peacekeeping operation in Darfur. *UNSC Res 1767*[56] states that 'there will be unity of command and control which, in accordance with basic principles of peacekeeping, means a single chain of Command'.[57] Indeed, UNAMID has a Joint Special Representative and is under the unified command and control of the Force Commander. The Force Commander is appointed by the AU in consultation with the UN but reports directly to the Joint Special Representative.[58]

In contrast, no case of joint responsibility can be made with regard to NATO's air strikes in support of the UN Protection Force (UNPROFOR).[59] The strikes were decided under the 'dual key' formula according to which the air strikes had to be approved by both the UNSG and the North Atlantic Council (NAC). However, there was no joint command or control over the operation. Also, no case of joint responsibility can be made with regard to the Rapid Reaction Force created by France, the UK, and the Netherlands to support UNPROFOR. The force was placed under UN command and control, thus engaging the latter's responsibility.[60] The Quick Reaction Force (QRF) in Somalia is another example. It served under US command and control (CENTCOM/CC) but its commander, Major-General Montgomery, was at the same time deputy commander of UNOSOM II, the UN operation. That command structure could not however support a conclusion of joint responsibility because, as the UNSG said, the US forces 'serve under two distinct

54 United Nations General Assembly, Report of the Secretary-General, 'Administrative and Budgetary Aspects of the Financing of the United Nations Peacekeeping Operations' (20 September 1996) UN Doc. A/51/389 adopted by *UNGA Res. 257* (17 July 1998) A/RES/52/247 paras. 18-19; A/CN.4/545 (n 12) 17-19.

55 A/CN.49/545 (25 June 2004) Intro, para. 3.

56 *UNSC Res. 1769* (31 July 2007).

57 Ibid. para. 7.

58 Letter dated 5 June from the Secretary General to the President of the Security Council, S/2007/307.Rev.1 (5 June 2007) paras. 56-57.

59 *UNSC Res. 836* (4 June 1993).

60 Letter dated 9 June 1995 from the Secretary General addressed to the President of the Security Council, UN Doc. S/1995/470 (9 June 1995). *Also see UNSC Res. 998* (16 June 1995).

structures, thus diffusing responsibility'.[61] Likewise, when EU missions use NATO resources and the DSACEUR (NATO) is appointed EU commander, wrongful conduct cannot be attributed to both the EU and NATO but to the institution on whose behalf the commander acts.[62] For example if DSACEUR acts as EU commander, the EU should be held responsible whereas if s/he actually follows NATO orders, the latter should bear responsibility. In similar vein, if a framework State is designated to lead an EU operation, acts will be attributed to that State depending on whether it exercises effective command and control over the force, or to the EU if the framework State acts under the command and control of the EU.

What transpires from the above is that joint responsibility is a rather remote possibility.[63] Some have argued that joint responsibility arises from the fact that military personnel have double allegiances; to the IO for the particular mission, and to their national State with which they maintain organic links. In fact, the UNSG opined that due to the fact that TCNs maintain exclusive criminal jurisdiction over their troops, the case can be made for joint responsibility.[64] Joint responsibility on that basis should however be rejected because jurisdiction over criminal or disciplinary matters does not establish any kind of control over the wrongful conduct which is what is required for attribution purposes. This has been rightly acknowledged by the ECtHR in the *Behrami* and *Saramati* cases where it recognised that even if TNCs retained some degree of control over their forces, this did not affect NATO's effectiveness and unity of command in operational matters.[65] The jurisdiction that a TCN retains on criminal and disciplinary matters means that its failure to exercise it will give rise to direct responsibility for breaching an obligation included in the agreement it signed with the UN. According to Article 25 of the Model Agreement between the United Nations and Member States Contributing Personnel and Equipment to the United Nations Peacekeeping Operations,[66] participating States 'agree' to exercise jurisdiction with respect to crimes or offences which may be committed by their military personnel.[67] Such omission will also give rise to responsibility irrespective of any agreement if it amounts to a breach of a State's

61 Further report of the Secretary General submitted in pursuance of para.graphs 19 and 19 of Resolution 794 91992) UN Doc. S/25354 of 3 March 1994 paras. 71-88; *UNSC Res. 814* (26 March 1993); United Nations, *The United Nations and Somalia 1992-1996* (1996) para. 129.

62 As the Superior Provisional Court of Vienna put it in another case: '[W]hat is decisive is not whose organ ... the person alleged to have caused the damage actually was, but rather in whose name and for whom (from a functional standpoint) that person was acting at the moment when the act occurred. What is decisive is therefore for whom the organ in question was acting at the relevant time'. *N.K v. Austria* 77 ILR 470 at 472.

63 A/CN.4/556 (n 52) 46; UN Doc. A/59/10 (n 14) 101.

64 UN Doc. A/51/389 (n 23) para. 44. Also L. Condorelli, 'Le statut de forces de l'ONU et le droit international humanitaire' (1995) 78 *Rivista di diritto internationale* 881 at 886.

65 *Behrami/Saramati* (n 9) para. 139.

66 *GCI-IV* (n 5).

67 'Model Agreement between the United Nations and Member States Contributing Personnel and Equipment to the United Nations Peacekeeping Operations' (23 May 1991) UN Doc. A 46/185.

customary law obligation to prosecute certain crimes such as the crime of genocide or war crimes.[68] However, such cases do not give rise to joint responsibility because the UN and the concerned State will be held responsible for different acts: the UN for the original wrongful conduct of the force whereas the State for its omission to exercise criminal or disciplinary jurisdiction with regard to this act. The State's failure to exercise criminal or disciplinary jurisdiction can also engage the responsibility of the UN or of any receiving IO for failing to ensure respect of IHL and human rights law which, as a customary law obligation, binds all IOs.[69] Again this is not a case of joint responsibility because the responsibility of the IO and that of the State derive from different primary acts and from different headings. More specifically, the State that for example fails to prosecute breaches of IHL defaults its primary international law obligation to prosecute and thus bears responsibility for that act alone, whereas the receiving IO breaches its obligation to ensure respect for IHL (by ensuring that States prosecute crimes) which is an obligation of due diligence. The above may however give rise to a situation of multiple responsibility whereby wrongful conduct is attributed to one actor engaging its responsibility but also engaging the responsibility of the other actor without being attributed thereto.

A situation that can support a claim of multiple attribution and responsibility is when an IO lacks legal personality.[70] Since international responsibility is 'an attribute of … international legal personality and [the] capacity to bear international rights and obligations',[71] an IO that lacks legal personality cannot bear obligations and thus responsibility. In this case it is the member States that can be held responsible. With regard to certain IOs, legal personality has been awarded by the constitutive treaties. For example the Economic Community of West African States (ECOWAS) constitutive treaties confer legal personality[72] to the organisation, and the same holds true for the Collective Security Treaty Organisation.[73] The AU is an organisation whose constitutive act is silent on the issue of personality; however, one can safely say that it has legal personality because it succeeded the OAU, which was endowed with legal personality.[74] By contrast, the Commonwealth of Independent States (CIS) does not have legal personality although again there are moves towards closer institutionalisation. According to its Charter, it is a framework for State cooperation, which is nei-

68 *Principles of International Law Recognised in the Charter of the Nuremberg Tribunal and in the Judgment of the Tribunal* affirmed by *UNGA Res. 95/I* (11 December 1946) Principle I; Article IV Genocide Convention; Article 129 GCIII; Article 146 GCIV.

69 GCI-IV (n 5).

70 A/CN.4/532 para. 27; *Case Concerning Certain Phosphate Lands in Nauru (Nauru v. Australia)* [1992] ICJ Rep. 240 at 258, para. 47.

71 UN Doc. A/51/389 (n 24) para. 6.

72 Article 88(1) Treaty of ECOWAS (28 May 1975).

73 Article 1 and 22 Charter of the Collective Security Treaty Organisation. <http://untreaty.un.org/unts/144078_158780/5/9/13289.pdf>. The CSTO was established in 2003 and its members at present are Russia, Armenia, Belarus, Kazakhstan, Kirgizstan, Tajikistan, Uzbekistan.

74 Article I of the General Convention on the Privileges and Immunities of the Organisation of African Unity 1965 CAB/LEG/24.2/13.

ther a State nor a supranational structure,[75] and most CIS peacekeeping operations, such as that in Tajikistan in 1993, were executed on the basis of bilateral or multilateral agreements signed within the framework of CIS but to which not all CIS States were parties.[76] Regarding the Organization for Security and Co-operation in Europe (OSCE), its status is rather ambivalent, although its institutionalisation has been rapid.[77] In order to disperse such ambivalence and strengthen the role of the OSCE, a working group was established to consider its legal personality, immunities and privileges; but the Convention on the international legal personality, legal capacity and privileges and immunities of the OSCE was not adopted. Thus one may say that its legal status remains undecided.

In the absence of a specific provision awarding or denying it, legal personality can be attributed on a functional basis if certain conditions are fulfilled. For example, when the issue of the legal personality of the UN was raised in the *Reparation* case, the ICJ said that it had legal personality because, among others, it pursues objectives, which require independent action and is endowed with permanent organs that have decision-making powers.[78] Although the legal personality of the UN is now well-established, the legal personality of other organisations may be debated.

One such organisation is NATO. For example, Yugoslavia brought suit against ten NATO member States in connection with NATO's campaign in Kosovo, claiming that NATO member States were 'jointly and severally responsible for the actions of the NATO military command structure'.[79] However, it is not clear whether Yugoslavia brought this action against NATO member States because NATO had no legal personality or because Yugoslavia did not recognise NATO's legal personality. Neither its submissions to the ICJ nor the ICJ's decision provide much enlightenment. The case of NATO presents certain complexity because there is a division between its political and military institutions. What is commonly referred to as the Organisation consists of the Council (and its subsidiaries bodies), which is endowed with legal personality by the Ottawa Agreement.[80] On the other hand, there are the Military Headquarters, which also enjoy legal personality.[81] The ques-

75 Article 4 and 5 of the CIS Charter (1995) 34 ILM 1279.

76 A. Smith Serrano, 'CIS Peacekeeping in Tajikistan' in J. Mackinlay and P. Cross, *Regional Peacekeepers: The Para.dox of Russian Peacekeeping* (United Nations University Press, Tokyo, 2003) 156.

77 N.D. White, *The Law of International Organisations* (2nd ed., MUP, Manchester, 2005) 52-53. *Also see* Sec 4 of the International Organisations Act 2005 (ch 20) and *OSCE Handbook* (October 2007) available at: <www.osce.org/item/22286.html>.

78 *Reparation for Injuries Suffered in the Service of the United Nations* (Advisory Opinion) [1949] ICJ Rep. 174 at 178-179.

79 Oral Pleadings of Serbia and Montenegro, *Legality of Use of Force* (*Serbia & Mont. v. Can.*) CR/99/14 (10 May 1999) and CR/2004/14 (21April 2004) paras. 10, 12-13.

80 Article I and IV of Agreement on the status of the North Atlantic Treaty Organization, National Representatives and International Staff signed in Ottawa (20 September 1951) No. 21805 Vol. 1307, 1-21805.

81 Article 10 Protocol on the Status of International Military Headquarters set up pursuant to the North Atlantic Treaty (Paris, 1952).

tion is whether NATO as a whole, including its military structures, has legal personality and whether its personality is international and objective. It is submitted here that on the basis of the *Reparation* criteria NATO has legal personality.[82] As a political/military structure, it pursues objectives, which require independent action, it has the capacity to conclude agreements,[83] it is endowed with permanent organs, which are distinct from its member States and can also take binding decisions within the framework of its constitutive treaty. Even if such decisions are adopted on the basis of unanimity, what is important is that these decisions are taken in accordance with NATO's constitutive document and carry out the provisions found therein. Its personality is also objective. The existence of legal personality does not however determine the extent of legal capacities that flow therefrom.[84] International organisations are derivative entities and although they may be endowed with legal personality, their legal rights and duties may be circumscribed. This applies to issues of responsibility as well, where States may agree to be held concurrently responsible with the IO[85] or may assume responsibility themselves. Indicative of the latter is the attitude towards issues of responsibility with regard to the Strategic Airlift Capability (2007). As NATO's SG noted:

> 1. Following our discussion during the Council meeting in Ministerial session regarding the Strategic Airlift Capability initiative, Ministers welcome and

82 *Branno v. Ministry of War*, 22 ILR 756; *Mazzati v. H.A.F.S.E. & Ministry of Def.*, 22 *ILR* 758; CR 2004/9 4.3; CR 2004/12 51. Also *see* Oral Pleadings of France in *Legality of Use of Force* (*Serbia & Mont. v. France.*) CR/2004/12 (20 April 2004) para. 51 and Oral Pleadings of Portugal in *Legality of Use of Force* (*Serbia & Mont. v. Portugal.*) CR/2004/9 (19 April 2004) paras. 4.3-4.8. *Contra* T. Gazzini, 'NATO's Role in the Collective Security System' (2003) 8 *JCSL* 231 at 240-242.

83 Article XXV of the North Atlantic Treaty Organization (n 80). Also *see* Agreement between the Republic of Bosnia and Herzegovina and the North Atlantic Treaty Organization Concerning the Status of NATO and its Personnel, (1996) 35 ILM 75.

84 '[T]he subjects of law in any legal system are not necessarily identical in their nature or in the extent of their rights'. *Repara.tions for Injuries* (n 78) 178.

85 There is a presumption against concurrent responsibility unless it is specifically provided for. *See* Article 6 of the Resolution of the *Institut de Droit International*, 'The Legal Consequences for Member States of the Non-Fulfilment by International Organisations of their Obligations Towards Third Parties', 66-II AIDI (1996) 445; International Chamber of Commerce, Court of Arbitration, 5 March 1984, *Westland Helicopters Ltd. And Arab Industrialisation Organisation, United Arab Emirates, Kingdom of Saudi Arabia, State of Quatar, Arab Republic of Egypt and Arab British Helicopters Company*, 80 ILR 595 at 610-613; *Westland Helicopters Ltd.* v. *Arab Industrialisation Organisation* 80 ILR 652 at 658 (Fed. Sup. Ct. 1988) (Switz). *Maclaine Watson v. Department of Trade and Industry* [1988] 3 All E.R. 257 (A.C.) at 306-7, 353, 332-334; *J.H. Rayner (Mincing Lane) Ltd. v. Department of Trade and Industry and others,* [1990] 2 A.C. 418 (H.L.) (Eng) at 480, 482, 512-513. Also Preliminary Objections of the Government of Australia in *Case Concerning Certain Phosphate Lands in Nauru (Nauru v. Australia* (December 1990) paras. 298-319. Oral Pleadings of Canada, *Legality of Use of Force* (*Serb. & Mont. v. Can.*) CR/99/27 (12 May 1999); Oral Pleading of Portugal, Ibid. CR/2004/18 (22 April 2004) paras. 4.3-4.6; Oral Pleadings of France, Ibid. CR/2004/12 (19 April 2004) para. 49-52.

endorse the legal and political commitment of member States of the NATO Airlift Management Organisation (NAMO) that member States of NATO that do not participate in NAMO shall bear no responsibility vis-à-vis NATO and third parties for the costs, expenses, and liabilities of any kind arising from the implementation of the Airlift Management Programme or the use and the maintenance of the SAC aircraft.

2. It is accordingly agreed that only the member States of NAMO shall jointly and directly assume responsibility vis-à-vis NATO, and shall bear any resulting cost and liability for the implementation of the Airlift Management Programme, notwithstanding the fact that NAMO will be established, by the Council, pursuant to Article 9 of the North Atlantic Treaty and within the meaning of the Ottawa Agreement and will share in the international legal personality of NATO as well as the juridical personality possessed by NATO by virtue of Article IV of the Ottawa Agreement.[86]

As far as the EU is concerned, the Treaty of Lisbon explicitly attributes legal personality to the EU[87] but prior to the Treaty, the EU could still have legal personality on the basis of the *Reparations* criteria.[88] More specifically, it has organs that can make binding decisions using various decision-making processes; it pursues certain objectives in foreign and defence affairs, and has international powers concerning treaty-making.[89] It should be said however that the practice with regard to claims arising out of its peacekeeping operations is somewhat ambivalent. According to certain agreements, claims should be presented to the entities that contributed to the mission: that is, to member States, third States or EU institutions.[90] On the other hand, there are agreements according to which claims should be brought to the Head of Mission and should be settled according to the mechanisms established by the Head of Mission and the Host Party.[91] These provisions refer to the period before the explicit conferment of legal personality to the EU and, more than that,

86 Strategic Airlift Capability (SAC) - Initiative Adoption of the NAMO charter, Note by the Secretary General (20 June 2007).

87 Article 47 Consolidated Version of the Treaty on European Union (2008) *Official Journal of the European Union*, 2008/C 115/01 (hereinafter referred to as CTEU).

88 *Tsagourias* (n 10) 121-123.

89 Former Article 24 and 38 of TEU. *See also* Articles 214-218 Consolidated Version of the Treaty on the Functioning of the European Union (2008) *Official Journal of the European Union* C115; A. Sari, 'The Conclusion of International Agreements by the European Union in the Context of the ESDP' (2008) 57 *ICLQ* 53.

90 For example Article 11 of Council Joint Action 2008/749/CFSP [2008] OJ L 252/39 (EU NAVCO) according to which 'The Member State which has seconded staff to the EU Coordination Cell shall be responsible for answering any claims linked to the secondment, whether from or concerning a staff member. The Member State in question shall be responsible for bringing any action against the seconded staff member'. Article 13(2) Council Action 2003/681/CFSP [2003] OJ L 249/66 (Proxima).

91 Cited in A. Sari, 'Status of Forces and Status of Mission Agreements under the ESDP: The EU's Evolving Practice' (2008) 29 *EJIL* 67, 94, n 191.

they are about the different ways of realising responsibility in peacekeeping.[92] As was said above, the consequences of legal personality may be different for different legal subjects.[93] Thus, although the EU has legal personality, its responsibility may variegate something that is not unique, as the preceding discussion on NATO has shown.

4. Circumstances Precluding Wrongfulness

Whereas a breach of an obligation which is attributed to an IO engages its responsibility, there are certain circumstances that preclude wrongfulness. With regard to military operations, the most relevant of the circumstances precluding wrongfulness are consent, necessity and self-defence.[94] Before examining the application of the aforementioned circumstances to military operations undertaken by IOs, it should be noted that they do not apply to violations of *jus cogens* norms.[95]

4.1. Consent

Consent to the commission of an act can preclude its wrongfulness.[96] For example, the deployment of military forces within a State would violate the rule on the non use of force and the rule on non-intervention in domestic affairs[97] if it takes place without UNSC authorisation, unless the State has given its consent. That is why peacekeeping forces are deployed with the consent of the host State.[98] That said, there are certain issues, which cause particular difficulties as far as consent is concerned. In order for consent to preclude wrongfulness, it should be valid and emanate from a competent authority. The main difficulty is thus in identifying the domestic authority that can legitimately give its consent to the deployment of military forces, something particularly complicated in situations of civil war. UN practice seems to give precedence to the established government while trying at the same time to involve

92 For example *see The Reform Treaty: the British Approach to the European Union Intergovernmental Conference* (Cm 7174, 2007); The House of Lords. Select Committee on European Union, tenth Report, 'The Treaty of Lisbon: an impact assessment' HL 62-I (March 2008) para. 2.58.

93 '[T]he subjects of law in any legal system are not necessarily identical in their nature or in the extent of their rights'. *Reparation for Injuries* (n 78) 178.

94 *Fourth report on responsibility of international organizations* (28th February 2006) A/CN.4/564

95 Article 25 DARIO (n 4); Article 26 ASR (n 4). *Legality of the Threat or Use of Nuclear Weapons, Advisory Opinion* of July 8, 1996 [1996] ICJ Rep para.. 79 *The Prosecutor v. Zoran Kupreškić and others*, Case No. IT-95-16-T,Trial Chamber Judgment (14 January 2000) para. 520.

96 Article 19 DARIO (n 4); Article 20 ASR (n 4); *Congo v. Uganda* paras. 42-54, 92-105.

97 UN Charter (n 1) Article 2(4) and Article 2(7). *Also see UNGA Res. 999* (ES-I) (4 November 1956) *UNGA Res. 1000* (ES-I) (5 November 1956) and *UNGA Res. 1001* (ES-I) (7 November 1956) with regard to UNEF I.

98 N. Tsagourias, 'Consent, Neutrality/Impartiality and the Use of Force in Peacekeeping: Their Constitutional Dimension' (2006) 11 *JCSL* 465 at 467-478.

other parties as a matter of political expediency. This is not however always successful. Related to the above is the problem of identifying the authority or authorities that can revoke such consent as well as that of establishing the consequences of any revocation. UN practice indicates that it is the government that can legitimately revoke consent and that such revocation will result in the force being withdrawn.[99]

That having been said, when it comes to violations of IHL, the obligation to respect and ensure respect of humanitarian law in all circumstances enunciated in Common Article 1 of the Geneva Conventions means that consent cannot be relied upon to preclude wrongfulness,[100] and the same holds true for non-derogable human rights.

4.2. Necessity

Necessity, the second circumstance precluding wrongfulness to be discussed here, precludes wrongfulness when it is the only means of safeguarding an interest against a grave and imminent peril.[101] However, with regard to military operations, a distinction should be made between necessity as a circumstance precluding wrongfulness and military necessity, which is a mainstream concept of the law of armed conflict.[102] IHL incorporates 'military necessity' within its rules which try to balance humanitarian considerations with military needs. This means that necessity cannot excuse departures from the laws of armed conflict unless it is allowed by a particular IHL rule.[103] Thus, in operations where IHL does not apply, such as in non-coercive peacekeeping missions, the state of necessity can be invoked to excuse, for example, an unauthorised use of force to the extent that such force is the only means of securing the material and human components of the operation against a grave and imminent danger. In contrast, when forces are engaged as combatants and IHL applies, necessity cannot be invoked unless it is specifically permitted by an IHL rule.

---

99 Report of the Secretary-General, 'Withdrawal of the United Nations Emergency Force', UN GAOR, Fifth Emergency Special Sessions, Annex, Agenda Item 5 (1967) UN Doc. A/6730.

100 *See also* Articles 51,52,131,148 GCI-IV. *Prosecutor v. Zoran Kupreskic and others*, Case No. IT-95-16-T, Judgement (Trial Chamber) (14 January 2000) para.. 519: 'As a consequence of their absolute character, these norms of international humanitarian law do not pose synallagmatic obligations, i.e. obligations of a State *vis-à-vis* another State. Rather (...) they lay down obligations towards the international community as a whole, with the consequence that each and every member of the international community has a 'legal interest' in their observance and consequently a legal entitlement to demand respect for such obligations'.

101 Article 24 DARIO (n 4); Article 25 ASR (n 4); *Case Concerning the Gabcikovo-Nagymaros Project (Hungary/ Slovakia)* [1997] ICJ Rep 4, para. 51-52; *Wall Advisory Opinion* (n 5) para. 140-142.

102 Y. Dinstein, *Military Necessity* (Encyclopaedia of Public International Law, vol. III) 395; UK Ministry of Defence, *The Manual of the Law of Armed Conflict* (Oxford University Press, Oxford, 2005) at 2.1-2.3; Yearbook of the International Law Commission (1980) Volume II Part Two 34-52; UN Doc. A/CN.4/498/ (1999) Add 2 para. 280.

103 *For example* Article 33(2) GC I; Article 49(2), Article 53, Article 55(3), Article 108(2) GCIV.

Military necessity has been used to exclude the liability of the UN for material damage caused during its peacekeeping operations. According to the UNSG, 'the liability of the Organization for property loss and damage caused by United Nations forces in the ordinary operation of the force is subject to the exception of 'operational necessity', that is, where damage results from necessary actions taken by a peacekeeping force in the course of carrying out its operations in pursuance of its mandates'. Also, the fact that damage was caused in itself may not necessarily engage the liability of the United Nations. Such liability would be entailed if the damage was caused in violation of international humanitarian law rules and could not be justified on grounds of 'military necessity'.[104] The use of military and/or operational necessity as circumstances excluding UN liability corresponds to the different situations peacekeepers may find themselves in, with military necessity covering war-like situations where peacekeepers act as combatants and with operational necessity covering all other situations.

An important issue that deserves further consideration is whether an IO can invoke necessity in order to deploy a military force within a State without the latter's consent. For example, can an IO other than the UN invoke necessity in order to deploy forces within a State to avert a humanitarian catastrophe? According to Article 24 DARIO the state of necessity can be invoked by an IO in order to safeguard 'an essential interest of the international community as a whole when the organisation has, in accordance with international law, the function to protect that interest'.[105] This formulation gives rise to a number of questions. The first set concerns the meaning of 'essential interest' and the relationship between the means used to protect such an 'essential' interest and the essentiality of the interest. For example, are humanitarian interests essential interests of the international community and if they are, does it mean that necessity can excuse any action to safeguard them, including the use of force?

The second set of questions concerns the availability of the plea of necessity to regional organisations. For example can the plea of necessity excuse their unauthorised humanitarian actions? If the protected interest should belong to the international community as a whole, regional organisations, in contrast to the UN which promotes international interests and can be equated with the international community, promote regional interests. It thus appears that they would not be able to invoke the plea of necessity in such circumstances. On the other hand, there are certain regional organisations such as the EU that promote international interests such as human dignity or international peace.[106] More than that, a legitimate question is whether regional peace or the regional protection of human rights can be separated from international peace or the international protection of human rights. One may say with reason that they are indivisible. Thus, if the determining test is the interna-

104 UN Doc. A/51/389 (n 23) paras. 13 and 16; *Third-party liability: temporal and financial limitations, UNGA Res. 52/247* (1996) para. 6. D. Shraga, 'UN Peacekeeping Operations: applicability of International Humanitarian Law and responsibility for Operations-Related Damage' (2000) 94 *AJIL* 406.

105 A/CN.4/L.687 (31 May 2006) 3.

106 Article 3 and 21 CTEU (n 86).

tional scope of the interests pursued by an organisation, it will be able to invoke the state of necessity in similar situations. This is the approach taken by the Rapporteur[107] although some states expressed misgivings due to the potential for abuse.[108]

As far as human rights are concerned, human rights treaties often permit derogations when there is a state of necessity such as war or other public emergency[109] but such derogations do not apply to all human rights. The question that immediately arises is whether IOs can derogate from human rights by invoking a state of necessity. It is submitted here that IOs can derogate from certain human rights to the extent that such derogations are justified by customary law. This is particularly relevant in cases of territorial administration, where an IO such as the UN can exercise jurisdiction over peoples and territory. That was the case for example in Kosovo, where war and public emergency were invoked by KFOR to justify extra-judicial detentions. In this case it was only the facts that were disputed by the European Commissioner of Human Rights, not the claim of derogation due to necessity.[110]

4.3. Self-Defence

Self-defence is another circumstance precluding wrongfulness[111] but its application to military operations undertaken by IOs raises a number of questions. One such question is whether IOs have a right to self-defence. The ILC seems to accept the view that the UN, and by implication other IOs, have a right to self-defence irrespective of whether the author of the attack is a State, another IO or individuals.[112] That said, the next question is whether an attack on an IO amounts to an armed attack as defined in Article 51 UN Charter or by customary law. If an armed attack is about the scope and effects of the attack, there may be cases where attacks on an IO's military forces can reach this threshold and trigger self-defence. All of the above, however, concern primary rules, not the secondary rules of the law on international responsibility. The same considerations apply to attacks on individual soldiers. The defence of individual soldiers against attacks on their person[113] does not raise any controversy because the defence of the person is a general principle of law. Self-defence as a circumstance precluding wrongfulness should refer to different situations but its definition in DARIO is not clear.[114] For example, the term 'defence of the mission' has often been inserted in resolutions establishing peacekeeping opera-

107 A/CN.4/610 (n 21) para. 67.

108 Thus China and the United States, A/C.6/62/SR.14, para. 8 and 82, respectively.

109 Article 4 ICCPR; Article 15 ECHR.

110 Mr Alvaro Gil-Robles (Commissioner for Human Rights) *Kosovo: The Human Rights Situation and the Fate of Persons Displaced from their Homes*, (16 October 2002) CommDH (2002)/11 paras. 97-103.

111 Article 20 DARIO (n 4); Article 21 ASR (n 4); *Wall Advisory Opinion* (n 5) paras. 139, 142; *also* Sep. Decl. Judge Burgenthal, Ibid. paras. 4-5 and Sep. Op. Judge Higgins, Ibid. paras. 33-35.

112 A/CN.4/564 (n 94) 5-7.

113 A/3943 (n 7) para. 179.

114 A/CN.4/610 (n 21) paras. 58-59.

tions.[115] This is a broad concept that includes the use of force to defend the mission's personnel, its objects or mandate. Such force is lawful if it has been authorised by the UNSC. It can also be justified under the rubric of self-defence as a primary rule depending on the scope and effects of the previous attack. If it has not been authorised by the UNSC or justified by the primary rule, it can very well be justified under the rubric of necessity, as seen above. Otherwise it can constitute a special case of defensive force whose wrongfulness can be precluded.

Be that as it may, a self-defence action does not free an IO from its humanitarian or human rights obligations since the *jus ad bellum* and the *jus in bello* are distinct legal regimes. Neither does self-defence preclude the wrongfulness of IHL violations. As was pointed out above IHL applies in all circumstances and as far as HRL is concerned, self-defence does not preclude the wrongfulness of violations of non-derogable human rights. Instead, it can apply to violations of derogable human rights.

8. Conclusion

This chapter has examined the criteria for attributing wrongful conduct to an IO in the course of military operations. Its main contention is that effective command and control is the determining criterion. This is a factual and pragmatic test that apportions responsibility by locating the direct perpetrator of the act. In this regard, it was argued that the UN cannot be held responsible for authorised operations and that the ECtHR's findings in the *Behrami* and *Saramati* cases are flawed. Another issue examined in this chapter is that of joint responsibility, where it was argued that it applies only to cases of joint effective command and control but that there may be cases where multiple responsibility may arise. Finally, the chapter dealt with consent, necessity and self-defence as circumstances precluding the wrongfulness of IHL and HRL violations and concluded that due to the nature of IHL and non-derogable human rights, the role of the aforementioned circumstances is more limited in this regard.

That having been said, there remain a number of problems that obstruct the realisation of such responsibility. One such obstacle is the uncertainty surrounding the scope and content of IHL and HRL obligations of IOs. Another is the absence of international adjudicatory mechanisms to effectuate such responsibility, compounded by the jurisdictional immunities that IOs enjoy at the national level. At the moment, ad hoc mechanisms are attached to military missions that deal with issues of compensation but these concern private law claims and should not be equated with adjudicatory mechanisms dealing with the international responsibility of IOs.[116] The difficulties in holding IOs to account has led individuals to pursue States indi-

115 'Report of the Panel on United Nations Peace Operations of 21 August 2000 (Brahimi Report)' UN Doc. A/55/305 paras. 48-51; High Level Panel Report, Report of the High Level Panel on Threats Challenges and Change, 'A More Secure World: Our Shared Responsibility' (2004) UN Doc. A/59/565, para. 213.

116 For the UN *see* 'Third-party liability: temporal and financial limitations' UNGA Res. 52/247 (20 June 1998); UN Doc. A/51/389 (n 23).

vidually or collectively but, as the *Behrami* and *Saramati* cases have shown, international courts often show deference to the needs of the international public order for peace and security.[117] Unless the issues identified above are addressed, the law on the responsibility of international organisations will not be able to fulfil its mission of promoting the rule of law in international relations.

117 *Brahrami* (n 111) paras. 144-152.

Conclusions

The complexity of IMMs and similar types of operations, as demonstrated in this book, means that different legal rules may apply to IMMs. There is no single legal regime. Clarifying the applicability of IHL where IMMs are deployed is one of the most important issues, as pointed out by the ICRC on many occasions. This is not just a matter of legal clarity; it is a matter of life or death for the victims, and potential victims, of armed conflicts. However, depending on the mandate of each IMM, different rules of IHL may apply, depending on the level of force authorised by the body which established the mission. Thus it may be necessary to take account of the law applicable to non-international armed conflict, to international armed conflict, the law of belligerent occupation and customary humanitarian law, with specific reference to common Article 3 to the four 1949 Geneva Conventions, as the minimum legal requirement.

However, the development of multi-functional operations, with different types of personnel and experts applying different rules that may be more suitable to fulfil their specific tasks, has been postulated as one way to overcome this impasse. While military personnel may use force and therefore apply IHL, civilian and police personnel are usually concerned with restoring civil society and democratic governance; therefore they would apply HRL. Despite this share of professional functions, the UN and other IOs have not clearly defined the set of rules that would apply in the context of PKOs and other military operations, including security, international policing and crises-response type operations. Furthermore, in some cases military units may operate in situations which fall below the threshold of armed conflict, and may occasionally be involved in policing and internal security operations, including anti-terrorist actions. In these cases, they may have to apply HRL when searching and detaining people, for instance.

The applicability of HRL in the course of IMMs seems less problematic, as these rules would apply always, with only a few exceptions where derogation is permitted because of a state of emergency. The obligations imposed on States and on their personnel acting officially abroad have been extended beyond national borders, despite some contradictory State practice. The issue of extraterritorial application of human rights obligations has been often used to clarify the type of obligations on a State's officers when acting abroad. However, states of emergency can be declared normally only by a government in response to threats that affect the survival of that particular State, and under specific, limited circumstances defined in the rel-

M. Odello and R. Piotrowicz (eds.), International Military Missions and International Law.
2011 Koninklijke Brill NV. Printed in The Netherlands. ISBN 978 9004 17437 5. pp. 267-271.

evant human rights treaties. In the case of international operations, a third State, or an IO, could not declare a state of emergency outside its own territory under HRL. Nonetheless, when the State, or a coalition of States, *de facto* effectively exercises control over a foreign territory it may be possible to admit that extra-territorial application of human rights obligations might be subject to some derogation, justified by the local situation. However, the suspension of HRL would not affect obligations under IHL, from which no derogation is permitted.

Furthermore, HRL, and the concept of R2P as one of the leading functions of IMMs under PKOs' mandate, is particularly relevant also when military contingents are deployed to protect the civilian population from different threats, in particular from armed violence and widespread violations of human rights. The protection of human rights has acquired particular significance because of abuses that have seen peacekeepers as potential violators of human rights, in particular concerning sexual abuse and detention. A clearer set of legal and procedural criminal rules applicable to individual perpetrators and commanders, defining their individual responsibility, should be defined. There are both international and national legal issues involved, including immunities for international personnel and criminal co-operation amongst States. These issues should be clarified, either in the form of an international agreement or in the special agreements between States and IOs, including formal Memorandums of Understanding clarifying the duties of TCCs regarding criminal action and prosecution powers.

Issues of *jus ad bellum* should also be clarified to understand the classification of the nature of the conflict or situation where IMMs operate. This may have a strong impact on the definition of the rules that should apply in the field, and it would certainly clarify several operational aspects of each operation. This also implies the need to clarify which rules apply to different types of personnel involved in IMMs. At present, this matter appears quite complicated and generates much confusion, in particular when dealing with the local population, which may be directly affected by actions of international personnel. There is a need to define the obligations of individual States and IOs regarding international responsibility for wrongful acts that may be committed by personnel acting under the mandate of IOs. This has become particularly relevant when dealing with criminal accountability and financial responsibility for acts committed by peacekeepers. In this context, both national and international criminal law can play a role, regarding the definition of crimes and the rules for the prosecution of those suspected of criminal acts.

Since the late 1990s, the UN Secretary-General has adopted two Bulletins that show the possible application of both areas of international law: the 1999 Bulletin, on the application of IHL, and the 2003 Bulletin, regarding the prohibition of sexual abuse and misconduct by peacekeepers. However, the two instruments are very general. The 2008 Capstone Doctrine, despite its reference to relevant principles and guidelines which should apply to PKOs, does not provide a proper set of rules that can be easily applied in the field by military personnel.

It is essential to understand which rules of IHL would apply in the field. This has to be clarified by TCCs and by the UN, or other IOs, through appropriate binding legal instruments. Until now, quite vague policy documents have addressed this issue, providing an unclear legal regulation of the matter. General reference to IHL and IHR obligations, without specifying their limits and content, makes the legal framework uncertain, the more that most IOs are not parties to major IHL and IHR treaties. However, customary international law can be of assistance as it would generally apply to IOs as subjects of the international system. Furthermore, States have different opinions regarding the applicability of both IIHL and HRL in the context of peace operations, which makes the substantive applicable law even more unclear. Their international responsibility may also be triggered as a parallel sanction regime against individuals who may commit crimes and violations of IHL and HRL. The qualification of the conflict where IMMs are deployed is also relevant to understanding the nature of the obligations for both States and IOs in the field. Human rights obligations should be stressed as well, as they may provide useful legal standards and guidelines for operations in the field and for the appropriate protections that troops and other international personnel should seek to ensure on the ground, mainly towards the civilian population. The issue of extraterritorial application of human rights international obligations for State officials and for IOs' personnel would need a stronger legal commitment at this stage. More extensive standards, going beyond the regulatory regime for armed conflicts *per se*, might be applicable in PKOs and other humanitarian missions, due to the reasons behind the justification of the use of force, and due to the humanitarian purposes of the operations, supported also by the idea of R2P as adopted by the international community.

Further difficulties are shown in cases of military operations in a maritime environment, where the Law of the Sea would apply. Even in this case, there is a need to clarify both terminological issues, defining the types of operations, and the definition of the international rules that may apply in that specific environment.

It is not possible at this stage to provide a detailed list of rules that would or should apply to different IMMs. The applicable rules depend also on the specific context and mandate that define the obligations of States, IOs and individuals in the field. From the study offered in this book, it can be seen that there are enough rules defined in great detail in existing branches of international law. The major problem that emerges is that clearer criteria regarding the application of the existing rules should be defined by appropriate international bodies which make use of IMMs, and by States that develop coalition missions with major military components. The assessment of which rules bind and apply to different components of IMMs has to be made under international law, so that other relevant matters, including issues of individual and international responsibility in cases of violation of international obligations, may be properly addressed.

Rules of Engagement are a useful practical and operational tool. However they have to be grounded on clear international obligations and have to match the international standards settled under IHL and IHRL. They are not meant to create new law and define new types of obligations for the troops on the ground. It is crucial that RoE be drafted in conformity with States' international obligations. Breach of these obligations would incur State responsibility.

Training is particularly relevant, as indicated in the case of scandals linked to sexual abuses by UN peacekeepers. Troops should be properly trained in different stages of their deployment. However, to provide proper training is not enough, if there is no clear definition of the applicable law in the different circumstances where

IMMs personnel are deployed and actively involved. Furthermore, the alleged cases of abuses that may have criminal and disciplinary dimensions should be properly addressed by military commanders under clear rules defining individual responsibility. Unfortunately, it seems that many governments have not taken sufficient action to tackle this important issue of military discipline, often abusing the protection offered by international immunities and the exclusive jurisdiction of the TCC. Only when these issues have finally been exposed have States reacted and the UN taken some (inadequate) measures.

This issue highlights the importance of defining accountability and international responsibility for actions of military personnel. There needs to be clarification of the command responsibility which may be under the TCC or under the relevant IO, and issues of concurrent accountability also have to be clarified. This is not only for the sake of legal certainty, but also to bring to justice those who commit crimes and abuses and to provide effective and adequate legal remedies to their victims, who are usually already affected by the situation in their country, and who often do not have the means to deal with complex legal matters.

Ideally, a binding international instrument clarifying the rules applicable to IMMs should be drafted and adopted. Failing or pending that, States, with the support of relevant IOs, could adopt policy instruments that would clarify the existing rules applicable to IMMs and PKOs. In fact, IOs should, where it is within their competence, ratify the relevant existing instruments. Customary rules should of course apply anyway but there may be ambiguity as to whether particular rules are binding on IMMs.

It is important that States and IOs define the chain of command and the issues related to co-ordination of their activities. This would clarify the responsibility and accountability of States, IOs and individuals responsible for violations of either IHL or IHRL. Concurrent responsibility is one way to address this problem, but when it comes to the legal determination of accountability, the confused state of affairs does not assist in the attribution of responsibility as different rules may apply depending on the effective command and control exercised over military contingents.

Finally, it would be appropriate to have a clearer terminology when dealing with IMMs and when they are deployed, in particular under the mandate of IOs. Peace-keeping, peace-enforcement, peace (support) operations, do not mean very much in legal terms. They have been partly defined in various policy documents. An agreed terminology ideally should provide a definition of the tasks and obligations of their components, in particular the military ones. The use of integrated and multifunctional operations has already clarified the tasks of each component, avoiding the need for military personnel to perform all the tasks associated with the conduct of the operation. However, it should be in the interest of military personnel to clarify their tasks when deployed in IMMs; furthermore they can reasonably expect a clear legal framework within which to operate, as well as to obtain the necessary training to ensure that operations are conducted in conformity with international law and provide the necessary protection for the civilian population.

Overall, the legal regime regarding IMMs is unnecessarily complex and highly unsatisfactory. While this book has clarified some matters, it has also shown that there is uncertainty in some areas, both about which law should apply and the extent to which that law may apply. Much work needs to be done, both by lawyers and policy makers, before we have a legal regime appropriate for the extremely important tasks of IMMs. The soldiers and those affected by their actions deserve better.

Select Bibliography and Cases

Articles

Altiparmak K, 'Bankovic: An Obstacle to the Application of the European Convention on Human rights in Iraq' (2004) 9 *JCSL* 213.

Amerasinghe CF, 'The Law of International Organizations: A Subject which Needs Exploration and Analysis' (2004) 1(1) *IOLR* 9.

Bellinger JB III & Haynes WJ II, 'A US government response to the International Committee of the Red Cross study Customary International Humanitarian Law' (2007) 866 *IRRC* 443.

Benvenuti P, 'Le respect du droit international humanitaire par les forces des Nations Unies: La Circulaire du Secretaire-Général' (2001) 105(2) *RGDIP* 355.

Benvenuti P, 'The ICTY's Prosecutor and the Review of the NATO Bombing Campaign against the Federal Republic of Yugoslavia' (2001) 12(3) *EJIL* 503.

Bertrand C, 'La nature juridique de l'organisation pour la sécurité et la coopération en Europe (OSCE)' (1998) 102 *RGDIP* 365.

Bloom ET, 'Protecting Peacekeepers: The Convention on the Safety of United Nations and Associated Personnel' (1995) 89 *AJIL* 621.

Boisson de Chazournes L and Condorelli L, 'Common Article 1 of the Geneva Conventions Revisited: Protecting Collective Interests' (2000) 837 *IRRC* 67.

Bongiorno C, 'A Culture of Impunity: Applying International Human Rights Law to the United Nations in East Timor' (2002) 33 *Columbia HRLR* 623.

Bothe M, 'Die Anwendung der Europäischen Menschenrechtskonvention in bewaffneten Konflikten – eine Überforderung?' (2005) 65 *Zeitschrift fur ausländisches und öffentliches Völkerrecht* 615.

Boustany K, 'Brocklebank: A Questionable Decision of the Court Martial Appeal Court of Canada' (1998) 1 *YIHL* 371.

Bouvier A, 'Convention on the Safety of United Nations and Associated Personnel: Presentation and Analysis' (1995) 309 *IRRC* 638.

Brown D, 'The Role of the United Nations in Peacekeeping and Truce Monitoring: What are the Applicable Norms' (1994) *RBDI* 559.

Burger J, 'International humanitarian law and the Kosovo crisis: Lessons learned or to be learned' (2000) 837 *IRRC* 129.

Campanelli D, 'The law of military occupation put to the test of human rights law' (2008) 871 *IRRC* 653.

Cerone J, 'Minding the Gap: Outlining KFOR Accountability in Post Conflict Kosovo' (2001) 12(3) *EJIL* 469.

Chinkin C, 'East Timor: A Failure of Decolonisation' (1999) 20 *AYIL* 50.

Chopra J, 'The UN's Kingdom of East Timor' (2000) 42(3) *Survival* 27.

Cockayne J and Malone D, 'United Nations Peace Operations: Then and Now', (2004) 9 *International Peacekeeping: The Yearbook of International Peace Operations* 1.

Cogen M, 'Correspondents' Report: Belgium' (1998) 1 *YIHL* 145.

Condorelli L, 'Le statut de forces de l'ONU et le droit international humanitaire' (1995) 78 *Rivista di diritto internazionale* 881.

Condorelli L and Boisson De Chazournes L, 'Common Article 1 of the Geneva Convention revisited: Protecting collective interests' (2000) 837 *IRRC* 67.

Cunning IR, 'Modernizing Customary International Law: The Challenge of Human Rights' (1991) 31 *Virginia Journal of International Law* 211.

Cunningham AJ, 'The European Convention on Human Rights, Customary International Law and the Constitution' (1994) 43 *ICLQ* 537.

Dannenbaum T, 'Translating the Standard of Effective Control into a System of Effective Accountability: How Liability Should be Apportioned for Violations of Human Rights by Member State Troop Contingents Serving as United Nations Peacekeepers' (2010) 51 *Harvard International Law Journal Online* 113.

Dennis MJ, 'Applying Human Rights Law and Humanitarian Law in the Extra-territorial War against Terrorism: Too Little, Too Much, or Just Rights? Application of Human Rights Treaties Extra-territorially to Detention of Combatants and Security Internees: Fuzzy Thinking all Around?' (2006) 12 *ILSA Journal of International and Comparative Law* 459.

Doswald-Beck L and Vité S, 'International Humanitarian Law and Human Rights Law' (1993) 293 *IRRC* 94.

Draper GIAD, 'The Relationship between the Human Rights Regime and the Laws of Armed Conflict' (1971) 1 *Isr.Y.B.Hum.Rts.* 191.

Dubois O, 'Implementation of International Humanitarian Law: Biannual Update of National Legislation and Jurisprudence – January to June 1998' (1998) 325 *IRRC* 729.

Dupuy PM, 'The Constitutional Dimension of the Charter of the United Nations Revisited' (1997) 1 *Max Planck Yearbook of International Law* 1.

Eagleton C, 'International Organization and the Law of Responsibility' (1950-I) 76 *Hague Recueil des Cours* 319.

Einarsen T, Gibney M and Roxstrom E, 'The NATO Bombing Case (Bankovic et al. v. Belgium et al.) and the Limits of Western Human Rights Protection' (2005) 23(1) *Boston University International Law Journal* 55.

Everly R, 'Reviewing Governmental Acts of the United Nations in Kosovo' (2007) 8(1) *German Law Journal* 21.

Fleck D, 'International Accountability for Violations of the Ius in Bello: The Impact of the ICRC Study on Customary International Humanitarian Law' (2006) 11(2) *JCSL* 179.

Freeman AV, 'Responsibility of States for the Unlawful Acts of their Armed Forces' (1956) 88 *Recueil des Cours de l'Académie de Droit International* 263.

Gazzini T, 'NATO's Role in the Collective Security System' (2003) 8 *JCSL* 231.

Gill TD, 'Legal and Some Political Limitations on the Power of the UN Security Council to Exercise its Enforcement Powers under Chapter VII of the UN Charter' (1995) 26 *Neth.Y.B. Int'l Law* 61.

Goulding M, 'The Evolution of United Nations Peacekeeping' (1993) 69 *International Affairs* 451.

Green LC, 'Humanitarian Law and the Man in the Field' (1976) 14 *Can.Y.B. Int'l Law* 96.

Greenwood C, 'International Humanitarian Law and United Nations Military Operations' (1998) 1 *YIHL* 3.

Greenwood C, 'Protection of Peacekeepers: The Legal Regime' (1996) 7 *Duke Journal of Comparative and International Law* 185.

Greenwood C, 'The Relationship Between *jus ad bellum* and *jus in bello*' (1993) 9 *Review of International Studies* 221.

Griffin M and Jones B, 'Building Peace through Transitional Authority: New Directions, Major Challenges' (2000) 7(4) *International Peacekeeping* 82.

Guéhenno JM, 'On the Challenges and Achievements of Reforming UN Peace Operations' (2002) 9(69) *International Peacekeeping* 69.

Happold M, 'Bankovic v. Belgium and the Territorial Scope of the European Convention on Human Rights' (2003) 3 *HRLR* 88.

Häußler U, 'Enforcing the Rule of Law: Military Contributions to Comprehensive Security' (2008) 8 *NZAFLR* 47.

Heintze H-J, 'On the Relationship between Human Rights Law Protection and International Humanitarian Law' (2004) 86 *IRRC* 798.

Henckaerts JM, 'Study on Customary International Humanitarian Law: A Contribution to the Understanding and Respect for the Rule of Law in Armed Conflict' (2005) 857 *IRRC* 175.

Hoffmann F and Mégret F, 'Fostering Human Rights Accountability: An Ombudsperson for the United Nations?' (2005) 11 *Global Governance* 43.

Kavaldjieva S, 'Jurisdiction of the European Court of Human Rights: Exorbitance in Reverse? Can, and Should, an Iraqi Victim of Human Rights Abuses Inflicted by U.K. Troops Have a Remedy in U.K. Courts under the European Convention of Human Rights' (2006) 37 *Georgetown Journal of International Law* 507.

Krieger H, 'A Conflict of Norms: The Relationship Between Humanitarian Law and Human Rights Law in the ICRC Customary Law Study' (2006) 11 *JCSL* 265.

Laursen A, 'NATO, the War over Kosovo, and the ICTY Investigation' (2002) 17 *American University International Law Review* 765.

Lavalle R, 'The Law of the United Nations and the Use of Force under Relevant Security Council Resolutions of 1990 and 1991 to Resolve the Persian Gulf Crisis' (1992) 23 *Neth.Y.B. Int'l Law* 3.

Leach P, 'The British Military in Iraq – The Applicability of the Espace Juridique Doctrine under the European Convention on Human Rights' (2005) 1 *Public Law* 448.

Levrat B, 'Le droit international humanitaire au Timor oriental: entre théorie et pratique' (2001) 841 *IRRC* 77.

Linderfalk U, 'The Effect of Jus Cogens Norms: Whoever Opened Pandora's Box, Did You Ever Think about the Consequences?' (2007) 18(5) *EJIL* 853.

Lobel J and Ratner M, 'Bypassing the Security Council: Ambiguous Authorizations to Use Force, Cease-Fires and the Iraqi Inspection Regime' (1999) 93 *AJIL* 124.

Lupi N, 'Report by the Enquiry Commission on the Behaviour of Italian Peacekeeping Troops in Somalia' (1998) 1 *YIHL* 375.

Mansson K, 'Book Review of *The UN, Human Rights and Post-Conflict Situations* by Nigel D. White and Dirk Klaasen (eds)' (2006) 17(5) *EJIL* 1033.

Mantouvalou V, 'Extending Judicial Control in International Law: Human Rights Treaties and Extra-territoriality' (2005) 9(2) *IJHR* 147.

Martinez JS and Marston Danner A, 'Guilty Associations: Joint Criminal Enterprise, Command Responsibility, and the Development of International Criminal Law' (2005) 93 *California Law Review* 75.

Megret F and Hoffmann F, 'The UN as a Human Rights Violator? Some Reflections on the United Nations Changing Human Rights Responsibilities' (2003) 25 *Human Rights Quarterly* 314.

Meron T, 'Agora: The 1994 US Action in Haiti: Extra-territoriality of Human Rights Treaties' (1995) 89 *AJIL* 78.

Mettraux G, 'US Courts-Martial and the Armed Conflict in the Philippines (1899-1902): Their Contribution to National Case Law on War Crimes' (2003) 1(1) *JICJ* 135.

Miltner B, 'Extraterritorial Jurisdiction Under the European Convention on Human Rights: An Expansion Under Isaak v Turkey?' (2007) 2 *EHRLR* 172.

Mole N, 'Issa v. Turkey: Delineating the Extra Territorial Effect of the European Convention on Human Rights?' (2005) 10 *EHRLR* 86.

Murphy R, 'United Nations Military Operations and International Humanitarian Law: What Rules Apply to Peacekeepers?' (2003) 14 *Criminal Law Forum* 153.

Nayar KMG, 'Human Rights: The UN and US Foreign Policy' (1978) 19 *HILJ* 813.

Odello M, 'Tackling Criminal Acts in Peacekeeping Operations: The Accountability of Peacekeepers' (2010) 15(2) *JCSL* 1.

Oliver GF, 'The Other Side of Peacekeeping: Peace Enforcement and Who Should Do It?' (2002) 8 *International Peacekeeping: The Yearbook of International Peace Operations* 99.

Opie RA, 'Human Rights Violations by Peacekeepers: Finding a Framework for Attribution of International Responsibility' (2006) 1 *New Zealand Law Review* 1.

Orakhelashvili A, 'Restrictive Interpretation of Human Rights Treaties in the Recent Jurisprudence of the European Court of Human Rights' (2003) 14 *EJIL* 529.

Orend B, '*Jus Post Bellum*: The Perspective of a Just War Theorist' (2007) 20 *Leiden Journal of International Law* 571.

Palwankar U, 'Applicability of International Humanitarian Law to United Nations Peacekeeping Forces' (1993) 294 *IRRC* 230.

Paris R, 'International Peacekeeping and the 'Mission Civilisatrice' (2002) 28 *Review of International Studies* 637.

Parks H, 'Air War and the Law of War' (1990) 32 *AFLR* 1.

Paust JJ, 'The U.N. Is Bound By Human Rights: Understanding the Full Reach of Human Rights, Remedies, and Nonimmunity' (2010) 51 *Harvard International Law Journal Online* 1.

Paust JJ, 'The Complex Nature, Sources and Evidences of Customary Human Rights' (1995) 25 *Georgia Journal of International and Comparative Law* 147.

Pedersen MP, 'Territorial Jurisdiction in Article 1 of the European Convention on Human Rights' (2004) 73 *Nordic Journal of International Law* 279.

Peters A, 'Compensatory Constitutionalism: The Function and Potential of Fundamental International Norms and Structures' (2006) 19 *Leiden Journal of International Law* 579.

Piacente N, 'Importance of the Joint Criminal Enterprise Doctrine for the ICTY Prosecutorial Policy' (2004) 2(2) *JICJ* 446.

Quénivet N, 'The Dissonance between the United Nations Zero-Tolerance Policy and the Criminalisation of Sexual Offences on the International Level' (2007) 7(9) *International Criminal Law Review* 657.

Quigley J, 'The United States and the United Nations in the Persian Gulf War: New Order or Disorder?' (1992) 25 *Cornell JIL* 1.

Ratner SR, 'Foreign Occupation and International Territorial Administration: The Challenges of Convergence' (2006) 16(4) *EJIL* 695.

Reinisch A, 'Securing the Accountability of International Organizations' (2001) 7 *Global Governance* 143.

Roberts A, 'Transformative Military Occupation: Applying the Laws of War and Human Rights' (2006) 100(3) *AJIL* 580.

Rostow EV, 'Until What? Enforcement Action or Collective Self-Defense?' (1991) 85 *AJIL* 506.

Rowe P, 'United Nations Peacekeeping Forces and Human Rights Violations: the Role of Military Discipline' (2010) 51 *Harvard International Law Journal Online* 69.

Ryniker A, 'Respect du droit international humanitaire par les forces des Nations Unies' (1999) 836 *IRRC* 795.

Sari A, 'The Conclusion of International Agreements by the European Union in the Context of the ESDP' (2008) 57 *ICLQ* 53.

Sari A, 'Jurisdiction and International Responsibility in Peace Support Operations: The Behrami and Saramati Cases' (2008) 8 *HRLR* 151.

Sassòli M, 'State responsibility for violations of international humanitarian law' (2002) 846 *IRRC* 401.

Schachter O, 'International Law in Theory and in Practice: General Course in Public International Law', (1982-V) 178 *Hague Recueil des Cours* 21.

Schachter O, 'United Nations Law in the Gulf Conflict' (1991) 85 *AJIL* 452.

Shraga D, 'UN Peacekeeping Operations: Applicability of International Humanitarian Law and Responsibility for Operations-Related Damages' (2000) 94(2) *AJIL* 406.

Simma B and Alson P, 'The Sources of Human Rights Law: Custom, Jus Cogens, and General Principles' (1988-1989) 12 *AYIL* 82.

Sohn L, 'The Human Rights Law of the Charter' (1977) 12 *Texas International Law Journal* 129.

Sohn L, 'Ideal to Law to Practice: The Universal Declaration Today and Tomorrow' (1999) 11 *Pace International Law Review* 71.

Stavrinides Z, 'Human Rights Obligations under the United Nations Charter' (1999) 3 *IJHR* 38.

Szablewska N, 'Non-state Actors and Human Rights in Non-international Armed Conflicts' (2007) 32 *South African Yearbook of International Law* 345.

Tarik AM, 'The Long Arm of the European convention on Human Rights and the Recent Development of Issa v. Turkey' 12(2) *Human Rights Brief* 9.

Thakur R, 'From Peacekeeping to Peace Enforcement: The UN Operation in Somalia' (1994) 32(3) *The Journal of Modern African Studies* 387.

Tsagourias N, 'Consent, Neutrality/Impartiality and the Use of Force in Peacekeeping: Their Constitutional Dimension' (2006) 11 *JCSL* 465.

Van Hegelson GJ, 'The Law of Armed Conflicts and the United Nations Peace-Keeping and Peace-Enforcing Operations' (1993) 6 *Hague Yearbook of International Law* 95.

Verdirame G, 'Compliance with Human Rights in UN Operations' (2002) 2(2) *HRLR* 265.

Vinuesa RE, 'Interface, Correspondence and Convergence of Human Rights and International Humanitarian Law' (1998) 1 *YIHL* 69.

Vité S, 'L'applicabilité du droit international de l'occupation militaire' (2004) 853 *IRRC* 9.

Von Heinegg WH, 'The United Nations Convention on the Law of the Sea and Maritime Security Operations' (2005) 48 *German Yearbook of International Law* 151.

Weingärtner D, 'Das UNIFIL-Mandat der Bundeswehr – politische und rechtliche Aspekte' (2007) *Journal of International Law of Peace and Armed Conflict* 116.

Wessel RA, 'The State of Affairs in WEU Security and Defence Policy: The Breakthrough in the Treaty of Nice' (2003) 8 *JCSL* 265.

Westhusing T, 'Taking Terrorism and ROE Seriously' (2003) 1 *J. Mil. Ethics* 4.

Weyembergh A, 'La notion de conflit armé, le droit international humanitaire et les forces des N.U. en Somalie (à propos de l'arrêt de la Cour militaire du 17 déc. 1997)' (1999) 79 *Revue de Droit Pénal et de Criminologie* 177.

White ND and Ulgen O, 'The Security Council and the Decentralized Military Option: Constitutionality and Function' (1997) 44 *NILR* 378.

Williamson JC, 'Establishing the Rule of Law in Post-War Iraq: Rebuilding the Justice System' (2004) 33 *Georgia Journal of International and Comparative Law* 229.

Zwanenburg M, 'Pieces of the Puzzle: Peace Operations, Occupation and the Use of Force' (2006) 45 *Revue de droit militaire et de droit de la guerre* 239.

Zwanenburg M, 'Compromise or Commitment: Human Rights and International Humanitarian Law Obligations for UN Peace Forces' (1998) 11 *Leiden Journal of International Law* 229.

Books

Arnold R and Quénivet N (eds), *International Humanitarian Law and Human Rights Law* (Martinus Nijhoff Publishers, Leiden-Boston, 2008).

Aust A, *Modern Treaty Law and Practice* (Cambridge University Press, Cambridge, 2000)

Boas G and Schabas W, *International Criminal Law Developments in the Case Law of the ICTY* (Martinus Nijhoff Publishers, Leiden, 2003).

Bowett DW, *United Nations Forces: A Legal Study of United Nations Practice* (Stevens, London, 1964).

Breau S, *Humanitarian Intervention: The United Nations and Collective Responsibility* (Cameron May, London, 2005).

Brownlie I, *Principles of Public International Law* (6th ed., Oxford University Press, Oxford, 2003).

Clark W, *Waging Modern War* (Public Affairs Books, New York, 2001).

Colombos CJ and Higgins R, *The International Law of the Sea* (2nd ed., Longmans, London, 1951).

Dallaire R, *Shake Hands with the Devil: The Failure of Humanity in Rwanda* (Carrol & Graf Publishers, New York, 2003).

Daniel DCF, Taft P. and Wiharta S. (eds), *Peace Operations: Trends, Progress, and Prospect* (Georgetown University Press, Washington D.C., 2008).

David E, *Principes de droit des conflits armés* (2e éd., Bruylant, Brussels, 1999).

De Wet E, *The Chapter VII Powers of the United Nations Security Council* (Hart Publishing, Oxford, 2004).

Diehl PF, *Peace Operations* (Polity Press, Cambridge, 2008).

Dinstein Y, *The Conduct of Hostilities under the Law of International Armed Conflict* (Cambridge University Press, Cambridge, 2004).

Doyle MW and Sambanis N, *Making War and Building Peace: United Nations Peace Operations* (Princeton University Press, Princeton, 2006).

Duffy H, *The War on Terror and the Framework of International Law* (Cambridge University Press, Cambridge, 2005).

Durch WJ and Tobias C. Berkman, *Who Should Keep the Peace? Providing Security for Twenty-First-Century Peace Operations* (The Henry L. Stimson Center, Washington DC, 2006).

Elliott LM and Cheeseman G (eds), *Forces for Good: Cosmopolitan Militaries in the Twenty-First Century* (Manchester University Press, Manchester and New York, 2004).

Evans M (ed), *Just War Theory. A Reappraisal* (Edinburgh University Press, Edinburgh, 2005).

Gazzini T, *The Changing Rules on the Use of Force in International Law* (Manchester University Press, Manchester, 2006).

Gray C, *International Law and the Use of Force* (2nd ed., Oxford University Press, Oxford, 2004).

Haksar U, *Minority Protection and the International Bill of Rights* (Allied, Bombay, 1974).

Häußler U, *Ensuring and Enforcing Human Security: The Practice of International Peace Missions* (Wolf Legal Publishers, Nijmegen, 2007).

Henckaerts JM and Doswald-Beck L, *Customary International Humanitarian Law* (ICRC and Cambridge University Press, Cambridge, 2005).

Ignatieff M, *Virtual War: Kosovo and beyond* (Chatto and Windus, New York, 2000).

Kalshoven F, *Constraints on the Waging of War* (ICRC and Martinus Nijhoff Publishers, Geneva, 1987).

Kelly MJ, *Restoring and Maintaining Order in Complex Peace Operations* (Kluwer, The Hague, 1999).

Kerr R, *The Military on Trial: the British Army in Iraq* (Wolf Legal Publishers, Nijmegen, 2008).

Knoops GJ, *The Prosecution and Defense of Peacekeepers Under International Criminal Law* (Transnational Publishers, New York, 2004).

Knoops GJ, *Defenses in Contemporary International Criminal Law* (Transnational Publishers, New York, 2001).

Kolb R, *Droit humanitaire et opérations de paix internationales* (2e éd., Helbring and Lichtenhahn, Basel, 2006).

Kolb R, Porretto G and Vité S, *L'application du droit international humanitaire et des droits de l'homme aux organisations internationales* (Bruylant, Brussels, 2005).

Kolb R, Porretto G and Vité S, *L'articulation des règles de droit international humanitaire et de droits de l'homme applicables aux forces internationales et aux administrations civiles internationales transitoires* (CUDIH, Geneva, 2003).

McCoubrey H and White ND, *The Blue Helmets: Legal Regulation of United Nations Military Operations* (Dartmouth, Aldershot, 1996).

Meron T, *Human Rights and Humanitarian Norms as Customary Law* (Clarendon Press, Oxford 1989).

Meyrowitz H, *Le principe de l'égalité des belligérants devant le droit de la guerre* (Éditions A. Pédone, Paris, 1970).

Murphy R, *UN Peacekeeping in Lebanon, Somalia and Kosovo* (Cambridge University Press, Cambridge, 2007).

Nordquist MH, Grandy NR, Nandan SN and Rosenne S (eds), *United Nations Convention on the Law of the Sea 1982. A Commentary*, Vol. III (Martinus Nijhoff Publishers, Dordrecht, 1995).

O'Connell DP, *The International Law of the Sea*, Edited by IA Shearer, 2 vols. (Clarendon Press, Oxford, 1982 and 1984).

Provost R, *International Human Rights and Humanitarian Law* (Cambridge University Press, Cambridge, 2002).

Rehman J, *International Human Rights Law. A Practical Approach* (Longman, Harlow, 2003).

Rivoli P, *The Travels of a T-Shirt in the Global Economy* (John Wiley & Sons, Inc., Hoboken, New Jersey, 2005).

Rogers APV, *Law on the Battlefield,* (Manchester University Press, Manchester, 1996).

Sandoz Y, Swinarski C and Zimmerman B, *Commentary on the Additional Protocols of 8 June 1977 to the Geneva Conventions of 12 August 1949* (ICRC and Martinus Nijhoff Publishers, Geneva, 1987).

Sarooshi D, *The United Nations and the Development of Collective Security* (Clarendon Press, Oxford, 1999).

Sassòli M and Bouvier A, *How Does Law Protect in War?* Volume I (ICRC, Geneva 2006).

Schachter O, *International Law in Theory and Practice* (Martinus Nijhoff Publishers, London 1991).

Schermers HG and Blokker NM, *International Institutional Law: Unity within Diversity* (3rd ed., Martinus Nijhoff Publishers, Boston 1995).

Schmitt MN and Pejic J (eds), *International Law and Armed Conflict: Exploring the Faultlines – Essays in Honour of Yoram Dinstein* (Martinus Nijhoff Publishers, Leiden-Boston, 2007).

Schwarzenberger G, *Power Politics: A Study of World Society* (3rd ed., Stevens, London, 1964).

Seyersted F, *United Nations Forces in the Law of Peace and War* (A.W. Sijthoff, Leiden 1966).

Shaw M, *International Law* (Cambridge University Press, Cambridge, 1997).

Smith RKM, *Textbook on International Human Rights* (3rd ed., Oxford University Press, Oxford, 2007).

Stahn C, *The Law and Practice of International Territorial Administration: Versailles to Iraq and Beyond* (Cambridge University Press, Cambridge, 2008).

Stahn C and Kleffner JK (eds), *Jus Post Bellum: Towards a Law of Transition From Conflict to Peace* (Cambridge University Press, Cambridge, 2008).

Stone J, *Legal Controls of International Conflict* (Stevens, London, 1954).

Tomuschat C, *Human Rights: Between Idealism and Realism* (Oxford University Press, Oxford, 2003).

Wallace RM, *International Law, Cases and Materials* (3rd ed., Sweet and Maxwell, London, 1997).

Walzer M, *Just and Unjust Wars* (Basic Books, New York, 2000).

White ND, *The Law of International Organisations* (2nd ed., Manchester University Press, Manchester 2005).

White ND, *The United Nations System: Towards International Justice* (Lynne Rienner Publishers, Boulder: CO, 2002).

Wilmshurst E and Breau S (eds), *Perspectives on the ICRC Study on Customary International Humanitarian Law* (Cambridge University Press, Cambridge, 2007)

Zwanenburg M, *Accountability of Peace Support Operations* (Martinus Nijhoff Publishers, Leiden, 2005).

Chapters

Aeschlimann A, 'Overview of protection Issues in the context of Multinational Peace Operations' in Faite A & Grenier JL (eds), *Expert Meeting on Multinational Peace Operations. Applicability of International Humanitarian Law and International Human Rights Law to UN Mandated Forces, Geneva, 11–12 December 2003* (ICRC, Geneva, 2004).

'Appendix to the Annex to the Protocol between the Arab Republic of Egypt and the State of Israel, 3 August 1981' reproduced in Siekmann RCR (ed.), *Basic Documents on United Nations and Related Peace-keeping Forces* (Martinus Nijhoff Publishers, Dordrecht, 1991).

Asseburg M, 'Der Bundeswehreinsatz im Libanon: Die Maritime Task Force im Rahmen von "UNIFIL plus"' in Mair St (ed), *Auslandseinsätze der Bundeswehr* (Leitfragen, Entscheidungsspielräume, und Lehren – SWP-Studie, Berlin, Stiftung Wissenschaft und Politik 2007).

Benvenuti P, 'The Implementation of International Humanitarian Law in the Framework of United Nations Peacekeeping Operations' in Roberts A (ed.), *Law in Humanitarian Crises*, Vol. I (European Commission, Office for Official Publications of the European Communities, Brussels 1995).

Bothe M and Dörschel T, 'The UN Peacekeeping Experience' in Dieter Fleck (ed.), *The Handbook of the Law of Visiting Forces* (Oxford University Press, Oxford, 2001).

Bothe M, 'Peace-keeping' in Simma B (ed.), *The Charter of the United Nations: A Commentary* (2nd ed., Oxford University Press, Oxford, 2002).

Bothe M, 'Syndicate Remarks' in Howard JJ and Oswald B (eds), *The Rule of Law on Peace Operations. A 'Challenges of Peace Operations' Project Conference* (Kluwer Law International, The Hague/London/New York, 2002).

Brown N, 'Issues Arising from Coalition Operations: An Operational Lawyer's Perspective' in Carsten MD (ed), *International Law and Military Operations*, 84 Naval War College International Law Studies Series (Naval War College, Newport, Rhode Island, 2008).

Buergenthal T, 'To Respect and Ensure: State Obligations and Permissible Derogations' in Henkin L (ed.), *The International Bill of Rights: The Convention on Civil and Political Rights* (Columbia University Press, New York, 1981).

Chesterman S, 'Virtual Trusteeship' in Malone DM (ed.), *The UN Security Council. From the Cold War to the 21st Century* (Lynne Rienner, London 2004).

Condorelli L and Boisson De Chazournes L, 'Quelques remarques à propos de l'obligation des Etats de "respecter et faire respecter" le droit international humanitaire "en toutes circonstances"' in Swinarski C (ed.), *Studies and Essays on International Humanitarian Law and Red Cross Principles in Honour of Jean Pictet* (Martinus Nijhoff Publishers, Geneva, 1984).

Dinstein Y, 'Military Necessity' in Bernhardt R (ed.), *Encyclopedia of Public International Law* (vol. III, North Holland, Amsterdam, 1997).

Dorronsoro G, 'The Security Council and the Afghan Conflict' in Lowe V, Roberts A, Welsh J and Zaum D (eds), *The United Nations Security Council and War* (Oxford University Press, Oxford, 2008).

Emanuelli C, 'Les forces des Nations Unies et le droit international humanitaire' in Condorelli L, La Rosa AM and Scherrer S (eds), *The United Nations and International Humanitarian Law* (Pedone, Paris, 1996).

Evans M, 'State Responsibility and the European Convention on Human Rights: Role and Realm' in Fitzmaurice M and Sarooshi D (eds), *Issues of State Responsibility before International Judicial Institutions* (Hart Publishing, Oxford, 2004).

Fassbender B, 'The Meaning of International Constitutional Law' in MacDonald R and Johnston D (eds), *Towards World Constitutionalism: Issues in the Legal Ordering of the World Community* (Martinus Nijhoff Publishers, Leiden, 2005).

Ferraro T, 'The Applicability of the Law of Occupation to Peace Forces' in *31st Round Table on Current Issues of International Humanitarian Law* (International Institute of Humanitarian Law, San Remo, 4 – 6 September 2008).

Garraway C, 'England Does Not Love Coalitions – Does Anything Change?' in Helm AM (ed.), *The Law of War in the 21st Century: Weaponry and the Use of Force* (Naval War College, Newport, Rhode Island, 2006).

Greenwood C, 'Historical Development and Legal Basis' in Fleck D (ed.), *The Handbook of Humanitarian Law in Armed Conflict* (Oxford University Press, New York, 1995).

Greenwood C, 'Customary international law and the First Geneva Protocol of 1977 in the Gulf Conflict' in Rowe P (ed.), *The Gulf War 1990-1991 in International and English Law* (Sweet and Maxwell, London, 1993).

Grenier JL, 'Extra-territorial Applicability of Human Rights Treaty Obligations to United Nations-mandated Forces' in Faite A and Grenier JL (eds), *Expert Meeting on Multinational Peace Operations. Applicability of International Humanitarian Law and International Human Rights Law to UN Mandated Forces, Geneva, 11-12 December 2003* (ICRC, Geneva, 2004).

Hampson F, 'Means and Methods of Warfare' in Rowe P (ed.), *The Gulf War 1990-1991 in International and English Law* (Sweet and Maxwell, London, 1993).

Häußler U, 'General Principles of International Humanitarian and Human Rights Law: A Tool to Overcome the War-and-Peace Divide in International Law' to in Bailliet CM (ed.), *Security: A Multidisciplinary Normative Approach* (Martinus Nijhoff Publishers, Leiden, 2009).

Hodgkinson DB, Hodgkinson SL, Noone DC and Noone GP, 'Human Rights Training to Law Enforcement Agents: A Key to PSO Success' in Arnold R (ed.), *Law Enforcement within the Framework of PSO* (Martinus Nijhoff Publishers, Leiden, 2008).

Hummer W, 'Untergang, "Entkernung" und Funktionsnachfolge Internationaler Organisationen – dargestellt am Beispiel der EGKS und der WEU' in Zehetner F (ed.), *Festschrift für Hans-Ernst Folz* (Neuer Wissenschaftlicher Verlag, Vienna, 2003).

Humphrey JP, 'The Universal Declaration of Human Rights: Its History, Impact and Juridical Character' in Ramcharan BG (ed.), *Human Rights: Thirty Years after the Universal Declaration* (Martinus Nijhoff Publishers, The Hague, 1979).

Kadelbach S, 'Jus Cogens, Obligations Erga Omnes and Other Rules – The Identification of Fundamental Norms' in Tomuschat C and Thouvenin JM (eds), *The Fundamental Rules of the International Legal Order: Jus Cogens and Obligations Erga Omnes* (Martinus Nijhoff Publishers, Leiden, 2006).

Kondoch B, 'Human Rights Law and UN Peace Operations in Post Conflict Situations' in White ND and Klaasen D (eds), *The UN, Human Rights and Post-Conflict Situations* (Manchester University Press, Manchester, 2005).

Lawson R, 'The Concept of Jurisdiction and Extra-territorial Acts of State' in Kreijen G et al (eds), *State, Sovereignty, and International Governanc*e (Oxford University Press, New York, 2002).

Lillich R, 'Civil Rights' in Meron T (ed.), *Human Rights in International Law: Legal and Policy Issues* (Clarendon Press, Oxford, 1984).

Lowe V, 'International Legal Issues Arising in the Kosovo Crisis' in Yee S and Tieya W (eds), *International Law in the Post-Cold War World; Essays in Memory of Li Haopei* (Routledge, London, 2001).

McConachie V, 'Coalition Operations: A Compromise or an Accommodation?' in Carsten MD (ed.), *International Law and Military Operations* (Naval War College, Newport, Rhode Island, 2008).

O'Boyle M, 'The European Convention on Human Rights and Extraterritorial Jurisdiction: A Comment on 'Life after Bankovic' in Coomans F and Kamminga M (eds), *Extraterritorial Application of Human Rights Treaties* (Intersentia, Antwerp, 2004).

Oeter S, 'Methods and Means of Combat' in Fleck D (ed.), *The Handbook of Humanitarian Law in Armed Conflict* (Oxford University Press, New York, 1995).

Parayre S, 'Beyond International Humanitarian Law: Aspects of the Applicability of International Human Rights Law' in Faite A and Grenier JL (eds), *Expert Meeting on Multinational Peace Operations. Applicability of International Humanitarian Law and International Human Rights Law to UN Mandated Forces, Geneva, 11–12 December 2003* (ICRC, Geneva, 2004).

Poole JL, 'Post-Conflict Justice in Sierra Leone' in Cherif Bassiouni M (ed.), *Post Conflict Justice* (Transnational Publishers, New York, 2002).

Quénivet N, 'The Role of the International Criminal Court in the Prosecution of Sexual Offences Committed by Peacekeepers' in Arnold R (ed.), *Law Enforcement within the Framework of PSO* (Martinus Nijhoff Publishers, Leiden, 2008).

Robertson HB, 'The Principle of the Military Objective in the Law of Armed Conflict' in Schmitt M (ed.) *The Law of Military Operation: Liber Amicorum Professor Jack Grunawalt* (Naval War College Press, Newport: Rhode Island, 1998).

Rostow N, 'Introduction to a special section on Coalition Operations' in Wall AE (ed.) *Legal and Etichal Lessons of NATO's Kosovo Campaign* (Naval War College, Newport: Rhode Island, 2002).

Schindler D, 'United Nations Forces and International Humanitarian Law' in Swinarski C (ed.), *Studies and Essays on International Humanitarian Law and Red Cross Principles in Honour of Jean Pictet* (Martinus Nijhoff Publishers, Dordrecht, 1984).

Schmitt M, 'Bellum Americanum: The U.S. View of Twenty-First Century War and Its Possible Implications for the Law of Armed Conflict' in Schmitt M and Green L (eds), *The Law of Armed Conflict: Into the Next Millenium* (Naval War College, Newport: Rhode Island, 1998).

Schmitt M, 'The Law of Armed Conflict as Soft Power: Optimizing Strategic Choice' in Schmitt M and Thomas AR (eds), *International Law Across the Spectrum of Conflict: Essays in Honour of Professor L.C. Green on the Occasion of his Eightieth Birthday* (Naval War College, Newport: Rhode Island, 2000).

Serrano AS, 'CIS Peacekeeping in Tajikistan' in Mackinlay J and Cross P (eds), *Regional Peacekeepers: The Paradox of Russian Peacekeeping* (United Nations University Press, Tokyo, 2003).

Shraga D and Zacklin R, 'The Applicability of International Humanitarian Law to United Nations Peacekeeping Operations. Conceptual, Legal and Practical Issues' in Palwankar U (ed.), *Report of the Symposium on Humanitarian Action and Peacekeeping Operations, 22 – 24 June 1994* (ICRC, Geneva, 1994).

Shraga D, 'The United Nations as an Actor Bound by International Humanitarian Law' in Condorelli L, La Rosa AM and Scherrer S (eds), *The United Nations and International Humanitarian Law* (Pedone, Paris, 1996).

Stein T, 'Coalition Warfare and Differing Legal Obligations' in Wall AE (ed.) *Legal and Etichal Lessons of NATO's Kosovo Campaign* (Naval War College, Newport: Rhode Island, 2002).

Strydom H, 'South Africa' in Gowlland-Debbas V (ed.), *National Implementation of United Nations Sanctions* (Martinus Nijhoff Publishers, Leiden, 2004).

Tavernier P, 'L'identification des Règles Fondamentales, un Problèm Résolu' in Tomuschat C and Thouvenin JM (eds), *The Fundamental Rules of the International Legal Order: Jus Cogens and Obligations Erga Omnes* (Martinus Nijhoff Publishers, Leiden, 2006).

Thürer D, 'Comments on Chapter 7 and 8' in Byers M and Nolte G (eds), *US Hegemony and the Foundations of International Law* (Cambridge University Press, Cambridge, 2003).

Tsagourias, N, 'EU Peacekeeping Operations: Legal and Theoretical Issues' in Trybus M and White N (eds), *European Security Law* (Oxford University Press, Oxford 2007).

Watkin K, 'Coalition Operations: A Canadian Perspective' in Carsten MD (ed.), *International Law and Military Operations* (Naval War College, Newport: Rhode Island, 2008).

White ND, 'Towards a Strategy for Human Rights Protection in Post-Conflict Situations' in White ND and Klaasen D (eds), *The UN, Human Rights and Post-Conflict Situations* (Manchester University Press, Manchester, 2005).

White ND, 'The United Nations and Democracy Assistance: Developing Practice within a Constitutional Framework' in Burnell P (ed.), *Democracy Assistance: International Co-operation for Democratization* (Frank Cass, London, 2000).

Zacklin R, 'The Use of Force in Peacekeeping Operations' in Blokker N and Schrijver N (eds), *The Security Council and the Use of Force* (Martinus Nijhoff Publishers, The Hague, 2005).

National Provisions

(UK) Ministry of Defence, *Peace Support Operations: JWP 3-50*, (Ministry of Defence, 1999).

(UK) Ministry of Defence, *The Military Contribution to Peace Support Operations: JWP 3-50* (2nd ed., Ministry of Defence, 2004).

(US) Statement by the President, 8 July 1950, United States Policy in the Korean Crisis, Dept. of State Publication No. 3922 (Washington, 1950).

(US) New Jersey State Act, 2C-3-4(a)-6C.

(US) US Navy, US Marine Corps, US Coast Guard, *The Commander's Handbook on the Law of Naval Operations* (Department of the Navy, 2007).

Cases

International Court of Justice (in chronological order)

Corfu Channel (United Kingdom v. Albania) Merits [1949] ICJ Rep 18.

Reparation for Injuries Suffered in the Service of the United Nations, Advisory Opinion [1949] ICJ Rep 174.

Nottebohm case (Liechtenstein v. Guatemala) [1954] ICJ Rep 4.

Effects of Awards of Compensation Made by the United Nations Administrative Tribunal, Advisory Opinion [1954] ICJ Rep 47.

Certain Expenses of the United Nations (Article 17, Paragraph 2, of the Charter), Advisory Opinion [1962] ICJ Rep 151.

South West Africa Cases (*Ethiopia v. South Africa; Liberia v. South Africa*), Judgement [1966] ICJ Rep. 6.

North Sea Continental Shelf, (*Federal Republic of Germany/Denmark; Federal Republic of Germany/Netherlands*) Judgment of 20 February 1969 [1969] ICJ Rep 3.

Barcelona Traction Case (*Belgium v. Spain*) [1970] ICJ Rep 4.

Legal Consequences for States of the Continued Presence of South Africa in Namibia, Advisory Opinion [1971] ICJ Rep 16.

Interpretation of the Agreement of 25 March 1951 between the WHO and Egypt, Advisory Opinion [1980] ICJ Rep 73.

Case Concerning Military and Paramilitary Activities in and against Nicaragua (*Nicaragua v. United States of America*) Merits [1986] ICJ Rep 14.

Case Concerning Certain Phosphate Lands in Nauru (*Nauru v. Australia*) [1992] ICJ Rep 240.

Legality of the Threat or Use of Nuclear Weapons, Advisory Opinion of 8 July 1996 [1996] ICJ Rep 226.

Case Concerning the Gabcikovo-Nagymaros Project (*Hungary v. Slovakia*) Merits [1997] ICJ Rep 51.

Legal Consequences of the Construction of a Wall in the Occupied Palestinian Territories, Advisory Opinion [2004] ICJ Rep 200.

Case Concerning Armed Activities on the Territory of the Congo (Democratic Republic of Congo v. Uganda) [2005] ICJ Rep 215.

International Criminal Tribunal for the Former Yugoslavia

Prosecutor v. Dusko Tadic, Case No. ITCY-94-1-A, Decision on the Defence Motion on Jurisdiction (10 August 1995).

Prosecutor v Dusko Tadic, Case No. ITCY-94-1-A, Judgment of Appeal Chamber (15 July 1999).

Prosecutor v. Enver Hadzihasanovic and Amir Kubura, Case No. ITCY-01-47-T, Judgment (15 March 2006).

European Court of Human Rights (in chronological order)

Lawless v. Ireland (Application No. 332/57) 1 July 1961, 2 ECHR 180.

X. v. Germany (Application No. 1611/62 25) September 1965, 8 *Yearbook of the European Convention on Human Rights* 158.

Cyprus v. Turkey (Application No. 6780/74 and 6950/75) 26 May 1975, *Decisions and Reports of the European Commission of Human Rights* (1975-2) 125.

Cyprus v. Turkey (Application No. 8007/77) 10 July 1978, Admissibility, *Decisions and Reports of the European Commission of Human Rights* (1978-13) 146.

Freda v. Italy (Application No. 8916/80) 7 October 1980, *Decisions and Reports of the European Convention of Human Rights* (1981) 250.

Reinette v. France (Application No. 14009/88) 2 October 1989, *Decisions and Reports of the European Convention of Human Rights* (1989-63) 189.

Chrysostomos, Papchysostomos and Loizidou v. Turkey (Application No. 15299/89, 15300/89 and 15318/89) 4 March 1991, *Decisions and Reports of the European Commission of Human Rights* (1991-68) 250.

Drozd & Janousek v. France and Spain (Application No. 12747/87) 26 June 1992, Series A No. 240.

Loizidou v. Turkey (Application No. 15318/89) Preliminary Objections of 23 March 1995, Series A No. 310 and Judgment of 8 December 1996, 70 *ECHR* 52.

Sánchez-Ramirez v. France (Application No. 28780/95) 24 June 1996, *Decisions and Reports of the European Convention of Human Rights* (1996) 155.

Aksoy v. Turkey (Case 100/1995/606/694) ECHR, Judgement of 18 December 1996.

Cyprus v. Turkey (Application No. 25781/94) 28 June 1996, (2001-IV) ECHR 81.

Selmouni v. France (Application No. 25803/94) 28 July 1999, 29 EHRR 403.

Öcalan v. Turkey (Application No. 46221/99) Admissibility of 14 December 2000.

Banković and Others v. Belgium and 16 Other Contracting States, (Dec.) [2001] [GC], No. 52207/99, ECtHR 2001-XII.

Cyprus v. Turkey (Application No. 25781/94) 10 May 2001.

Gentilhomme v. *France*, [2002] European Court of Human Rights (ECtHR) No. 48205/99, (14 May 2002).

Ilascu and others v.Moldova and Russian Federation (Application no. 48787/99) Judgment of 8 July 2004, ECHR 318.

Issa v. Turkey (Application No. 31821/96) 16 November 2004 (2005) ECHR 71.

Isaak and Others v. Turkey (Application No. 44587/98) Admissibility Decision of 28 September 2006.

Behrami v. France (Application No. 71412/01) *and Saramati v. France, Germany and Norway* (Application no 78166/01) Grand Chamber Decision on Admissibility of 2 May 2007.

Human Rights Committee

Delia Saldias de Lopez v. Uruguay, Communication No. 52/1979, 29 July 1981, UN Doc. CCPR/C/OP/1 (1984).

Lilian Celiberti de Casariego v. Uruguay, Communication No. 56/1979, 29 July 1981, UN Doc CCPR/C/OP/1 (1984).

UN Human Rights Committee, Concluding Observations: Israel, UN Doc. CCPR/C/79/ Add. 93 (18 August 1998).

UN Human Rights Committee, Concluding Observations: Belgium UN Doc. CCPR/C/79/ Add.99 (19 November 1998).

UN Human Rights Committee, Concluding Observations: The Netherlands, UN Doc. CCPR/CO/72/NET (27 August 2001).

UN Human Rights Committee, General Comment No. 31 on Article 2 of the Covenant: The Nature of the General Legal Obligation Imposed on States Parties to the Covenant, UN Doc. CCPR/C/74/CRP.4/Rev.6 (21 April 2004).

UN Human Rights Committee, Concluding Observations: Serbia and Montenegro, UN Doc. CCPR/CO/81/SEMO (12 August 2004).

UN Human Rights Committee, Concluding Observation on UNMIK, UN Doc. CCPR/C/ UNK/1 (14 August 2006).

Other International Courts

Affaire des biens britanniques au Maroc espagnol (*Espagne contre Royaume-Uni*) (1925) 2 RIAA 615.

European Commission for Democracy through Law, *Opinion on Human Rights in Kosovo: Possible Establishment of Review Mechanisms*, Opinion No. 280/2004, CDL-AD (2004) 033, 11 October 2004.

ECJ, *Yassin Abdullah Kadi v. Council of the European Union and Commission of the European Communities*, Case T-315/01, 21 September 2005.

ICTR, *Prosecutor v. Jean-Paul Akayesu*, Case No. ICTR-96-4-T, Judgement (2 September 1998).

International Chamber of Commerce, *Westland Helicopters Ltd. v. the Arab Organization for Industrialization, United Arab Emirates, Kingdom of Saudi Arabia, State of Quatar, Arab Republic of Egypt and Arab British Helicopter Company* (ICC case 3879), 23 ILM (1984) 1701.

PCIJ, *Case Concerning the Factory at Chorzów (Germany v. Poland)*, Claim for Indemnity, Merits, Judgement No. 13 of 13 September 1928, Series A, No. 17.

National Cases

(Austria) *N.K. v. Austria*, Vienna Superior Provincial Court (26 February 1979) 77 *ILR* 470.

(Belgium) *Coelus en Baert*, C.M., 17 December 1997, II, 3, D, *J.T.*, (1998) 289.

(Canada) Law-Reports of Trials of War Criminals, The United Nations War Crimes Commission, Volume IV, London, HMSO, 1948, Case No. 22, The Abbaye Ardenne Case Trial of S.S. Brigadefuhrer Kurt Meyer, Canadian Military Court, Aurich, Germany, 10/28 Decemebr 1945, available at http://www.ess.uwe.ac.uk/WCC/meyer.htm

(Canada) *Major A.G. Seward v. Her Majesty the Queen*, Court Martial Appeal Court of Canada, 27 May 1996, available at <http://csc.lexum.umontreal.ca/en/bulletin/1996/96-11-08.bul/96-11-08.bul.html>.

(Canada), *Her Majesty the Queen v. Private D. J. Brocklebank*, Court Martial Appeal Court of Canada, 2 April 1996, 134 *DLR* (4th).

(Canada) *Amnesty International Canada and British Columbia Civil Liberties Association v. Chief of the Defence Staff for the Canadian Forces, Minister of National Defence and Attorney General of Canada*, 2008 FC 336, 12 March 2008.

(Germany) *The Varvarin Case*, District Court at Bonn, Judgment, 10 December 2003, Case No. 1 O 361/02.

(Germany) Higher Regional Court at Cologne (Oberlandesgericht), Judgment, 28 July 2005, Case No. 7 U 8/04.

(Italy) *Branno v. Ministry of War*, Italian Court of Cassation (1954) 22 ILR 756.

(Italy) *Mazzanti v. H.A.F.S.E. & Ministry of Def.*, Tribunal of Florence (1954) 22 ILR 758.

(The Netherlands) Dutch Supreme Court, HR (29 September 2002) NJ 2003 35.

(United Kingdom) *Nissan v. Attorney-General,* Queen's Bench Division (1967) 2 All ER 200.

(United Kingdom) *Attorney-General v. Nissan,* House of Lords (1969) 1 All ER 629.

(United Kingdom) *Al-Skeini et al. v. Secretary of State for Defence* (2007) UKHL 26.

(United States) *Filartiga v. Pena-Irala*, 630 F. 2d 876 (2d Cir. 1980) 883.

(United States) *De Sanchez v. Banco Central de Nicaragua*, 770 F.2d 1385, 1397 (5*th* Cir. 1985).

(United States) *Restatement (Third) of the Foreign relations law of the United States*, 1987, Section 702(a)-(g).

(United States) *Siderman de Blake* v. *Republic of Argentina*, 965 F.2d 699, 719 (9th Cir. 1992).

(United States) *Rasul v. Bush*, 542 U.S. 466 (2004) and *Omar et al. v. Secretary of the United States Army et al.*, 479 F. 3d 1 (D.C. Cir. 2007).

UN Documents

Security Council Resolutions (in chronological order)

UNSC Res. 83, Complaint of Aggression upon the Republic of Korea (27 June 1950).

UNSC Res. 84, Complaint of Aggression upon the Republic of Korea (7 July 1950).

UNSC Res. 217, Question Concerning the Situation in Southern Rhodesia (20 November 1965).

UNSC Res. 221, Question Concerning the Situation in Southern Rhodesia (9 April 1966).

UNSC Res. 425, Israel-Lebanon (19 March 1978).

UNSC Res. 426, Israel-Lebanon (19 March 1978).

UNSC Res. 678, Iraq-Kuwait (29 November 1990).

UNSC Res. 687, Iraq-Kuwait (3 April 1991).

UNSC Res. 713, Socialist Federal Republic of Yugoslavia (25 September 1991).

UNSC Res. 727, Socialist Federal Republic of Yugoslavia (8 January 1991).

UNSC Res. 751, Somalia (24 April 1992).

UNSC Res. 787, Bosnia and Herzegovina (16 November 1992).

UNSC Res. 794, Somalia (3 December 1992).

UNSC Res. 814, Somalia (26 March 1993).

UNSC Res. 827, Tribunal of Former Yugoslavia (25 May 1993).

UNSC Res. 872, Rwanda (5 October 1993).

UNSC Res. 940, On Authrization to Form a Multinational Force under Unified Command and Control to Restore the legitimately elected President and Authorities of the Government of Haiti and Extension of the Mandate of the UN Mission in Haiti (31 July 1994).

UNSC Res. 1244, On the Situation relating Kosovo (10 June 1999).

UNSC Res. 1272, On the situation in East Timor (25 October 1999).

UNSC Res. 1310, On the situation in the Middle East (27 July 2000).

UNSC Res. 1337, On the situation in the Middle East (30 January 2001).

UNSC Res. 1365, On the situation in the Middle East (31 July 2001).

UNSC Res. 1368, Threats to International Peace and Security caused by Terrorist Acts (12 September 2001).

UNSC Res. 1373, Threats to International Peace and Security caused by Terrorist Acts (28 September 2001).

UNSC Res. 1391, The situation in the Middle East (28 January 2002).

UNSC Res. 1428, The situation in the Middle East (30 July 2002).

UNSC Res. 1483, The situation between Iraq and Kuwait (22 May 2003).

UNSC Res. 1496, The situation in the Middle East (31 July 2003).

UNSC Res. 1511, The Situation between Iraq and Kuwait (16 October 2003).

UNSC Res. 1525, The situation in the Middle East (30 January 2004).

UNSC Res. 1540, Non Proliferation of Weapons of Mass Destruction (28 April 2004).

UNSC Res. 1542, The Question Concerning Haiti (MINUSTAH) (30 April 2004).

UNSC Res. 1546, The Situation between Iraq and Kuwait (8 June 2004).

UNSC Res. 1559, The situation in the middle East (2 September 2004).

UNSC Res. 1565, The Situation Concerning the Democratic Republic of Congo (1 October 2004).

UNSC Res. 1583, The situation in the Middle East (28 January 2005).

UNSC Res. 1614, The situation in the Middle East (28 July 2005).

UNSC Res. 1655, The situation in the Middle East (31 January 2006).

UNSC Res. 1674, Protection of Civilians in Armed Conflict (28 July 2006).

UNSC Res. 1701, The situation in Middle East (11 August 2006).

UNSC Res. 1769, Reports of the Secretary-General on the Sudan (31 July 2007).

UNSC Res. 1773, The situation in Middle East (24 August 2007).

UNSC Res. 1816, The situation in Somalia (2 June 2008).

UNSC Res. 1832 The situation in Middle East (27 August 2008).

UNSC Res. 1838, The situation in Somalia (7 October 2008).

UNSC Res. 1846, The situation in Somalia (2 December 2008).

UNSC Res. 1848, The situation in Middle East (12 December 2008).

UNSC Res. 1851, The situation in Somalia (16 December 2008).

General Assembly Resolutions

UNGA Res. 5/376, The Problem of the Independence of Korea (7 October 1950).

UNGA Res. 5/498, Intervention of the Central's People Government of the People's Republic of China in Korea (1 February 1951).

UNGA Res. 25/2625, Declaration on Principles of International Law concerning Friendly Relations and Co-operation among States in accordance with the Charter of the United Nations (24 October 1970).

UNGA Res. 29/3314, UN Definition of Aggression (14 December 1974).

UNGA Res. 30/3452, Declaration on the Protection of all Persons from being Subjected to Torture and other Cruel, Inhuman or Degrading Treatment or Punishment (9 December 1975).

UNGA Res. 34/169, Code of Conduct for law Enforcement Officials (17 December 1979).

UNGA Res. 49/59, UN Convention on the Safety of United Nations and Associated Personnel, Annex (9 December 1994).

UNGA Res. 52/247, Third-party Liability: Temporal and Financial Limitations (17 July 1998).

UNGA Res. 60/1, 2005 World Summit Outcome (24 October 2005).

UNGA Res. 56/83, Responsibility of States for Internationally Wrongful Acts (12 December 2001).

UNGA Res. 60/147, Basic Principles and Guidelines on the Right to a Remedy and Reparation for Victims of Gross Violations of International Human Rights and Serious Violations of International Humanitarian Law (21 March 2006).

Other UN Documents

DPKO, *General Guidelines for Peace-Keeping Operations* (United Nations, New York 1995).

DPKO, *Guidelines for the Development of ROE for UNPKO* (United Nations, March 2002).

'Guidance on Integrated Missions', Note from the Secretary General Kofi Annan (9 February 2006).

UN Doc. A/3943, Report of the Secretary-General. 'Summary Study on the Experience derived from the Establishment and Operation of UNEF I' (9 October 1958).

UN Doc. A/45/594, Report of the Secretary-General, 'Model Status-of-Forces Agreement for Peace-Keeping Operations' (9 October 1990).

UN Doc. A/46/185, Report of the Secretary-General, 'Model Agreement between the United Nations and Member States contributing Personnel and Equipment to United Nations Peace-Keeping Operations' (23 May 1991).

UN Doc. A/47/277- S/24111, 'An Agenda for Peace: Preventive Diplomacy, Peacemaking and Peace-keeping', Report of the Secretary-General pursuant to the Statement adopted by the Summit Meeting of the Security Council on 31 January 1992 (17 June 1992).

UN Doc. A/49/681, Report of the Secretary-General, 'Command and Control of United Nations Peacekeeping Operations' (21 November 1994).

UN Doc. A/50/60- S/1995/1, 'Supplement to An Agenda for Peace: Position Paper of the Secretary-General on the Occasion of the Fiftieth Anniversary of the United Nations' (25 January 1995).

UN Doc. A/51/389, Report of the Secretary-General, 'Administrative and Budgetary Aspects of the Financing of the United Nations Peacekeeping Operations' (20 September 1996), reproduced at 37 ILM 700 (1998).

UN Doc. A/51/950, 'Renewing the United Nations: A Programme for Reform' (14 July 1997).

UN Doc. A/54/549, 'Report of the Secretary-General pursuant to General Assembly Resolution 53/35: The Fall of Srebrenica' (15 November 1999).

UN Doc. A/55/305, S/2000/809, 'Report of the Panel on United Nations Peace Operations' (21 August 2000) (The Brahimi Report).

UN Doc. A/56/326, 'Road Map Toward the Implementation of the United Nations Millennium Development Goals' (6 September 2001).

UN Doc. A/56/767, Special Committee on Peacekeeping, 'Comprehensive review of the whole question of peacekeeping operations in all their aspects' (28 March 2003).

UN Doc. A/58/10, 'Report of the International Law Commission on the Work of its 57th Session, 5 May – 6 June and 7 July – 8 August 2003' (2003).

UN Doc. A/59/10, 'Report of the International Law Commission on the Work of its 56th Session, 3 May – 4 June and 5 July – 6 August 2004' (2004).

UN Doc. A/59/565, Report of the High Level Panel on Threats Challenges and Change, 'A More Secure World: Our Shared Responsibility' (2 December 2004).

UN Doc. A/59/661, Report of the Secretary-General, 'Investigation by the Office of Internal Oversight Services into Allegations of Sexual Exploitation and Abuse in the United Nations Organization Mission in the Democratic Republic of the Congo' delivered to the General Assembly (5 January 2005).

UN Doc. A/59/710, Report of the Secretary-General, 'A Comprehensive Strategy to Eliminate Future Sexual Exploitation and Abuse in United Nations Peacekeeping Operations' (24 March 2005).

UN Doc. A/59/2005, Report of the Secretary-General, 'In Larger Freedom: Towards Development, Security and Human Rights for All' (21 March 2005).

UN Doc. A/61/645 Annex III, 'We are United Nations Peacekeeping Personnel' and Annex IV, 'Code of Personal Conduct for United Nations Peacekeeping Personnel' (18 December 2006).

Un Doc. A/6730, 'Report of the Secretary-General on the Withdrawal of the United Nations Emergency Force', UN GA Official Records, Fifth Emergency Special Sessions, Annex, Agenda item 5 (26 June 1967).

UN Doc. A/CN.4/233, 'Second Report on State Responsibility', 22nd session of the International Law Commission (20 April 1970).

UN Doc. A/CN.4/246, 'Third Report on State Responsibility' in (1971) 2 *Yearbook of the International Law Commission* 272.

UN Doc. A/CN.4/532, 'First Report on Responsibility of International Organizations', ILC, Fifty-fifth Session (2003).

UN Doc. A/CN.4/541, 'Second Report on Responsibility of International Organizations', ILC, Fifty-fifth Session (2004).

UN Doc. A/CN.4/545, 'Responsibility of International Organizations. Comments and Observations received from International Organizations', ILC, Fifty-fifth Session (2004).

UN Doc. A/CN.4/556, 'Responsibility of International Organizations. Comments and Observations received from Governments and International Organizations', ILC, Fifty-seventh Session (2005).

UN Doc. A/CN.4/564, 'Fourth Report on Responsibility of International Organizations', ILC, Fifty-eighth Session (2006).

UN Doc. A/CN.4/L.687, 'Responsibility of International Organizations. Titles and Texts of the Draft Articles adopted by the Drafting Committee on 31 May 2006', ILC, Fifty-eighth Session (2006).

UN Doc. E/CN.4/Sub.2/2005/42, Commission on Human Rights, 'Administration of Justice, Rule of Law and Democracy: Working Paper on the Accountability of International Personnel Taking Part in Peace Support Operations' (7 July 2005).

UN Doc. S/6597, 'Letter dated 6 August 1965 from the Secretary-General addressed to the Acting Permanent Representative of the Union of Soviet Socialist Republics' (6 August 1965).

UN Doc. S/23363, 'Further Report of the Secretary-General Pursuant to Security Council Resolution 721' (5 January 1992).

Un Doc S/25354, 'Further Report of the Secretary-General submitted in pursuance of paragraphs 18 and 19 of Resolution 794' (3 March 1993).

UN Doc. S/11052/Rev.1, 'Report of the Secretary-General on the Implementation of Security Council Resolution 340' (27 October 1973).

UN Doc. S/1999/1257, 'Report of the Independent Inquiry into the Actions of the United Nations during the 1994 Genocide in Rwanda' (16 December 1999).

UN Doc. S/1999/779, 'Report of the Secretary-General on the United Nations Interim Administration Mission in Kosovo' (12 July 1999).

UN Doc. S/2000/460, 'Report of the Secretary-General on the Implementation of the SC Resolutions 425 and 426' (22 May 2000).

UN Doc. S/2005/167, 'Seventeenth Report of the Secretary-General on the United Nations Organization Mission in the Democratic Republic of the Congo' (15 March 2005).

UN Doc. S/2006/730, 'Report of the Secretary-General on the Implementation of the SC Resolution 1701' (12 September 2006).

UN Doc. S/2006/933, 'Letter dated 1 December 2006 from the Secretary-General addressed to the President of Security Council' (1 December 2006).

UN Doc. S/2007/147, 'Report of the Secretary-General on the Implementation of the SC Resolution 1701' (14 March 2007).

UN Doc. S/2007/392, 'Report of the Secretary-General on the Implementation of the SC Resolution 1701' (28 June 2007).

UN Doc. S/2008/135, 'Report of the Secretary-General on the Implementation of the SC Resolution 1701' (28 February 2008).

UN Doc. S/2008/425, 'Report of the Secretary-General on the Implementation of the SC Resolution 1701' (27 June 2008).

UN Doc. S/2008/715, 'Report of the Secretary-General on the Implementation of the SC Resolution 1701' (18 November 2008).

UN Doc. S/PRST/2000/21, 'Statement by the President of the Security Council' (18 June 2000).

UN Doc. S/PV.5511, 'Record of the SC 5511th meeting of 11 August 2006.

UN Doc. S/PV.5733, Record of the SC 5733th meeting of 24 August 2007.

UN Doc. ST/SGB/1999/13, 'Secretary-General's Bulletin on Observance by United Nations Forces of International Humanitarian Law' (6 August 1999).

UNMIK Regulation 2001/9 'On a Constitutional Framework for Provisional Self-Government in Kosovo' (18 June 2001).

UNMIK Regulation No. 1999/1 'On the Authority of the Interim Administration in Kosovo' (25 July 1999).

UNMIK Regulation No. 1999/24 'On the Law Applicable in Kosovo' (12 December 1999).

UNTAET Regulation No. 1999/1 'On the Authority of the Transitional Administration in East Timor' (27 November 1999).

European Communities Legislation

Council Joint Action 2003/681/CFSP of 29 September 2003 on EUPOL Proxima, (2003) OJ L 249/66.

Council Joint Action 2008/851/CFSP of 10 November 2008 on a European Union military operation to contribute to the deterrence, prevention and repression of acts of piracy and armed robbery off the Somali coast, (2008) OJ L 301/33.

Treaties, Statutes and Agreements

Additional Protocol I to the Geneva Conventions of 12 August 1949, and Relating to the Protection of Victims of International Armed Conflicts, Geneva (adopted 8 June 1977, entered into force 7 December 1978), 1125 UNTS 3.

Additional Protocol II to the Geneva Conventions of 12 August 1949, and Relating to the Protection of Victims of Non-International Armed Conflicts, Geneva (adopted 8 June 1977, entered into force 7 December 1978), 1125 UNTS 109.

African Charter on Human and Peoples' Rights (adopted 27 June 1981, entered into force 21 October 1986), OAU Doc. CAB/LEG/67/3 Rev. 5.

Agreement between the United Nations and Sierra Leone Concerning the Status of the United Nations Mission in Sierra Leone (4 August 2000) 2118 UNTS.

Agreement between Ethiopia and the United Nations Concerning the Status of the United Nations Mission in Ethiopia and Eritrea (23 March 2001) 2141 UNTS.

Agreement between the United Nations and the Government of Sudan Concerning the Status of the United Nations Mission in Sudan (28 December 2005) 2351 UNTS.

Agreement on the Status of the United Nations Assistance Mission (UNAMIR) (5 November 1993) 1748 UNTS.

American Convention on Human Rights (adopted 22 November 1969, entered into force 18 July 1978) 1144 UNTS 123.

American Declaration of the Rights and Duties of Man, Res. XXX, adopted by the Ninth International Conference of American States (2 May 1948), *Basic Documents Pertaining to Human Rights in the Inter-American System*, OEA/Ser.L.V/II.82 doc.6 rev.1 at 17 (1992).

Charter of the Commonwealth of Independent States (22 June 1993) [2005] 34 ILM 1279.

Convention (IV) Respecting the Laws and Customs of Wars on Land and its Annex: Regulations Concerning the Laws and Customs of War on Land The Hague (adopted 18 October1907, entered into force 26 January 1910) [1910] UKTS 10.

Convention Against Torture and Other Cruel, Inhuman or Degrading Treatment or Punishment (approved by the general Assembly for consensus 10 December 1984, entered into force 26 June 1987) 1465 *UNTS* 85.

Convention on Cluster Munitions, Dublin (adopted 30 May 2008, entered into force on 1 August 2010) [2009] 48 ILM 354, available also at: <http://www.clusterconvention.org/>.

Council of Europe, European Convention for the Protection of Human Rights and Fundamental Freedoms (as amended through November 1998) (adopted 4 November 1950) 213 UNTS 221.

EU, Consolidated versions of the Treaty on European Union and of the Treaty establishing the European Community (24 December 2002), OJ C 325.

General Framework Agreement for Peace in Bosnia and Herzegovina, Annex IA [1996] 35 ILM 75.

Geneva Convention (I) for the Amelioration of the Condition of the Wounded and Sick in Armed Forces in the Field, Geneva (adopted 12 August 1949, entered into force 21 October 1950) 75 UNTS 31.

Geneva Convention (II) for the Amelioration of the Condition of the Wounded, Sick and Shipwrecked Members of Armed Forces at Sea,Geneva (adopted 12 August 1949, entered into force 21 October 1950) 75 UNTS 85.

Geneva Convention (III) relative to the treatment of Prisoners of War, Geneva (adopted 12 August 1949, entered into force 21 October 1950) 75 UNTS 135.

Geneva Convention (IV) relative to the protection of Civilian Persons in Time of War, Geneva (adopted 12 August 1949, entered into force 21 October 1950) 75 UNTS 287.

International Covenant on Civil and Political Rights (adopted 16 December 1966, entered into force 23 March 1976) 999 UNTS 171.

Ottawa Convention on the Prohibition of the Use, Stockpiling, Production and Transfer of Anti-Personnel Mines and on their Destruction (adopted 18 September 1997, entered into force 1 March 1999) 2056 UNTS 211.

Rome Statute of the International Criminal Court (adopted 17 July 1998, entered into force 1 July 2002) 2187 UNTS 3.

Statute of the International Criminal Tribunal for the Former Yugoslavia, adopted by UNSC Res 827 (25 May 1993) 32 ILM 1159.

Statute of the Special Court for Sierra Leone, adopted by UN Doc S/2002/246 (16 January 2002) 2178 UNTS 138.

The International Law Commission's Articles on State Responsibility for Internationally Wrongful Acts (2001), submitted to the UN General Assembly with UN Doc A/56/10, Report of the International Law Commission on the Work of its 53rd Session (23 April-2 June and 3 July-10 August 2001).

UN Charter, San Francisco (adopted 26 June 1945, entered into force 24 October 1945).

UN Convention on the Law of the Sea, Montego Bay (adopted 10 December 1982, entered into force 16 November 1984) 21 ILM 1261.

UN Convention on the Prohibitions or Restrictions on the Use of Certain Conventional Weapons Which May Be Deemed to be Excessively Injurious or to have Indiscriminate Effects, Geneva (adopted 10 October 1980, entered into force 2 December 1983) 1342 UNTS 168.

UN, Universal Declaration of Human Rights, adopted by UNGA Res 3/217 (10 December 1948).

Vienna Convention on the Law of Treaties (adopted 22 May 1969, entered into force 27 January 1980) 1155 UNTS 331.

Reports

Afghanistan Independent Human Rights Commission Report, 'Violations of International Humanitarian Law in Afghanistan: Practices of Concern and Example Cases', available at: <http://www.aihrc.org.af/IHL_practices_and_examples_final_Coalition_Vioalatioin.pdf>.

Amnesty International, 'Report on Sierra Leone' (2000), available at: <http://www.unhcr.org/refworld/publisher,AMNESTY,,SLE,3ae6aa127,0.html>.

Canada, Commission of Inquiry into the Deployment of Canadian Forces to Somalia, 'Dishonoured Legacy: The Lessons of the Somalia Affair', Report of the Commission of Inquiry into the Deployment of Canadian Forces to Somalia (Ottawa, Minister of Public Works and Government Services Canada - Publishing, June 1997), available at: <www.dnd.ca/somalia/somaliae.htm>.

Council of Europe, Parliamentary Assembly, 'Areas where the European Convention on Human Rights cannot be implemented', Doc. 9730 (11 March 2003).

Council of Europe, Commissioner for Human Rights, 'Kosovo: The Human Rights Situation and the Fate of Persons Displaced from Their Homes', Report by Mr. Alvaro Gil-Robles, Commissioner for Human Rights, 16 October 2002, CommDH(2002).

Department of National Defence and the Canadian Forces, 'Report of the Somalia Commission of Inquiry', available at: <http://www.forces.gc.ca/somalia/vol2/v2c22e.htm>.

Eide EB, Kaspersen AT, Kent R and von Hippel K, 'Report on Integrated Missions: Practical Perspectives and Recommendations' (Independent Study for the Expanded UN ECHA Core Group, May, 2005).

'Final Report to the ICTY Prosecutor by the Committee Established to Review the NATO Bombing Campaign against the Federal Republic of Yugoslavia' (1999), available at: <http://www.un.org/icty/pressreal/nato061300.htm>.

Human Rights Watch, 'Off Target; The Conduct of War and Civilian Casualties in Iraq', available at: <http://www.hrw.orgreports/2003/usa1203/usa1203.pdf>.

Human Rights Watch, 'We'll Kill You if You Cry. Sexual Violence in the Sierra Leone Conflict' (2002) available at: <www.hrw.org/reports/2003/sierraleone/sierleon0103.pdf>.

Human Rights Watch, 'Better Late than Never: Enhancing the Accountability of International Institutions in Kosovo' No. 2, June 2007, available at: <http://www.hrw.org/en/node/82371/section/1>.

ICTY, Office of the Prosecutor, *Final Report to the Prosecutor by the Committee Established to Review the NATO Bombing Campaign against the Federal Republic of Yugoslavia* (13 June 2000).

ILC Draft on Responsibility of States for Internationally Wrongful Acts, Annex to General Assembly Resolution 56/83 (12 December 2001).

Informal Expert Paper for the Office of the Prosecutor, 'The Principle of Complementarity in Practice' (ICC-OTP 2003) available at: < http://www.icc-cpi.int/iccdocs/doc/doc654724.PDF>.

ICRC, Report on 'Treatment by the Coalition Forces of Prisoners of War and Other Persons Protected by the Geneva Conventions in Iraq During Arrest, Internment and Interrogation'(February 2004), available at: <http://msnbcmedia.msn.com/i/msnbc/Sections/News/International%20News/Mideast%20and%20N.%20Africa/Iraq%20conflict/Red%20Cross%20report.pdf>.

ICRC, 'International Humanitarian Law and the Challenges of Contemporary Armed Conflicts' (30th International Conference of the Red Cross and Red Crescent, Geneva, 26 – 30 November 2007).

ICRC, 'How is the Term "Armed Conflict" Defined in International Humanitarian Law?', Opinion Paper, March 2008.

Jones B and Cherif F, 'Evolving Models of Peacekeeping: Policy Implications and Responses', External study prepared for the Best Practices Unit (UN Department of Peacekeeping Operations, 2004).

NATO, *Peace Support Operations*, Allied Joint Publication (AJP) 3.4.1, (July 2001).

Ombudsperson Institution in Kosovo, 'Special Report No. 1 on the compatibility with recognized international standards of UNMIK Regulation No. 2000/47 on the Status, Privileges and Immunities of KFOR and UNMIK and Their Personnel in Kosovo' (18 August 2000).

Ombudsperson Institution in Kosovo, 'Special Report No. 2, on Certain Aspects of UNMIK Regulation No. 2000/59 Amending UNMIK Regulation No. 1999/24 on the Law Applicable in Kosovo' (27 October 2000).

Ombudsperson Institution in Kosovo, 'Special Report No. 5 on Certain Aspects of UNMIK Regulation No. 2001/17 on the Registration of Contracts for the Sale of Real Property in Specific Geographical Areas of Kosovo' (22 August 2001).

REDRESS – Seeking Reparation for Torture Survivors, 'Memorandum to the UK Ministry of Defence on the Aitken Report: An Investigation into cases of deliberate abuse and unlawful killing in Iraq 2003 and 2004' (31 January 2008), available at: <http://www.redress.org/publications/Memo%20on%20Aitken%20Report%2031%20Jan%2008.pdf>.

Resolution of the Council of Delegates, 'Centenary Congress of the International Red Cross' reprinted in (1963) 31 *IRRC* 514.

Resolution XXV, 'Application of the Geneva Conventions by United Nations Emergency Forces', 20th International Conference of the Red Cross, Vienna, 1965, reprinted in *Handbook of the International Red Cross and Red Crescent Movement* (13th ed., Geneva 1994) 748.

'The Application of the Geneva Conventions by the Armed Forces Placed at the Disposal of the United Nations', Memorandum of the ICRC to the Governments of States Party to the Geneva Conventions and Members of the United Nations, reprinted in (1961) 9 ICRC 489.

The Challenges Project, *Meeting the Challenges of Peace Operations: Cooperation and Coordination* (Elanders Gotab, Stockholm, 2005).

'The Damning Red Cross Report of February 2004', in EIR Vol. 31, Nr. 20 (21 May 2004) available at: <http://www.larouchepub.com/eirtoc/2004/eirtoc_3120.html >.

'The (Taguba) Report on the Treatment of Abu Ghraib Prisoners in Iraq' (2004), available at: <http://www.npr.org/iraq/2004/prison_abuse_report.pdf>.

UK Ministry of Defence, 'The Aitken Report: An Investigation into Cases of Deliberate Abuse and Unlawful Killing in Iraq in 2003 and 2004' (25 January 2008) available at: <http://www.mod.uk/NR/rdonlyres/7AC894D3-1430-4AD1-911F-8210C3342CC5/0/aitken_rep.pdf>.

UN, *Human Rights Standards and Practice for the Police. Expanded Pocket Book on Human Rights for the Police* (United Nations Publications, Geneva, 2004) reproduced at: <http://www.ohchr.org/Documents/Publications/training5Add3en.pdf>.

UN, *The Blue Helmets: A Review of United Nations Peacekeeping* (3rd ed., United Nations Department of Public Information, New York, 1997).

UN, DPKO, Department of Field Support, *United Nations Peacekeeping Operations: Principles and Guidelines* (DPKO, New York, 2008).

US Department of Defense, 'Dictionary of Military and Associated Terms: Joint Publication 1-02' (12 April 2001 as amended in 2005).

US Department of State, 'Second and Third Report Concerning the International Covenant on Civil and Political Rights' (21 October 2005) available at: <http://www.state.gov/g/drl/rls/55504.htm>.

US Government Printing Office, Final Report to Congress: 'Conduct of the Persian War' (Washington DC, 1992).

US Joint Chiefs of Staff, 'Joint Doctrine for Multinational Operations: Joint Publication 3-16' (7 March 2007), reproduced at <www.dtic.mil/doctrine/jel/new_pubs/jp3_16.pdf>.

Working Papers

Cameron L, 'Accountability of International Organisations Engaged in the Administration of Territory', Dissertation, University Centre for International Humanitarian Law, 13 February 2006.

Center on International Cooperation at New York University, 'Annual Review of UN Peace Operations 2008', Briefing Paper, available at: <http://www.cic.nyu.edu/internationalsecurity/docs/Final2008briefingreport.pdf>.

General (ret) Dr. Naumann K, *Towards a Grand Strategy for an Uncertain World. Renewing Transatlantic Partnership* (Noaber Foundation, 2007) reproduced at: <http://www.gmfus.org/doc/GrandStrategy.pdf >.

Hansen W, Ramsbotham O, and Woodhouse T, 'Hawks and Doves: Peacekeeping and Conflict Resolution', (Berghof Research Centre for Constructive Conflict Management, 2004).

Isberg J, United Nations Mission in the Democratic Republic of Congo (MONUC), 'Psychological Fitness - Experiences from UN Military Peace, Enforcement Operations in the DRC April 2003 – January 2005' reproduced at: <http://www.dtic.mil/cgi-bin/GetTRDoc?AD=ADA472816&Location=U2&doc=GetTRDoc.pdf>.

Uerpmann R, 'International Law as an Element of European Constitutional Law: International Supplementary Constitutions', Jean Monnet Working Paper 9/03, Max Planck Institute for Comparative Public Law and International Law, Heidelberg, 2003.

Other Online Sources

Joint Declaration on UN-EU Co-operation in Crisis Management, 24 September 2003 available at <http://ochaonline.un.org/Coordination/FieldCoordinationMechanisms/TheFribourgProcess/EuropeanCoordinationProcess/tabid/1393/language/fr-FR/Default.aspx>.

Joint NATO-WEU Operation SHARP GUARD, available at <http://www.nato.int/IFOR/general/shrp-grd.htm>.

Koelebl S, 'NATO High Commander Issues Illegitimate Order to Kill', *Spiegel Online International* (28 January 2009) reproduced at: <http://www.spiegel.de/international/world/0,1518,604183,00.html >.

NATO's Comprehensive Political Guidance, Endorsed by NATO Heads of State and Government at the Riga Summit on 29 November 2006), available at: <http://www.nato.int/docu/basictxt/b061129e.htm>.

NATO's Strategic Concept, Approved by the Heads of State and Government participating in the meeting of the North Atlantic Council in Washington D.C., 24 April 1999, available at: <http://www.nato.int/docu/pr/1999/p99-065e.htm>.

NATO, Operation Active Endeavour, available at: <http://www.afsouth.nato.int/JFCN_Operations/ActiveEndeavour/Endeavour.htm>.

OSCE Handbook (October 2007), available at: <www.osce.org/item/22286.html>.

The NATO Glossary, Allied Administrative Publication No. 6 – AAP-6 (2008), available at <www.nato.int/docu/stanag/aap006/aap6.htm>.

Wells M, 'How Smart was this bomb' *The Guardian* (19 November 2001), reproduced at: <http://www.guardian.co.uk/media/2001/nov/19/mondaymediasection.afghanistan>.

WEU, *Petersberg Declaration*, 9 June 1992, available at: <http://www.weu.int/documents/920619peten.pdf>.

Index

G

H

I

www.ingramcontent.com/pod-product-compliance
Lightning Source LLC
LaVergne TN
LVHW010631300926
849162LV00001B/125